Good Catholics

Good Catholics

THE BATTLE OVER ABORTION IN THE
CATHOLIC CHURCH

Patricia Miller

UNIVERSITY OF CALIFORNIA PRESS
Berkeley   Los Angeles   London

The publisher gratefully acknowledges the generous support of the General Endowment Fund of the University of California Press Foundation.

The publisher gratefully acknowledges the generous support of Jamie Rosenthal Wolf, David Wolf, Rick Rosenthal, and Nancy Stephens as members of the Publisher's Circle of the University of California Press Foundation.

University of California Press, one of the most distinguished university presses in the United States, enriches lives around the world by advancing scholarship in the humanities, social sciences, and natural sciences. Its activities are supported by the UC Press Foundation and by philanthropic contributions from individuals and institutions. For more information, visit www.ucpress.edu.

University of California Press
Berkeley and Los Angeles, California

University of California Press, Ltd.
London, England

Library of Congress Cataloging-in-Publication Data

Miller, Patricia, 1964–
 Good Catholics : the battle over abortion in the Catholic Church / Patricia Miller.
  pages cm
 Includes bibliographical references and index.
 ISBN 978-0-520-27600-0 (cloth : alk. paper) — ISBN 978-0-520-95827-2 (e-book)
 1. Abortion—Religious aspects—Catholic Church—History. 2. Catholic Church—United States. 3. Church and state—United States. I. Title.
 HQ767.3.M56 2014
 241'.6976—dc23   2013035084

Manufactured in the United States of America

23 22 21 20 19 18 17 16 15 14
10 9 8 7 6 5 4 3 2 1

To my parents,
Madelyn S. Miller
and John J. Miller

Contents

Acknowledgments

Writing a book makes you acutely aware of how much any creative endeavor is more than the work of one person. Writing a book about history doubles this awareness, because you are of necessity telling the stories of other people. Writing a book about people who have been neglected by history, especially women, leaves you in awe of the many people whose shoulders you are standing on in your own life, even if you don't know their names. This book tells the story of some of these people, the women and men—many previously unknown—who contributed to the Catholic reproductive rights movement, with the hope that they will be acknowledged by history.

I thank the many individuals who generously shared their time with me to recount their involvement in the movement. As any historian knows, firsthand historical recollections are a precious commodity, a fact that I was reminded of when I would track down a source only to discover that she or he had passed away just a few months earlier. I will always regret not being able to tell their stories.

I also thank the librarians and archivists who assisted me, in particular those at the Pennsylvania State Archives, the Sophia Smith Collection at Smith College, and the Rockefeller Center Archives.

This book truly would not have been possible without the involvement of several people at Catholics for Choice. Jon O'Brien knew that this was a story that needed to be told and made it possible for me to spend eighteen months working in the CFC archives to tell it. David Nolan graciously assisted me with locating material in the archives and tracking down interviewees. Sara Morello was an invaluable sounding board and all-around supporter of the project.

Kristin Luker's interest and support in this project was also essential to its realization. Her feedback on early drafts was invaluable. Our many conversations on the arc of the history of the reproductive rights movement were enlightening and inspiring. Her willingness to include me in her network of scholars was both gracious and indispensible.

I also express my gratitude to Naomi Schneider at the University of California Press for her willingness to publish a book on a controversial subject by a first-time author. Thanks as well to Christopher Lura for his good-natured editorial assistance, to project editor Francisco Reinking, and to Pam Suwinsky for her thoughtful copyediting of the book.

Both my parents passed away during the course of writing this book. My debt to them is too deep to acknowledge properly. Everything I know about Catholicism and politics was born from many long conversations around our dining room table.

Finally, this book would not have been possible without the continued support, insight, and good humor of my husband Anthony Spadafore and the constant companionship, and reminders that the most important thing in life is a good walk with those you love, of my Chesapeake Bay retriever Rosie.

Introduction

Everything you need to know about the Catholic Church and women can be ascertained from the front doors of St. Patrick's Cathedral in New York City. There, six notable American Catholics are immortalized in statues set in the massive bronze doors of the entryway. St. Joseph and St. Patrick occupy the uppermost niches; the martyred Jesuit Isaac Jogues resides in the middle left panel. The three remaining statues occupying the middle right panel and the lowermost reaches of the door are of women. There is Kateri Tekakwiyha, a Mohawk-Algonquian convert to Catholicism who is best known for taking a vow of chastity and dying a virgin at age twenty-four. There is Elizabeth Ann Seton, the founder of the Sisters of Charity, who is famous for being the first native-born American saint. And there is Mother Cabrini, an Italian nun known for her charity work among poor Italian immigrants. All three are now recognized by the church as saints for their various works and purported miracles, although neither Seton nor Tekakwiyha was a saint when the doors were dedicated in 1949.

Virgin, saint, and nun. This is how the Catholic Church sees the ideal woman: chaste, selfless, dedicated to serving others. And positioned decidedly below men in the hierarchy of the sexes. Pope John Paul II was a huge proponent of this idealized view of women, and it has permeated

1

the official theological discourse of the church since the beginning of his reign in 1978. He was forever extolling the special "genius" of women to serve others. "For in giving themselves to others each day women fulfill their deepest vocation," he wrote in his Letter to Women. He had to do theological gymnastics to explain why women were just as "human" as men but could not be priests because they weren't the same as men; they were "different and complementary" and fulfilled their authentic "reign" as wives and mothers.[1]

Although the church lionizes motherhood as woman's true role and purpose, having babies involves the messy realities of sex, which the Catholic Church has never been very good at grappling with. It has always considered celibacy a holier state than marriage.[2] Sex is associated with the fall of man; with sin; with Eve, the temptress. This central contradiction of Catholicism is embodied in the Virgin Mary: virgin and mother, a state unachievable by actual flesh-and-blood women. For some 2,000 years the Catholic Church has tried, largely in vain, to reconcile its horror of sex with the realities and necessity of human reproduction, most notably by attempting to proscribe any sexual activity not directly related to reproduction or any interference with the generative process that would sever sex from the sanction of pregnancy—the only thing, so the church fathers believed, which prevented the world from being consumed by unbridled lust, lost in a frenzy of fornication.

It is women who have borne the brunt of these proscriptions, limited in their ability to control their fertility just as the settled lifestyle and relatively stable food supply of the agricultural revolution decreased the interval between pregnancies and dramatically increased the number of children a woman could expect to bear in her lifetime.[3] At the same time, the church denied women the agency to modify these restrictions on fertility management to better fit the realities of bearing and raising children. They were prevented from studying theology or becoming priests, which meant they could not rise through the ranks to become members of the magisterium—the bishops and cardinals, and ultimately the pope—who determine church doctrine. This book is the story of how women asserted their agency by reinterpreting Catholic doctrine to better capture its historical and theological nuance regarding sex and reproduction and their lived reality as members of the church. It is not the story of women alone; men also took part in the process of developing and promoting a progressive theology that recognized birth control and abortion as moral options. But they are of necessity its locus for the simple reason that lack of access to abortion and contraception is felt more keenly by women and by that fact alone the relationship between women and the Catholic Church is uniquely fraught.

The Catholic Church officially has prohibited abortion and birth control throughout most of its history, although, as I show, not for the reasons most people think and with a surprising lack of distinction between the two. Today, the issue of abortion has come to define, and in many ways divide, the Roman Catholic Church. But when I was growing up in a middle-class Catholic community in the northern New Jersey suburbs in the 1970s and 1980s, no one mentioned abortion. Priests did not inveigh against it from the pulpit on Sundays. The teachers in the parochial schools I attended, many of them nuns, managed to discuss religion, politics, and human sexuality without ever saying the word. I never knew a single person in our large and vibrant parish who went to an anti-abortion march nor saw a single piece of anti-abortion literature. And our parish was not an exception. I had cousins and friends in parishes throughout the Irish, Italian, and Polish enclaves of North Jersey; my brother and sister went to different Catholic high schools than I did; my family attended mass at different shore churches over the course of many summers (where the priests not only never mentioned abortion, but gave mercifully short, doctrine-free sermons designed to get the faithful to the beach with all due haste). Abortion was not something most Catholics worried or talked about. How, I wondered, did that change? How did abortion go from being a non-issue in the lives of most Catholics to the issue that defines Catholicism today? And what effect has this elevation of abortion as a central concern had on the church and on the United States at large? This book attempts to answer these questions.

As I sought answers, I was surprised to find how much unrecognized influence the hierarchy of the Catholic Church in America, the bishops and cardinals of the U.S. Conference of Catholic Bishops, has had on the anti-abortion movement. This book details how they created the modern anti-abortion movement to camouflage their own lobbying against the expansion of abortion rights and then lost control of the movement at the very moment that *Roe v. Wade* made it essential. It shows how the U.S. bishops created the use of abortion as a wedge issue in modern presidential campaigns, a tactic that was picked up and used with stunning success by the Christian Right. And it shows how despite the high-profile anti-abortion activism of the Christian Right over the past thirty years, it is the Catholic bishops who in many ways have been the most persistent and successful opponents of legalized abortion.

Good Catholics tells the story of the nearly fifty-year struggle in the Catholic Church over abortion, as progressives and conservatives battled it out over the moral acceptability of the procedure and whether Catholics have the right to disagree with the leadership of the church on the issue. It is the interwoven story of two forces. On one side is the all-male leadership of the church—the pope and the bishops who compose the magisterium, which is popularly known as the "hierarchy" (and which progressive Catholics are quick to note is not the "church," which is made up of the hierarchy and the lay Catholics who receive their teaching). On the other side are Catholics—lay, consecrated religious, and clerical—who believe that there is room in Catholic teaching and tradition for Catholics to support abortion rights and even to chose abortion as a moral option. They have not only provided a crucial backstop to the political power of the hierarchy both nationally and internationally but have helped modern Catholics deal realistically with difficult issues like comporting church doctrine with democratic participation. I show that the way these two forces have interacted over the past five decades on the issue of abortion has affected not only the Catholic Church but also the very woof and warp of U.S. politics in ways that are not widely recognized.

The book is divided into two halves. The first half traces the development of a distinctly Catholic pro-choice movement. It tells the story of the first Catholic women to publicly challenge the hierarchy on the practice of birth control and abortion in an era when it was widely assumed that all Catholics believed what the magisterium told them to believe. It simultaneously traces the development of the secular abortion rights movement through the 1960s and 1970s to show how it interacted with nascent Catholic feminism to create a Catholic movement in support of abortion rights. It then details the struggle of this movement and its flagship organization, Catholics for a Free Choice ([CFFC], which is now known as

Catholics for Choice [CFC]), to establish itself in the 1970s and 1980s and the concurrent maturation and professionalization of the abortion rights movement. The first half concludes by recounting the historic battle over abortion and dissent occasioned when conservative bishops called out vice presidential candidate Geraldine Ferraro during the 1984 presidential election for her support of CFFC's contention that good Catholics, including Catholic politicians, can support abortion rights. The result was a landmark statement on abortion and pluralism that changed forever the perception of abortion and Catholics.

The second half of the book details how the U.S. bishops' conference evolved into a freestanding political lobby that aggressively represents its own interests in the political process, a transformation that most Americans were unaware of until the bishops almost derailed President Barack Obama's health reform effort with their insistence that it contain new limits on abortion funding. It shows how the 1984 confrontation over pro-choice Catholics triggered an unprecedented Vatican crackdown on dissent in the church that raged from the mid-1980s onward. I illustrate how this war against progressive dissent changed the church and moved the hierarchy away from balanced, reasonable participation in the political process toward a tacit alliance with the Republican Party. This alliance eventually evolved into a far-right coalition comprising the Catholic bishops, conservative elements of the GOP, and the Catholic and Christian Rights that seeks to further limit access to abortion, undercut support for family planning, and create new rights for religiously affiliated organizations in civil society. In particular, I argue, Pope John Paul II's deliberate conflation of abortion and contraception eventually "infected" the Christian Right and led to the current anti–birth control environment that threatens funding for Planned Parenthood and other efforts to ensure access to contraception.

The remainder of the book shows how the hierarchy's political absolutism has played out in a number of areas, from highly charged UN conferences on development and women's issues, to health care in the United States, where hospitals affiliated with the church provide health care to one out of six Americans in any given year and church-affiliated health maintenance organizations (HMOs) participate in government-financed public health plans yet are expected to follow the limitations that the hierarchy puts on the provision of reproductive health services. The book details how the Catholic Church got involved in health care and how the bishops control what services can be provided. It also shows how the bishops have fought for exemptions to allow Catholic health and social service agencies to refuse to provide reproductive health services or serve populations they find morally objectionable, a quest that came to a head in a dramatically public manner when the U.S. bishops challenged the Obama administration's mandate that all health insurers make contraceptives available to women free of charge.

This book addresses many of today's hot-button questions about the separation of church and state and the role of religion in the public square. Are Catholic public officials obligated by their religion to try and insert Catholic doctrine into law? Are the Catholic bishops participating inappropriately in the political process when they consistently and harshly criticize one political party for disagreeing with select aspects of Catholic teaching on reproductive health while giving the other party a pass on social justice issues? What concessions does the civil system need to make for matters of religious doctrine like the Catholic ban on contraception, especially when most Catholics don't follow the doctrine and the bishops wish to impose it on non-Catholics?

Good Catholics recounts a history of protest and persecution that has never been pulled together in one narrative and demonstrates the profound and surprising influence that the battle over abortion in the Catholic Church has had on the U.S. political system. The role of the hierarchy in creating the highly politicized political climate over abortion has not been well recognized, nor has the successful effort to create a space for pro-choice Catholicism, which has provided an important underpinning for Catholic politicians who favor abortion rights and had a profound cultural affect on the practice of Catholicism. I demonstrate how a relatively small number of committed individuals were able to effect change in society through the careful leveraging of a powerful, but controversial, idea in a number of areas: the media, state and national policymaking bodies, and international forums.

The sources I draw on to tell this story reflect my own background as a journalist, specialist in women's health policy, and independent scholar with a special interest in using primary sources to reconstruct historical events involving women, whose grassroots stories are often neglected by mainstream history. This book draws on the previously unexamined archival resources of Catholics for Choice, a repository of primary documentation of the abortion rights movement going back to the early 1970s and the only archive with extensive holdings related to the Catholic abortion rights movement; interviews with key participants in many of the events detailed; contemporaneous news coverage; and secondary sources, particularly early Catholic feminist texts and accounts of the early women's and reproductive rights movements; and scholarly texts to create a narrative history of the Catholic reproductive rights movement.

In the end, this book is the history of an idea, an incredibly controversial, groundbreaking idea—that good Catholics can support abortion rights—and the people who have fought a nearly fifty-year battle to assert its legitimacy. Their success in doing so has important implications not just for Catholics and not just for women, but for anyone interested in religious pluralism in our democracy.

PART I   The History of an Idea

1 The Four Wise Women

Years later, when the remembrance of so many other things had faded, the memory still remained crisp in her mind. She saw herself lying in the hospital bed, bleeding, writhing in agony. She remembered clawing at the curtain surrounding the bed, trying get help, certain she was going to die. Finally she managed to cry out, "God dammit, I can't die. I have five children."

Her cries roused her roommate, who summoned a doctor. The doctor managed to staunch the bleeding from the hematoma that had resulted from the birth of her fifth child. It was not an unexpected complication. She had hemorrhaged after giving birth to her fourth child. The doctors had warned her against any more pregnancies, but she was a devout Catholic and the church said that using birth control was a sin. So another pregnancy had followed quickly on the heels of the last, and a little over a year later she was again in danger of dying and leaving her children motherless. As she lay helpless on her bed, Jane Furlong Cahill made a decision. "I decided that the pope can have all the kids he wanted. I was through," she said.[1]

After that she used the Pill, which had only just become available, and eventually she got a tubal ligation to permanently end her childbearing ability. It was a controversial choice for a Catholic woman in 1964, but especially so for Cahill, who was one of the first women formally trained in Roman Catholic theology and knew that the church made no exception to its teaching that Catholics could never use artificial methods of contraception. The only acceptable form of birth control for Catholics, both then and now, is natural family planning, which relies on calculating a woman's infertile period during her menstrual cycle and only having sex on those days. The "rhythm method," as natural family planning was called in the early 1960s, was notoriously unreliable, however, which made it a poor option for women like Cahill who really, really didn't want another child. In 1963, Catholic physician John Rock reported that couples using the rhythm method experienced rates of unplanned pregnancy that were two to three times higher than those using other methods of contraception. According to the church, Cahill's only option if she absolutely, positively wanted to avoid pregnancy, even for life-threatening reasons, was to stop having sex with her husband altogether.[2]

The Catholic Church's absolute ban on modern methods of contraception is inextricably linked to its views on sex and marriage. The church fathers who laid out the founding doctrine of the religion were always squeamish about the idea of sexual intercourse; they considered chastity a holier state. But at the same time, they recognized that it was neither possible nor practical to suggest that most people abstain from sex. Corralling sex within marriage was better than unbridled fornication. Hence, it was "better to marry than to burn with passion," according to the Apostle Paul. But even within marriage, the Christian fathers' acceptance of sex was grudging. Influenced by the Stoics, they looked to nature to determine the purpose and moral limits of bodily functions like sex. Hence, sex within marriage was only moral if it was used for its "natural" purpose of procreation. They taught that Christians were not to have sex for pleasure or when pregnancy was impossible, such as when a woman was already pregnant. The belief that procreation sanctified sex automatically excluded the possibility of using withdrawal, contraceptive potions, or crude devices—all of which were common and widely used in the early Christian world—to frustrate conception.[3]

The first formal theological condemnation of contraception was made by St. Augustine in the early 400s, when he declared that it is "a procreative purpose which makes good an act in which lust is present" and that married people who contracept "are not married." It was a proclamation that would guide Catholic thinking about contraception for the next 1,500 years as the Augustinian doctrine was gradually codified by the church.[4]

In 590, Pope Gregory the Great decreed that married couples who mixed pleasure with procreation in sexual intercourse "transgressed the law." The first church legislation forbidding contraception appeared in the 600s in a canon that specified a penance of ten years for any woman who took "steps so that she may not conceive." The church's reaction to the distinctly non-procreative ethic of courtly love in medieval Europe and Catharism, a Christian sect that rejected the Catholic sacraments, including marriage, further hardened its insistence on the procreative purpose of sex. By 1400, Augustine's doctrine on contraception was the rule within the church.[5]

Despite its longevity, Cahill wasn't the only Catholic woman questioning the teaching on birth control. In 1964, another budding theologian named Rosemary Radford Ruether published an article titled "A Catholic Mother Tells: 'Why I Believe in Birth Control'" in the *Saturday Evening Post*, bringing the issue straight into the living rooms of Main Street America. Ruether took the church to task for failing to acknowledge that in modern marriages couples didn't have sex just for the purpose of having children. She also revealed what many Catholic couples were saying privately: the rhythm method not only didn't work but put extraordinary strain on otherwise happy marriages. "A man and a wife may follow all the current methods for predicting the time of ovulation, they may be armed with an arsenal of slide rules, thermometers, glucose tests, they may abstain for the proscribed period with dogged perseverance, and they may still find that the method has failed. . . . The rhythm method keeps couples in a constant state of tension and insecurity," she wrote.[6]

Ruether, who was just embarking on a promising career as a theologian and already had three young children, wrote of her own failure with the method and the desperation of other women who found themselves pregnant when they didn't want to be, including a friend who was in despair after finding herself pregnant for the sixth time in seven years. Like many women of her day, Ruether realized that controlling her fertility with a fairly high degree of certainty was essential to her ability to steer her own

Figure 1. Theologian Rosemary Radford Ruether was one of the first Catholic women to publicly challenge the hierarchy's teaching on birth control. (Courtesy of Rosemary Ruether)

life. "I see very clearly that I cannot entrust my destiny just to biological chance. As a woman who is trying to create a happy balance of work and family, I know effective family planning is essential. A woman who cannot control her own fertility, who must remain vulnerable to chance conception, is a woman who cannot hope to be much more than a baby-machine," she wrote.[7]

Her analysis made her the first Catholic woman to publicly critique the church's ban on birth control. But Cahill and Ruether were not alone in concluding that the church's dictum on contraception was an anachronism. By the mid-1960s, more and more Catholic women were using "artificial" methods of contraception. In 1955, just under half of all Catholic women had never used any method of birth control, including rhythm. But ten years later, by 1965, fewer than one-quarter of Catholic women had never attempted to control births. Of the married Catholic women who did attempt family planning in 1955, slightly over half had most recently used the rhythm method, while just over one-quarter used appliance contraceptives like condoms or diaphragms. This was almost exactly opposite the general population of white women, where just over half of all women used appliance contraceptives and fewer than one-quarter used rhythm.

But with the approval of the birth control pill in 1960, Catholic women began abandoning the rhythm method for the certainty of oral contraceptives. By 1965, only 36 percent of Catholic women practicing family planning were using rhythm; 20 percent were using the Pill and another 25 percent were using other modern methods. All total, by the time Ruether wrote her article nearly half of all Catholic women were using contraceptive methods forbidden by the church.[8]

Lay Catholics weren't the only ones concluding that the ban on contraception made little sense in the modern world. Catholic theologians and bishops were also suggesting it was time to revisit the teaching. Two developments spurred their willingness to question the ban. One was a change in how the church viewed the purpose of marital sex. The church had held since Augustine's time that the primary purpose of sex within marriage was procreation. A secondary purpose was expressed in the negative: to prevent fornication. But gradually a more positive view of sex crept in that allowed that pleasure and the expression of conjugal love could be part of the equation. In 1951, Pope Pius XII formally admitted that it was okay for married couples to enjoy sex: "In seeking and enjoying this pleasure, therefore, couples do nothing wrong."[9]

The church's view of marriage was evolving in tandem. Increasingly it viewed marriage as having two ends: procreation and the "ontological completion of the person" within the union of marriage. This meant that many of the old prohibitions against "sterile" sex within marriage, that is, sex that could not produce offspring, such as sex during pregnancy, no longer held. If some limited forms of non-procreative sex within marriage were now considered licit and sex was acknowledged to have more than one purpose in marriage, this raised the question of whether in general each and every act of intercourse within marriage necessarily had to be procreative.[10]

The second reason many theologians believed that the church could approve modern contraceptives was because it had already approved the idea of family planning when it approved the rhythm method. As Ruether noted in her *Saturday Evening Post* article, the church's distinction between "natural" family planning and contraceptives was "theologically meaningless." If, she said, it was morally acceptable to "divorce sex from impregnation" with the rhythm method, "it would then seem to make little difference whether the egg and sperm are separated by barriers of space or of time, and whether the couple use times of natural sterility or use bodily hormones to create temporary artificial sterility."[11]

The church's incongruence on the issue of family planning dated back to 1930 and the papal encyclical *Casti Connubi* (On Christian Marriage), which was specifically written to address the growing acceptance of birth control throughout the Western world. The invention of vulcanized rubber in the 1830s had made possible the production of cheap, effective condoms. The first diaphragms were developed in the 1880s. For the first time, fairly reliable methods to prevent conception were widely available. Margaret Sanger's crusade to bring contraceptives to the teeming tenements of the lower East Side made birth control front-page news in the United States and helped publicize its availability. Family planning leagues sprung up to promote the new technology and make it available to the poor. The acceptance of birth control reflected not just its increased availability but the reality that larger families were no longer economically viable, or necessary, in the post-agrarian era. It also reflected the growing acceptance of the idea of companionate marriage—that marriage was more than just an economic arrangement for the production of children, but an emotional partnership.

The tipping point was reached in 1930, when the Anglican Church, which at the time was the most influential Christian church in the West, officially approved the use of birth control by married couples. Other Protestant denominations soon followed, signaling that contraceptives had gained moral and social legitimacy. With birth control gaining widespread acceptance, the Catholic Church had to respond. On the very last day of 1930, Pope Pius XI issued *Casti Connubii*. In it, he firmly restated the absolute Augustinian prohibition on contraception and denounced the idea that the primary purpose of marriage was anything other than producing and raising children. He condemned contraception as "base and intrinsically indecent" and said that it "violates the law of God and nature, and those who do such a thing are stained by a grave and mortal flaw."[12]

The encyclical was read to ban all known forms of contraception: withdrawal, the use of condoms or diaphragms, douching after intercourse, and folk contraceptive potions.[13] However, the pope appeared to give approval to a birth control method that had been rattling around since the ancient Greeks but had seen a spike in interest since the discovery of female ovulation in the mid-1800s: timing sexual intercourse to coincide with a woman's naturally occurring sterile period.[14] The method had limited practical application at the time because science had yet to figure out exactly when during the menstrual cycle women ovulated, although some couples did try to put it into practice—often with unsatisfactory results.[15]

But all that changed in the early 1930s, right around the time of *Casti Connubii*, when scientists finally determined when ovulation typically occurred, allowing for the development of the rhythm method. It was far from perfect, but it did offer a way to at least slow the growth of a family without resorting to contraceptives. The Vatican earlier had indicated preliminary acceptance of rhythm, but growing interest in the method elevated the question of whether it was acceptable under Catholic doctrine to a pressing theological concern.[16]

The question was not definitively answered until 1951 by Pope Pius XI's successor, Pius XII. In an address to the Italian Catholic Society of Midwives, he declared that the "observance of the sterile period can be licit" if done for serious reasons. He said, however, that serious indications for limiting births included "medical, eugenic, economic, and social" reasons, which went far beyond the reasons traditionally accepted by even the most liberal of Catholic theologians for refraining from sex to limit family size: extreme poverty or a serious threat to the woman's health. In doing so he gave the Catholic Church's stamp of approval to the idea of couples purposely manipulating the size of their family for the sake of the family's overall well-being. In case there should be any doubt as to what he meant, a month later he confirmed, "We have affirmed the lawfulness and at the same time the limits—in truth quite broad—of a regulation of offspring."[17]

So by 1960 the church had made three key admissions: that sexual intercourse within marriage played a role that was not limited to procreation; that it was acceptable to limit family size for a number of reasons; and that it was licit to use the naturally occurring sterile period to do so. Enter Catholic physician John Rock, who helped to develop the birth control pill. By designing a contraceptive that used hormones already present in a woman's body to mimic the natural infertility of a pregnant woman, he hoped the Vatican would find a theological basis to approve the method. In 1958, when the Pill was already being tested on human populations, Pius XII said its use would be acceptable "as a necessary remedy because of a disease of the uterus or the organism" even if had the secondary effect of causing sterility. This meant women could use the Pill to treat painful periods or excessive bleeding, which became a popular early theological work-around for Catholic women who wanted to use it.

Theologians also speculated that the Pill could be used to regulate irregular menstrual periods to make the rhythm method work more effectively—which led to an extensive theological discussion about what constituted an irregular enough menstrual cycle to qualify. Of course, that raised the question that if the Pill was allowed to make the menstrual cycle regular enough to permit the reliable use of rhythm, why not just permit the use of the Pill?[18]

Pius XII appeared to condemn such use in 1958, but the question only gained steam with the Food and Drug Administration's approval of the Pill in 1960 and evidence that many Catholic women were using it without waiting for instruction from the Vatican. Theologians began cautiously suggesting that the Pill could be lawful under Catholic doctrine as long as it wasn't used for "hedonistic purposes."

In 1963 the bishops of the Netherlands called for discussion of the question of oral contraception use at the upcoming Second Vatican Council. Three European theologians wrote articles in 1963 and 1964 for respected theological journals that concluded that it was licit to use hormonal contraceptives to regulate births.[19] A rash of books appeared during the same period criticizing the hierarchy's complete prohibition of birth control. Former Bombay Archbishop Thomas Roberts declared there was no theological basis for the church's ban in *Contraception and Holiness*, which included essays by Ruether and other theologians. The ban was also criticized by a Georgetown University theologian in *Contraception and Catholics* and by lay Catholics in *The Experience of Marriage*, in which thirteen Catholic couples wrote about trying to use the rhythm method, and *What Modern Catholics Think about Birth Control*. Father Bernard Häring, who was considered the dean of Catholic moral theology, wrote that Pius XII's informal statement prohibiting use of the Pill as a regular form of birth control should not be taken as the last word and said that the church should seriously examine whether use of the Pill would help married couples practice responsible parenthood.[20]

In 1966, John Noonan published *Contraception,* his sweeping history of the evolution of Catholic contraception theology, in which he concluded that Christian doctrine "did not have to be read in a way requiring an absolute prohibition" on contraception. He said that the doctrine was a reflection of the times in which it had been developed, in which society sought to promote the sanctity of marriage and place limits on sexual behavior and in which "slavery, slave concubinage, and the inferiority of women were important elements of the environment affecting sexual relations." He noted the "profound" changes in church doctrine regarding marriage and marital intercourse and said this should affect the way the church viewed contraception. "[I]t is a perennial mistake to confuse repetition of old formulas with the living law of the Church," he warned.[21]

Traditionalist theologians held fast to the distinction between artificial and "natural" contraception, arguing that rhythm was acceptable because it did not interfere with the integrity of the act of intercourse (although many proponents of the Pill argued that it was acceptable because it didn't physically interfere with intercourse like other contraceptives). The debate over contraception emerged as the major issue facing the Catholic Church. Popular publications wrote about the "Catholic Revolution" and the "Growing Unrest in the Catholic Church" as the controversy became the subject of widespread discussion.[22]

With the debate raging, Cahill and Ruether weren't content to sit on the sidelines and hope that the church fathers would eventually get around to changing the rules. They wanted to have a hand in formulating the rules. They were among the first women in the United States to get advanced degrees in theology—the study of church doctrine and teaching to arrive at the essential truths of the faith. As they studied the church's teaching regarding women—rules that forbade women from becoming priests, required women to "submit" to their husbands, and forbade the use of contraceptives—they began to suspect that these rules had less to do with the Catholic faith and more to do with the ways that the church and society had traditionally viewed women.

Historically women were seen as lesser versions of men in every way. They were thought to be less intelligent and less emotionally developed. Traditional reproductive beliefs dating back to Aristotle held that men contributed the spark of life, the soul, to an embryo through semen, while women contributed only the raw physical matter through their menstrual blood. The equal role of the sperm and egg in reproduction—therefore of the male and female—had not been recognized until 1875 and the old misunderstanding had tainted thinking about women for centuries. Pioneering feminist theologians like Cahill and Ruether sought to tease out what was real in Catholic doctrine and what were simply long-standing societal prejudices against women.

In 1966, Cahill published one of the first serious feminist theological treatments of the issue of contraception in a religious journal. Titled "Contraception and Eve," it took a fresh look at the story of Adam and Eve as it applied to contraception. In it, Cahill questioned why Adam, who is punished for the fall of man by having to "work by the sweat of his brow," is allowed to use labor-saving devices to mitigate his punishment, while Eve, who is punished by an increase in the number and frequency of her pregnancies, is not allowed to use contraception "to put reasonable control back into women's role as human wife and mother." In this light, Cahill said, instead of being considered an affront against nature, contraception could be considered a form of redemption for women and "part of the restoration of women and men and marriage itself in Christ." It was an example of how women could bring a completely different reading to traditional Catholic theology—one that was, not surprising, more sympathetic to the needs of women and the real-life demands of pregnancy and childrearing.[23]

In 1967, Ruether published her first book, *The Church against Itself*, in which she lamented the inability of the church to "delve deeply enough to create a viable theology of radical change" on issues like birth control because of its irrational commitment to outdated doctrines from the past. But the real thunderclap came in 1968, with the publication of Mary Daly's *The Church and the Second Sex*.[24]

Daly was a classmate of Cahill's at St. Mary's College, a women's Catholic college that in the mid-1950s became the first in the United States to grant advanced degrees in theology to women. After she received her doctorate in theology from St. Mary's, Daly went to Switzerland to study at the University of Fribourg for her doctorate in sacred theology, the highest Catholic theological degree. No university in the United States would grant the degree, which allows theologians to teach theology or canon law at Catholic universities and seminaries, to a woman. It prepares theologians to participate in the highest levels of theological debate within the church, which is essential to creating and interpreting church doctrine. Daly said the church's historical refusal to allow women access to a theological education was part of its systematic exclusion from leadership and decision-making roles in the church and "perpetuated an atmosphere in which theologians—all male—felt no pressure to give serious attention to the problems of the other sex."[25]

Daly was propelled in her groundbreaking critique of sexism in the Catholic Church by her own difficulty in obtaining a theological education and her experience at the Second Vatican Council, the historic worldwide church meeting called by Pope John XXIII in the early 1960s to discuss how the Catholic Church could modernize and, in his words, open the windows to "let in some fresh air." Despite pronouncements about a new era of openness in the church and a greater role for lay Catholics, women were largely excluded from Vatican II. There were no women among the thousands of bishops, theologians, canon lawyers, lay observers and observers from other religions who were the official attendees at the first two sessions of the council. This prompted Belgium Cardinal Leo Jozef Suenens to ask, "Why are we even discussing the reality of the church when half of the church is not even represented here?"

Eventually fifteen women were invited to attend the third and fourth sessions of the council as "auditors," but their role was largely restricted to observing the sessions. There was even a separate café constructed for their use to segregate them from the male conference attendees and the "real" action of the conference.[26]

Daly was in Rome in the fall of 1965 for the last session of the council, just another doctoral student among the throngs of students, journalists, and Catholics from around the world attending the historic "carnival" that was Vatican II—part ecclesiastical conference, part free-ranging theological debate on the past and future of the church, part Catholic pageant. The excitement was palpable as liberal Catholics like Daly eagerly anticipated "the greatest breakthrough in nearly two thousand years" as the church "came bursting into open confrontation with the twentieth century." They hoped that the church would shake off the constraints of its dusty dogma and become what they knew it could be—a powerful force for good and social justice in the modern world.[27]

Daly borrowed a press pass from a journalist friend to attend one of the major conference sessions at St. Peter's Basilica. What she saw sitting in the press box changed her view of the church, and her life, forever: "I saw in the distance a multitude of cardinals and bishops—old men in crimson dresses. In another section of the basilica were the 'auditors': a group which included a few Catholic women, mostly nuns in long black dresses with heads veiled. The contrast between the arrogant bearing and colorful attire of the 'princes of the church' and the humble, self-depreciating manner and somber clothing of the very few women was appalling. Watching the veiled nuns shuffle to the altar to receive Holy Communion from the hands of a priest was like observing a string of lowly ants at some bizarre picnic."[28]

The Vatican would shortly decree in The Church in the Modern World (Gaudium et Spes), one of the key products of Vatican II, that "every type of discrimination," including discrimination based on sex, was wrong. It would also recognize for the first time that women should be free to "embrace a state of life, or to acquire an education or cultural benefits equal to those recognized for men."[29] But the reality of how the church viewed women was on display in Rome. Not only were women denied a meaningful role in the conference itself, but female observers were harassed and discriminated against by members of the hierarchy. A female reporter sitting among male journalists on the main conference floor was removed by a Vatican official and told that she had to sit in the balcony. A woman who was an expert on global poverty was denied her request to address the council and was replaced by a man. Another woman was prevented from receiving communion at a mass during Vatican II. For Daly, it was as if a veil had been lifted from her eyes. She finally saw how the church really viewed women: "as not quite human."[30]

Daly returned to Fribourg to begin work on The Church and the Second Sex, her groundbreaking effort to excavate the roots of sexism in Catholicism. It would become The Feminist Mystique for American

Catholic women. In it, she showed that many of the foundational texts of Catholicism, from the Bible to the writings of church fathers like Augustine and Aquinas, were seeped in a "fierce misogynism" under which women were viewed as inferior and subordinate to men. These views went as far back as the story of creation of Eve from Adam's rib. St. Paul said that "man was not made from women, but woman from man. Neither was man created for women, but woman for man." Pauline doctrine was widely interpreted throughout the Bible to mean that women were subservient to men in the natural order of things.[31]

It was also widely held that women were mentally and physically inferior to men. Aquinas called women "defective" and "misbegotten" and said "the image of God is found in man, not in woman."[32] The writings of these men, Daly said, "have been used over the centuries as a guarantee of divine approval for the transformation of women's subordinate status from a contingent fact into an immutable norm of the feminine condition."[33]

Under this paradigm, women's only value, and their salvation for leading men into sin in the Garden of Eden, was the one thing nature had equipped them to do: bear children. At the same time, said Daly, the all-male priesthood had a horror of anything related to the physical aspects of sexuality because of the church's emphasis on celibacy as a holier state than marriage and the association of sex with the fall of man. Women were considered polluted by their close association with sex and childbearing. Tertullian called women "the devil's gateway."[34] As a result, they were quarantined from contact with certain aspects of the church. Hence the old ritual of "churching," in which a women had to be purified after giving birth in order to return to church, and the prohibition against women entering the inner sanctum of the alter to serve as altar girls or lectors. "Valued chiefly for their reproductive organs, which also inspired horror, and despised for their ignorance, they were denied full personhood," wrote Daly.[35]

The result, said Daly, was the Catholic Church's particular myth of the "eternal feminine," which demonized women in the flesh as gossipy, simple-minded, and sinful even as they were lionized in the abstract as paragons of obedience and submissiveness who found "generic fulfillment in motherhood." This myth was used to justify women's subordinate position in the church—and until recently in society—and closed the church to the type of theological evolution that would allow it to grapple more effectively with modern issues affecting women, like the use of birth control.[36]

The warnings of both Ruether and Daly about the church's inability to evolve and take a more realistic view of women and sexuality were fulfilled the same year *The Church and the Second Sex* was published, when Pope Paul VI issued *Humanae Vitae* (Of Human Life), his long-awaited encyclical on birth control use. In 1963, Pope John XXIII, who had succeeded Pius XII, appointed a commission that would eventually comprise fifty-five members, including five married Catholic women, theologians, priests, and physicians, to study the question of whether the church's teaching on artificial contraception should be changed. There is some indication that he created the commission as a way to isolate the incendiary issue of birth control from the Vatican II proceedings, which were already dealing with a number of controversial doctrinal issues, and had no real intention of changing the policy on birth control.

Originally there were no lay members on the commission, but when they were added they were all married Catholic couples drawn from conservative Catholic family organizations who could be expected to mirror the hierarchy's position on contraception. The commission studied Catholic teachings on contraception and marriage and heard from its lay members on the realities of using the rhythm method. Contrary to the assertions of the hierarchy that the rhythm method, with its continual obsession with fertile periods and the timing of sexual intercourse, was a way to bring couples closer together and strengthen marriages, they heard that it stressed marriages and drove couples apart.

They also heard from the women on the commission about the importance of sex in marriage beyond procreation and the burdens of repeated or poorly timed pregnancies. After a series of hearings, the commission voted overwhelmingly to recommend that the ban against artificial means of birth control be lifted. After all, the church had accepted the idea of birth control, so why not give couples a better way to practice it if it would strengthen marriages and families?[37]

Unhappy with the direction of the commission, the Vatican packed the last commission meetings with fifteen bishops to formulate the final recommendation to the pope. But even the bishops voted nine to three (three abstained from voting) to change the teaching, concluding that the popes' previous teaching on birth control were not infallible and that the traditional theological basis for the prohibition of contraception was invalid. They declared that responsible parenthood was an essential part of modern marriage and that the morality of sexual acts between married couples were not dependent "upon the direct fecundity of each and every particular act" but must be viewed within the totality of the marriage relationship.[38]

Despite the commission's years of work and theologically unassailable conclusion that the church's teaching on birth control was neither infallible nor irreversible, Pope Paul stunned the world on July 29, 1968, when he reaffirmed the church's ban on modern contraceptives in *Humanae Vitae*. He declared that "each and every marital act must of necessity retain its intrinsic relationship to the procreation of human life."[39]

The pope had deferred to a dissenting minority report prepared by four conservative theologian priests on the commission that maintained contraception was a "sin against nature" and a "shameful and intrinsically vicious act." These theologians said that the church could not change its teaching on birth control because admitting the church had been wrong about the issue for centuries would raise questions about the moral authority of the pope, especially on matters of sexuality, and the belief that the Holy Spirit guided his pronouncements. "The Church cannot change her answer because this answer is true. . . . It is true because the Catholic Church, instituted by Christ . . . could not have so wrongly erred during all those centuries of its history," they wrote.[40]

As one of the conservative theologians famously asked one of the female members of the commission, what would happen to "the millions we have sent to hell" for using contraception if the teaching were suddenly changed?[41]

But another reason lurked behind the official explanation about why the teaching could not be changed: maintaining the link between sex and procreation was essential to the maintenance of the traditional, subordinate role of women. Maintaining the traditional family, in which men were leaders in the world outside the home and women were confined to the domestic realm by the demands of young children and repeated pregnancies, was a key concern of the Catholic Church. In the mid-1950s the

Catholic bishops made headlines when they condemned married working mothers for deserting their children and helping to destroy the home. Allowing women to regulate their fertility was dangerous to what the church considered the natural order of things: women as receptors of God's will as expressed through the acceptance of pregnancy.[42]

Stanislas De Lestapis, a Jesuit sociologist who was one of the four authors of the minority report, first warned against what he termed the "contraceptive mentality" in his 1961 book *Family Planning*. He said allowing women the freedom to regulate when they got pregnant would lead to a decline in women's maternal instinct and a hostility toward children, increased female promiscuity, and "confusion between the sexes." In the 1960s his fears about contraception were influential only among the members of the Vatican inner circle who were working to hold the line on contraception, but in the coming decades they would find currency with a much more influential figure and come to dominate much of the church's thinking about sexuality.[43]

Humanae Vitae came as a shock to Catholics, who had seen other aspects of the church—like the Latin mass and the teaching that Catholicism was the only road to salvation—change as a result of Vatican II and widely expected the contraception ban to be lifted. It seemed that the church was perfectly willing to evolve doctrine—except when it affected women.

The day following the encyclical's release, eighty-seven leading Catholic theologians released a statement condemning it, saying it relied on out-moded conceptions of papal authority and natural law. They said the encyclical was not infallible and because it was "common teaching in the Church that Catholics may dissent from authoritative teachings of the magisterium when sufficient reasons for doing so exist," Catholics couples "may reasonably decide according to their conscience that artificial contraception in some circumstances is permissible."[44] This statement was eventually signed by 600 Catholic theologians and was part of an unprecedented torrent of dissent that greeted the papal encyclical. Many of the world's most noted theologians dissented from the encyclical, including Richard McCormick, Bernard Häring, Hans Küng, and Edward Schillebeeckx. There were public statements of dissent from the theologi-cal faculties at Boston College, Fordham University, Marquette University, and the Pope John XXIII National Seminary. Bishops' conferences in the

United States, Canada, Belgium, Germany, the Netherlands, France, and Holland also issued statements saying that Catholics who found it impossible to follow the teaching could use birth control in good conscience.[45]

The outcry over *Humanae Vitae* only further reinforced the belief of Catholic feminists that the church's teaching regarding sexuality had little to do with theology. Anthony Padovano, the theologian who authored the response by the U.S. bishops, agrees. "*Humanae Vitae* was really not dealing with contraception. It was dealing with the authority and prestige of the magisterium," he said. To Daly, Ruether, and Cahill the birth control encyclical was just more evidence that nothing would change in the church unless women made their voices heard.[46]

. . . . .

When Elizabeth Farians was young, she couldn't figure out why no one ever asked her what she wanted to be when she grew up. Somewhere along the line, she figured out it was because for a Catholic girl growing up in the Midwest in the midst of the Great Depression there were only two choices: wife and mother or nun. But Betty, as she was known, chafed against the restrictions placed on women. Women weren't expected to think or play too hard, which didn't suit her. She was a born scholar, winning scholarships and making the dean's list semester after semester even as she crammed high school and college into three years each for fear she would have to drop out and go to work to help support her family, who were so poor that at one point they lived in friend's basement. She was also a talented athlete. She excelled at softball, basketball, and track and field at a time when women were discouraged from playing competitive sports.

After college, Farians got a master's degree in education and worked as a physical education teacher for girls, encouraging them to get involved in team sports, which she believed promoted self-confidence and leadership in women. She helped organize some of the first community sports leagues for girls in Cincinnati and, deeply influenced by the social justice teachings of the Catholic Worker movement, racially integrated them, a local first. But Farians had the feeling she was destined for something greater; she had a strong religious bent and wanted to be "dedicated" to

Figure 2. Elizabeth Farians as a young theologian. Farians was one of the first women in the United States to receive a theology degree. (Courtesy of Elizabeth Farians)

something larger than herself but didn't want to live the restricted life of a nun.[47]

The answer came when she heard that the first theology program for women had opened. "That was a tremendous breakthrough for women," she recalled. "This new school meant that women no longer had to listen to men telling them they were inferior mentally and spiritually, or that women's supposed inferiority was by divine design." At St. Mary's she became fast friends with another firecracker of a young theologian—Mary Daly. Together they relished the opportunity to study the foundational texts of Catholicism and receive the kind of education that had formerly been reserved only for men. Both Farians and Daly understood what this meant. For the first time, Farians said, "Women could speak with authority in religious circles, and even talk back."[48]

After graduating, Farians struggled to find acceptance in the all-male world of Catholic theology. She taught Thomistic philosophy (the teaching of St. Thomas Aquinas) at the University of Dayton with the understanding that she would be "allowed" to teach theology after two years. When she pressured the school to live up to their agreement, she was fired. She

Figure 3. Elizabeth Farians in Rome in July 1964, shortly before the start of the third session of the Second Vatican Council. (Courtesy of Elizabeth Farians)

was the first woman accepted into membership in the Catholic Theological Society, but when she showed up at their annual banquet in 1966 the priest at the door threatened to call the police if she didn't leave. Father Charles Curran, a well-known progressive theologian who would soon be the leader of the opposition to *Humanae Vitae,* personally escorted her inside the meeting, officially integrating the society.

Farians was an activist by nature. Like fellow theologian Ruether, she took part in some of the early civil rights protests in the South, compelled by Catholic social justice teaching to join the nonviolent movement for African American equality. By the mid-1960s her own experiences with discrimination led her to begin agitating for change in the church. In 1965 she helped Frances McGillicuddy organize the U.S. chapter of the St. Joan's Alliance, a UK-based Catholic feminist organization that had successfully pushed for the inclusion of women auditors at Vatican II. St. Joan's focus was on getting women into the priesthood as a way of ensuring equity in the church. It was the first progressive Catholic laywomen's organization in the United States and included Daly and Jane Cahill.

In 1966, while she was teaching at Sacred Heart University in Bridgeport, Connecticut, Farians created the Ecumenical Task Force on

Women and Religion to bring together Protestant and Catholic women to tackle the issue of sexism in religion. When she heard that Betty Friedan, the author of *The Feminist Mystique,* had started the National Organization for Women (NOW) to "bring women into full participation in the mainstream of American society" and was going to be in Bridgeport, she called her up and asked to meet. Over a drink in the bar of the Bridgeport railroad station, Farians convinced Friedan that religion was a "root cause" of women's oppression and should be included as a core issue for the largely secular women's rights movement. At NOW's next annual meeting, the Task Force on Women and Religion was added as one of NOW's seven founding task forces and Farians was elected to the NOW board of directors.[49]

Farians began applying her experience with protests, which by the late 1960s had become a staple of activism across a range of issues from civil rights to the Vietnam War, to the fight for women's rights in the church. Farians had taken part in both traditional labor protests and NOW's groundbreaking protests of institutional sexism—from all-male "executive" flights and tap rooms that prohibited women to companies like Colgate-Palmolive that kept women from the best-paying jobs by barring them from positions that required lifting more than thirty-five pounds.

Farians was there when NOW picketed the *New York Times* for the common newspaper practice of segregating classified ads by sex, with the high-paying management and executive jobs reserved for men and the low-paying secretarial and administrative jobs the province of women. "I remember going into the *New York Times* building with our hands full of newspapers and just dumping them until the editors couldn't open their doors—they wouldn't talk to us or do anything about the classified ads so we organized a protest," she said.[50]

In 1968, the NOW task force, which included McGillicuddy and Daly, called for a "National Unveiling" to protest the Catholic tradition of requiring women to cover their heads in church, which it considered a sign of women's subjugation. The following April the "Easter Bonnet Rebellion" took place at a church in Milwaukee where a priest had criticized a woman from the pulpit for not covering her head. Some fifteen women approached the priest to receive communion during Easter mass, removed their purposely large hats, placed them on the communion rail, and proceeded to receive communion in what is believed to be "first church demonstration for women's rights."[51]

When a new Catholic missal was published in 1970 that allowed women to serve as lectors at mass for the first time, but only if no man was available and required them—unlike laymen—to stand outside the holiest part of the altar, Farians was enraged. She organized the "Pink & Ash" protest. A copy of the new regulation was ceremoniously cremated and the ashes were tied in a pink ribbon and sent to Cardinal John Dearden, head of the National Conference of Catholic Bishops (NCCB), at the bishops' annual meeting. A poem by Farians was included that read:

> We have burnt your sacred books.
> Your latest oppressive words.
> We are sick with your pomp and male prerogative.
> We are weary of your callous stance toward women in the church.
> You have raped us of our rights.
> And preached that it was in the name of God.[52]

By 1970 Farians, with her quick wit, outspoken demeanor, and knack for protest, was the national voice of Catholic feminism. "Some day soon some pastor is going to tell a woman she can't read the epistle and she's going to pop him one," she told the *New York Times* with her typical flair.[53] Farians's outspokenness came with a price, however. In 1970 she was fired by Loyola University for her feminist protest activities. She had taken the job at Loyola after being fired by Sacred Heart University for inviting a Vietnam War protester who had burned his draft card to address her class. Daly had suffered a similar fate after the publication of *The Church and the Second Sex*, but the faculty at Boston College had relented and rehired her after protests against her dismissal shook the campus. Farians wasn't so lucky and found herself out of work and struggling to maintain her theological career. She wrote to one friend that the "personal struggle has been lonely and depressing." She attempted to quit the NOW task force to concentrate on teaching, but the board refused her resignation because her work was so critical.[54]

Farians sought dialogue with the church. In 1970 she collected the most prominent Catholic feminist groups, including the NOW Women and Religion Task Force, the St. Joan's Alliance, the National Coalition of

American Nuns, which represented feminist women religious, and several smaller groups into the Joint Committee of Organizations Concerned with the Status of Women in the Church. Farians badgered the NCCB to meet with the committee about discrimination against women in the church. In August 1970, the committee was granted a meeting with the newly formed liaison committee of the NCCB, which was the first time the bishops met with women about women's role in the church. They presented the bishops with a list of demands that included "the moral condemnation of sexism, an end to sex discrimination by the church, and an affirmative action program for women."[55]

When the committee received no response from the NCCB, Farians showed up at their annual meeting in 1971, where she castigated the bishops for refusing to end sexism in the church. "Because of the sex equals sin syndrome which permeates the church and the almost total identification of women with this, women have been excluded from meaningful participation in the church . . . Women want their God-given rights of personhood restored," she said.[56]

The bishops may have disregarded Farians, but she got the attention of someone else who was concerned about the voice of women in the church as it related to another, even more controversial matter and was following the work of these four wise women—Cahill, Ruether, Daly, and Farians—with increasing interest. By the early 1970s, Farians had shown how to use creative liturgical protests to highlight sexism in the church. Ruether had gone public with what many Catholic women were feeling about the church's irrational position on birth control. Cahill had offered the first substantial theological criticism of the church's position on birth control from a woman's perspective. Daly had excavated the roots of the church's misogyny and sparked a feminist revolution within the church. But it would take a fifth woman to harness the work of these pioneering women and bring it to bear in the one area that no one was talking about in the church: abortion.

2 The Dread Secret

By the time Pope Paul VI announced his decision in 1968 to continue the church's ban on contraceptives, contraception was on its way to becoming a non-issue for most Catholics. "I don't care what the pope says. . . . I have made my decision," one Catholic housewife told the *New York Times*. Apparently many Catholic women agreed, because their use of "artificial" methods of contraception continued to increase throughout the late 1960s and early 1970s. By the mid-1970s, some 60 percent of Catholic women would be using methods of birth control not sanctioned by the church. But there was another issue on the horizon that could not be so easily ignored: abortion.[1]

In the late 1960s, abortion was not yet a major issue in the United States. In fact, abortion wasn't discussed at all, at least not publicly. When newspapers were forced to refer to it, usually in a story about the death of a woman from a back-alley abortion, they used the euphemism "an illegal operation." Abortion was regulated by the states, and every state banned the procedure except to save a woman's life, except for a few states that allowed it for severe threats to a woman's health. The federal government was largely silent on the issue of abortion except for the nineteenth-century Comstock anti-obscenity law, which made it illegal to distribute information about the procedure. But the fact that abortion was illegal didn't mean it didn't exist. In fact, abortion had always existed in America—what changed was how society viewed and regulated it. And after nearly a hundred years of trying to hide the reality of abortion by banishing it to back alleys and referring to it euphemistically, it came roaring back into the public consciousness in the 1960s.

The historical record tells us that abortion has been practiced to some degree in every society, and America is no exception. During the colonial era every community had midwives and folk healers who would have known about herbal abortifacients such as hellebore and savin. Widely circulated home medical guides also directed women to common abortifacients and listed traditional methods thought to bring on miscarriage, including bleeding, vigorous horseback riding, and hot baths. Physicians knew basic methods to induce abortion, such as dilating the cervix or introducing an irritant to the uterus. But abortion was likely not widely practiced. Many of the folk techniques for inducing miscarriage were of limited effectiveness, and herbal abortifacients like savin could be deadly if used incorrectly. And the demand for abortion would have been low in early America. People got married young and large families were desirable in a rural, agrarian society. Even a premarital pregnancy was not terribly ruinous for a young woman as long as the father of the baby stepped up and married her, which the community took pains to ensure happened whenever possible.[2]

When women did turn to abortion it was generally to hide evidence of an illegitimate pregnancy when there was no prospect of marriage. But even then early abortion was not considered an especially serious legal or moral matter. There were no laws banning abortion, and under common law terminating a pregnancy before quickening—the point at which a woman can feel the fetus moving, usually sometime between the fourth and fifth month of pregnancy—wasn't a crime because the fetus wasn't considered a living person yet. Inducing abortion before quickening was widely referred to as restoring blocked or obstructed menstruation, which shows that most people in early America considered early fetuses to be part of the women's reproductive process, not individual human beings. Because only a woman could know whether her pregnancy had quickened, abortions were performed quietly by women themselves or by trusted folk practitioners and were believed to be limited to unwed women, there was little interest in making the procedure illegal.

This began to change as the country transitioned from a rural, farm-based society to an urban, industrialized society. Large families became less desirable and economically viable, but birth control methods were still primitive and unreliable. There were condoms, first made from sheepskin and other animal skins and then newly invented vulcanized rubber, but these were prone to failure, were uncomfortable, and had an unsavory association with prostitutes. Douching after sexual intercourse was the most popular form of birth control, but it was inconvenient, especially since many homes didn't have running water or indoor bathrooms. It could be effective in preventing conception if an effective spermicide like vinegar was used, but many women used water or other substances that were completely ineffective. Early iterations of diaphragms and vaginal sponges were difficult to use, especially for modest Victorian women, and not reliable. Women also attempted to use primitive versions of the rhythm method, which was often spectacularly ineffective because science had yet to figure out exactly when a woman's infertile period was.

Yet despite these limitations, the fertility rate for married women declined dramatically throughout the nineteenth century from just over seven children in 1800 to just under four by 1900. The consensus of social historians is that women used a combination of early contraceptive methods, abortion, and pressure on their husbands to refrain from sexual activity to affect this decline.[3]

The incidence of abortion as a method of fertility control increased markedly as the industrial and urban revolutions picked up steam. It was easy to access thanks to a proliferation of abortion providers in rapidly growing cities and the availability of mail-order patent abortifacients, although these varied in quality from completely useless to extremely dangerous. Women could also visit their local drugstores for abortifacient preparations compounded by their neighborhood druggist or turn to the time-honored emmenagogic recipes in popular home medical guides.[4] In his landmark book on the history of abortion, James Mohr estimates that the abortion rate went from one abortion for every twenty-five or thirty live births in the years from 1800 to 1830 to "as high as one abortion for every five or six live births by the 1850s and 1860s."[5]

Public awareness of the procedure skyrocketed. By mid-century, newspapers were full of thinly veiled ads for abortionists who treated "female complaints" and patent medicines with names like "French Renovating Pills" that promised to "restore the menstrual flow."[6] Newspaper readers were treated to salacious stories about notorious abortionists like New York's Madam Restell, a former seamstress who performed surgical abortions and sold patent abortifacient pills. Her services were so popular that she had branch offices in Boston and Philadelphia. In one Boston newspaper alone in 1845 there were ads from four doctors offering abortions.[7]

Just as important as the skyrocketing number of abortions was who was having them. Prior to 1840, abortion had been almost exclusively linked to illegitimacy. But the women procuring abortions in the mid-nineteenth century were married women from the Protestant middle and upper classes who simply didn't want any more children; they were using abortion as a method of birth control. A substantial percentage of Madam Restell's clients were "married women of good social standing." In 1854 the *Boston Medical and Surgical Journal* complained that abortion was no longer "exclusively performed upon unmarried women, who fly to the abortionist in the hope of being able to conceal their shame and degradation, but even married women who have no apology for concealment, and who only desire to rid themselves of the prospective cares of maternity." An early study of abortion in New York City estimated that married women accounted for 75 to 90 percent of abortions.[8]

That well-off, married women would seek to avoid having children was a shock to many people. To them it wasn't about women attempting some control over their fertility when a new baby would otherwise come along every year or two. It was about women shirking their God-given role as mothers. Social commentators and legislators complained about women who wanted a life of "ease" and "fashion" rather than the traditional pleasures of a full nursery. They also worried about the declining birthrate among native-born white women just as waves of Catholic immigrants, who had a notoriously high birthrate, were inundating America's shores. "Do [our native women] realize that in avoiding the duties and responsibilities of married life, they are, in effect, living in a state of legalized prostitution? Shall we permit our broad and fertile prairies to be settled only by the children of aliens?" asked a legislator in Ohio.[9]

Doctors were especially concerned about the burgeoning abortion rate. Not only did they have the same fears as others of their class that women were losing their taste for motherhood, but they were eager in the early days of the professionalization of medicine to flaunt their scientific expertise to differentiate themselves from unlicensed "irregular" physicians and folk practitioners like midwives—both of whom traditionally provided abortions—and to assert a leadership role in society. Through popular tracts, home medical guides, and medical journals, doctors set out to discredit quickening as a folk notion. They argued that abortion was immoral at all stages of gestation because it was impossible to tell when fetal life began. Under the auspices of the newly formed American Medical Association, doctors began a crusade to alert Americans to the immorality of abortion and end its practice. They lobbied state legislatures across the country to pass laws banning abortion at any stage of pregnancy except in the rare instances where it was needed to save the life of the woman.[10]

This first "pro-life" campaign, which argued that concern for fetal life trumped women's traditional prerogative to manage early and mid-term pregnancies, was one of the most successful legislative assaults in American history. Between 1860 and 1900, state after state banned abortion. By the dawn of the twentieth century abortion was illegal in every state.[11]

Abortion did not, however, go away. As surgery became safer and the Comstock Act ended the trade in patent abortifacients, surgical abortion supplanted traditional herbal concoctions. The procedure became the purview of physicians, who now decided who qualified for abortions under the narrow therapeutic exception for saving a woman's life. There were doctors who interpreted the law liberally to find reasons to perform abortions for women who wanted them—often by overstating the threat a particular medical condition like pernicious vomiting, diabetes, tuberculosis, or a heart problem posed to a patient's life. Throughout the first half of the twentieth century, most cities and larger towns had one or more trusted abortionists who went about their practice largely unmolested by legal authorities and who received referrals from established physicians for what they considered a regretful but necessary service. One doctor who practiced in the era remembered, "Every doctor—let's put it frankly—who wanted to help people had to have an abortionist he trusted."[12]

Especially during the economic hardships of the Great Depression, doctors who provided abortions became more willing to perform the procedure for "social reasons" such as economic distress, and both single and married women turned to abortion with increasing frequency. A Kinsey Institute study of 5,000 married white women found that they aborted just under 25 percent of their pregnancies during the depths of the Depression in 1930, and that 85 percent of these abortions were performed by physicians.[13]

Once again abortion was widespread, especially among married women, and once again there was a counterreaction. Beginning in the 1940s and coinciding with the emphasis on women's return to domesticity and childrearing after the Depression and Second World War pushed them into the workforce, there were widespread crackdowns on physician abortionists throughout the United States and "[r]aids of abortionists' offices became the national norm during the 1940s and 1950s."[14]

By the early 1950s the procedure had been driven almost completely underground, where it became the purview of unscrupulous, unlicensed providers. At the same time, hospitals created abortion review committees to regulate the provision of legal therapeutic abortions. A woman who wanted an abortion had to go to a doctor, who had to go before a committee of three or more colleagues and get permission to do the abortion. The entire process was designed to embarrass women and discourage abortion; there often were several examinations as well as detailed questioning about the woman's personal life and her reasons for wanting an abortion.[15]

Technically abortion was legal only for threats to a woman's life, which was a medical rarity by the second half of the twentieth century. But sympathetic doctors would stretch the indications to advocate for the procedure for a woman whose well-being was threatened by a pregnancy, especially if she was ill or impoverished or already had a large family. Some doctors also would perform an abortion for a woman who had been exposed to German measles, which could cause deformed fetuses. Doctors also used psychiatric grounds to justify abortions for women who supposedly threatened suicide if they had to carry their pregnancy to term, under the broad interpretation of protecting their lives. This became an increasing popular strategy to provide legal abortions as other avenues closed, especially for unmarried college students who faced expulsion and social ruin if their pregnancies were discovered. "By the 1960s, it was widely known that a woman might obtain an abortion if she found the right psychiatrists and the right words," said Leslie Reagan in her history of illegal abortion.[16]

But getting a hospital abortion was not easy. Review committees were in the business of protecting the reputations and legal standing of hospitals and physicians, not in making abortion accessible. Their decisions about which women "qualified" for an abortion reflected the values of the time, which included the disapproval of premarital sex and a strong emphasis on women's role as mothers. Many hospitals had abortion "quotas" that placed a limit on the number of abortions they would perform. Review boards were also notoriously inconsistent from hospital to hospital. Two similar cases could be handled very differently by two different hospitals.[17] Hospitals in conservative areas or with Catholic physicians on the review boards were especially likely to refuse just about all abortions.[18] The rigors of abortion committee review had a chilling effect on the number of legal abortions performed in hospitals, which plunged from 30,000 in 1940 to 8,000 in 1964.[19]

Women with money had more options than women without. They were more likely to get legal hospital abortions because of their access to well-connected private physicians and their ability to pay for the multiple consultations that were often required. "It all depended on who you were. As long as you were the banker's daughter, the doctor's daughter, the golf buddy's daughter, it was always taken care of," one doctor recalled.[20]

At one hospital in New York City between 1951 and 1962, 88 percent of abortions performed were for patients of private physicians, while the largely African American and Hispanic ward patients got only 12 percent of abortions.[21] Women also could get illegal but safe abortions from reputable private physicians who did abortions on the side for a select clientele, but they were expensive. A 1955 survey of nine cities found the average cost of an abortion was $200 to $500 (approximately $1,600 to $4,000 today). By 1967, women in New York City were paying as much as $1,500.[22]

Women also could go to illegal but generally well-run clinics in Mexico or Puerto Rico—the Puerto Rico option being so popular with women from the East Coast that flights traveling the route were nicknamed the "D&C Express" in reference to the dilation and curettage technique used for abortions. Similarly, there was a popular route between the West Coast and Japan, where abortion was legal and easily arranged. But going abroad for an abortion took considerable time and money, so it was out of reach for most women.

The vast majority of women who were determined to get rid of unwanted pregnancies turned to the black market of underground abortionists, which was often a dangerous and humiliating experience. Women had no way of knowing whether the person performing the abortion was a doctor or was in any way qualified to do the procedure. Butchers, barbers, and salesmen were arrested for performing illegal abortions. Many of the doctors who turned to the trade in illegal abortions had fallen from the graces of the medical profession because of alcoholism, addiction, or incompetence. Women faced unsanitary conditions, sexual exploitation, and providers who were drunk. "It was a filthy operation," one woman said, recalling the "flophouse where this M.D. kept an office just for this purpose. The office itself was filthy, he smelled of booze. . . . When it was over, he tried to kiss me."[23]

Some women were picked up on street corners and blindfolded for the trip to the abortionist, adding to their overwhelming sense of powerlessness. Some of the abortionists were kind, or at least professional; many others were not. A college student who got an abortion in a small New England town got a lecture from the doctor on the evils of sinning before he performed the abortion. "There is no nurse, no anesthetic, you're tied down with rope," she recalled.[24]

Unsanitary conditions, ill-trained providers, and little medical followup turned what was a simple, safe procedure when performed correctly in a clean setting into a crapshoot of potential complications: perforated uterus, which was almost always fatal, raging postoperative infection, which a woman had a slightly better chance of surviving if she got immediate medical treatment, or permanent infertility. To add insult to injury, a woman who was hospitalized with post-abortion complications could expect a visit from the local police threatening her with jail time and demanding to know who performed the procedure, which deterred many women from seeking care even when they were desperately ill.[25]

Yet women still took the risk and suffered the consequences. In 1967 alone, 10,000 women were admitted to New York City municipal hospitals suffering from botched abortions. One doctor remembered that the gynecological ward at the New York-area hospital where he worked was supposed to have 64 beds but had 140 beds "all up and down the hallways." The beds were always full. Residents working a twenty-four-hour shift would get ten to twelve abortion-related admissions.[26]

Some of these women had incomplete abortions or abortion-related infections from procedures performed by incompetent abortionists. Many others suffered from botched, self-inflicted abortions—the ultimate act of desperation for women too poor or too ashamed to even seek out an illegal provider. Without the folk wisdom and emmenagogic recipes of midwives and other traditional healers to guide them, woman attempted to abort themselves with caustic solutions of Lysol or soap. They inserted catheters, knitting needles, coat hangers, or whatever else was at hand into their uteruses in an attempt to cause a miscarriage. All methods were incredibly dangerous. Abortion activist Bill Baird never forgot being in a New York City hospital in 1963 when a screaming woman covered in blood came stumbling down the corridor with an eight-inch piece of wire coat hanger protruding from her uterus. The woman died, becoming another one of the abortion-related deaths that accounted for nearly half of maternal mortality in New York City in the early 1960s.[27] Nationally, illegal abortions were estimated to kill anywhere between 1,000 and 10,000 women annually.[28]

That women were willing to risk illegal abortions speaks to the almost impossible calculus between the risks the procedure posed and the burden of an unplanned pregnancy—be it expulsion from college, another mouth to feed when there already wasn't enough to go around, the public shame of premarital sex in the chill dawn of the sexual revolution, or the fear deep in a woman's bones that either her sanity or health would not endure if she had to bear another child. But many, many women took the risk. In his influential 1966 book *Abortion,* Lawrence Lader estimated that well over 1 million illegal abortions were performed annually in the United States. He called abortion "the dread secret of our society."[29]

In 1962, Sheri Finkbine, the popular host of a local children's program in Phoenix and a mother of four, became a national symbol of the irrationality of abortion laws when doctors denied her an abortion after she unknowingly took the drug thalidomide, which had just been discovered to cause severe birth defects (the doctors originally approved the abortion but got cold feet when Finkbine went public in an attempt to warn other women about the dangers of thalidomide). Several years later a German measles outbreak had abortion back in the headlines, when women who had contracted the disease sought abortions for what they feared were deformed fetuses and doctors were threatened with prosecution for providing them. By then, the public health scandal of illegal abortion-related deaths and injuries, the injustice of denying the procedure to poor women when their richer sisters could find ways to work the system, and the inhumanity of forcing women to give birth to severely deformed children created a groundswell of support to reform abortion law. Physicians, the very people who had gotten abortion banned in the first place, began to push for changes to allow them to legally perform the abortions they had always done rather than relying on the subterfuge of the hospital review committee.[30]

In 1962, the American Law Institute (ALI) introduced model abortion reform legislation that recommended legalizing abortion for conditions that threatened the physical or mental health of the woman, in cases of severely deformed fetuses, and for rape or incest. The reform legislation still required a second doctor in addition to the doctor performing the procedure to certify that the procedure met the criteria.[31] It also denied abortion for women who simply wanted to terminate an unwanted pregnancy. As one proponent of the reform law explained at hearings on the proposal, the ALI would not sanction abortion for "some girl who goes out and gets herself in trouble and wants to get out of it by abortion."[32]

This began a state-level push to reform abortion laws. California became the first state to consider abortion reform in 1961, but the effort quickly ran into opposition from local members of the Catholic clergy and Catholic professional groups like the Catholic Physicians' Guild, which also opposed a 1964 reform effort. By the time the bill was reintroduced in 1966, the Catholic hierarchy had joined efforts to fight any change in abortion law, which would forever change the politics of abortion, and the trajectory of politics itself, in the United States.[33]

·   ·   ·   ·   ·

The Catholic bishops of the United States have been organized as a national entity since 1919, when the National Catholic Welfare Conference was established to advocate for Catholic interests in a country that was often hostile to Catholics. Since their large-scale arrival in America in the 1800s, Catholics had been viewed with suspicion because their primary allegiance was believed to be to the Vatican in Rome, not to the United States. Many also worried that the Catholic bishops would try to influence civil law to reflect Catholic doctrine. Throughout the nineteenth and the first half of the twentieth centuries, anti-Catholic discrimination was widespread. Few Catholics could be found in boardrooms, elite schools, or country clubs. Catholics largely lived apart from mainstream Protestant society, with their own working-class neighborhoods and schools organized around parish life. Local bishops were powerful figures whose authority over the faithful was unquestioned, and the hierarchy worked to emphasize the patriotism of their flock and protect them from discrimination.

The post–World War II era brought widespread change to this parochial world. Catholics assimilated into the mainstream, leaving their urban neighborhoods for the suburbs and gaining entry to institutions once reserved for WASPs, including the ultimate pinnacle of American achievement, the presidency itself, with the election of John F. Kennedy. The power of the bishops and the church began to decline, as did the need for them to protect Catholics from the outside world. The church convened the Second Vatican Council from 1962 to 1965 to discuss how it should respond to these changes and how it should relate to the modern world.

Vatican II urged the hierarchy to move beyond protecting the narrow interests of a Catholic minority to take a new, more engaged role in the modern world and confront broader social problems. It also recommended the establishment of national bishops' conferences that could assert the collective authority of the bishops at a national level. This was especially important in the United States, where the locus of government power had shifted to the federal level as a result of President Franklin Delano Roosevelt's New Deal and President Lyndon Johnson's Great Society programs. In 1966, the U.S. bishops replaced the loosely organized

National Catholic Welfare Conference, in which membership had been voluntary and participation desultory, with the National Conference of Catholic Bishops (NCCB), which officially represented all U.S. bishops. It also created an administrative arm for the bishops' conference, the United States Catholic Conference, giving the Catholic Church a fully staffed, highly centralized presence in Washington, D.C.[34]

The social issues that Vatican II urged the bishops to focus on were economic development, the fostering of peace in an age of nuclear weapons, and, most significant for the history of the church and the United States, abortion.[35] No issue would capture the attention of the Catholic hierarchy quite like abortion. The movement to legalize abortion challenged not just the hierarchy's prohibition against abortion as an "unspeakable crime," but also its belief that sex needed to be linked to procreation to preserve the sanctity of marriage. The bishops had long seen the maintenance of conventional sexual morality—even for non-Catholics—as their special purview. In 1921, as birth control was gaining widespread acceptance, New York Archbishop Patrick Hayes got the police to shut down a public discussion of contraception sponsored by the Voluntary Parenthood League. He defended his action as a "public duty" carried out not in a "sectarian spirit," but in the broad interest of protecting society from the pernicious effects of family limitation.[36]

They may have lost the battle over birth control, but the bishops had a new, even more consequential fight on their hands. From the mid-1960s onward, members of the Catholic hierarchy turned much of their attention to preventing the further legalization of abortion. As abortion reform gained momentum in California in the mid-1960s, the Diocese of Los Angeles hired Spencer-Roberts Associates, the political consulting firm that managed Ronald Reagan's successful gubernatorial campaign, to lobby against the measure. It organized the first "Right to Life" League, which was named by a local bishop based on wording from the Declaration of Independence, consisting of Catholic clergy and a handful of local anti-abortion activists. The idea was to create the appearance of widespread Catholic grassroots opposition to abortion reform so that it didn't look like Catholic opposition was a top-down effort, which might have reawakened fears about the Catholic hierarchy trying to impose its values in a pluralistic society.

When the abortion reform measure was reintroduced in the California Legislature 1967, these anti-abortion activists were flown by Spencer-Roberts to Sacramento to testify against the bill.[37] The abortion reform bill passed anyway and was signed by Governor Reagan, but the "Right to Life" movement had been concocted just as the fight over abortion reform was heating up. In 1967, fully half the states considered legislation to liberalize abortion law; three states in addition to California—Colorado and North Carolina, and Mississippi—liberalized their laws along the lines recommended by the ALI.[38]

The bishops moved aggressively to halt the momentum of abortion reform. They successfully pressured the governor of Indiana to veto a reform measure. When a bill to liberalize New York State's abortion law was introduced in early 1967 by influential Democratic assemblyman Albert H. Blumenthal, the eight Catholic bishops of New York State issued a joint pastoral letter that was read aloud at every mass in the state beseeching Catholics to fight the liberalized law "with all their power."[39] The bill was subsequently killed in committee, and the speaker of the assembly, who was Catholic, ousted Blumenthal as chair of the Democratic Advisory Committee at the behest of the Catholic bishops.[40]

That same year the Catholic hierarchy began to construct a national grassroots network to oppose liberalization of abortion laws. The NCCB gave the U.S. Catholic Conference's Family Life Bureau $50,000 to start a program to coordinate national anti-abortion activities, laying the groundwork for what would become the anti-abortion movement.[41] Under the direction of Father James McHugh, the Family Life Bureau monitored state-level abortion reform efforts and held regional meetings to organize anti-abortion activists. Most significant, it hired political consultant Martin Ryan Haley, who "worked behind the scenes to help state Catholic conferences and dioceses set up pro-life groups and trained members how to talk to state legislators."[42]

The NCCB also encouraged individual bishops to develop right-to-life groups. The bishops provided local groups, which were often just one or two activists, with places to meet, administrative support, free publicity in church bulletins and, perhaps most invaluably, exhortations from the pulpit for Catholics to work to oppose abortion.[43]

As a result of these activities, most of the earliest anti-abortion groups can be traced directly to the Catholic hierarchy. The Pennsylvania Catholic Conference created an Ad Hoc Committee on Abortion in 1967, which in 1969 became Pennsylvanians for Human Life, which had local chapters managed by priests.[44] That same year, the Right-to-Life League of Southern California was incorporated by the anti-abortion activists organized by the Archdiocese of Los Angeles.[45] Lansing Bishop Alexander Zaleski encouraged local parishes to form Right-to-Life Committees when advocates began pushing for reform legislation in Michigan in 1969. The Michigan Catholic Conference's Right-to-Life Committee was particularly active and effective. In 1970, it helped defeat Republican state senator Lorraine Beebe, the legislature's most outspoken advocate of abortion reform. It was also pivotal in defeating 1972's Proposal B, which would have allowed abortion in the first twenty weeks of pregnancy.[46] Anti-abortion activists receiving assistance from the church also founded pro-life groups in Virginia and New York.[47]

In 1968, the bishops' Family Life Bureau created the National Right to Life Committee (NRLC) as a formal structure to coordinate the activities of local right-to-life groups and to give the fledgling pro-life movement a national presence. It would become the single most powerful anti-abortion group nationally and was wholly a creation of the Catholic bishops.

The NRLC was the answer to the bishops' biggest political problem: the widespread perception that they were the anti-abortion movement.[48] In fact, when a coalition of anti-abortion groups were gearing up to oppose the Michigan ballot proposal, even the head of the Michigan Catholic Conference advised them to pick a Protestant woman as its leader to avoid the impression that the group was a tool of the bishops.[49] Officially, the NRLC was independent of the bishops' conference and headed by Juan Ryan, a Catholic lawyer from New Jersey. But it worked closely with the Family Life Bureau and received significant financial assistance from the bishops.[50]

Despite opposition from the Catholic bishops, a tide of abortion reform swept the nation between 1967 and 1970, as twelve states—mainly those without a strong Catholic Conference—reformed their abortion laws.[51] Most of these early abortion reform efforts were championed by men who were interested in making abortion more "humane" by broadening the circumstances under which doctors could legally perform the procedure. But the late 1960s brought a new constituency interested in changing abortion law: women. Like Jane Cahill and Rosemary Ruether, women increasingly saw controlling their fertility as essential to their ability to be equal in society and realize their full potential as individuals. The connection was not always obvious. When Betty Friedan founded the National Organization for Women (NOW) in 1966, the board didn't want to wade into the thorny issue of abortion reform, preferring to tackle safer issues like employment discrimination. But increasingly women realized that personal issues like abortion were as important to women's rights as workplace equality. On a practical level, the ability to control their fertility was essential to women's ability to access the higher education and workforce opportunities that had been reserved for men. On an emotional level, women began to acknowledge that they were angry that they were the ones who had to pay such a high price for an unwanted pregnancy.

It's hard to conceive of what a starkly different world it was for women in terms of sexuality and reproduction in the mid-1960s. The Pill had been introduced only in 1960, and although it was already rewriting the rules of sexual behavior, it still had its limitations. Early oral contraceptives had very high doses of estrogen, which caused side effects for many women and led them to discontinue use. Access to birth control also was limited by law. As late as 1965, twenty-nine states had laws limiting access to contraceptives. Some banned birth control from being advertised or information about birth control being distributed. Others allowed only doctors or pharmacists to distribute contraceptives and banned drugstores from selling condoms. Many states banned minors from buying contraceptives. Social convention also played a role. Many doctors would not prescribe contraceptives to unmarried women because they were afraid of promoting promiscuity, and many pharmacists kept condoms behind the counter for the same reason.[52]

A handful of Catholic states like Connecticut and Massachusetts still banned birth control even for married couples. The right of married couples to use contraception was not officially sanctioned until 1965 in the *Griswold v. Connecticut* Supreme Court decision, which recognized the right of privacy within marriage. Unmarried couples would have to wait until 1972's *Eisenstadt v. Baird* to be granted the same right. It was a society in flux. The old strictures were gradually falling away as the sexual revolution gained steam, but women did not yet necessarily have the tools to take advantage of the newfound sexual liberation that was being espoused.

At the same time, out-of-wedlock pregnancy and promiscuity in women were harshly judged and still had the power to alter the course of a woman's life. "You can't imagine what it was like," said sociologist Kristin Luker, who has studied attitudes about abortion and was herself a college student in the late 1960s, of the sheer terror brought about by an unplanned pregnancy in the days before *Roe v. Wade*. "The choices were to have an illegal abortion or to be sent away to the Midwest to have the baby," she said. Beyond that, there was the social approbation heaped on a woman who had an illegitimate pregnancy. "You can't believe how dirty and tainted the whole thing was—not the abortion, but the sex. In those days, sex was dirty. It was women's job to control it. If you got knocked up you had to pay the price," she recalled.[53]

Adoption was encouraged as the alternative to abortion for unmarried girls and women who got pregnant, but the adoption system could leave them feeling as disempowered as an illegal abortion. A woman who taught at a home for unwed mothers in the 1960s recalled the continual stream of middle-class young women sent from towns across America to hide the shame of their illegitimate pregnancies. Once safely removed from the prying eyes of the neighbors, the girls found themselves isolated in a "crummy Victorian mansion with twenty other women, each with a belly as full as hers, with backaches, varicose veins, stretch marks, piles, and a matching story of failure and loss."[54]

The girls were cloistered away until they delivered their babies. They were kept busy with art projects, endlessly constructing what the art teacher called "fear totems": tiny clay models with "strangely distorted breasts and bellies." They gave birth in the stark maternity wards of the local hospitals, attended only by strangers. Their newborns were whisked away after delivery to prevent any attachment from forming. A woman who got emotional and threw a fit about seeing her baby could find herself locked up in the psychiatric ward to preserve her "emotional tranquility." The home, the woman concluded, existed to punish "fallen" women, a form of oppression, she wrote with inestimable sadness, that was known "only to women."[55]

Unwanted children, back-alley abortions, crummy maternity homes—these were the choices, and they all seemed designed to punish women for sexual transgressions, for not wanting any more children, sometimes it seemed for just being women. But the legislative and public policy systems were still largely run by men. In February 1969, when New York State was again considering a reform bill, the joint Public Health Committee held a hearing in New York City. The panel consisted of fourteen men and one woman—a Catholic nun. Women sat mutely in the audience watching men discuss their reproductive lives.

But just as a white-haired former judge finished speaking, a woman named Kathy Amatniek stood up in audience and shouted, "All right, now let's hear from some real experts—the women."

Then Amatniek made a demand that was just gaining currency among feminists: "Repeal the abortion law, instead of wasting more time talking about these stupid reforms." A dozen other women stood up and began shouting to be heard on the issue as the men on the panel "stared over their microphones in amazement."[56]

Their outburst ensured that the otherwise staid hearing got media coverage.[57] Women were so incensed over their exclusion from the hearing that the feminist group Redstockings organized an all-women abortion "speak-out" at the Washington Square Methodist Church. There women on the panel did something that no women had done before: they went public about their abortions. They told of the fear, pain, and humiliation they endured. Then a really extraordinary thing happened. "[W]omen got up and started telling about their abortions from the middle of the audience," recalled Irene Peslikis, who helped organize the hearing. She said it was like a "bomb" went off. "All of the sudden they realized that this was something that had been bothering them for the longest time," she said.[58]

The publicity from the speak-out galvanized women across the country. They held abortion speak-outs in their living rooms. They questioned why they disproportionately suffered the consequences of sexual activity, why they had to risk their lives or health to get an illegal abortion or beg a man for a legal abortion. The result of this consciousness-raising was a sea change in how women perceived the politics of abortion. They started to see access to abortion as a right, an expression of their full personhood, not a favor to be granted by men. Women began pushing for what only a few years earlier had been considered a radical idea: removing doctors as the gatekeepers of abortion and allowing women to make the abortion decision. Feminists soon were calling for "abortion on demand" in a repudiation of the existing abortion model.[59]

The first organization to campaign openly for repeal of abortion laws in the early 1960s was the Society for Humane Abortion, founded by Patricia Maginnis. Maginnis suffered through three horrific illegal abortions after her contraception failed. She became a pioneer in getting people to discuss abortion openly. She traveled around California presenting classes on self-abortion and providing referrals for abortion providers in Mexico, hoping to get arrested to challenge state laws banning the provision of information about abortion. "At the time, even mentioning the word abortion was taboo and the mass media avoided the word completely. In California it was a felony even for the medical profession to discuss abortion techniques," she recalled.[60]

But Maginnis and her colleagues were just a tiny voice preaching what seemed an outlandish idea. But gradually, as the women's movement gained steam and the pure inanity and inhumanity of the current abortion situation became clear, abortion repeal came to the forefront of the women's rights movement. In 1967, NOW agreed to include "the right of women to control their reproductive lives" as one of eight planks in a Bill of Rights for women.

Speaking at the First National Conference on Abortion Laws in 1969, which led to the establishment of the National Association for Repeal of Abortion Laws (NARAL), the first national abortion rights organization, Betty Friedan spoke the words that would become a rallying cry for a generation when she asserted that "there are certain rights that have never been defined as rights, that are essential to equality for women. . . . The right of women to control her reproductive process must be established as a basic and valuable human civil right." Like her feminist colleagues, she dismissed the idea of abortion reform: "Don't talk to me about reform—reform is still the same—women, passive object. Reform is something dreamed up by men."[61]

Figure 4. Father Bob Drinan, dean of Boston College Law
School, advocated repealing all abortion laws pertaining to the
first two trimesters as the nation debated abortion reform in
1967. He said there was no such thing as a Catholic position on
abortion jurisprudence. (AP/Charles Gorry)

Repeal also found favor with some male abortion reformers like
NARAL cofounder Laurence Lader, who realized that reform, which
would allow only marginally more abortions, was an inadequate response
to the problem of illegal abortions. In 1970 the repeal movement gained
steam when it received the backing of several influential mainstream
organizations: Planned Parenthood, the President's Commission on the
Status of Women, and the YWCA.[62]

Repeal also found support from another, more surprising quarter.
Influential Jesuit law professor Robert Drinan created a stir when he said
that from the perspective of Catholic moral teaching it would be better for
all abortion laws to be repealed than for the government to be in the business of deciding who should and should not be born, as it would be forced

to do under reform measures. He advocated the complete repeal of laws prohibiting abortion in the first twenty-six weeks of pregnancy, with abortion treated as homicide thereafter.[63]

With support for repeal growing, Friedan and the New York chapter of NOW decided the time was ripe to push for repeal in New York State. It was a long shot. In a state that was 40 percent Catholic, the Catholic Church had used its clout in the legislature to turn back abortion reform efforts in 1967 and 1968. In addition, only four of the state's 207 legislators were women. They found a sympathetic legislator, however, in one of them: Connie Cook, a Republican from upstate New York.

Cook believed that a repeal measure was viable because it bypassed legislative arguments over the details of reform (some legislators wanted to allow abortions only for women who had four or more children, others refused to allow it for deformed fetuses, and so on) and would rally women. "The reason why they could never get any votes for reform is that reform is a terrible approach. When you pull in the State in any way—establishing grounds or hospital committees or any of that stuff—women are not interested. They'd rather go to an illegal abortionist," she said.[64]

Cook introduced a bill in 1969 that would strike all mention of abortion from the New York State penal code. This was the vision of repeal preferred by most of the New York feminists. Not only would it leave the abortion decision entirely to women, but it would allow nonphysicians to perform abortions, which the women felt was necessary to make the procedure truly accessible. The bill failed to get out of committee, however, and Cook went back to the drawing board.

After consulting with colleagues in the legislature and Lader about what realistically could pass, she came back with a revised bill in 1970 that returned abortion to the penal code but allowed women to make the decision about abortion up through the first twenty-four weeks of pregnancy (which was the historic division in New York State law between second-degree and first-degree abortion—tracking the traditional distinction between pre- and post-quickening abortion) but banned it thereafter except to save a woman's life. The bill also required doctors to perform the procedure.

The proposed measure cleaved the feminist community. Some thought the bill was a pragmatic adjustment that could pass and make abortion much more widely available. The more radical feminists, however, warned that allowing the government to put any conditions on abortion access was a mistake. They feared it would enable the gradual erosion of abortion rights as more and more conditions were added. Groups like New Yorkers for Abortion Law Repeal, which was the NOW New York abortion lobby, actively opposed the Cook bill and pleaded for abortion advocates to hold out for a measure that would give women the absolute right to control their reproductive destinies.

The radical feminists' analysis may have been correct in the long term, but in the short term they didn't have the votes in the legislature. The bulk of the feminist and abortion reform communities coalesced around the Cook bill, not wanting to lose the opportunity to pass what was by far the most liberal abortion measure in the nation. Immersed in the fight over a bill for parochial school aid, the bishops were caught flatfooted when the repeal bill began to move through the legislature with surprising speed. They were unable to halt its momentum despite a last-minute onslaught of pastoral letters and priests who singled out pro-repeal legislators as "murderers."

Despite ferocious lobbying from the Catholic hierarchy and after a dramatic last-minute vote switch by a legislator in a conservative, heavily Catholic district, who stood to gravely acknowledge that he was signing his political death warrant but said in good conscience he could not be the person to let the bill fail, the New York Legislature passed the law on April 9, 1970. Governor Nelson Rockefeller signed the bill in spite of a last-minute plea from New York Cardinal Terence Cooke.[65]

The New York bill was essentially a compromise between the repeal and reform positions. It became the model for broad-based abortion legalization when it was in effect codified by the U.S. Supreme Court in *Roe v. Wade*. But in many ways the fight over abortion in New York was just beginning.

·   ·   ·   ·   ·

The passage of the abortion bill was a rude awaking to Catholic pro-life forces in New York. The Right to Life Committee of New York State was galvanized by the loss and immediately began organizing to repeal the repeal. Membership in the group surged; within two years it had morphed from a tiny letter-writing organization into a major lobbying force of some 300,000 members organized into fifty chapters around the state.

The energized committee began flexing its political muscle in the 1972 legislative elections. It brought abortion opponents to the halls of the Capitol every day the legislature was in session to strong-arm legislators. "They didn't merely furnish the legislators with their information and point of view and ask them to consider the question on the merits, they brought it down to a question of political survival," said Alfred Moran, executive vice president of Planned Parenthood.[66]

As a result of pressure from the right-to-life forces, nine legislators who originally supported the abortion reform law voted to repeal the law in the spring of 1972. Only a veto by Governor Rockefeller—in which in a clear reference to the Catholic Church he noted that it is not "right for one group to impose its vision of morality on an entire society"—kept the measure intact.[67]

The near-death experience of the New York State abortion law was a wake-up call to abortion rights activists. They had long considered the Catholic bishops their single biggest opponent and now had to face a surging Catholic grassroots pro-life movement—Catholics made up 85 percent of the New York Right to Life Committee. By 1970 there was a right-to-life committee in just about every state. Between 1970 and 1973, after a string of successes, abortion reform efforts failed in state after state, most of them heavily Catholic. "If it weren't for the Catholic Church, the law would have been changed years ago," groused one legislator after three failed attempts to liberalize abortion law in Ohio.[68]

Supporters of legal abortion had good reason to fear the power of the Catholic Church. The hierarchy had been the most formidable opponent of the legalization of birth control. Once contraception gained acceptance in the 1930s, the bishops couldn't do much about middle-class women who received birth control through private physicians for "health" reasons, which the courts declared legal. They did, however, prevent the opening of public birth control clinics in northeastern cities that served largely immigrant and poor populations, blocked state legislatures from legalizing birth control, and turned back efforts to provide federal funding for family planning programs for the poor.[69] Their efforts on birth control didn't falter until the 1960s, when the popularity of the Pill and the widespread acceptance of contraception finally overwhelmed their lobbying.[70]

Although the abortion liberalization movement had been worried about the Catholic Church for some time, most activists were reluctant to attack the church directly for fear it would allow the bishops to hide behind charges of anti-Catholicism. But there was a way to rebut the bishops on abortion without running the danger of being called anti-Catholic: have other Catholics do it.[71]

As early as 1965, after attending a meeting of the Yorkville Democratic Club in New York and finding that most of the club's officers were Catholic and supported abortion reform, Lader espoused a strategy of splitting progressive lay Catholics from the hierarchy on the issue of abortion. As part of the push for the New York repeal measure, NARAL created an organization called New York State Catholic Women for Abortion Repeal, which was made up of seventy-five Catholic leaders. The group sent telegrams to every state senator saying that although many members personally opposed abortion, we "believe our church should not impose its will on our non-Catholic neighbors." It was the first Catholic group to back abortion reform, but it was little more than a letterhead organization.[72]

As abortion politics heated up in the wake of the passage of the New York law, the need for a credible, grassroots Catholic movement in favor of the legalization of abortion only became more acute. But publicly taking on the bishops on a matter on which they had staked so much of their ecclesiastical authority was a far cry from using birth control in the privacy of your own bedroom. As Father Drinan noted in 1968, "No Catholic group in America to date has advocated 'liberalization' for the civil law regulating abortion nor has any group even expressed the opinion that Catholics are free to select their own views on the matter."[73]

But that changed in 1971 in Pennsylvania. Pennsylvania had a powerful Catholic Conference and influential individual bishops. In 1965, when the State Office of Public Assistance recommended allowing staff to provide family planning counseling to low-income women, Archbishop John Krol decried it as a "dangerous experiment on the lives of the poor," and the Pennsylvania Catholic Conference (PCC) organized a successful campaign against the program. Between 1967 and 1970, the PCC managed to stymie abortion reform efforts by using its legislative power in Harrisburg and through the creation of Pennsylvanians for Life.[74]

Despite the opposition, however, reform efforts picked up steam after 1970, due to the success of the New York repeal bill and the election of a pro-reform governor. In September 1971, an organization calling itself Roman Catholics for the Right to Choose announced its support for the repeal measures before the state assembly. Mary Robison, the group's chair, said, "It appears . . . at least in the public mind—that opponents of abortion law repeal are Roman Catholics. Many undoubtedly are. But many Roman Catholics do not agree with the stand taken by our church in this regard."[75]

Roman Catholics for the Right to Choose was the first explicitly Catholic abortion rights organization and marked a new chapter in the evolving effort to legalize abortion, as Catholics for the first time went public with their support of abortion rights. The organization sent the assembly a petition in favor of repeal with the names of 500 Catholics. It said that while not all the signers found abortion "personally acceptable," they were in agreement "in our belief that our Church should not attempt to use civil law to impose its moral philosophy upon our non-Catholic neighbors."[76]

In December, Governor Milton Shapp announced the formation of an Abortion Law Commission to recommend changes to the law. Jane Cahill was living in Philadelphia, having recently completed a postdoctoral fellowship in religion at the University of Pennsylvania. She tried unsuccessful to get herself appointed to the commission but secured a spot to testify at one of four public hearings held by the commission.

In February 1972, Cahill presented the first detailed progressive theological defense of the morality of abortion at a public hearing in Harrisburg. She explained that the theory of delayed hominization, or the gradual ensoulment of the fetus, "was held by some of the greatest theologians in the Catholic Church and is still held by a goodly proportion of theologians today," and said this theory negated the hierarchy's absolutist contention that early abortions have always been considered murder by the church. She listed a number of contemporary theologians who were questioning the "one-dimensional nature" of the hierarchy's ban on abortion and called for the liberalization of abortion law to allow for abortions in the first trimester "when the woman felt in conscience justified in having it," and noted that later abortions could be "both morally and medically justifiable."[77]

Cahill's testimony brought her instant notoriety. Archbishop Krol reportedly referred to her as "the abortion woman." She engaged in a heated exchange of letters with Father John Foley, the editor of the diocesan newspaper *The Catholic Standard & Times,* over the theological validity of her testimony. Her testimony also caught the attention of someone else, a former stockbroker and NOW volunteer in New York City who would soon unite the work of Cahill, Rosemary Ruether, Mary Daly, and Elizabeth Farians into a far-reaching movement to challenge the hierarchy on the issue of abortion.[78]

3 Pope Patricia

Patricia Fogarty McQuillan was born in 1924, four years after the Nineteenth Amendment gave women the right to vote. She came of age at the start of the Second World War. She was one of the first women to be employed by United Aircraft Laboratories as a chemist. When the call went out for women to join the armed forces to "free a man to fight," she joined the Marines, where she repaired aircraft engines for the duration. After the war, she got an economics degree from Columbia University, worked for the IRS, and eventually became a stockbroker—one of the few women in the almost all-male world of finance. Along the way she married and had a daughter.

It was in many ways a stupefying time to be a smart, ambitious woman in America. Professional women were few and far between, and there was intense pressure on young women to get married at an early age and con-centrate on childbearing and housekeeping. In the 1950s, the average bride was twenty years old, which was younger than the age at which women got married in the late nineteenth century. Larger families also came into vogue. More than half of all women in 1955 said the ideal family was four or more children, versus just one-quarter of women who wanted families that large in the early 1940s.[1]

In 1963 Betty Friedan's *The Feminist Mystique* questioned the assumption that women were destined only for the domestic sphere and named the "problem with no name"—the boredom and dissatisfaction that plagued many housewives. Friedan said women would be more fulfilled if they were free to pursue careers outside the home. The publication of *The Feminist Mystique* converged with other great social forces that were rewriting the rules for women. The Pill freed women from the pressures of endless or unexpected pregnancies, allowing them for the first time to direct their lives independent of their reproductive systems. "Before 1960, when they didn't have anything but a lousy diaphragm, women were helpless creatures. They were just victims of circumstances. . . . And then, when they began to get [better contraception] you could just see them getting into jobs, planning their lives," said one woman OB/GYN who had been treating patients since the 1940s.[2]

Women began to enter the workforce in larger numbers—some out of choice and some out of necessity as the divorce rate increased, perhaps as women sought to escape marriages they had rushed into ten years earlier for fear of being an "old maid" by age twenty-five.[3] But here they found their options limited, because women largely were relegated to low-paying secretarial and administrative jobs. Higher-paying professional jobs were reserved for men. Women who wanted to advance in the workplace or in higher education also faced questions about their childbearing plans under the assumption that they would marry and abandon their careers.[4]

It was an era of brutal but casual sexism: stewardesses were forced to retire when they married or turned thirty-two because they no longer were fetching or available enough to do their jobs; pregnant (married) teachers could be fired because their students might be scandalized by their growing bellies; and some restaurants didn't allow women in during "business" hours. Some states still didn't allow married women to own property or enter into contracts. A married woman couldn't open a credit card or take out a loan in her name.

There was also formidable social pressure on women to stay at home. Day care was virtually nonexistent and leaving children in the care of someone else to go to work was frowned upon unless a woman was widowed or divorced. The belief that women shouldn't be working or were just waiting for a husband to come along justified employers paying them far less than men. Three-quarters of working women were at the very bottom of the job market.[5]

Prompted by Freidan, women began noticing the ways that the structures of society kept them from reaching their full potential and they began demanding changes. The second-wave feminist movement—so named because the first wave was the initial agitation for women's suffrage—was born. McQuillan, who had divorced and started her own financial advisory service, was an eager recruit to this new movement. After she sold her business in 1969, she became a full-time volunteer for the National Organization for Women's (NOW's) flagship New York chapter, where she was part of a coterie of groundbreaking second-wave feminists that included Freidan and Democratic representative Bella Abzug. McQuillan worked on mainstream feminist issues like employment discrimination and antiquated divorce laws that favored men. But she also was interested in an issue that the largely secular feminist movement ignored: religion.

To McQuillan, the relationship between what she saw as the patriarchal oppression of religion and the resulting lack of female agency in society was obvious. She struggled to reconcile her faith with church teachings that she found harmful to women. Like Mary Daly, she delved into the early writings of the church for answers. "I was shocked at the blame placed on women . . . for being sinful, harmful, evil people," she said.[6]

Like Jane Cahill, McQuillan came to believe that the bishops were wrong when they said that the church had always taught that abortion was murder and that Catholics could never support its legalization. From her research, she realized that the church's absolute ban on abortion was only a hundred years old and that the church had held varying positions on abortion that, like the ban on contraception, reflected cultural exigencies and contemporary attitudes about women and sex. "Abortion has nothing to do with religion. It is just politics, wanting to control women and keep them in their place," she concluded.[7]

In general, the Catholic Church has always taught that abortion is a sin. The *Didache* from around A.D. 100 named abortion among the principle sins, saying, "You shall not slay the child by abortions." It bookmarked the sin of abortion, however, with two other sins the church viewed in a similar light: the practice of *pharmakeia,* or the use of drugs or potions, particularly abortifacients or contraceptives, and infanticide, which was widespread in the ancient world, often in the form of exposure, or leaving unwanted infants outside. Like contraception and infanticide, abortion was associated with sins of the flesh, especially fornication, and circumventing the procreative purpose of sex. It was also linked to a general, widespread disregard for human life in the Greco-Roman world that early Christians sought to counter. Some early Christian writers called abortion an affront to God because it destroyed what he created but didn't consider it murder.[8]

Throughout most of the church's history, from about A.D. 400 onward, most theologians and moralists made a distinction between early and late abortion. The general belief was that abortion was homicide only after the fetus had received a soul. Neither Augustine or Aquinas, two of the church's most important theologians, taught that early abortion was homicide because they believed that the fetus was not ensouled in the first stage of pregnancy. This idea of "delayed hominization"—that the soul entered the fetus sometime during its development and not at conception—was the predominant belief throughout much of the history of Catholicism. It tracked the Aristotelian belief that the human soul underwent three stages of development: vegetable, animal, and eventually, human. The church most commonly held that the fetus was ensouled after forty days, although Aristotle taught that it took ninety days for the female fetus to be ensouled. Delayed hominization tracked the popular notion of "quickening"—that the fetus acquired human value as the pregnancy progressed. Nonetheless, Augustine taught that abortion, like contraception and infanticide, was a "sin against marriage" because it destroyed the procreative purpose of sex.[9]

The first collection of canon law from 1140 specified that abortion was homicide only when the fetus was "formed," or had a soul. As a result, penances for early abortion were similar to those for using contraceptives. One pope, Sixtus V, tried to equate abortion with homicide, largely in an attempt to reduce widespread prostitution in Rome. He declared in the 1588 bull *Effraenatum* that abortion at any stage of pregnancy (as well as the use of contraceptive drugs) was homicide and punishable by excommunication. But the prohibition was a failure and was overturned three years later by his successor, Gregory XIV, who found the stand not in keeping with previous theological views.[10]

Theologians throughout the history of the church also recognized abortions to save a woman's life as licit, in keeping with the principle that it is sometimes lawful to take a life to save one's own. Some theologians even posited that this would extend to a woman aborting a fetus to save her life if her family would likely kill her if they found out she was pregnant as the result of illicit sex, such as in a premarital pregnancy.[11]

But beginning in the 1600s the church started to move toward the idea that the fetus was ensouled at the moment of conception. This belief would pick up steam over the next centuries, influenced by the decline of Aristotelian thought as science discovered that human generation occurred from the combination of the sperm and egg. At the same time, the central teaching authority of the church, in the form of the Vatican, was becoming more powerful. The regional theologians who once held sway over moral philosophy were replaced by the authority of the pope; instead of many strands of thought, increasingly there would be only one.

There also was concern in the church about the declining birthrate in Catholic countries like France and what was assumed to be the rising incidence of abortion and contraception. It was perhaps no coincidence then, that in 1869, just as medical doctors in the United States were accelerating their crusade against abortion, Pope Pius IX issued the bull *Apostolicae Sedis*, which dropped the traditional distinction between ensouled and unensouled fetuses and said that abortion at any stage of pregnancy was punishable as a homicide by excommunication. This was officially codified by the church in 1917 in the revised Code of Canon Law.

By 1900, the Vatican also had ruled that abortions to save the life of a woman, even one facing "certain and imminent death," were never allowable. By the second half of the twentieth century, the Vatican was claiming that the church had always considered abortion murder and had always banned it completely. This gave widespread credibility to the view that the Catholic position on abortion was unchanged and unchangeable.[12]

While the hierarchy claimed an unchanged and unchangeable position on the morality of abortion, it was clear by the early 1970s that progressive currents in the church were moving in another direction. In 1973, noted theologian Charles Curran, who had led the opposition to *Humanae Vitae*, wrote, "[T]here is a sizable and growing number of Catholic theologians who disagree with some aspects of the officially proposed Catholic teaching that direct abortion from the time of conception is always wrong."[13]

A 1972 study of priests in New York State found that "priests are not so nearly unanimous about Church teaching on abortion as has been assumed. . . . [E]ven among those who uphold the Church teaching, there is disagreement as to whether their beliefs should be translated into restrictive legislation." The study found that nearly 40 percent of the priests surveyed disagreed or had doubts about the church's teaching on abortion; more than half of priests younger than thirty-five expressed disagreement or doubts.[14]

To McQuillan, it was clear that this emerging progressive theological perspective on abortion, as well as existing support for legalized abortion among the Catholic laity, would have to be made manifest to prevent New York's reform law from being overturned. What was needed was an explicitly Catholic abortion rights organization. "We were driven to organize because all of the polls indicated that anywhere between 68 percent and 90 percent of Catholic people, women and men, thought that there should be no criminal and restrictive laws against women who wanted or needed an abortion. In the interest of sanity and dignity we felt compelled to counteract the false propaganda," she told an audience in 1973.[15]

By the fall of 1972, as the battle over repeal of New York's law raged, McQuillan was drafting version after version of a manifesto for her new organization and reaching out to prominent Catholic feminists like Elizabeth Farians, Cahill, and Daly for support. Daly had renounced Catholicism in 1971, when, after preaching a sermon at Harvard's Memorial Church, she led women in an "exodus" from what she had concluded was a hopelessly patriarchal institution, but she remained a guiding force for Catholic feminists like McQuillan. Farians had participated in the exodus, yet she kept some ties to church reform efforts and was happy to advise McQuillan. "Abortion wasn't one of my issues, but I was in favor of what she was doing and helped her get it going," said Farians.[16]

With her deep understanding of Christian theology and ground-level experience in feminist protest tactics, Farians was invaluable. McQuillan also drew from her experience working with the irrepressible Frances McGillicuddy, the founder of the U.S. chapter of St. Joan's International

Alliance, who proudly called herself a "thorn in the side of the hierarchy." In August 1973, McQuillan joined McGillicuddy in a picket of St. Patrick's Cathedral to protest against the reading from Ephesians that said wives should be submissive to their husbands.[17]

In December, McQuillan announced the formation of Catholics for the Elimination of All Restrictive Abortion and Contraception Laws to protect legal abortion in New York, lobby for the elimination of all references to abortion and contraception in New York's criminal code, and "dispel the myth that all Catholics, or even a majority, favor restrictive abortion and contraception laws." (New York had repealed a measure in 1965 that banned the sale and manufacture of contraceptives but replaced it with a law limiting the sale of contraceptives to pharmacists, banning sales to minors, and forbidding contraceptive advertising.) McQuillan had found her calling. "I am an activist, thoroughly involved in the most revolutionary of all revolutions in history—the women's struggle to emancipate themselves religiously, spiritually and politically from sinful patriarchal oppression," she said.[18]

But beyond her passion for equality for women and anger at the sexism embedded in the teachings of the hierarchy, McQuillan brought little to the table that matched the power and resources of the Catholic Church. She had scant organizing experience, no friends with deep pockets to fund her new organization, and no experience with lobbying. She also was dying. She had metastatic breast cancer; the invasion of the cancer into her bones caused a hunch in her shoulders and was slowly draining her life away. But to her the need to organize Catholics was so obvious, the cause so righteous, and the facts so overwhelmingly in her favor that to do otherwise was not an option.

No sooner had McQuillan announced the formation of the organization than the landscape changed dramatically with the January 1973 *Roe v. Wade* decision. The U.S. Supreme Court determined that the right to privacy as found in the due process clause of the Fourteenth Amendment of the Constitution encompassed a woman's decision about abortion. The court also found, however, that this right was not absolute and that the state had an interest in protecting fetal life as the pregnancy progressed. As a result, it said that the state may not regulate abortion in the first trimester and may only regulate it to protect the health of the woman in the second trimester. States could regulate abortion in the third trimester to protect the life of the fetus, except when necessary to protect a woman's life or health.

The court hewed closely to the traditional common-law distinction between abortions before and after quickening, allowing them in the first two trimesters and prohibiting them in the third trimester after quickening except in serious circumstances. The court rejected the view that abortion should be banned because life begins at conception, noting that most Western religions generally hold that "life does not begin until live birth" and that even in Catholicism the theory of delayed hominization was official dogma from the Middle Ages until the nineteenth century.[19]

The *Roe* decision negated state-level laws restricting abortion and legalized abortion through the second trimester. It followed the New York model by striking a balance between those who would repeal all abortion laws and those who felt the state had an interest in the regulation of abortion. Although elated in the short term, McQuillan realized the gains of *Roe* could be temporary if an organized anti-abortion movement, fueled by the Catholic hierarchy and its followers, was allowed to gain momentum. For although many viewed the legalization of abortion as a fitting response to a social and medical injustice and a long overdue acknowledgment of the moral agency of women, to others it was an irreconcilable affront to their most deeply held values about the meaning of motherhood and family. They immediately began to organize to pass a constitutional amendment to ban abortion, swelling the ranks of the anti-abortion movement. If passage of the New York law lit a fire under the pro-life movement, *Roe* was a nuclear bomb.[20]

For the U.S. bishops, *Roe* was the ultimate provocation. It not only challenged their moral authority in the area of human sexuality but threatened their now-tenuous hold on the reproductive behavior of Catholics. They wasted no time in condemning *Roe*. John Krol, by this time a cardinal and president of the National Conference of Catholic Bishops (NCCB), called it an "unspeakable tragedy" with "disastrous implications for our stability as a civilized society." The NCCB made headlines when it declared unequivocally that Catholics must oppose abortion and that any Catholic who obtained an abortion, persuaded others to have one, or performed the procedure would be automatically excommunicated from the Catholic Church.[21]

By the time abortion was officially legal, the fledging Catholics for the Elimination of All Restrictive Abortion and Contraception Laws was holding its first meeting. By February 1973, McQuillan was claiming a membership of nearly 1,000, including several nuns.[22] She also had help in her new endeavor when fellow NOW volunteer Joan Harriman joined her. Harriman was more political than McQuillan, having lobbied for the original New York State abortion reform bill in 1967 and having managed the campaign offices of Senator James Buckley of the Conservative Party, whom she disavowed after he became a prominent anti-abortion supporter. She also had a flair for publicity. The previous summer she had well-known bachelor philanthropist Stewart Mott named Non-Parent of the Year, crowned him in a wreath of laurel leaves, and paraded him and his non-parent "queen" down Fifth Avenue in a hansom cab to publicize the National Organization for Non-Parents, which was promoting the then-radical idea that individuals and couples could have fulfilling lives without children.

In August, McQuillan and Harriman got their first opportunity to tout Catholic support for legal abortion when the CBS television network decided to rebroadcast a controversial episode of the popular sitcom *Maude* in which the title character, who has an accidental late-life pregnancy, decides to have an abortion. The U.S. bishops charged that the episode, titled "Maude's Dilemma," advocated abortion and called on Catholics to pressure their local CBS affiliates to drop the rerun. As a result, most of the program's advertisers dropped out and some forty CBS affiliates decided not to air the episode. On August 21, Catholics for the Elimination of All Abortion and Contraceptive Laws ran an ad in the *Los Angeles Times* cosigned by seventeen pro-choice and religious groups headlined "Maude's Dilemma Is Your Problem Too!" in which it asked, "Is it proper for one religious group to dictate to everyone else what they can or cannot view on television."[23]

It was the first time that a group of lay Catholics had publicly challenged the bishops on the issue of abortion. The ad brought letters from Catholics all over the country asking how they could support abortion rights. That, combined with the *Roe* decision, signaled to McQuillan that her organization had outgrown its original focus on New York State. She and Harriman began making plans to take the Catholic abortion rights movement national. They came up with a new name for the organization to reflect its expanded mission: Catholics for a Free Choice (CFFC).[24]

The new organization made its national debut in October 1973 in *Ms.* magazine's first article on abortion rights, which listed CFFC as one of the key organizations for readers to contact to keep abortion safe and legal. The article noted that the Catholic Church was giving the anti-abortion movement moral, financial, and political support. McQuillan received hundreds of phone calls and letters as the result of the article, launching Catholics for a Free Choice as a national organization.[25]

. . . . .

January 22, 1974, was an unseasonably balmy day in New York City. A little after noon, Patricia McQuillan made her way up the steps of St. Patrick's Cathedral, the great neo-Gothic bastion of Catholic ecclesiastical power and immigrant pride. At the top of the stairs, just under the great bronze doors of the cathedral, she turned to face a crowd of several dozen supporters as hundreds of curious tourists and office workers looked on from Fifth Avenue. McQuillan was resplendent, with her hunched figure cloaked in white ersatz vestments adorned with a giant stained-glass pendant. The pendant was in the shape of a Venus symbol with an equal sign in the center—the unofficial symbol of the feminist movement that had so captured the lives and imaginations of women like McQuillan. All eyes were on McQuillan as a white-and-gold cardboard miter emblazoned with a Venus symbol was ceremoniously lowered onto her head. With that, McQuillan declared herself Her Holiness Pope Patricia the First.

The newly minted pope wasted no time in delivering her first encyclical. "The Catholic Church's stand on abortion . . . is only 100 years old, is strictly political and has nothing to do with 'religion' as taught by Jesus," Pope Patricia declared. She called Jesus the first feminist, "who rebelliously taught the equality of women under religious and civil law."[26]

As if that wasn't enough to make the six archbishops entombed beneath the altar of St. Pat's turn in their graves, McQuillan declared that because the church taught that "women are the source of all evil and are not full persons," women would "no longer accept the erroneous dictates of the magisterium or the 'teaching authority' of the church regarding women."

Figure 5. Catholics for a Free Choice founder Patricia Fogarty
McQuillan is crowned Pope Patricia on the front steps of
St. Patrick's Cathedral in New York City on the first anniversary
of *Roe v. Wade.* (Corbis)

As cameras whirred and several news crews jockeyed for position,
McQuillan raised her arm and blessed the assembled flock "in the name of
the mother, daughter and holy grandmother."[27]

And so it came to pass that the first anniversary of the *Roe* decision was
commemorated by a mock investiture of a woman pope on the doorstep of
traditional, patriarchal Catholicism. The crowd of women surrounding
McQuillan didn't look like heretics, in their hose and heels and their good
winter coats, with their neat, middle-aged coiffures and sensible purses.
But they were undertaking one of the most dramatic rebellions in the history of modern religion. By symbolically anointing a woman pope, they
were declaring themselves equal to the hierarchy and announcing their
intention to challenge the right of the bishops to speak for all Catholics,

especially Catholic women, on abortion. "We, the female church hierarchy today, uphold the Supreme Court's decision on abortion and support it as the moral, humane and supreme law of the land," McQuillan said.[28]

The crowning of Pope Patricia was an instant sensation and the indelible image of the first anniversary of *Roe v. Wade.* "It created an uproar," recalls Pat Carbine, who was busy only ten blocks away working on *Ms.* magazine. "What she did was brilliant. In New York it was a big deal."[29]

The photo of McQuillan before the doors of St. Patrick's in her feminist vestments and miter appeared in *Time* and *Newsweek* magazines (although *Time* found the demonstration in "bad taste," which prompted McQuillan to write a letter to the editor correcting the impression that the crowing was intended to be derogatory). It also appeared in the New York *Post,* daily papers from Cleveland to Germany, and on the front page of the *National Catholic Reporter.* Pope Patricia got saturation coverage on all the local New York television and radio stations and a mention in the *New York Times* coverage of the *Roe* anniversary, heralding the birth of a new element in the fight over abortion: a Catholic abortion rights movement.

McQuillan needed all the publicity she could get. At the very moment she was climbing the steps of St. Patrick's, some 6,000 anti-abortion protesters were gathering 225 miles to the south in Washington, D.C., for the first national right-to-life march. And as passionate as McQuillan was in her belief that reproductive rights were essential to the emancipation of women, the individuals assembled at the Capitol fervently believed that legalizing abortion signaled the moral ruination of the nation. To them, *Roe* overturned one of society's most basic tenets: that killing an unborn child was murder and could never be condoned except in the direst circumstances. And despite the fact that the historical evidence shows that just about all societies practiced abortion—or, in some cases its evil twin, infanticide—and that illegal abortions in the United States numbered 1 million per year before *Roe,* they persisted in the somewhat Pollyannaish belief that abortion was a recent phenomenon ushered in by the permissiveness of the 1960s that could be reversed.

The Washington, D.C., demonstration was organized by the leaders of the right-to-life movement to display the electoral clout of abortion opponents. Most of the protestors were Catholic and had been recruited through their parishes or parochial schools. They had been bused in from all over the Northeast—a hundred buses from New York City and twenty-three from Pittsburgh—and from as far away as Minnesota to lobby for quick action on a constitutional amendment to ban abortion. Yet when the story of the first anniversary of *Roe* was written, this large and heavily orchestrated anti-abortion demonstration was eclipsed by the sensational photo of the beatific Pope Patricia. Harriman crowed to a supporter about the publicity she generated with the crowning and said that not seeing 6,000 anti-abortion demonstrators was "very important strategically."[30]

It was a stunning publicity coup for a nascent organization that had no office, board, or even a piece of letterhead to its name. It built on the protest work of Farians and McGillicuddy and the feminist movement's successful use of demonstrations in the 1960s and early 1970s that combined street theater and social and political commentary. "Those demonstrations were like civil rights demonstrations. It was women's opportunity to say it's not us that are screwed up, it is the system," said sociologist Kristin Luker. "It was as if you spent your life sitting at the back of the bus and drinking from segregated water fountains and all the sudden you don't have to do it—suddenly everything seemed possible."[31]

McQuillan and Harriman spent the first few months of 1974 building on the publicity of the crowning to get CFFC up and running. McQuillan was the philosopher of the movement, working to shape the theology of the Catholic pro-choice movement, and the face of the organization, making appearances to promote the still surprising idea that Catholics could support legal abortion. "There's no doubt but that some of the things I will say today will shock and dismay some of you because I'm going to bring up a few truths that they didn't dare teach us as girls and women in Catholic school," she told one audience.[32]

Harriman worried about the nuts and bolts. She found a lawyer to handle the organization's nonprofit incorporation, arranged meetings in Washington to coordinate strategy with the National Organization for Women (NOW), the National Abortion Rights Action League (NARAL), which was the renamed and expanded National Association for the Repeal of Abortion Laws, and the newly formed Religious Coalition for Abortion Rights (RCAR). She successfully begged some office space from Planned Parenthood. Most important, she made pleas for funding, because the tiny organization didn't have enough money in the bank to print the letterhead it had ordered. She wrote to the executive director of RCAR that CFFC was "inoperative" and would "go under" if it didn't receive funding. Her pleas worked. In addition to a $6,000 grant from RCAR, CFFC received $1,000 from NARAL, and Methodist minister Rodney Shaw, founder of the Population Institute, sent out a letter appealing for funding for the organization.[33]

By March 1974, CFFC had supporters in thirty states and chapters being formed in six more. In April, CFFC elected its first board of directors, which consisted of McQuillan as president, Harriman as vice president, and Glenn Ellefson-Brooks, who worked in NOW's legislative office in Washington, as secretary. Farians was a director and Cahill and Rosemary Ruether were appointed to a thirteen-member advisory committee that also included Sister Gloria Fitzgerald and Jesuit priest Joseph O'Rourke.[34]

By June, brochures and letterhead were printed, and CFFC debuted the first issue of its newsletter *Conscience,* which announced, "We have an office of our own! After almost a year of hard work, typewriters that wouldn't work, Xerox machines 40 blocks away, house cats knawing [*sic*] on our papers . . . we now have spanking new headquarters of our own, a desk, a typewriter and a telephone."[35]

But McQuillan would not live to see the organization she gave birth to grow beyond its infancy. On June 24, 1974, just five months after she stood on the steps of St. Patrick's to launch a movement that would rattle the bones of the Catholic hierarchy, McQuillan died in Germany, where she had gone in a last-ditch attempt at treatment for her cancer.

For the women who had worked side by side with her for the past few years, and for the nascent pro-choice Catholic movement, the loss was immeasurable. She was both the head and the soul of the movement. At her funeral mass at St. Jeanne Baptiste Church in New York, Farians eulogized her as a woman who transcended her own experience of dying to join the "age-old, on-going struggle for the freedom and dignity of women" and by doing so helped "all women to bring into reality our full being—or if you will, to bring women into our more perfect image of God."[36]

·   ·   ·   ·   ·

The loss of McQuillan came at a critical time for the Catholic abortion rights movement. The Catholic bishops were working overtime to consolidate their position as the voice of the anti-abortion movement. In March, four Catholic cardinals, including NCCB president Krol, testified back-to-back as the opening witnesses at the first congressional hearing on a constitutional amendment to ban abortion. They dominated television coverage of the event and made headlines when they refused to back an abortion ban because it made an exception for abortions to save the life of a woman. In his testimony, Krol asserted the bishops' authority to speak for Catholics and non-Catholics alike on abortion: "We do not propose to advocate sectarian doctrine but to defend human rights. . . . [W]e believe that what we say expresses the convictions of many Americans who are members of other faiths and of no faith."[37]

The cardinals' show of force, however, backfired by creating the impression that the Catholic hierarchy was trying to impose its morality on all Americans. Tensions with other religions over the bishops' claims to represent a universal morality had been brewing for some time. A month before the Senate hearing, the general board of the American Baptist Churches had criticized the Catholic hierarchy for supporting anti-abortion legislation, saying such measures "violate the theological and moral sensitivities, and hence the freedom, of other church bodies."[38]

The cardinals also roiled other anti-abortion opponents. "[T]rotting out the American Catholic Church's brass before cameras and reporters is not the best way to prove to the public that abortion is not a religious issue, or more specifically a Roman Catholic issue," noted the wife of one Lutheran pastor who was left to testify after the reporters had gone home.[39]

Tensions over the bishops' attempts to dominate the anti-abortion movement came to a head in 1972, when the bishops tried to centralize control of the movement under the auspices of the National Right to Life Committee (NRLC), which was at the time a loose coalition of state and local right-to-life groups. The bishops deemed the organization part of their newly created Office of Pro-Life Activities and appointed one of their staffers as its head.[40]

The bishops' move did not sit well with many right-to-life leaders, who feared the bishops' overt involvement posed a strategic problem for the movement by allowing people to dismiss opposition to abortion as a political manipulation of the hierarchy. Even some heavily Catholic right-to-life committees kept their political distance from the church, even as they accepted help with funding and organizing. "In the last session, somebody suggested bringing Bishop Sheen up for a communion breakfast with the legislators. I said I'd much rather have a bar mitzvah on the Capitol steps," said Ed Golden of New York's influential right-to-life group.[41]

Added to the reluctance of pro-life groups to identify as Catholic for political reasons was the reality that increasingly many no longer were. The anti-abortion movement was starting to attract new participants, especially conservative Protestants from midwestern states, which saw a surge in the formation of nonsectarian anti-abortion organizations between 1970 and 1972.

Groups like People Taking Action Against Abortion in Michigan, which was founded by a Presbyterian woman, and Minnesota Citizens Concerned for Life, which was headed by Dr. Fred Mecklenburg and his wife Marjory, both Methodists, quickly became powerful ecumenical anti-abortion organizations. These groups were wary of the top-down organization being imposed on the movement by the bishops, believing that independent state organizations without a Catholic label would be more potent in the fight against abortion.[42]

These tensions erupted at a NRLC board meeting in December 1972, when the board approved a proposal by the Mecklenburgs to divorce itself from the bishops' conference and reorganize as an independent, nonsectarian, national organization. The bishops had lost control of their creation just when they needed it most. They would need to rebuild their anti-abortion efforts from scratch. Less than a week after *Roe*, the NRLC met in Washington to craft a strategy to overturn *Roe*, while the bishops met separately to plot their own course.[43]

The bishops decided to launch their own campaign to push for a "human life" amendment. The NCCB voted in November 1973 to create the National Committee for a Human Life Amendment (NCHLA), declaring passage of a pro-life constitutional amendment "a priority of the highest order."[44] The bishops' new organization created immediate friction with the NRLC, which charged that the creation of the bishops' committee proved "the Catholics are trying to control the pro-life movement."[45]

While the anti-abortion movement grew in size and strength, the fledgling abortion rights movement languished. Much of the grassroots firepower for the pre-*Roe* abortion repeal efforts had come from the feminist and population movements, which now turned their attention to other priorities, such as passing the Equal Rights Amendment. Only a handful of dedicated abortion rights groups—NARAL, CFFC, and RCAR—existed, augmented by backing from groups like NOW and Planned Parenthood. The smaller groups like CFFC struggled with funding, organization, and administration. Many of the women who ran these organizations didn't receive salaries. McQuillan never took any kind of remuneration for her work and Harriman was paid on a project basis only if there was some funding available. Activists working for these groups often paid their day-to-day expenses out of their own pockets, which could be a stretch for women who didn't work outside the home or had only modest salaries. Some CFFC state organizers struggled to pay $10 for dues and a $5 handling and postage charge for bulk mailings of brochures.

In addition, long-distance phone calls and plane tickets were prohibitively expensive in the early 1970s and there was no e-mail or even fax machines, so communication among activists and groups was largely carried out face-to-face or by mail, which was cumbersome. Many of the early CFFC volunteers and board members never met one another or set foot in the New York office. In the summer of 1973, board member Ellefson-Brooks, who was CFFC's Washington representative, wrote longingly to Harriman that if she could ever afford it, she would like to come to New York for the day "to acquaint myself with what is going on there and how you handle things."[46]

The responsibility for keeping CFFC alive fell on Harriman, who was elected president after McQuillan's death. In August, national events presented CFFC with an opportunity make news when a priest in Marlborough, Massachusetts, refused to baptize a baby because the baby's mother had been quoted in the local paper as saying she supported the opening of an abortion clinic in the town. Her priest pressured her to recant her support for abortion rights in exchange for the baptism of her son, but the woman, Carole Morreale, refused.

CFFC arranged for Father Joseph O'Rourke to go to Marlborough and baptize the baby on the steps of the church where the baptism had been refused in front of some 300 spectators. The baptism became national news, with coverage by the *New York Times,* the wire services, *Time*

Figure 6. Father Joseph O'Rourke baptizes Nathaniel Morreale in front of his parents' church after Nathaniel was denied baptism because his mother, Carole, voiced support for abortion rights. CFFC president Joan Harriman is to the left of O'Rourke. (AP)

magazine, and ABC Evening News, providing CFFC with a much-needed jolt of publicity. Meta Mulcahy, another NOW volunteer who had joined CFFC as membership coordinator and quickly became an integral part of the organization, wrote to a supporter that she thought the publicity from the baptism would force the hierarchy to reexamine their teachings "in light of the society we live in" or risk alienating the laity.[47]

Mulcahy's belief was emblematic of the thinking in the early years of the movement that public pressure would force the bishops and the Vatican to take a more reasonable stance on abortion and contraception. Instead of bowing to public pressure, however, the Jesuit order, reportedly under pressure from the Vatican, dismissed O'Rourke in early September with little fanfare and no opportunity for him to make a defense of his actions, establishing a pattern of purging dissenters that would accelerate throughout the 1970s and 1980s, eventually making open support of CFFC or abortion rights by priests or nuns a dim memory.[48]

September also brought continued testimony in the U.S. Senate on a proposed constitutional amendment to ban abortion. Harriman had worked all summer to ensure Catholic supporters of abortion rights would be represented. On September 12, 1974, O'Rourke and Cahill testified before the U.S. Senate Subcommittee on the Constitution regarding proposed constitutional amendments to ban abortion. O'Rourke told the committee that "the majority of the Catholic laity and, in his opinion, Catholic theologians and a large number of parish priests approved of abortion in certain circumstances other than when necessary to save the life of the mother."[49]

In her testimony, Cahill said the church had a double standard of sexuality morality for men and women that resulted in the degraded position of women in relation to sexuality that was manifest in the hierarchy's prohibition of abortion and contraception. "Such a stand is designed to leave women at the mercy, not only of her biological makeup, but also at the mercy of a celibate hierarchy, who claim the right to damn her eternally if she uses methods such as artificial birth control, sterilization or abortion to protect herself against unwanted or dangerous pregnancies," she said. She said the real issue was the refusal of the hierarchy "to recognize women as real persons, complete human beings, who are quite capable of making their own decisions regarding abortion."[50]

It was the first time CFFC had a national audience for its pro-choice Catholic theology, but without the bishops present, media coverage of the hearing was limited. Cahill's testimony didn't go to waste however. It was developed into a pamphlet titled "Abortion: The Double Standard." It was the first extensive published rationale for pro-choice Catholicism and would remain CFFC's most requested publication for the rest of the decade.

Ensuring that there was pro-choice Catholic representation at the hearing was one of Harriman's last acts at CFFC. In January 1975, she stepped down as president to head up a new Catholic sexuality educational organization that she founded called Catholic Alternatives. The movement had lost its founding duo.[51]

Harriman was replaced as president by board member Jan Gleason, who was one of CFFC's most committed state activists. The attractive, outspoken wife of a prominent La Jolla, California, plastic surgeon, Gleason had seen the effects of a lack of education about and access to reproductive health care while working as a pediatric nurse at Chicago's Cook County Hospital. "How can a priest, or a comfortable, middle-aged woman who is being supported by a husband ever realize the many needs women have for abortion. . . . If abortion is once again made illegal, it will only revive the back street butchers who until recently profited and thrived," she said.[52]

Gleason's outspoken support of abortion rights soon attracted the attention of San Diego Bishop Leo Maher, who had taken a hard line on abortion, ordering a six-point anti-abortion declaration to be read in all the churches in his diocese on the first anniversary of *Roe*. When Maher heard that a woman who was president of CFFC and a member of NOW was serving as a lector at All Hallows Church, he ordered Gleason dismissed, the strongest action to date by a member of the hierarchy against a lay supporter of abortion. He then issued a "pastoral letter" ordering priests to deny communion or roles as lectors to anyone who admitted to being a member of a "pro-abortion" group until she or he renounced support of abortion rights. Maher's move was the first attempt by a member of the Catholic hierarchy to turn the sacrament of communion into a political cudgel to discipline abortion rights supporters. His communion edict unleashed a firestorm of criticism inside and outside of the Catholic Church. The following Sunday some 125 women who purposely identified themselves as pro-choice members of NOW or CFFC were denied communion in churches throughout the diocese. Gleason, the original source of the prohibition, declined to take part in the protest for fear of politicizing the sacrament, explaining, "I don't think the communion service is the proper place to bring about change in the church's cruel and archaic position on this subject."[53]

The publicity generated by the Morreale and Maher controversies would be a high-water mark for the Catholic pro-choice movement in the 1970s. Short on funds and lacking the leadership and inspiration of McQuillan and the press savvy of Harriman, the movement increasingly foundered. The tiny New York office that McQuillan and Harriman were so proud of was no longer staffed. Gleason was three times zones away from New York and lacked any administrative support. The coterie of Catholic feminist thinkers and activists who had given the movement so much of its early energy drifted away, buffeted by personal and professional challenges. Cahill and Farians struggled to find work as theologians. Cahill eventually became a psychiatric social worker and left active participation in the movement. Farians, who had been fired from several teaching positions at Catholic universities for her views, severed her remaining ties with the Catholic reform movement, abandoned her efforts to find common ground with the bishops, and moved back to her hometown of Cincinnati and the house she grew up in, where she became a pioneering animal rights and vegan activist. Ruether followed Harriman to Catholic Alternatives, where she served on the board, and then, as that project faltered, drifted away from formal involvement with the Catholic pro-choice movement.[54]

At the same time the Catholic pro-choice movement was foundering, the hierarchy was becoming increasingly aggressive. In November 1975, frustrated at the lack of progress in passing a constitutional ban on abortion, which had yet to make it out of committee in Congress, the NCCB released its Pastoral Plan for Pro-Life Activities. The plan called for "well planned and coordinated action by citizens at the national, state and local levels" to pressure legislators to pass an abortion ban. It laid out a blueprint for a national Catholic political machine dedicated to anti-abortion lobbying, with "the development in each congressional district of an identifiable, tightly knit and well-organized pro-life unit."[55]

The pastoral plan was an attempt by the bishops to give its anti-abortion lobbying efforts what they had been missing since the NRLC broke its ties to the NCCB: a grassroots Catholic constituency to pressure legislators on abortion. Getting Catholics to rally around the cause of recriminalizing abortion had proved a hard sell. NCHLA head Robert Lynch admitted that the hierarchy itself was deeply divided on the abortion issue, priests and nuns were reluctant to lend their weight to what was seen as a conservative Republican cause, and many Catholics were apathetic about abortion. He concluded, "Unless and until the overwhelming majority of Catholics can be moved to do something, the cause is in trouble."[56]

The Pastoral Plan for Pro-Life Activities drew immediate criticism as an unprecedented attempt by the bishops to use the faithful to assert their will in a pluralistic society. Few believed the bishops' protestations that they wouldn't control the local anti-abortion groups. Bishop Tomas

Gumbleton of Detroit accused the NCCB of "trying to have it both ways" by distancing themselves from formal control of the groups while trying to use them as a political tool.[57]

The *National Catholic Reporter* called it a "highly political act." It warned, "If the bishops have created a Catholic party ... they have unleashed a fearsome thing."[58] In October 1977 an ecumenical group of 200 theologians released a "Call to Concern" in which they said they were "saddened by the heavy institutional involvement of the bishops of the Roman Catholic Church in a campaign to enact religiously based anti-abortion commitments into law . . . . [W]e view this as a serious threat to religious liberty and freedom of conscience."[59]

The bishops forged ahead. Organizers from the NCHLA created grass-roots right-to-life political action committees (PACs) in almost half the nation's congressional districts that "involved thousands of sympathetic Catholics in right-to-life activity, including letter-writing, meeting with elected officials, conducting candidate and voter education projects and developing efficient phone networks."[60]

The bishops' move to prioritize abortion had the effect of politicizing the issue during a presidential election in which the Catholic vote was increasingly courted. The Republicans saw an opportunity to use the issue of abortion to break Catholics away from the New Deal coalition of conservative southerners and northern ethnic Catholics and African Americans that was by the early 1970s beginning to fray. President Richard Nixon's political team had pioneered the leveraging of the abortion issue to appeal to Catholics. In 1971 Nixon touted the "sanctity of human life" when he directed the Department of Defense to rescind regulations allowing therapeutic abortions at military hospitals.[61] Then in May 1972, during the run-up to the presidential election, Nixon voiced his personal support for efforts to repeal New York's abortion reform law in a letter to New York's Cardinal Cooke that was conveniently leaked to the public. A *New York Times* editorial said, "Historians should find it hard to locate a parallel instance of a President openly working through a particular church in influence the action of a state government."[62]

That same year, Nixon, who had been supportive of family planning programs and created a commission on the effects of population growth, "publicly disavowed the prochoice findings of his own presidential commission on population" to appeal to Catholics, who in turn ditched their traditional alliance to the Democratic Party in the election of 1972.[63]

In 1976, both Republican President Gerald Ford and Democratic nominee governor Jimmy Carter found themselves fighting over the Catholic vote—and the endorsement of the bishops they believed could deliver it. Carter was thought to have a "Catholic problem" because he was a born-again Southern Baptist. Ford needed to carry the heavily Catholic Northeast and upper Midwest to counter Carter's hold on the South.

As a result, abortion, which the bishops had elevated to their number one issue for Catholics, became a political hot potato. Americans were treated to the spectacle of both presidential candidates—neither of them Catholic—genuflecting before the bishops for their benediction. It was a lost cause for Carter given the Democratic Party's official pro-*Roe* stance, which the bishops condemned as "morally offensive," but he nevertheless sought a meeting with the NCCB executive committee and tried to mollify them by noting his personal opposition to abortion. When that failed to get the bishops' blessing, he backpedaled on his opposition to an anti-abortion constitutional amendment, telling the bishops he would support a "partial amendment," which didn't cut it either. The bishops told the assembled press waiting breathlessly for the outcome of the meeting that they were "disappointed" with Carter's position on abortion.[64]

Ford, who was believed to be personally pro-choice, embraced the Republican Party's call for a constitutional amendment to overturn *Roe*. After a meeting with the bishops in which he confirmed his support of an anti-abortion amendment that would return the issue to the states, he received what was widely perceived as the tacit backing of the bishops, despite the fact that the rest of the GOP platform was diametrically opposed to nearly all the bishops' other positions on issues like poverty and nuclear weapons.

CFFC criticized efforts by both candidates to pander to the bishops on abortion to win the Catholic vote: "The candidates' responses to the Bishops patronizes Catholic voters by seeing them as sheep being led by their hierarchy. Most Catholics will vote on a wide range of issues." The fact that Carter won the election—including 56 percent of the Catholic vote—proved that the bishops could not deliver the Catholic vote with their endorsement, which was widely criticized as an inappropriate intrusion into politics, but would not dampen the efforts of politicians to court Catholics or their leaders.[65]

With the center of gravity on abortion now clearly in Washington and the New York office nonoperational after the resignation of Mulcahy in early 1976, CFFC relocated its headquarters to the Capital in November 1976. It hired Virginia Andary to lobby for the organization (which was incorporated as a nonprofit lobby) and run the office on a part-time basis.

Much of Andary's energy—and the energy of the abortion rights movement as a whole—was taken up with trying to unsuccessfully block the federal Hyde Amendment, which banned Medicaid from paying for abortions for low-income women except in cases of rape, incest, or when the woman's life was at stake.[66]

It was a critical moment in the history of abortion rights because it created a blueprint for how access to abortion could be limited without a constitutional ban, and the Catholic hierarchy was a major force in its passage. NCHLA lobbyist Mark Gallagher was a key player in the behind-the-scenes legislative maneuvering over the amendment in 1977, as the all-male House and Senate conference committee squabbled over whether exceptions to the funding ban should be made for "forced rape" or just "rape," or whether there should be an exception for serious threats to a woman's health as well as her life. "Every time the Senate conferees make a compromise offer, Mr. Gallagher quietly walks to the conference table to tell a staff aide to the 11 House conferees whether the proposal is acceptable to the bishops. His recommendations are invariably followed," the *New York Times* reported.[67]

The bishops poured funding into the NCHLA's Hyde efforts. The NCHLA was supposedly independent from the NCCB for tax purposes, but in his history of the political activity of the American bishops, Timothy Byrnes noted that the separation was "more formal than real."[68] Half of $900,000 raised by the committee between January 1976 and March 1977 came from the bishops and the other half came directly from dioceses, dwarfing the $250,000 raised by the NRLC in 1976. Political fundraising under the auspices of the church was happening in conservative dioceses. "[N]ever before has one church, under orders from its leadership, financed a political campaign to the extent of half its funds," noted abortion rights pioneer Lawrence Lader. [69]

By the time the Hyde Amendment passed in 1977, CFFC, like the abortion rights movement as a whole, was largely playing defense. The loss on Hyde was devastating. "We have lost for now and our opposition has been given a real boost. We have learned a bitter lesson," wrote Andary.[70]

The organization's tiny budget of $20,000, which came from a grant from a single donor, just paid Andary's part-time salary. It had no other staffers and no regular programs, although requests still poured in to Andary for information about pro-choice Catholicism and she doggedly replied to them all. Dedicated individuals ran a handful of local CFFC chapters, but earlier efforts to organize chapters by state or congressional district to create a forceful lobbying presence had petered out. Upheaval also continued internally. In May 1977, Gleason resigned as president to run for a city council seat in San Diego. Joe O'Rourke, who had been unsuccessful in his battle with the Vatican to be reinstated as a Jesuit, became the president. The controversial, charismatic priest was guaranteed press coverage whenever he spoke, but planning and administration were not his strong suit and the tiny movement sagged further. There were complaints among board members about factionalism and a heavy-handed approach by some of the New York members, who had formed a New York chapter that was more active than the national organization.[71]

Burned out by the demands of running the organization single-handedly, Andary resigned in February 1979. *Conscience,* the one constant since the earliest days of CFFC, ceased publication. O'Rourke announced his intention to step down as president in June 1979. The tiny organization was adrift, unstaffed, underfunded, and in real danger of going under and ending the work that Patricia McQuillan had begun with her dying breath just as new threats to legalized abortion were evolving.

4 Coming of Age

At the same time that the board of Catholics for a Free Choice (CFFC) was casting about for a new executive director to replace Virginia Andary, Patricia McMahon was visiting Ireland on a monthlong vacation that mixed a search for her heritage with some soul-searching about the next steps of her career. But the much-anticipated trip quickly turned into a personal political odyssey as she experienced what it was like to live in a country that was essentially a theocracy, with the moral tenets of the Catholic Church written into the law and the patriarchy of the church woven deeply into the culture.

McMahon found a "strange, strangled, twisted expression of sexuality" that affected men and women alike. "If Irish women were trapped by the ban on all forms of birth control and the laws forbidding divorce, Irish men seemed hopelessly ensnared in the paradox that all women were either Madonnas or whores," she said. Men berated her for shirking her duty to marry and have children and assumed she was an "acceptable sexual target" because she was single and traveling alone. "Clearly the Catholic Church sought to control sexuality and in the process did a pretty good job of demonizing women," she said, stunned at how the faith that had taught her about social justice "could become a tyrant and agent of injustice."[1]

McMahon returned home determined to work for women's reproductive rights "as the most fundamental issue in the emancipation of women from patriarchal rule."[2] It was perhaps fate when she heard that CFFC was looking for an executive director. The tiny organization was in bad shape. "The organization was very close to going out of business," said Carol Bonosaro, who was president of the board at the time. "There was $15,000 in the treasury and little prospect of raising significantly more." She recommended using the remaining money to hire a new director with the understanding that he or she would have to raise additional money to be able to keep the job and hire staff. Bonosaro met with McMahon and was soon convinced that she had the right person. "What was important was her entrepreneurial spirit, her willingness to take on the task," said Bonosaro.[3]

But what McMahon found when she took over the organization was dispiriting. "[O]nly a handful of the Directors then in office seemed to believe we were a viable organization and had enthusiasm that was communicated to me . . . I sat alone in my little office surrounded by stacks of papers wondering if perhaps I had been a madwoman to take the job," she wrote to a board member.[4]

McMahon's immediate challenge was Pope John Paul II's first visit to the United States in October 1979. The election of Polish Cardinal Karol Wojtyla to the papacy in October 1978 was a major turning point for Catholicism. If Vatican II had opened the windows of the church to let in the fresh air of modernity, it seemed that John Paul was determined to slam them shut.[5]

From the outset, John Paul made it clear that he intended to enforce doctrinal orthodoxy on the issues of women and sexuality and assert a highly centralized style of leadership that left little room for dissent. He set the tone just one month into his papacy when he condemned abortion and suggested that women ended pregnancies because of societal pressure to keep families fashionably small. He also made it clear that women would continue to be barred from leadership positions within the church, affirming the church's ban on female priests as unchangeable.[6]

Conservatism was also in the air in the United States. The right wing had been intellectually ascendant in the Republic Party since Barry Goldwater unsuccessfully ran for president in 1964, but, largely focused on the issues of states' rights and fiscal conservatism, had failed to garner widespread electoral support. The bishops' elevation of abortion as the most important issue for Catholics in the 1976 presidential election and the widespread perception that they backed the Republican candidate as a result gave conservative political strategist Paul Weyrich a road map for creating a new conservative political alliance that leveraged abortion as a wedge issue.

Weyrich realized that abortion could be used to unite otherwise disparate political constituencies into a powerful electoral coalition that could rival the New Deal coalition that had dominated U.S. politics since President Franklin Roosevelt. The abortion issue neatly exploited the resentments of traditionalist Americans who felt alienated by the progressive values of the 1960s and '70s. It encapsulated their fears of the feminist movement and the spread of sexual permissiveness, which threatened patriarchal values, and a distrust of the federal government imposing liberal values on their families and communities. "Weyrich made abortion into a legitimate conservative issue, providing the justification for conservatives to form a fifth column within the right-to-life movement," wrote Connie Paige in her history of the right-to-life movement.[7]

At the time, the main organization of the movement, the National Right to Life Committee (NRLC), had impressive numbers, claiming some 11 million members in 3,000 chapters. But this didn't necessary translate into electoral success in banning abortion. "[T]he Right to Life Committee doesn't have the political sophistication it needs to accomplish its goal," said Weyrich.[8]

Weyrich knew the movement needed to be part of a "winning coalition" that could get conservative politicians elected. His "brilliant innovation," according to Paige, was to rebrand the right-to-life movement the "profamily" movement. "This allowed conservatives to broaden right-to-life concerns to cover what they saw as the proper role of government with respect to family matters, and its cost," she said.[9] Now the coalition could encompass groups battling challenges to patriarchy, such as those opposed to the Equal Rights Amendment and government-funded day care; those concerned about the decline of traditional sexuality, such as opponents of abortion and gay rights; anti-government overreach crusaders, such as the opponents of gun control; the get-tough-on-crime crowd, which included opponents of gun control and proponents of the death penalty; and the traditional conservative groups fighting for smaller government and lower taxation.

This coalition could push conservative social goals but also the long-time conservative fiscal goals of rolling back regulations designed to protect the environment, consumers, and workers, and lowering taxes on the wealthy. "We talk about issues that people care about like gun control, abortion, taxes and crime," said Weyrich. "Yes, they're emotional issues, but that's better than talking about capital formation."[10]

The only problem was, the NRLC wasn't playing ball. It was a single-issue organization resolutely focused on obtaining a constitutional amendment to ban abortion. So Weyrich aligned with organizations like the Life Amendment Political Action Committee and the American Life League (ALL) that were willing to espouse a broader, more radical socially conservative agenda than the NRLC and link these issues to abortion. The Life Amendment Political Action Committee and ALL were run by two conservative Catholics, Paul Brown and his wife, Judie, a former NRLC staffer who broke away from the NRLC to create ALL as a vehicle for the emerging "New Right."[11]

Then Weyrich and Republican direct mail wizard Richard Viguerie, who also was advising ALL, reached out to fundamentalist televangelists Jerry Falwell and Pat Robertson to draw their millions of conservative evangelical Protestant followers into the coalition. Evangelicals had eschewed political involvement for most of the twentieth century but became politically activated by a 1978 IRS ruling revoking tax exemption for segregated Christian academies in the South, which made them receptive to Weyrich's arguments about government overreach and a lack of local control over traditional values. These evangelical Protestants, when linked with conservative, anti-abortion Catholics, who had been politicized about the abortion issue by the bishops, and a smaller number of Orthodox Jews and Mormons, comprised a new electoral coalition that Weyrich famously called the "moral majority."[12]

This new supercharged electoral coalition loomed as a far more serious threat to abortion rights than the NRLC or even the bishops because of the sheer number of voters it potentially encompassed. Despite its increased public profile in the 1970s, the right-to-life movement had been surprisingly ineffective in moving the needle on a constitutional ban because of the lack of an effective electoral constituency as well as infighting among anti-abortion forces. Backers of an abortion ban had been divided from the start between hardliners, such as the NRLC, which wanted a "human life" amendment that would confer personhood on fetuses from the "moment of conception," and pragmatists, including many in Congress, who thought the most attainable solution was to return the issue to the states and let them decide whether or not to ban abortion.

The hardliners were further split among those who would make an exception for the life of the woman and instances of rape or incest, those who would make an exception only for a woman's life, and those who would make no exception at all. Even these hardest of hardliners could not agree how to define the "moment of conception": Was it when the egg was fertilized or implanted in the uterus? This distinction mattered as to whether the intrauterine contraceptive device would be considered an abortifacient. Robert Lynch, then head of the bishops' National Committee for a Human Life Amendment (NCHLA), complained in 1976 of the "terrible and at times scandalous disunity that exists among pro-life partisans," noting that there were "six national pro-life organizations, each with a different form of amendment, each with a different political plan, each refusing generally to communicate or work with the other."[13]

The Catholic bishops also were split between those who favored a potentially more attainable states-rights amendment, even if it kept some abortions legal, and those who would settle for nothing less than a complete national ban on all abortions. When they initially testified before Congress in March 1974, the bishops appeared to take a hard line, saying they wouldn't back a ban if it made an exception for the life of the woman. But in September 1975, Senator Quentin Burdick (D-ND) introduced a measure drafted by the NCHLA that would have thrown the issue back to the states. And in 1976, NCCB president Joseph Bernardin reportedly threatened to cut off support to Ohio right-to-life groups if they didn't stop pressing for a human life amendment because the bishops' lobbyist was pushing for a states' rights amendment. Shortly after leaving the NCHLA to study for the priesthood in 1976, Lynch wrote in *America* that the bishops had "shown considerably more flexibility on the issue" than other pro-life groups, "refusing to close the door on any legislative proposal that would in effect restore some measure of protection to the unborn."[14]

Now the abortion rights movement was facing organized, politically sophisticated opposition, but it was hardly up to the challenge. The coalition of abortion rights groups included single-issue groups like CFFC, the National Abortion Rights Action League (NARAL), and the Religious Coalition for Abortion Rights (RCAR), and broader groups like Planned Parenthood, Zero Population Growth, the National Organization for Women (NOW), and the American Civil Liberties Union (ACLU) that worked on abortion along with other issues. These groups were loosely organized into the Abortion Information Exchange, but with limited funding, staffing, and membership, as well as divided priorities, these groups lacked lobbying clout. In addition, many of the people running the organizations had come from the volunteer ranks and had little professional political experience—hardly a match for the sophisticated political strategists who created the Moral Majority.

In 1980, the religious right helped to catapult Ronald Reagan into the White House and swing the Senate to the Republicans. For the first time since *Roe v. Wade*, opponents of abortion controlled the presidency and the Senate. In the ultimate political irony, the Catholic bishops had by their unstinting opposition to abortion helped bring into power a determined conservative movement that opposed almost everything that the Catholic Church stood for—compassion for the poor and immigrants, opposition to the death penalty, and concern for the environment. The right had successfully used the bishops' anti-abortion agenda to "cloak a conservative political agenda in religious imagery and rhetoric" and catapult itself into power.[15]

·   ·   ·   ·   ·

As the religious right was gearing up for the pivotal presidential election of 1980, the new pontiff made his first trip to the United States. He was enthusiastically received. There was nonstop media coverage of his every move and the huge crowds that greeted him, but few were making the link between the pomp of the papal visit and the growing gulf between the sexual ethics of Americans and the Vatican. John Paul II was outspoken in his condemnation of abortion and birth control during the six-city tour, saying abortion strikes a blow at the "whole of the moral order" and telling parents that they were selfish to limit the size of families for their own comfort. At his final mass on the Mall in Washington, D.C., he called both abortion and birth control threats to "human life," the initiation of his efforts to conflate abortion and birth control and associate both with moral decline.[16]

McMahon decided to use the pope's visit to highlight the disparity between what he was preaching and what most Catholics actually thought about abortion and birth control by running an ad in the *Washington Post* on the day of the pope's mass in Washington. It was the first time that the Catholic pro-choice movement had been on the offensive in nearly five years. The ad congratulated the pope for his work on behalf of religious liberty around the world but asked him to tell the bishops to stay out of politics: "We ask you to instruct the Roman Catholic hierarchy to observe the separation of church and state in the U.S. and to refrain from their attempt through political action to impose Church teaching on all citizens."[17]

"The bishops and the right-to-life at that time were shaping the debate, and it was necessary to counter the bishops by demonstrating that the rank and file of Catholic women were not in fact adhering to the rules on birth control and that many Catholic women had abortions and did not believe they were going to hell as a result," said McMahon.[18]

In addition to putting the movement on the offensive for the first time in years, McMahon also worked to attract funding to the struggling organization. Before she resigned, Virginia Andary had successfully lobbied the CFFC board to create a separate educational organization that would be eligible to receive foundation funding. By the end of her first year, McMahon had raised $250,000 for the CFFC Education Fund, including $75,000 from the Sunnen Foundation for a series of educational brochures on Catholics and abortion. It was an extraordinary amount for an organization whose budget had never been more than $20,000.[19] "Funders were glad to see a pro-choice Catholic perspective and wanted it visible in the debate," McMahon said. "They thought CFFC was a necessary voice."[20]

Technically CFFC was still organized as a lobbying organization, but it never had the resources to build the political base to make that a reality. "I met with Geraldine Ferraro when she was a member of Congress and asked her to ally herself publicly with CFFC," recalled McMahon. "She gave me the quick and basic political lesson that I should have expected. She said, 'Can you deliver votes in my district, can you bring people to me who will help when the priests or the bishops in my district go after me for supporting a woman's right to choose?' Of course I knew that CFFC would never raise the money to do that kind of work nationally and was convinced it wasn't what we should be doing. Publications, public speaking and convening like-minded groups of people around the country seemed the most important thing that CFFC could do at the time," said McMahon.[21]

Agreeing that the future of the organization was in educational efforts, in 1980 the board voted to change the name of the main CFFC organization to the Catholic Lobby for Abortion Rights and change of the name of the CFFC Education Fund to Catholics for a Free Choice, essentially swapping out the old lobby for the new educational organization. With new funding in hand, McMahon opened an office, hired a staff of four to assist her, including a public affairs director and a community outreach coordinator, restarted publication of *Conscience,* and replaced board members to increase diversity and bring a fresh perspective to the organization. CFFC was reborn and reenergized. "In a word, Pat saved CFFC from extinction and started the organization on a solid path of achievement and recognition," said Bonosaro.[22]

.   .   .   .   .

The first big test of the new pope's effect on church teaching regarding sexuality was the October 1980 World Synod of Bishops, when the U.S. bishops shocked the synod by asking for a reexamination of the 1968 encyclical *Humanae Vitae.* San Francisco Archbishop John Quinn, who was head of the National Conference of Catholic Bishops (NCCB), said priests were losing credibility because they couldn't discuss the issue of birth control realistically with their parishioners. He cited a recent poll by sociologist Father Andrew Greeley that found that three-quarters of Catholic women used birth control and that the intransience of the Vatican on the issue was alienating record numbers of Catholics.[23] He called for the study of a more flexible approach to Catholics who decided to use contraception, within a doctrine of what he called "responsible parenthood."[24]

The decade between the issuance of *Humanae Vitae* and John Paul II's ascendance to the papal throne had seen a sort of "Don't ask, don't tell" accommodation on birth control. Most Catholics used birth control, and their priests knew better than to ask them about it. This was not an unusual accommodation to unworkable Catholic doctrine, according to theologian Anthony Padovano. "The general Vatican approach to something highly controversial is to make your statement and then ignore it," he said.[25]

For instance, around the time of Vatican II, Pope John XXIII, who was under pressure to do something to placate conservatives in the church, mandated that Latin had to be used exclusively in every theology class in Catholic seminaries. But many instructors didn't even know Latin. "Throughout the world the Catholic theologians just ignored it or they would say two lines in Latin and do the rest in English," said Padovano, adding, "That's how contraception would have gone if John Paul II had not come in."[26]

Instead, John Paul made opposition to contraception a "militant part of his papacy," according to Padovano. The Vatican responded sharply to Quinn that there was no need to study the contraceptive ban. A chastised Quinn was forced to publicly clarify that he was not challenging *Humanae Vitae* and that he didn't favor any change to the policy on contraception. At the end of the synod, the bishops pledged their allegiance to *Humanae Vitae*, reaffirming it as "prophetic" and saying that it just needed to be better explained to Catholics.

Vatican observer Father Francis X. Murphy wrote that that the pope's closing speech at the synod signaled that he intended to "dismiss the achievement of the majority of the Church's theologians in their attempt to update Catholic moral thinking."[27]

Murphy's prediction was correct. The pope followed up on the synod with his apostolic exhortation *Familiaris Consortio* (On the Christian Family in the Modern World), in which he laid out his vision for marriage and the family. While acknowledging that families were changing and there was greater attention being paid to "the quality of interpersonal relationships in marriage, to promoting the dignity of women, to responsible procreation," he condemned birth control as a manipulation and degradation of human sexuality.

He also warned about the emergence of a "contraceptive mentality" that placed independence and personal satisfaction over the complete self-giving required by God of Catholic couples. The pope had reached back to the warnings of Jesuit theologian Stanislas De Lestapis, one of the dissenters from the majority report of the Papal Birth Control Commission, about the negative personal and societal effects of contraception to justify his conflation of abortion and contraception as part of a societally destructive pattern of selfishness, especially on the part of women.[28]

.   .   .   .   .

The U.S. hierarchy also reflected the new hard line of the Vatican on reproductive issues in another area: the provision of reproductive health services by Catholic hospitals. All U.S. health care institutions affiliated with the Catholic Church are governed by a set of rules promulgated by the U.S. bishops called the *Ethical and Religious Directives for Catholic Health Care Services* that were first made official in 1971.[29]

The *Directives* codified the church's ban on the provision of abortion, contraceptive sterilization for men (vasectomy) and women (tubal ligation), and all artificial methods of contraception. Some hospitals, however, continued to look for some leeway to provide tubal ligations for women whose health or life might be endangered by a future pregnancy, especially in rural areas where the Catholic hospital was the only accessible facility. In 1974, the Vatican's Congregation for the Doctrine of Faith weighed in and said hospitals should not perform such sterilizations because they were still contraceptive in nature, but the *Directives* were not revised and some hospitals continued to quietly provide the procedure if a woman would be endangered by a future pregnancy or was likely to bear a child with a serious genetic disorder.

In 1978, the Sisters of Mercy, who ran the largest nonprofit health system in the country, tested how far the Vatican would go to enforce the ban on sterilizations and the autonomy of hospital administrators to decide what is in the best interest of their patients. At the time, tubal ligation was becoming an increasingly popular form of birth control; by 1982, it would be the most popular form of contraception for married women. With requests for sterilization increasing at their hospitals, the sisters decided that good medical ethics required that they provide the procedure when the patient and her doctor determined it was "essential to the overall good of the patient" because the position of the fallopian tubes after childbirth makes it easy to perform the procedure as a minor surgery. Otherwise the woman would have to undergo a second surgical procedure at a later date at another hospital, which the sisters felt was an unjustifiable risk to the patient.

Apparently the Sisters of Mercy were not alone in their decision that serving the medical needs of their patients overrode Vatican dictates. A 1979 study found that 20 percent of Catholic hospitals were performing sterilizations and nearly half of all Catholic hospitals said they wanted to perform them.[30]

When the Vatican learned that the Sisters of Mercy were planning to implement a policy formally allowing tubals in their hospitals, it threatened to dismiss their entire leadership and put all their hospitals, schools, and other projects under Vatican control. The sisters backed down, fearing that Vatican would dismantle many of their other progressive programs and policies, and banned the performance of tubals at their hospitals.[31]

With the controversy over the Sisters of Mercy's move still fresh and the demand for tubals increasing, in July 1980 the NCCB issued a revised directive on female sterilization affirming that Catholic hospitals could not perform the procedure on any patient for any reason, even if a woman's life would be endangered by a subsequent pregnancy.[32]

The new directive allowed hospitals to perform tubal ligations only for "grave reasons extrinsic to the case," such as a hospital being threatened with closure if it did not perform sterilizations. A commentary accompanying the directive suggested that couples who were worried that a pregnancy would endanger the life or health of the woman or result in a child affected by a genetic disorder "forgo the genital expression of their love" rather than resort to the "evil" of sterilization.[33]

It was becoming clear that one of the hallmarks of John Paul's reign would be a crackdown on public displays of dissent from official church teaching. Dissent on the issue of abortion was even more unacceptable than dissent on contraception—especially when it came from a priest—and in the late 1970s the most high-profile dissenter from Vatican teaching on abortion was Jesuit priest Robert F. Drinan.

Drinan had written a series of commentaries on abortion and Catholic teaching when the issue of abortion reform was heating up in the 1960s, suggesting that it was preferable under Catholic teaching that the law be silent on the issue of early abortion rather than try to determine which abortions were and were not permissible. He also was outspoken in his belief that the Catholic Church shouldn't attempt to use the U.S. civil code to enforce its moral beliefs. He called the bishops' statements on the legality of abortion "inappropriate intrusions in a pluralistic society."[34]

At the same time, Drinan believed passionately that the church should bring its social justice witness to bear in the public square. He decided to run for Congress when the opportunity arose to represent his liberal Massachusetts district. Generally the Vatican prohibited priests from holding public office, but Drinan managed to wrangle permission from his local superiors. He was first elected to the House of Representatives in 1970 and became an outspoken opponent of the war in Vietnam and a proponent of human rights around the world.

Drinan also opposed efforts to limit access to abortion, voting against the Hyde Amendment and a constitutional amendment to ban abortion. By the late 1970s, high-profile conservative Catholics like Republican representative Bob Dornan (CA) were complaining to the Vatican that Drinan's pro-choice position was an embarrassment to the church. In May 1980, Pope John Paul II ordered Drinan to withdraw his candidacy for a sixth term in Congress, making clear that he would have to sacrifice his vocation if he disobeyed the pope. Reluctantly Drinan stepped down. A clear message had been sent that this pope would not tolerate dissent on abortion from those publicly identified as Catholics.[35]

While Drinan's progressive voice was silenced in the public square, the bishops were free to continue their high-profile politicking on abortion. After Ronald Reagan's election as president, they made it clear they expected to see action on an amendment to ban abortion to pay back Catholics for their support of the president. "The president-elect promised that an amendment would be part of his program. We would hope to see it as early as possible," said NCCB president Quinn.[36]

As expected, the election of conservative Republicans who were deeply in the electoral debt of the religious right created new momentum for a constitutional amendment to ban abortion. The two Senate committees most critical to the passage of such an amendment were now in the hands of staunch abortion opponents: South Carolina's Strom Thurmond, who chaired the Senate Judiciary Committee, and Utah's Orrin Hatch, who chaired the Judiciary Committee's Subcommittee on the Constitution.

In September 1981, Hatch introduced the "Human Life Federalism Amendment," which would overturn *Roe* and give Congress and the states "concurrent power to restrict and prohibit abortions." Hatch hoped to attract support from anti-abortion pragmatists and weakly pro-choice legislators who didn't want to be seen as supporting abortion on demand but who wouldn't support a human life amendment. Passage of the federalism amendment would leave states free to ban or limit abortion by a simple majority vote in the legislatures, which was a much lower hurdle than passing a constitutional amendment.

Two months later, NCCB president Archbishop John Roach and Cardinal Terence Cooke, chair of the bishops' Committee on Pro-Life Activities, testified before Congress to endorse the Hatch Amendment. It marked the first time that the bishops had endorsed a specific constitutional amendment on abortion. Although the amendment did not meet their long-standing goal of conferring personhood on fetuses, Roach said the bill "has the great merit of being an achievable solution."[37]

The bishops pledged to "mobilize" American Catholics on behalf of the measure. CFFC held a press conference immediately following the bishops' endorsement in which McMahon called it a "misrepresentation of the beliefs of a majority of Catholics in this country." She said, "No one is pro-abortion but three-quarters of the Catholic population is pro-choice."[38]

The next day the bishops' endorsement of the Hatch measure was front-page news in the *New York Times*—as was McMahon's criticism of the bishops' position. It marked the ascendance of the Catholic pro-choice movement in its modern iteration to the national stage—a fact that was not lost on Cardinal Cooke. Two weeks later he complained, "It is news to me that any Catholic people would call themselves fine Catholics if they are Catholics for a Free Choice."[39] It was the first time the bishops had ever recognized the existence of an organized movement of pro-choice Catholics. In late November 1981, the NCCB made its first official statement on CFFC, dismissing the organization as "small number of people claiming some affiliation with the Roman Catholic Church" that "carries no official status within this church."[40]

It was the beginning of efforts to discredit the Catholic pro-choice movement as de facto illegitimate because it did not have the imprimatur of the hierarchy and disagreed with it on abortion. These themes were quickly amplified in the conservative Catholic press when the *National Catholic Register* carried an "exposé" on CFFC that accused the organization of being a "sham" masquerading as a "spontaneous coming together of Catholic women who dissent from official church teaching" that falsely asserted to represent a majority of Catholics.[41]

By the end of 1981, McMahon had put CFFC on the road to stability, established its first professional staff, and returned it to the national stage just when its presence was critical. But the nonstop work had taken its toll. McMahon was burnt out and ready to move on. "It was a very intense burden," she said. She had brought credibility to the movement as a national organization representing pro-choice Catholics. "When I was first at CFFC, the *New York Times* would run an occasional story referring to 'a group calling itself Catholics for a Free Choice.' By the time I left, the *Times* reference was simply, 'According to Catholics for a Free Choice,'" she said.[42]

.   .   .   .   .

McMahon left the organization at a critical time. Hatch had introduced a measure that would give the states the right to ban abortion by a simple majority vote in the legislature. The bishops directed significant institutional support to the passage of the Hatch Amendment, telling parish priests to participate in the "Life Roll" campaign coordinated by the NCHLA, which including handing out lobby cards at masses.[43]

But not everyone in the anti-abortion movement was on board with the Hatch Amendment. Most of the rank-and-file right-to-life movement, including the NRLC, wanted to hold out for passage of a human life amendment that would confer legal personhood on fetuses. Two such amendments were introduced in early 1980, one by Senator Jesse Helms

(R-NC) and one by Representative Dornan that made no exceptions and a second version that made an exception only to prevent the death of a woman. But as with previous versions of such amendments, both lacked enough support in Congress to move forward. Helms then switched tactics and in early 1981 introduced a bill that would simply have Congress declare "scientific evidence demonstrates the life of each human being begins at conception."[44]

With the Helms and Hatch measures both active in Congress and the bishops suggesting that Catholics were strongly behind the Hatch measure, the Catholic pro-choice movement couldn't afford to sit on the sidelines. CFFC needed new leadership. It didn't have to go far to find it. The board hired Frances Kissling, who had been a member of the board since 1980, as executive director in early 1982.

Kissling grew up in a working-class Catholic neighborhood in Flushing, New York, attended parochial school, and wanted to be a nun from childhood. She was attracted to the life of a nun not because of the sisters' religious devotion but because they were the "most liberated women" she knew. "They didn't have to worry about a husband. They didn't have kids. They were well educated. Many of them were fascinating in their idiosyncrasies as well as in their knowledge and intelligence," she recalled.[45]

But the bitter realities of the church's sexual politics were also with her from a young age. Kissling's mother had divorced and remarried, which meant she wasn't allowed to participate in the church—she drove her four children to mass every week and dropped them off. Kissling spoke with a sympathetic priest about the situation, who said he would see what he could do. The priest told Kissling's mother that she could return to the church if she promised to live in a sexually celibate relationship with her husband, but she would have to receive communion in secret to avoid a scandal. "I was outraged," Kissling recalled, sensing that it was wrong that "somebody has to go to the kitchen door to receive the sacraments," even though she couldn't fully comprehend the sacrifice her mother was being asked to make.[46]

Kissling joined the Sisters of Saint Joseph when she was nineteen, but her growing doubts about the church's hypocrisy on the issues of sexuality and divorce caused her to leave the order after nine months. After college, she found her way to the front lines of the movement to provide women with access to abortion. She ran one of the first legal abortion clinics in New York. She worked overseas, first with the International Pregnancy Advisory Services and Marie Stopes to open the first legal abortion clinic in Austria and then in Mexico to help open an illegal clinic. In the mid-1970s she became the first executive director of the National Abortion Federation, the professional association of abortion providers. After the Hyde Amendment passed, she cowrote *Rosie: The Investigation of a Wrongful Death,* which documented the first known death from the Hyde restrictions on federal abortion funding. She was organizing an Abortion Rights Action Week when McMahon approached her about joining the CFFC board in 1980. Kissling wasn't a practicing Catholic at the time and struggled with the decision, finally deciding that she would join, reenter the world of Catholicism, and find out if she was Catholic.

When the opportunity came to lead the organization, Kissling saw a unique opportunity. "I always felt that the abortion rights movement lacked a moral dimension," she said, because it concentrated more on rights than morality. "I was very interested in the fact that Catholics for a Free Choice was a space where the moral dimensions of the issue could be explored. I also believed that social change occurs at the margins, not in the center," she said, and the small, little-known organization offered the freedom to pursue her vision.[47]

Kissling came to CFFC at a watershed moment for the organization and the abortion rights movement. "The recognition that *Roe v. Wade* did not settle the issue had sunk in . . . and that defending *Roe v. Wade* and the right to abortion would be long-term," said Kissling.[48]

The ascendency of a socially conservative Republican Party determined to roll back *Roe* was a wake-up call for the movement. "On the day after the conservative Republicans took over, phones jangled in the offices of abortion rights leaders in Washington, D.C., and New York," *Ms.* magazine reported. By the time Kissling was settling in at CFFC, the loosely organized pro-choice coalition that had struggled to beat back the Hyde Amendment in the 1970s was "a tightly knit organization, plotting, in monthly meetings, a common strategy and a unified attack."[49]

In addition to CFFC, NARAL, Planned Parenthood, RCAR, NOW, and the ACLU, the pro-choice coalition included new players, such as Voters for Choice, the Ms. Foundation for Women, and the National Abortion Federation. Many of the existing organizations had seen a change of leadership. This new generation of abortion rights leaders was professionally experienced and politically savvy. Where the early abortion rights pioneers had been outsiders on the Hill, pushing a lonely and unpopular cause, the movement now found friends on the inside, in the offices of pro-choice senators like Bob Packwood (R-OR), Patrick Moynihan (D-NY), Lowell Weicker (R-CT), and Ted Kennedy (D-MA).

The threat to abortion rights poised by the right also swelled interest in the abortion rights movement. NARAL saw its membership soar from 8,000 in 1977 to 90,000 in 1980 and to 140,000 by 1982. Its political action committee (PAC) raised $400,000 in the first half of 1982, as much as it had in the previous two years total.[50]

The legislative battle over the Helms and Hatch Amendments raged throughout 1982 as the pro-choice coalition worked to mobilize their grassroots supporters and raise PAC money for pro-choice senators. When it became apparent that Helms didn't have enough backing to move the human life measure through Congress, he attached it as a rider to a bill to raise the debt ceiling. This legislative end run resulted in an historic filibuster led by Packwood that transfixed the Capital for nearly a month. The Helms measure was narrowly defeated in mid-September, largely due to the efforts of the unified pro-choice coalition. "For the first time, pro-choice groups did a first-rate job of lobbying," Packwood said, summing up the consensus that the movement had finally come of age.[51]

Shortly after the defeat of the Helms Amendment, Hatch pulled his states' rights amendment in a tacit admission that the bishops' promised Catholic support for the measure had failed to materialize. In addition to being damaged by a lack of grassroots support, bitter divisions within the NCCB over the measure helped undermine the impression that there was unified Catholic support behind it.[52]

Although CFFC played a role in the emerging pro-choice coalition that helped defeat Hatch and Helms, spreading pro-choice materials from other organizations throughout the progressive Catholic community, Kissling wanted to differentiate the organization from strictly secular pro-choice groups. "Catholics for a Free Choice has a unique role in the pro-choice movement. We address the abortion issue in its complexity, and draw into the discussion other issues—sexuality, contraception and the separation of church and state," she said when she became president.[53]

Kissling also moved to integrate CFFC into the budding community of Catholic reform organizations that was forming. CFFC hadn't had a strong connection to this movement since the early 1970s, when Patricia McQuillan was alive and working with early reformers like Elizabeth Farians and Frances McGillicuddy. Since that time new organizations had been created to advocate for reforms in the church, including women priests and the recognition of the rights of gay and lesbian Catholics. In addition, women religious organized into groups like the National Coalition of American Nuns and the National Assembly of Religious Women had become increasingly outspoken, going so far as to publicly oppose the Hatch and Helms Amendments.

In November 1982, CFFC held a press briefing at the NCCB's annual meeting in conjunction with the Women's Ordination Conference and the National Coalition of American Nuns on women's issues in the church, including the ordination of women. Not since Farians's ill-fated efforts to get the bishops to discuss women's issues in the early 1970s had Catholic reformers appeared at a meeting of the bishops' conference to offer a feminist perspective on the issues.[54]

Kissling also worked to bring new energy to the CFFC board, bringing in individuals who brought a more explicitly Catholic and feminist perspective to the organization. She recruited Marquette University theologian Dan Maguire and feminist theologian Mary Hunt, founder of the Women's Alliance for Theology Ethics and Ritual (WATER), to the board. She also brought back Rosemary Radford Ruether, who had recently testified in favor of abortion rights at a congressional hearing on Helms's human life bill and was about to release her pioneering book *Sexism and God Talk*. In it, Ruether offered a critique of traditional Christian theology from a feminist perspective—a reimaging of the Bible and Christianity from a woman's point of view. The book created what the *New York Times* called the first "full-fledged feminist theology" within a Christian context.[55]

An explicitly feminist theology was necessary in Catholicism, according to Ruether, because the Catholic Church "has the most explicit and enforced theology that really impeded access to abortion and reproductive rights in general."[56] It was this linking of feminist Catholic theology to reproductive rights that would in many ways define CFFC. In her first column for *Conscience*, Kissling wrote, "It is the one-dimensional role of women *in the church* that reinforces the one-dimensional approach of the Church's teaching on abortion."[57]

The association of cutting-edge progressive theologians like Ruether, Hunt, and Maguire with the Catholic pro-choice movement elevated it from a bystander in debates over Catholic theology to a participant that could make significant contributions. One area in which there was a glaring need was information about the decision to have an abortion from the Catholic perspective. CFFC was receiving calls on almost a daily basis from women with questions about the morality of abortion. The church had "ignored dealing with this issue in a pastoral way," said Kissling, which resulted in a lack of guidance for pregnant Catholic women considering abortion.[58]

Maguire and his wife, Marjorie, who also was a theologian, undertook the development of a guide to ethical decision making about abortion within a Catholic context. "Abortion: A Guide to Making Ethical Choices," was published in late 1983. It was written in question-and-answer format and tackled questions like how to go about forming one's conscience on abortion and whether a Catholic would be excommunicated for having an abortion. "The idea of doing it in a catechism was very Catholic," explains Dan Maguire. "It was written so all kinds of people could read it and get good theological opinions stated understandably."[59]

The guide was instantly in demand by abortion clinics and student health centers around the country. "Clinics were probably the biggest consumers of our materials," notes Mary Jean Collins, who joined CFFC as director of public affairs in the mid-1980s. "The clinics really needed them for their patients; they sought out these materials to help Catholic patients dealing with guilt about abortions. It was all about making Catholics comfortable with the choices they were making when the church said it was wrong," she said.[60]

For their part, the bishops were struggling to regain the high ground on questions of morality after their implicit endorsement of the anti-abortion Republican Party had helped catapult into office many lawmakers who were diametrically opposed to their progressive agenda on other issues. In

1983, the NCCB released a much-anticipated statement on the morality of nuclear war. *The Challenge of Peace: God's Promise and Our Response* was the result of a lengthy consultative process within the bishops' conference and with theologians, laypeople, and lawmakers. It condemned all potential uses of nuclear weapons except as a deterrent within a framework of working toward their eventual elimination, essentially backing liberal calls for a nuclear "freeze."

The Challenge of Peace was a stunning rebuff of the Reagan administration's muscular nuclear policy, which asserted the right to use nuclear weapons in a variety of situations—including as a first strike and in conventional warfare. The statement was warmly welcomed by liberals and the Democratic Party, who had backed nuclear disarmament and were happy to have an issue that once again allowed them to find common ground with the Catholic Church.

Cardinal Joseph Bernardin of Chicago, who had just been named head of the NCCB's Pro-Life Committee, followed up on *The Challenge of Peace* with a speech at Fordham University in December 1983 in which he famously said that the statement was a starting point for developing a "consistent ethic of life" that recognized the moral linkage of all "life" issues like abortion, nuclear war, and poverty. "I am convinced that the pro-life position of the church must be developed in terms of a comprehensive and consistent ethic of life. . . . I am committed to shaping a policy of linkage among the life issues," he said.[61]

Beyond Bernardin's theological interest in finding consistency in Catholic teaching, the consistent ethic was also, according to historian Timothy Byrnes, "a political strategy designed to prevent a recurrence of either the bishops' divisive and partisan role of 1976 or their distorted, indirect role of 1980," when the religious right co-opted the abortion issue. Bernardin wanted to eliminate the opportunity for either political party or individual candidates to use Catholic teaching piecemeal by creating a unified theological framework.[62]

Like many progressive organizations, CFFC welcomed the bishops' statement on nuclear war and the effort to move beyond single-issue politics. At a press conference commemorating the tenth anniversary of *Roe v. Wade*, Kissling said that the open, collegial process used to formulate the nuclear statement was a model for how the bishops should operate on important matters of policy and stood in stark contrast to their heavy-handed approach to abortion. Bernardin sharply rebuffed Kissling's suggestion in a column in *The Chicago Catholic,* noting that the nuclear question "raises a host of new and complex questions for the church," while the church's position on abortion "is crystal clear and has been from the beginning." He concluded, "If Catholics for a Free Choice wants to dialogue on these matters, I'm all for it. But I flatly reject the idea that there is room for dissent about the immorality of abortion."[63]

Just the fact that Bernardin felt it necessary to respond to Kissling illustrated that by 1983 the bishops were wary about the emergence of a viable Catholic pro-choice movement that might challenge their authority over abortion teaching. The movement had found its footing and its voice.

5 The Cardinal of Choice

It was clear that the role of religion in government would be a major factor in the 1984 presidential election, largely because of a backlash against the influence of the religious right. *Time* magazine noted that "the prominence and complexity of religious issues may [be] greater than in any previous election."[1]

Democratic nominee Walter Mondale, who had been President Jimmy Carter's vice president, squared off with President Ronald Reagan about the right's leveraging of religion to push its policy agenda. Mondale accused Reagan of breeching the wall separating church and state, while Reagan defended policies that would increase the public role of religion, such as allowing prayer in public schools, as appropriate and good for a nation that had strayed too far from its Christian roots. The Catholic bishops largely stayed on the sidelines of the argument, apparently somewhat chagrined that their emphasis on abortion as their overriding public policy issue had helped bring to power a Christian Right that cared little for the poor, sought to undercut unions and the rights of labor, and mocked environmentalism—all traditional concerns of the church.

Cardinal Joseph Bernardin's "consistent ethic of life" was an attempt to walk back the widespread perception that the bishops cared only how a candidate voted on abortion. But as the party conventions approached in the summer of 1984, it became clear that not all the bishops were on board with Bernardin's philosophy. At a news conference in late June, newly appointed New York Archbishop John O'Connor said that he didn't believe candidates should be evaluated on a number of issues and declared that a Catholic "in good conscience cannot vote for a candidate who explicitly supports abortion." Religion writer Jim Castelli said that with those comments, O'Connor, who occupied the most high-profile pulpit in the nation, "shredded the seamless garment," and cast abortion back into the spotlight in a presidential election year. O'Connor's comments came just as Mondale announced his pick of New York representative Geraldine Ferraro, who was Catholic, as his vice presidential choice, a move he hoped would help draw ethnic Catholics back to the Democratic Party.[2]

O'Connor's remarks drew him into a highly publicized running battle of words with New York governor Mario Cuomo (D), who criticized both O'Connor and Reagan for politicizing religion and O'Connor for asserting that Catholics couldn't vote for pro-choice politicians.[3]

Then in August, National Conference of Catholic Bishops (NCCB) president Bishop James Malone of Youngstown, Ohio, released a statement asserting the primacy of the church's teaching on abortion and saying that politicians couldn't separate their private morality from their public policy positions. Cuomo fired back: "There is a Catholic law on homosexuality. There is a Catholic law on birth control. There is a Catholic law on abortion. I accept the Catholic law. There is no Catholic law on what you have to do about imposing birth control on others."[4]

Catholic politicians had been struggling with the question of how to separate their personal beliefs about Catholic moral teaching with the application of that teaching in the public policy arena as far back as 1964, when the abortion question first emerged into the public eye. That summer, with Senator Ted Kennedy (D) running for reelection and Robert Kennedy (D) running for a Senate seat in New York, the Kennedy family summoned prominent Catholic theologians and a bishop to their family compound in Hyannis Port, Massachusetts, to hash out the issue. The Kennedys wanted to "formulate a political stance on abortion that would be compatible both with Catholic teaching and with the political climate of the country."[5]

The leading progressive theologians of the era were present, including Robert Drinan, who was then dean of Boston College Law School, Richard McCormick, Charles Curran, and J. Giles Milhaven. "The theologians worked for a day and a half among ourselves at a nearby hotel," recalled former Jesuit Milhaven. "In the evening, we answered questions from the Kennedys and Shrivers. Though the theologians disagreed on many a point, they concurred on certain basics," he said.[6]

The theologians agreed with McCormick's assertion that "the translation of a rigorously restrictive ethics of abortion into law was unlikely to be enforceable or to achieve its positive goals without significant attendant social evils." The theologians also concurred with the church's teaching that abortion was immoral in all circumstances but agreed that it wasn't feasible to translate this into public policy. They decided that the best course in terms of public policy would be to back the American Law Institute's abortion reform measure, which would allow abortion in some circumstances, such as when the life or the health of the woman was threatened or in cases of rape, incest, or fetal malformation. Thus they established the theological framework that allowed Catholic policymakers to make a distinction between their personal beliefs about abortion and the application of these beliefs in public policy in a pluralistic society.[7]

Somewhat prophetically, however, when the theologians met with the Kennedys to present their recommendations, the lone bishop present "summed up the whole discussion and then—serenely and in good faith—claimed as a consensus the opposite of what the theologians had been saying," recalled Milhaven.[8]

This disconnect between what theologians believed was considerable flexibility in the application of the church's abortion teaching in society at large and the hierarchy's insistence that it be translated literally into public policy was on full display twenty years later as the 1984 presidential election drew close. On September 5, Archbishop Bernard Law of Boston called a news conference to release a statement by the eighteen bishops of New England that said abortion was the "critical issue" in the campaign and should be voters' central concern. In an explicit rebuff to Bernardin's "seamless garment," the statement said, "While nuclear holocaust is a future possibility, the holocaust of abortion is a present reality."[9]

Then on September 9, Archbishop O'Connor stunned the political world by calling out Ferraro by name for saying "things about abortion relevant to Catholic teaching which are not true." He charged that "she has given the world to understand that Catholic teaching is divided on the subject of abortion."[10]

Ferraro was astounded by the charge. She had said that she accepted the church's teaching that life begins at conception, and although she was pro-choice in her policy choices, she had never publicly disagreed with the church's teaching on abortion. After she spoke to O'Connor, it became clear that he was referring to a cover letter that Ferraro had signed introducing a monograph produced from a congressional briefing Catholics for a Free Choice (CFFC) had held two years earlier.

The September 1982 briefing on "The Abortion Issue in the Political Process" was in many ways CFFC's coming-out party on Capitol Hill, introducing the organization to Catholic legislators as one that could help them communicate to constituents about a difficult issue and provide a sound, progressive theological analysis of the abortion issue. "It is critical that our policy makers hear reasoned and objective experts speak to the arguments presented by the bishops," said CFFC president Frances Kissling of the briefing.[11]

Speakers included religion columnist Jim Castelli, who provided an analysis of the bishops' ill-fated attempts to pass a human life amendment; pollster Greg Martire, who presented polling evidence showing that a majority of Catholic women supported legalized abortion; and political strategist Ken Swope, who had advice for pro-choice politicians on communicating to constituents about abortion.[12]

In addition, Marquette University theologian Dan Maguire reviewed the "theological basis for Catholic pluralism on abortion." Maguire asserted that there was "no one 'Catholic' position" on abortion and said that any effort to present "*the* Catholic position on abortion is fallacious and theologically ungrounded." He argued that the Catholic doctrine of probabilism, which says that in matters of conscience a doubtful moral obligation may not be imposed on the faithful, enshrines the right of dissent from the hierarchy's teachings. He concluded that because there was legitimate debate on the abortion issue, it met the test of an issue on which the faithful could dissent from the hierarchy. Because of this uncertainty, he said, Catholic legislators could support abortion rights as a matter of public policy, even if they were personally opposed to abortion.[13]

The invitation to the briefing, which was signed by Ferraro and Representatives Leon Panetta (D-CA) and Tom Daschle (D-SD), said it would demonstrate that "the Catholic position on abortion is not monolithic and that there can be a range of personal and political responses to the issue." This was repeated in a cover letter to the monograph produced from the briefing and signed only by Ferraro, which was the specific instance of the phrase that O'Connor took exception to.[14]

Following his criticism, Ferraro assured O'Connor that she believed the reference was to the beliefs of Catholics on abortion, not church doctrine, but this failed to assuage him, nor did a further public statement that she accepted that the Catholic position was monolithic but that she believed "there are a lot of Catholics who do not share the view of the church."[15]

Ferraro was stunned by the controversy and not alone in wondering why O'Connor was suddenly making a two-year-old cover letter a central issue in a presidential campaign. O'Connor claimed that the letter had been recently mailed to him. Kissling suspected that the letter was sent to O'Connor by Doug Johnson, the legislative director of the National Right to Life Committee (NRLC), to stir up trouble for the Democratic ticket. NBC News reported that Reagan campaign officials orchestrated the attack against Ferraro, using intermediaries to contact members of the hierarchy and urging them to criticize the candidate.[16]

Regardless of how O'Conner got the letter, Ferraro's public dissent on the abortion issue had become, according to Kissling, "a visible sign of the Church's inability to control the Catholic people," and the bishops were not about to back down.[17]

Press coverage of the back-and-forth between Ferraro and O'Connor, coming on the heels of extensive coverage of the O'Connor–Cuomo dust-up, pushed the question of abortion and religion into the spotlight in the heat of an election year and created a political firestorm. The press and leaders of other faiths raised questions about the propriety of the bishops crawling into the political trenches, especially after Cardinal John Krol gave the invocation at the Republican convention, which again gave the unavoidable impression that the hierarchy favored the Republican Party. It also raised the legitimate question of the role of religion in public life, in particular Catholicism, which, unlike most other religions, has very specific rules that relate to public issues like abortion and a powerful hierarchy to lobby for them.

It was an issue that many thought settled with John F. Kennedy's historic 1960 speech to the Greater Houston Ministerial Association. In that speech, Kennedy sought to assuage concerns that as a Catholic president he would push the Vatican's agenda in American public policy.[18] "I believe in an America that is officially neither Catholic, Protestant nor Jewish— where no public official either requests or accepts instructions on public policy from the Pope, the National Council of Churches or any other ecclesiastical source—where no religious body seeks to impose its will directly or indirectly upon the general populace or the public acts of its officials," he said.[19]

Now, twenty-five years later, with Catholics firmly entrenched in the policy and professional classes and fears of "Papism" a distant memory, the Catholic hierarchy was asserting exactly the opposite: that Catholic public officials did have an obligation to listen to them and attempt to put Catholic teaching into law.

As the election neared, the controversy showed no signs of dying down. Anti-abortion protesters dogged Ferraro. Supporters showed up at her rallies with "I'm Catholic and I'm Pro-Choice" and "Nuns for Ferraro" signs. Krol and Buffalo Bishop Edward Head appeared at rallies with Reagan, while Scranton Bishop James Timlin denounced Ferraro for her "absurd" pro-choice views after she made a campaign stop in that city. Abortion was a hot topic during the presidential debates, with Reagan asserting it was close to murder and Mondale raising the specter of Jerry Falwell picking Supreme Court justices. Abortion was now, according to the *New York Times,* officially a "profoundly divisive" issue in American politics.[20]

With the question of how Catholic lawmakers were to apply religious dogma in a pluralistic society still unsettled, Cuomo gave a landmark address on the subject at the University of Notre Dame in mid-September. In it, he sought to draw a distinction between what Catholics believed as Catholics and how Catholic policymakers should act when representing society as a whole, saying that Catholics should not impose their morality on others. "My church and my conscience require me to believe certain things about divorce, birth control and abortion. My church does not order me, under pain of sin or expulsion, to pursue my salvific mission according to a precisely defined political plan," he said.[21]

Even before the Cuomo and Ferraro controversies, Kissling and Dan and Marjorie Maguire had been working on the idea of developing a sign-on statement on abortion and Catholicism that would make public the division within Catholicism on the morality of abortion. Putting "official" Catholics such as theologians, nuns, and priests on record as saying there was a diversity of opinion on abortion in the church would give all Catholics who supported legal abortion, but especially pro-choice Catholic public officials, legitimacy for their position. At the annual meeting of the Society of Christian Ethics in January 1983, Kissling and the Maguires drafted a statement on Catholics and abortion dissent that was circulated among the Catholic ethicists in attendance. Some fifteen agreed to serve as a sponsoring committee to recruit other signatories, with the idea of eventually publishing the statement. "The idea was to create a major challenge that was international in scope," said Dan Maguire.[22]

The Catholic Committee on Pluralism and Abortion included Kissling, novelist Mary Gordon, who was on the CFFC board, the Maguires, and theologians Mary Hunt, Elizabeth Schüssler Florenza, Milhaven, and Rosemary Radford Ruether. In March 1984, CFFC provided funding to mail the statement to the members of the Catholic Theological Society of America, the Catholic Biblical Association, and the College Theology Society, which represented approximately 2,000 Catholic theologians. As a result, 55 theologians agreed to sign the statement; another 77 said they agreed with it but were afraid they would lose their jobs if they signed it. Some notable progressive theologians, such as Charles Curran, who had led opposition to the encyclical *Humanae Vitae* and who had questioned the bishops' assertion that all abortions were immoral, didn't sign the statement, feeling it went too far in asserting the morality of abortion in circumstances beyond cases of rape, incest, or life endangerment.

The Ferraro controversy seemed custom-made to publicize the "Catholic Statement on Pluralism and Abortion," and the committee decided to publish it as a full-page ad in the *New York Times*. As word of the imminent publication of the statement circulated among women's groups, a number of nuns signed on as well, many to demonstrate support for Ferraro, with some going so far as to send last-minute telegrams to beat the publication deadline.

On Sunday, October 7, the statement ran in the *New York Times* with the signatures of ninety-seven Catholic scholars, theologians, priests, and nuns under the headline "A Diversity of Opinions Regarding Abortion Exists Among Committed Catholics." The statement read in part: "Continued confusion and polarization within the Catholic community on the subject of abortion prompt us to issue this statement. Statements of recent Popes and of the Catholic hierarchy have condemned the direct termination of pre-natal life as morally wrong in all instances. There is the mistaken belief in American society that this is the only legitimate Catholic position. In fact, a diversity of opinions regarding abortion exists among committed Catholics."[23]

The statement noted that "a large number of Catholic theologians hold that even direct abortion, though tragic, can sometimes be a moral choice." The statement called for "candid and respectful discussion on this diversity of opinion within the Church" and said that "Catholics should not seek the kind of legislation that curtails the legitimate exercise of the freedom of religion and conscience."[24]

The impact of the statement was immediate. "It was so public and such a challenge to the Catholic hierarchy," said Dan Maguire. "It was a major event in the history of Catholic ecclesiology. It broke the myth of Catholicism being a monolith on moral issues."[25]

The controversy that had raged over abortion and the church now reached a fever pitch. In an extraordinary period between early October and early November 1984, the divisions within the church were laid bare for all the world to see. On one side were progressive bishops, who didn't want to emphasize abortion because it aligned the church with a political party that contradicted Catholic teaching in just about every other way. These bishops emphasized the church's social justice mission, particularly the preferential option for the poor and nonviolence, as being the most crucial aspect of the church's witness in the world. They also took a Vatican II approach to authority in the church, which stressed the role of the whole Catholic community in receiving and validating the teachings of the hierarchy. As a result, they were reluctant to force Catholic public officials to take what was

A DIVERSITY OF OPINIONS REGARDING ABORTION EXISTS AMONG COMMITTED CATHOLICS.

A CATHOLIC STATEMENT ON PLURALISM AND ABORTION.

Continued confusion and polarization within the Catholic community on the subject of abortion prompt us to issue this statement.

Statements of recent Popes and of the Catholic hierarchy have condemned the direct termination of pre-natal life as morally wrong in all instances. There is the mistaken belief in American society that this is the only legitimate Catholic position. In fact, a diversity of opinions regarding abortion exists among committed Catholics:

- A large number of Catholic theologians hold that even direct abortion, though tragic, can sometimes be a moral choice.
- According to data compiled by the National Opinion Research Center, only 11% of Catholics surveyed disapprove of abortion in all circumstances.

These opinions have been formed by:

- Familiarity with the actual experiences that lead women to make a decision for abortion;
- A recognition that there is no common and constant teaching on ensoulment in Church doctrine, nor has abortion always been treated as murder in canonical history;
- An adherence to principles of moral theology, such as probabilism, religious liberty, and the centrality of informed conscience, and
- An awareness of the acceptance of abortion as a moral choice by official statements and respected theologians of other faith groups.

Therefore, it is necessary that the Catholic community encourage candid and respectful discussion on this diversity of opinion within the Church, and that Catholic youth and families be educated on the complexity of the issues of responsible sexuality and human reproduction.

Further, Catholics — especially priests, religious, theologians, and legislators — who publicly dissent from hierarchical statements and explore areas of moral and legal freedom on the abortion question should not be penalized by their religious superiors, church employers, or bishops.

Finally, while recognizing and supporting the legitimate role of the hierarchy in providing Catholics with moral guidance on political and social issues and in seeking legislative remedies to social injustices, we believe that Catholics should not seek the kind of legislation that curtails the legitimate exercise of the freedom of religion and conscience or discriminates against poor women.

In the belief that responsible moral decisions can only be made in an atmosphere of freedom from fear or coercion, we, the undersigned,* call upon all Catholics to affirm this statement.

To assist in our work please check one or more boxes below and send this coupon to:
The Catholic Committee c/o
Catholics For A Free Choice, Inc.
2008 17th Street N.W.
Washington, DC 20009

☐ I want to help you reach more people with this message. Here is my tax deductible contribution of $_____

☐ Please send me additional literature.

☐ Please add my name to your Catholic Statement on Pluralism and Abortion.

NAME_____

ADDRESS_____

CITY/STATE/ZIP_____

PHONE_____

This ad is a project of the Catholic Committee. It has been paid for by Catholics For A Free Choice, Inc. Make your check payable to Catholics A Free Choice, Inc.

CATHOLIC COMMITTEE ON PLURALISM AND ABORTION

Anthony Battaglia, Ph.D., Associate Professor, California State University • Roddy O'Nell Cleary, D. Min., Campus Ministries, University of Vermont • Joseph Fahey, Ph.D., Professor, Manhattan College • Elizabeth Schüssler Florenza, Ph.D., Professor, University of Notre Dame • Mary Gordon, M.A., author of Final Payments and Company of Women • Patricia Hennessy, J.D., New York City • Mary Hunt, Ph.D., Women's Alliance for Theology, Ethics and Ritual • Frances Kissling, Executive Director, Catholics for a Free Choice • Justus George Lawler, Executive Editor, Academic Bookline, Winston-Seabury Press • Daniel C. Maguire, S.T.D., Professor, Marquette University • Marjorie Reiley Maguire, Ph.D., Fellow in Ethics and Theology, Catholics for a Free Choice • J. Giles Milhaven, Ph.D., Professor Brown University • Rosemary Radford Ruether, Ph.D., Professor, Garrett Evangelical Theological Seminary, IL • Thomas Shannon, Ph.D., Professor, Worcester Polytechnic Institute, MA • James F. Smurl, Ph.D., Professor, Indiana University

OTHER SIGNERS

Agnes P. Albany, M.A., Chestnut Hill College, PA • Everett Ballmann, Minot State College, ND • Michael H. Barnes, Ph.D., University of Dayton, OH • Barbara Bemache-Baker, Ph.D., Loomis Institute, CT • Kathryn Bissell, Wider Opportunities for Women, MD • Mary C.I. Buckley, S.T.D., St. John's University, NY • Ronald Burke, Ph.D., University of Nebraska at Omaha, NB • Mary J. Byles, Ph.D., Maryville College, MO • Ann Carr, Ph.D., University of Chicago Divinity School, IL • Rev. Joseph M. Connolly, S.T.L., pastor, Archdiocese of Maryland, MD • Margaret Cotroneo, Ph.D., University of Pennsylvania, PA • Patty Crowley, Chicago Catholic Women, IL • Barbara A. Cullom, Ph.D., Quixote Center, VA • Maryann Cunningham, S.L., Colorado • Mary Louise Denny, S.L., MO • Daniel DiDomizio, Marian

College, WI • Maurice C. Duchaine, S.T.D., San Francisco, CA • Emmaus Community of Christian Hope, NJ • Margaret A. Farley, Yale Divinity School, CT • Darrell J. Fasching, Ph.D., University of South Florida, FL • Barbara Ferraro, Sisters of Notre Dame, WV • Maureen Fiedler, Ph.D., S.L., Catholics for the Common Good, MD • Silvio E. Fittipaldi, Ph.D., Pastoral Institute of Lehigh Valley, PA • George H. Frein, Ph.D., University of North Dakota, ND • Lorine M. Getz, Ph.D., Somerville, MA • Kevin Gordon, Director, Consultation on Homosexuality, Social Justice and Roman Catholic Theology, CA • Jeannine Gramick, School Sisters of Notre Dame, NY • Christine E. Gudorf, Ph.D, Xavier University, OH • Terry Hamilton, Woodstock/St. Paul Roman Catholic Community, NY • Jack Hanford, Th.D., Ferris State College, MI • Kathleen Hebbeler, Dominican Sister of the Sick Poor, OH • Patricia Hussey, Sisters of Notre Dame, WV • Caridad Inda, Council of Women Religious, MD • Dorothy Irvin, S.T.D., Dunbar, NC • Fr. Janey Kaelin, O.F.M., Cincinnati, OH • Janet Kalven, Loveland, OH • Elizabeth Nelson Keating, Yale University, CT • Pat Kenoyer, S.L., Loretto Women's Network, MO • Joseph E. Kerns, S.T.D., Center for Christian Living, VA • Paul F. Knitter, Th.D., Xavier University, OH • Joseph A. LaBarge, Ph.D., Bucknell University, PA • Eleanor V. Lewis, Ph.D., Baltimore, MD • Wayne Lobue, Ph.D., Gilmour Academy, OH • Agnes Mary Mansour, Ph.D., Lansing, MI • Roseann Mazzeo, S.C., NJ • Bro. Ray McManaman, F.S.C., Lewis University, IL • Kathleen E. McVey, Ph.D., Princeton Theological Seminary, NJ • John A. Melloh, S.T.L., Milwaukee, WI • Joe Mellon, M.A., University of Notre Dame, IN • Diane Neu, M.Div., S.T.M., Co-director Women's Alliance for Theology, Ethics and Ritual, Washington, DC • Jeanne Noble, National Assembly of Religious Women, MD • Sr. Margaret Nulty, Sisters of Charity of New Jersey • Kathleen O'Connor, Ph.D., Maryknoll School of Theology, NY • Margaret A. O'Neill,

Ed.D., Sisters of Charity of New Jersey, NJ • Ronald D. Pasquariello, Ph.D., Marist Brothers, Washington, DC • Richard Penaskovic, Ph.D., Auburn University, AL • Gerald A. Pire, M.A., Seton Hall University, NJ • Stanley M. Polan, S.T.L., Franklin Pierce College, NH • Dolly Pomerleau, Catholics for the Common Good, MD • John E. Price, S.T.L., Evanston, IL • Donna Quinn, National Coalition of American Nuns, IL • Jill Raitt, Ph.D., University of Missouri, MO • Maureen Reiff, Chicago Catholic Women, IL • John G. Rusnak, Ph.D., Phoenix, AZ • Mary Savage, Ph.D., Albertus Magnus College, CT • Jeanne Schaberg, Ph.D., University of Detroit, MI • Mary Jane Schutzius, Federation of Christian Ministries, Association of the Rights of Catholics in the Church, MO • Ellen Shanahan, Ph.D., Rosary College, IL • Emily Ann Staples, University of Minnesota, MN • Marilyn Thie, Sisters of Charity of New Jersey, Colgate University, NY • Sr. Rose Dominic Trapasso, Lima, Peru • Sr. Margaret Ellen Traxler, National Coalition of American Nuns, IL • Marjorie Tuite, Church Women United, NY • Alan F. Turner, Association for the Rights of Catholics in the Church, Valley Forge, PA • Judith Vaughan, National Assembly of Religious Women, CA • E. Jane Via, Ph.D., J.D., University of San Diego and Superior Court of San Diego, CA • Gerald S. Vigna, Ph.D., Pennsauken, NJ • Ann Patrick Ware, M.A., National Coalition of American Nuns, NY • Sallie Ann Watkins, National Coalition of American Nuns, CC • M Jo Weaver, Ph.D., Indiana University, IN • Virginia Williams, S.L., MO • Arthur E. Zannoni, Ph.D., University of Notre Dame Extension Program, IN

*Organizational affiliations are listed for purposes of identification only. Partial listing. This statement has been signed by many other Catholics. In addition, 75 priests, religious and theologians have written that they agree with the Statement but cannot sign because they fear losing their jobs.

Figure 7. The Catholic Statement on Pluralism and Abortion ran in the *New York Times* on October 7, 1984.

in effect a "loyalty oath" on the issue of abortion, preferring the pastoral role of teaching and guiding rather than mandating.

On the other side were the conservatives, who would brook no dissent on abortion and were determined to bring errant Catholic politicians to heel. Maintaining the hierarchy's authority on doctrine related to women and sexuality was their highest priority, as well as restoring a pre–Vatican II authoritarian leadership structure under which the dictates of the hierarchy were unquestioned and absolute.

In the end, the controversy came down to one question: Who was a "good" Catholic? On the one hand, progressives in the church, both clerical and lay, held that someone could be a good Catholic if they believed in the articles of faith and lived the teachings of Christ—concern for thy neighbor, for the poor, for the world. And although some progressives believed that abortion is a sin, they also believed strongly in the right of individual conscience and didn't think it appropriate for the church to impose its morality in specific policy positions in the temporal world. The conservatives, on the other hand, were asserting that to be a good Catholic one had to assent absolutely to the hierarchy's position on abortion and act accordingly in the public square, whether by refusing to vote for pro-choice politicians or seeking laws that inserted Catholic doctrine into the civil code.

On October 14, without responding formally to the Statement on Pluralism and Abortion, NCCB president Malone tried to walk back the impression that the bishops were telling Catholics not to vote for pro-choice politicians. "We do not seek the formation of a voting bloc, nor do we pre-empt the right and duty of individuals to decide conscientiously whom they will support for public office," he said.[26]

But two days later, O'Connor said that the church expected Catholic public officials to make "a statement opposing abortion on demand and a commitment to work for a modification of the permissive" abortion laws. Less than a week later, the liberal wing struck back. Led by Detroit Auxiliary Bishop Thomas Gumbleton, twenty-three progressive bishops criticized their fellow conservative bishops for elevating the issue of abortion above nuclear war. Two days after that, Cardinal Bernardin gave a speech at Georgetown University reiterating his "consistent ethic of life" view and criticizing the single-issue focus on abortion. "We obviously do not have a consensus on this point at present even within the church," he said, and noted that "relating convictions to policy choices is a complex process."[27]

Two weeks later, Mondale and Ferraro lost the election in a landslide. The team was hobbled by a range of problems that included Mondale's ineffectiveness as candidate in the face of Reagan's continued popularity and issues related to the Ferraros' finances and income taxes, so it is difficult to assess the affect of the abortion controversy. White Catholics, who accounted for 24 percent of the electorate, went 58 percent to 41 percent for Reagan, which was a higher percentage than in 1980, when Catholics also split in favor of Reagan. The abortion issue, however, apparently did not drive their votes. Only 8 percent said abortion was the most important issue to them—41 percent said the most important issue was the economy and 32 percent said arms control, while 18 percent said it was fairness toward the poor, which seemed to buttress the contention of progressive bishops that Catholics were inclined to vote on a range of social issues.[28]

It took until mid-November, when the bishops met at their annual meeting, for them to officially condemn the *New York Times* ad: "The members of the Committee on Pluralism and Abortion present a personal opinion which directly contradicts the clear and constant teaching of the church about abortion, a teaching which they as Catholics are obliged to accept."[29]

At this point, lay dissent from the official Catholic position on abortion had been in the headlines for months, along with stories about how Catholics' views on contraception, abortion, premarital sex, and women priests had evolved while the hierarchy remained mired in the past. It was a public relations disaster for the hierarchy.

Unable to deny the evidence of significant dissent from its most treasured positions, the Vatican began to pressure the dissenters who were under its direct authority to retract their support of the statement, apparently hoping that by expunging their signatures they could erase the controversy. The twenty-four nuns of various orders, two brothers, and one of the two priests who signed the statement received a letter in late November from the Vatican's Sacred Congregation for Religious and Secular Institutes saying that the signers were "seriously lacking in 'religious submission of will and mind' to the Magisterium" and demanding that they make a public retraction or face dismissal. (The other priest who signed was a diocesan priest and didn't come under the jurisdiction of the congregation.)[30]

It was an unprecedented step by the Vatican in the modern history of the church. "The letter was about our lack of submission; clearly it was about blind obedience to the pope," said Barbara Ferraro, one of the nuns who received the letter.[31]

The two brothers and the priest backed down almost immediately. The Vatican had no direct authority over the lay theologians who signed the ad. This left the twenty-four nuns, all of whom refused to recant their support, as the target of the Vatican's wrath. Soon the newspapers were full of stories about nuns being threatened with expulsion from their orders if they didn't renounce the ad. One was already a casualty. Sister Ann Carr, a theologian who was serving as a consultant to the bishops as they drafted a pastoral letter on the role of women in the church, was told by the bishops to resign from her position.

For the Vatican, the Statement on Pluralism and Abortion was about more than its position on the morality of abortion—it was about its ability to maintain authority in a church that had been on a path toward a more democratic, less hierarchical structure since Vatican II. "Under the present papacy there is a full-scale effort to roll the Church back to the pre-Vatican II concept of Catholicism as a monarchial chain of command, rather than a community of people who have differences," wrote Ruether. "Control over nuns, particularly American nuns, is seen as a particular priority in this effort to restore a monolithic church," she noted, because well-educated, autonomous women religious in self-governing communities did not fit with the Vatican's conception of nuns as "submissive and silent servants of the clerical hierarchy."[32]

With the "Vatican 24" refusing to back down and the Vatican determined to make its point, a series of protracted negotiations between the Vatican and the nuns' superiors ensued. Cardinal Jean Jerome Hamer, head of the Vatican's Congregation for Religious and Secular Institutes, visited the United States in the summer of 1985 to press for retractions. He said the nuns had caused a "scandal" and must make statements "indicating adherence to the teaching of the church."[33]

In October 1985, Cardinal Bernardin issued a statement from the NCCB saying that the nuns were disobeying God's law. Still no nun budged. In November, apparently surprised by the continued resistance of the nuns and looking for a way to settle the matter, the Vatican indicated that it would accept "clarifications" from the nuns on their positions on abortion rather than outright retractions.[34]

Lay signers found themselves under a different, more subtle, kind of pressure. Four female theologians who signed the ad were asked to meet with their local bishops—reportedly at the request of the Vatican—to discuss "doctrinal matters." The Thomas More Society of San Diego cancelled a lecture by one of the four, Jane Via, at the request of the local bishop. She was warned she would not be allowed to speak at any Catholic institution in the diocese unless she retracted her support for the statement. Florenza saw speaking engagements dry up, as did Dan Maguire. His engagements at four summer theological institutes, including those at Boston College and Villanova University, were cancelled, wiping out his entire 1985 summer lecture schedule.[35]

Maguire was stunned by the blowback. "There is a shunning going on like the Amish do—a blacklisting like during the McCarthy period in the '50s," he charged.[36]

Worried about the implications of the cancellations for academic freedom, the American Association of University Professors convened a special committee to look into the universities' actions. The committee concluded that the cancellations were "representative of a more widespread determination to suppress dissent on the abortion issue."[37]

The *New York Times* ad was a pivotal event in Catholic history because it showed just how the Vatican worked to suppress dissent. "For the public it was an educational tool without parallel, but for the signers there was an enormous price tag—some of which continues to this day in terms of career opportunities," said Hunt.[38]

It was not the only instance of the Vatican using its authority to whitewash abortion dissent. In 1983, Sister Agnes Mansour was forced by the Vatican to choose between remaining a Sister of Mercy and her position as director of the Michigan Department of Social Services, where she administered the state's Medicaid program. A tiny portion of Medicaid funding—less than 1 percent of the department's budget—went for abortions for poor women. Mansour, who had been a nun for twenty-eight years and was a founder of the Catholic social justice lobby Network, personally opposed abortion but felt the good she could do for the poor in the job greatly outweighed any complicity with abortions. She obtained the backing of the leadership of the Sisters of Mercy to take the position when the governor offered it to her in late 1982. Once her leadership of the department became controversial because of the nominal administration of abortion funding, she requested a leave of absence from her order for the duration of her tenure in an attempt to find a compromise that would satisfy the Vatican.

Despite her efforts, Mansour was summoned to a meeting with Bishop Anthony Bevilacqua in May 1983 at the personal request of Pope John Paul II and ordered to resign her position or face dismissal from the Sisters of Mercy. Two days later Mansour asked to be released from her vows with "deep regret," saying that to accede to the Vatican's wishes would violate her conscience and allow "church intrusion into state affairs."[39]

For many, the issue had evolved from the right to dissent from the hierarchy on abortion to the right to dissent period. In late 1984, Kissling began working with some of the signers of the Statement on Pluralism and Abortion to build public support for the "Vatican 24." At a January meeting, they agreed to publish a "Declaration of Solidarity" under a new steering committee, the Committee of Concerned Catholics. The committee drafted a statement and began circulating it in the spring of 1985 as word spread of the reprisals, planning to run it in early October to mark the anniversary of the first ad.[40]

As word of the new statement spread, a backlash began brewing. The *National Catholic Reporter* ran an editorial in September under the headline, "Don't Sign the Abortion Ad," saying it would "cause more conflict and inhibit meaningful dialogue." It said the campaign was "a deceitful, dishonest and divisive effort by a small, single-issue group" to return abortion to center stage just when the U.S. bishops had made great strides in "multi-issue leadership." It implied that the nuns had been victimized by the first ad and said no one benefited from it "except Catholics for a Free Choice—which reaped a rash of publicity."[41]

Kissling called the editorial a classic example of Catholic "red baiting," in which "malevolent 'pro-abortionists' manipulate and dupe" well-intentioned nuns and theologians. "Suffice it to say," she wrote, "that rumors of my or

CFFC's power are greatly exaggerated." She noted that it was the bishops' clumsy attempts to manipulate the abortion issue in the political process that precipitated the first ad. She accused the *National Catholic Reporter* of being complicit in the Vatican's attempt to impose self-censorship on the issue of abortion and of drawing attention away from the real issue—the abuse of ecclesiastical power.[42]

As the controversy heated up in the fall of 1985, some who agreed to sign the second ad withdrew their names, saying they feared their support would be misconstrued as supporting abortion. Some signers of the original *New York Times* ad declined to sign the second ad for fear of reprisals. Another original signer wrote that she disagreed with the strategy but would sign her name because she didn't want to give the impression she had withdrawn her endorsement. The second ad had been slated to run in October 1985, but with the atmosphere in the Catholic community incredibly charged, the Committee of Concerned Catholics held off after the publication of the *National Catholic Reporter* editorial as, according to Marjorie Maguire, a "gesture of good will."[43]

But in early January 1986, Mary Ann Sorrentino, executive director of Planned Parenthood of Rhode Island, revealed that the Diocese of Providence had excommunicated her the previous June for activities related to the "sinful termination of human life." Sorrentino kept the news of the excommunication to herself until a local priest denounced her on a television program as "Public Enemy No. 1 of all babies being killed in the womb in Rhode Island."[44]

Calling the excommunication of Sorrentino the last straw, the committee decided to go ahead and run the ad. The "Declaration of Solidarity" appeared in the *New York Times* on March 2, 1986. A total of 1,000 signers, including five priests and forty nuns, affirmed their "solidarity with all Catholics whose right to free speech was under attack." The ad was signed by three of the original Vatican 24: Patricia Hussey, Barbara Ferraro, and Rose Dominic Trapasso. The ad noted that the reprisals against the signers of the original *New York Times* ad "consciously or unconsciously have a chilling effect on the right to responsible dissent within the church; on academic freedom in Catholic colleges and universities; and on the right to free speech and participation in the U.S. political process." It continued, "We believe that Catholics who, in good conscience, take positions on the difficult questions of legal abortion and other controversial issues that differ from the official hierarchical positions act within their rights and responsibilities as Catholics and as citizens."[45]

With the unresolved cases of the Vatican 24 back in the news as the result of the ad, the Vatican began negotiating in earnest with the superiors of the various nuns, and, for the first time, directly with some of the sisters. Under the pressure of five-hour meetings with Archbishop Vincenzo Fagiolo of the Congregation for Religious and Secular Institutes, some of the nuns agreed to carefully worded statements designed to mollify the Vatican. Some nuns' superiors struck agreements with the Vatican without revealing to the nuns exactly what had been agreed to in their names. The superior of one Sister of Mercy assured Rome that the nun was in agreement with the church's teaching. The Vatican announced that the nun had retracted her support of the ad, only to have the nun publicly deny the assertion.[46]

In July, the Vatican announced that it had accepted "public declarations of adherence to Catholic doctrine on abortion" from twenty-two of the twenty-four nuns, although eleven of these women immediately and publicly disagreed that they had made any such declaration. It appeared that the Vatican was attempting to isolate the two remaining unrepentant signers, Notre Dame de Namur Sisters Ferraro and Hussey, who ran a homeless shelter in Charleston, West Virginia.[47]

Ferraro and Hussey had been summoned to meet with Fagiolo in March at the same time that other nuns were successfully pressured to sign statements. When they got to the meeting, Fagiolo told them that they must put into writing that they supported the hierarchy's position on abortion or they could no longer be nuns. Over the next couple of hours, the two sat through a surreal experience as Fagiolo asked them what their "mommies and daddies" would think if they were removed from their order, excused himself to pray for them, and held Hussey's hand and stroked her arm. "If a higher up did that in any other setting, I would have slapped him in the face. But you knew in the context of that meeting you couldn't do it," she said.[48]

Despite the pressure, Hussey and Ferraro refused to make a statement, suspecting, as in the case of other nuns, that the Vatican would misrepresent

Figure 8. Barbara Ferraro and Patricia Hussey, who eventually
left the Sisters of Notre Dame de Namur over the Vatican's
insistence that they recant their support for the Catholic
Statement on Pluralism and Abortion. (Courtesy of Barbara
Ferraro and Patricia Hussey)

it as a retraction of support for the Statement on Pluralism and Abortion. By
July, the Vatican was threatening formal disciplinary action against the two
nuns if they didn't recant their support of the ad. The nuns' superiors refused
to discipline Ferraro and Hussey, saying the ad was a call for dialogue, not
an endorsement of abortion.[49]

Eventually, after two more years of stress and negotiations, the Vatican
did back down, but Ferraro and Hussey resigned from their order anyway,
saying they no longer recognized the church they had loved. By that time
the issue of the right to dissent from the hierarchy had become a full-
blown crisis that would consume the church.

The *New York Times* ad and its aftermath were watershed moments in
the history of pro-choice Catholicism. From the time in 1964 when
Rosemary Ruether first went public with her use of birth control, the

entire point of the Catholic pro-choice movement had been to make public the fact that Catholics used and supported contraceptives and abortion and that Catholic doctrine supported this choice. With the Statement on Pluralism and Abortion, there was no longer any doubt that there was a significant pro-choice voice within Catholicism. "[T]he ad and the resulting dispute effectively and finally put to rest the myth that Catholics, especially professional Catholics . . . share the belief of the Vatican and the U.S. bishops that abortion is to be absolutely prohibited both legally and morally," wrote Kissling and Hunt. The ad, they said, "ended the hegemony of both bishops and male clerics as the public interpreters of Catholic teaching."[50]

Kissling had succeeded in fulfilling McQuillan's vision of creating a vibrant movement that united lay Catholics, activists, theologians, and religious women and men to provide an alternative voice to the bishops. "When CFFC was founded in 1973, the goal had been for the American people, particularly political leaders, to understand that the bishops did not speak for Catholics and that Catholics could and did support the right to choose. With the ad, that task was definitively accomplished," she noted.[51]

The controversy over the ad made CFFC, and especially Kissling, the face of progressive Catholic dissent. Media coverage of the organization increased dramatically. Dan Maguire was widely quoted in the press on the nuances of the progressive theological position on abortion, and Kissling became the go-to person on the politics of abortion in the church. With her national profile soaring, she was dubbed the "Cardinal of Choice" in an August 1986 profile in the *Washington Post Magazine*. "Just a few years ago no one ever heard of CFFC," Dan Maguire told the *Washington Post*. "Now it's a very major factor in Catholic life."[52]

·   ·   ·   ·   ·

The *New York Times* ad and the subsequent controversy put CFFC and the pro-choice Catholic movement on the map. For the first time there was credible, organized Catholic opposition to the assertions of the U.S. bishops that they alone represented Catholic thought about abortion. This was especially important for the media, who now had a place to go that gave

voice to Catholic dissent, and for pro-choice politicians. But its prominence also made the organization a target. The bishops were not happy to
have competition on the issue of abortion. In fact, much of their authority
in the public sphere had come from the perception that they spoke for all
Catholics on the issue and the implication that to cross the bishops was to
risk alienating Catholic voters. They couldn't afford to have an organization continually reminding people that they didn't speak for a significant
proportion of Catholics.

In addition, CFFC's success in highlighting divided Catholic opinion on
abortion was bringing attention to similar divides in the church on the
issues of divorce and remarriage for Catholics, women and married
priests, and greater acceptance of homosexual Catholics. These were not
discussions the bishops wanted to have. Their response was to attempt to
discredit the pro-choice Catholic movement by attacking CFFC as a thinly
veiled front for secular organizations that promoted widespread abortion
and anti-Catholicism.

In November 1985, Richard Doerflinger, the assistant director of the
NCCB Office of Pro-Life Activities, published a long critique of CFFC in
the progressive Jesuit magazine *America*. He charged that CFFC was being
used by the "pro-abortion" lobby as "part of a political strategy for under-
mining the Catholic Church's efforts against the abortion industry." He
attacked the theological basis of the *New York Times* ad, denying that the
church had ever based its abortion dogma on the point at which a fetus was
ensouled, and suggested that the signers had been duped into supporting
a pro-abortion organization. He pointed to the fact that only about 3 percent of CFFC's 1983 income of $222,000 came from membership dues,
thereby accusing CFFC of being a tool of "pro-abortion" and "population
control" groups rather than a genuine outlet for "home-grown Catholic
dissent."[53]

Doerflinger tried to discredit the organization's funders, charging that
the Sunnen Foundation, which had given CFFC $70,000 in 1983, was
founded "on the profits from Emko contraceptive foam" and was a longtime supporter of population control initiatives: that the Brush Foundation,
which gave CFFC $30,000, was founded "by a eugenics enthusiast and
colleague of Margaret Sanger"; and that the Ford Foundation, which gave
$25,000, was "a major funding source for population control groups."[54]

In a rebuttal that *America* refused to publish, Marjorie Maguire noted that only "someone who is employed by an anti-contraceptive organization such as the NCCB could seriously think that the mere mention of Margaret Sanger, Planned Parenthood, contraceptive foam, or population planning groups would strike terror into the soul of any Catholic and clinch his argument that CFFC is bent on evil purposes."[55]

Another point of attack over funding designed to make CFFC's funders seem unsavory was that it had accepted funding from *Playboy* magazine. CFFC had received $10,000 from the Playboy Foundation in 1982 and in 1983, as had a number of other progressive organizations, including the NAACP and the American Civil Liberties Union. As Kissling noted at the time, the organization realized that taking money from *Playboy* could be problematic for a feminist group but "made a judgment that taking Playboy money was a matter of reparations, and provided an opportunity to do some good with that money." Despite the fact that the organization had only accepted $20,000 over a two-year period in the early 1980s, anti-abortion groups would continue to intimate for years that *Playboy* was a major or ongoing funder of the organization in an attempt to conflate sexual licentiousness and abortion rights.[56]

The problem of membership had been a sticky one for CFFC and one that its critics increasingly took aim at, suggesting it was not a legitimate social movement. By the early 1980s, CFFC claimed a membership of about 5,000, but a quick calculation of its membership income suggests that even that number was overstated—although CFFC had always been generous about renewing membership, and subscriptions to *Conscience*, for those who couldn't pay membership dues. It lacked the budget for the kind of large-scale, ongoing direct mail membership effort that would be needed to reach a widely dispersed constituency like Catholics.

In addition, Catholics were not the kind of classic "aggrieved" population that made organization easy. Most Catholics could quietly go about their business using contraception, having abortions if needed, and voting for pro-choice candidates without ever missing mass. Very few people felt compelled to stand up to their local priests, never mind the bishops, on these issues as long as they could do what they wanted in the privacy of their homes. Studies show that in general "opponents of abortion feel more strongly about the issue than those supporting abortion rights."

Surveys in the early 1980s found only 16 percent of strongly pro-choice Catholics felt it was one of the most important issues versus 43 percent of strongly anti-abortion Catholics. As a result, the "small minority of Catholics who follow the church's absolutist position are much more politically involved than the majority of Catholics who approve of abortion."[57]

"People could be 100 percent pro-choice but they weren't going to take on the church," said Mary Jean Collins, who was director of public affairs for CFFC in the mid-1980s. "The polling was always in favor of Catholics not supporting the bishops, but they would not look them in the eye and picket their own church," she noted.[58]

And there was another factor at work that Kissling noted in a *Conscience* editorial shortly after she became president of CFFC. "We believe that Catholic women's reluctance to seek publicly to secure the right to choose abortion is attributable to our unconscious acceptance, *when it comes to our own rights,* of the 'role' the church fathers have assigned to us—that of servant to others," she wrote. "[I]in the case of lay women, many of us are afraid that if we speak out on the abortion issue, the automatic assumption on the social level is that the reason we fight for this right is that we are sexually active, which is evil, and we may need the ability to get rid of the evidence."[59]

Sociologist John McCarthy noted that it was the initial organizing done by the Catholic bishops that made the anti-abortion movement a more effective grassroots force than the pro-choice movement. The bishops were able to capitalize on the existing dense social infrastructure of the church to create a movement that eventually took on a life of its own, while the pro-choice movement, lacking an infrastructure to build on, became more reliant on professional social movement organizations, advertising, public relations, and direct mail to demonstrate support for abortion rights.[60]

By 1985, CFFC's board had decided to do away with membership altogether and to work strictly as an educational organization. Under Kissling's leadership, CFFC was less worried about getting rank-and-file Catholics to fill out a membership form and more interested in finding creative ways to make visible Catholic support for abortion rights. This was in keeping with the evolving role of social movement organizations, which play a critical role in any movement. If protestors and passion are the flesh of social movements, social movement organizations are the muscle and sinew. They keep movements going, especially in the lean years when the public isn't paying attention to a particular issue. They attract funding, which allows them to support a staff and a small cadre of thinkers and activists who develop the intellectual basis of the movement and educate lawmakers and key constituencies.

By the mid-1980s, most of the major social movements—civil rights, women's rights, environmentalism—had evolved from spontaneous movements run by loosely aggregated individuals with little formal training to being largely conducted by professionalized organizations. These organizations had full-time professional staff, a small or largely paper membership, and outside funding sources such as foundations.[61]

CFFC fit this model. It had a professionalized staff and worked with a cadre of leading progressive theologians and activists, publishing their work and organizing conferences to spread their ideas. It had a strong media component, which it leveraged to publicize pro-choice Catholic thought. "We knew that the *New York Times* was our best friend. The struggle over reform in the Catholic Church was going to take place on the pages of the newspapers and on the TV and the radio because we didn't have access to church mechanisms, so we need to use secular mechanisms to get the message out," said Kissling.[62]

The organization also had a core of some two dozen state-level activists who organized grassroots activists, wrote letters to the editor, kept in touch with legislators and organized local educational programs, and the support of several thousand individual donors, with major funding coming from foundations aligned with its issues.

By the mid-1980s, the abortion rights movement was a coalition of professionalized social movement organizations, each with its own unique role to play. The National Abortion Rights Action League was the political arm, making visible electoral support for abortion rights. Planned Parenthood was the reproductive health service provider. The National Abortion Federation represented abortion clinics. CFFC was a counterbalance to the bishops and an informational resource for pro-choice Catholic politicians. "The way in which CFFC became extremely important was that we gave the politicians the writings of the theologians that said there were legitimate arguments on the pro-choice side.

This had tremendous impact in Congress for elected officials; it gave them someplace to go," said Collins.[63]

It was this very success at becoming an established, professionalized part of the abortion rights movement and a source of legitimacy for pro-choice Catholics that the bishops were attacking to suggest that CFFC was somehow less than legitimate. The mid-1980s saw a spate of articles attacking CFFC. The conservative *National Catholic Register* did a two-part exposé in 1984 that repeated old charges about pro-choice foundation funders and a progressive theological take on abortion. In 1986, *The Wanderer*, a far-right Catholic newspaper, published a study by a short-lived organization calling itself the National Catholic Action Committee that charged CFFC was "[c]reated by elements of the abortion rights movement" as part of a "deliberate strategy of engendering and exploiting anti-Catholic sentiment for political purposes." These attacks received little notice outside of conservative circles but were harbingers of a more organized countermovement to come.[64]

The conservatives' attacks on CFFC mirrored real anxiety about the growing legitimacy of pro-choice Catholicism. Doerflinger hinted at the bishop's concern when he charged that CFFC's *Abortion: A Guide to Making Ethical Choices*, was "openly competing with the bishops in forming individual consciences." He also charged that the organization's activities, from the 1979 *Washington Post* ad when the pope visited Washington, to the 1982 press conference criticizing the bishops' endorsement of the Hatch Amendment, to the *New York Times* ad, were "designed to counteract the Catholic Church's public policy impact by presenting itself as something akin to an alternative religious denomination."[65]

CFFC had been successful in giving voice to an alternative view of Catholicism at a time when the bishops were increasingly concerned that they were losing control over Catholics, who were more and more likely to pick and choose which rules to follow, giving birth to a new term: "cafeteria Catholics." A 1985 CBS/*New York Times* poll found that 79 percent of Catholics believed that a person could be a "good" Catholic even if he or she disagreed with church teaching on abortion, birth control, and divorce.[66]

"Certainly never in the history of Catholicism have so many Catholics in such apparent good faith decided that they can reject the official teaching of the church as to what is sexually sinful and what is not, and to do so while continuing the regular practice of Catholicism and even continuing the description of themselves as good, strong, solid Catholics," wrote Catholic sociologist Father Andrew Greeley.[67]

But instead of backing off and trying to find a way to reconcile the growing divide in the church, the Vatican would double down on its strategy of trying to purge dissent from the church.

PART II The Bishops' Lobby

6 The Bishops' Lobby

The election of 1984 and the Catholic Statement on Pluralism and Abortion began a new era for the Catholic abortion rights movement. It moved from the edges of the abortion debate to a very public confrontation with the Catholic hierarchy over the issue of who had the right to interpret Catholic doctrine. The stakes were high for the Vatican, which asserted that it alone held this right. With its authority challenged, the hierarchy began an unprecedented, church-wide crackdown on any deviation from its official doctrine, removing priests and theologians who dared to dissent.

In July 1986, the National Conference of Catholic Bishops (NCCB) announced that it was reevaluating the appointment of Jesuit theologian Rev. Michael Buckley to head its Committee on Doctrine because he, along with twenty-two other theologians, had signed a letter nine years earlier dissenting from the Vatican's 1977 proclamation that women could never be priests. That same month it was made public that Father James Provost, a noted canon lawyer, had seen his application for tenure at Catholic University held up for more than a year because he had questioned the hierarchy's positions regarding women's ordination and divorced Catholics receiving sacraments. He received tenure after he agreed to make a public statement that church doctrine was controlled by the hierarchy and publish articles clarifying his positions.[1]

Noted Catholic University theology professor Father Charles Curran received no such reprieve. In August 1986, the Vatican revoked his authority to teach Catholic theology, effectively ending his career at any Catholic university, because Curran refused to recant his views that contraception, divorce, homosexuality, and abortion could be moral in certain circumstances. He also held that he had the right to dissent from church teachings that were not deemed infallible, which none of the teachings regarding sexuality were. "It should be evident that the positions taken by me are neither radical or rebellious but are in the mainstream of contemporary Roman Catholic theology," he said.[2]

More than 600 Catholic theologians signed on to a statement of support for Curran that declared the right of theologians to dissent from non-infallible teaching. Catholic University, however, removed Curran from the faculty in 1987 despite the fact that he had tenure, raising alarm among Catholic and non-Catholic academics about academic freedom at Catholic universities.[3]

Father Terrance Sweeney also saw his career in the Catholic Church come to an end in August 1986. He resigned from the Jesuits rather than comply with a Vatican demand that he destroy his research on the attitudes of bishops toward mandatory celibacy for priests and women's ordination. His survey of U.S. bishops—to which nearly half of all U.S. bishops responded—found that one-quarter would support allowing priests to marry, while fewer than 10 percent supported the ordination of women.[4]

The shock over the disciplining of Curran was still reverberating when in September the Vatican took the unprecedented step of stripping Seattle archbishop Raymond Hunthausen of his authority regarding issues of morality, turning power over to Auxiliary Bishop Donald Wuerl. The Vatican accused Hunthausen, a liberal antiwar activist, of failing to sufficiently enforce Vatican doctrine in the areas of homosexuality, birth control, and premarital sex. Among his sins, he had allowed Dignity, an organization of gay Catholics, to celebrate mass in St. James Cathedral, Catholic hospitals in his diocese to perform sterilizations for non-Catholic women, and divorced Catholics who had remarried to receive communion.[5]

Even children were not immune from the wave of near hysteria over dissent that swept through the Catholic Church in 1986. An eleven-year-old girl was expelled from St. Agnes Roman Catholic School in Toledo, Ohio, after she refused to recant her support for abortion rights. She had attended a demonstration against a bill that would require parental consent for a minor to receive birth control counseling and signed on to an ad commemorating the thirteenth anniversary of *Roe v. Wade*. Her priest demanded that in order to avoid being expelled from the sixth grade, she write a letter to the school's principal saying she didn't personally support abortion.[6]

The atmosphere over dissent was so charged that in March 1987 a delegation of American bishops that included Cardinals John O'Connor and Joseph Bernardin went to Rome ahead of the pope's planned September visit to the United States to confer with Vatican officials on handling the tension caused by the crackdown. One bishop warned the pope against scolding Americans on their lack of adherence to the hierarchy's teaching, saying the issue needed to be handled in a "sensitive manner." Despite the warnings of U.S. bishops, the theme of the pope's visit was clear: the Vatican intended to enforce orthodoxy on moral views; there would be no dissent tolerated. "It is in the United States more than any place else in the world that the church is defining its role in modern, secular society," said one Vatican advisor.[7]

Not surprisingly, the issue of the right to dissent continued to consume the church. In February 1989, 163 of the world's leading Catholic theologians, including Bernard Häring, Hans Küng, and Edward Schillebeeckx, published the Cologne Declaration, in which they decried the Vatican's heavy-handed, centralized approach to church governance and its crackdown on legitimate theological inquiry as an overreach of the pope's authority. "If the Pope does what does not belong to his office, he cannot demand obedience in the name of Catholicism," they declared, charging that the pope was conflating the teaching on birth control with the articles of faith to squelch dissent.[8]

In March 1989 the pope met with thirty-five U.S. archbishops in an extraordinary four-day summit to discuss the state of relations between the Vatican and the American Catholic Church. The meeting sprung from the hierarchy's dissatisfaction with the way the Hunthausen case had been handled, although Hunthausen's authority had been largely restored in a deal that included appointing a coadjutor bishop to the diocese and an agreement by Hunthausen to cease the liberal practices he sanctioned.[9]

At the meeting, some prelates spoke to the need to present church teachings in the spirit of the American traditions of pluralism and freedom of thought. They heard back from the Vatican that the real problem was their failure to sufficiently enforce doctrinal orthodoxy. "[D]issent from church doctrine remains what it is—dissent," said Cardinal Joseph Ratzinger, the head of the Vatican's Congregation for the Doctrine of the Faith, which guards doctrine on faith and morals. It was Ratzinger who oversaw the Hunthausen and Curran cases and was the most enthusiastic enforcer of the pope's brand of orthodoxy. Specifically noted by Ratzinger at the meeting as obstacles to American obedience were "radical feminism," theologians with too much authority, and the television program *Dallas*.[10]

The following June, Ratzinger issued a more definitive statement on theologians, stating that they had no right to dissent publicly from the hierarchy's teachings, even on general moral teachings not considered infallible. "The first reaction of many if not most theologians will be to dissent from that document on dissent," quipped noted Notre Dame theologian Rev. Richard McCormick.[11]

·　　·　　·　　·　　·

Despite the continued controversy over the right to dissent from church teaching on abortion, the U.S. bishops largely refrained from interference in the 1988 presidential election. Abortion was not a major factor in the contest between Vice President George H. W. Bush and Massachusetts governor Michael Dukakis. The Christian Right found itself without a standard-bearer in the general election after televangelist Pat Robertson, who had carried the anti-abortion flag, lost his bid for the Republican nomination after a brief surge early in the primaries. Cardinal Bernardin, who championed the "consistent ethic of life" approach to the bishops' involvement in public policy over a single-issue focus on abortion, chaired the NCCB's Committee on Pro-Life Activities and kept the abortion politics quiet.

But the issue returned to center stage in July 1989 with the Supreme Court's decision in *Webster v. Reproductive Health Services,* a landmark decision that upheld a Missouri law that restricted the use of public funds and facilities for abortion and required doctors to test for viability in cases of later-term abortions.[12]

The *Webster* ruling, while not overturning *Roe*, allowed states to impose a variety of new restrictions on abortions designed to make them harder to obtain. It was the beginning of a piecemeal strategy to limit access to abortion. No longer would opponents of abortion have to hit the high bar of a supermajority for a constitutional amendment to ban abortion; they could restrict access to abortion through laws passed by simple majority votes in state legislatures. Justice Harry Blackmun, who authored the *Roe* decision, warned in his dissent that a "chill wind blows" for a woman's right to legal abortion.[13]

The decision revitalized the anti-abortion movement, which had seen its image eroded by a series of violent clinic protests.[14] It also invigorated abortion opponents within the U.S. bishops' conference. At their annual meeting in November, the bishops unanimously passed a resolution hailing the *Webster* decision and calling for a renewed effort to ban abortion. They also for the first time officially rebuked pro-choice Catholic public officials: "No Catholic can responsibly take a 'pro-choice' stand when the 'choice' in question involves the taking of an innocent human life." The bishops elected hard-core anti-abortion Cardinal O'Connor to replace Bernardin as head of the pro-life committee, telegraphing their intent to reenter the fight over abortion. Both Bernardin and incoming NCCB president Archbishop Daniel Pilarczyk of Cincinnati speculated that bishops might mete out ecclesiastical sanctions against pro-choice Catholics.[15]

They were correct. In mid-November, San Diego Bishop Leo Maher, who in 1975 had denied communion to women who supported abortion rights, issued an edict denying communion to pro-choice California State Senate candidate Lucy Killea. But his move backfired when Killea, who was a Democrat, won in a heavily Republican district. Nonetheless, Los Angeles Cardinal Roger Mahony and Orange County Bishop Norman McFarland said they would impose sanctions against Catholic politicians who exhibited "flagrant" support of abortion rights.[16]

In Montana, Bishop Elden Curtiss asked four Catholic state officials to fill out a questionnaire explaining their support of abortion rights. Suddenly, bishops around the country found themselves being asked if they would excommunicate pro-choice Catholic politicians. What followed over the next six months was what political commentator John McLaughlin called "a full court press" against pro-choice politicians "the likes of which has never been seen by American Catholics."[17]

In January 1990, New York Auxiliary Bishop Austin Vaughan warned Governor Mario Cuomo that he was "in danger of going to hell" unless he changed his position on abortion. Shortly thereafter, Brooklyn Bishop Thomas Daily barred Cuomo from speaking in any parishes in his diocese (Cuomo already had been barred from speaking in parishes in the Archdiocese of New York).[18]

O'Connor also moved in the early months of 1990 to make his mark as the new head of the NCCB's Committee on Pro-Life Activities. He tried at the bishops' March meeting to get approval for concrete sanctions against pro-choice Catholic politicians but failed to get enough backing to submit his proposal for a vote. Instead, in a move that apparently pleased both hard-core abortion opponents and the more moderate members of the conference, the board approved a proposal to hire a public relations firm to conduct a national anti-abortion campaign. The news that the NCCB had hired the PR firm of Hill & Knowlton to conduct a $5 million campaign to influence public opinion against abortion sparked an immediate outcry—both over the cost of the campaign and the appropriateness of the bishops behaving in such a brazenly political manner. "In a church that is having difficulty keeping inner-city parishes open . . . spending $5 million on this seems a totally inappropriate use of money and may make a lot of Catholics, even those who agree with them on abortion, very unhappy," said Frances Kissling.[19]

O'Connor found himself subject to a new round of criticism in June, when he published a twelve-page statement in the New York archdiocesan newspaper that explicitly threatened pro-choice politicians with excommunication. He wrote that "where Catholics are perceived not only as treating church teaching on abortion with contempt but helping to multiply abortions by advocating legislation supporting abortion or by making public funds available for abortion . . . bishops may consider excommunication the only option."[20]

The statement caused a political uproar, with both Republicans and Democrats expressing concern that such measures would cast doubt on the political independence of Catholics and effectively bar them from government service. O'Connor said his statement had been misinterpreted; but the meaning was clear: the anti-abortion hardliners were back in control at the bishops' conference and had pro-choice Catholic public officials in their crosshairs.

Around the country, priests condemned pro-choice politicians from the pulpit and warned them to avoid communion or parish activities. In March, Archbishop Pilarczyk told Catholic abortion providers that they shouldn't receive communion. Guam Archbishop Anthony Apuron threatened to excommunicate any Catholic senator in that territory's legislature who voted against what would be the most restrictive abortion legislation in the United States. The Diocese of Providence, Rhode Island, cancelled a talk that state representative Patrick Kennedy (D) was scheduled to give at a mother–daughter breakfast because of his support of abortion rights. The bishop of Las Vegas refused to let a pro-choice candidate for attorney general speak to a government class at a Catholic school.[21]

In April, the eighteen Catholic bishops of Pennsylvania sent out a pastoral letter saying that public figures "cannot be a Catholic in good standing in the church while publicly rejecting and advocating the abandonment of its teaching." A pro-choice candidate running for the Pennsylvania Assembly was fired from her volunteer position coordinating a day care program at her local church in what she called an "openly political" move designed to "intimidate other Catholics." Another local candidate in Pennsylvania was removed from her position as president of her parochial school board, and the monsignor of Our Lady of Lourdes in Montgomery County, Maryland, ordered a candidate for the Maryland House of Delegates to resign from the parish council. In early June, Bishop John Myers of Peoria, Illinois, said that pro-choice Catholics should abstain from receiving communion.[22]

The same month, Bishop Rene Gracida of Corpus Christi, Texas, issued a formal decree of excommunication against Rachel Vargas, the director of a local clinic that provided abortion services, for sinning "against God and humanity and against the laws of the Roman Catholic Church." It was the first official decree of excommunication regarding abortion. "My excommunication was clearly a political gesture . . . to silence all Catholics on the issue of abortion," said Vargas.[23]

This period marked a major broadening of the bishops' condemnation of pro-choice Catholic politicians. The attacks on Geraldine Ferraro and Mario Cuomo in the mid-1980s had been made primarily by O'Connor and Bernard Law of Boston and demonstrated a definite split within the bishops' conference about how to handle the issue of public dissent on abortion. By the early 1990s, denunciations of pro-choice public officials had spread throughout the country and were now officially joined by the bishops' conference. The conference itself was becoming more conservative as older progressive bishops retired at the mandatory age of seventy and were replaced with conservatives picked by Pope John Paul II, who had exclusive authority to appoint bishops and elevated only those who favored his restrictive, absolutist positions on sexuality.

As a result of this increasing hierarchical conservatism, coupled with the systematic stifling of dissent, the church began to ossify from within. The vibrant theological discussions that had characterized the 1960s and 1970s were silenced. Young Catholics shied away from vocations; seminary enrollment was only one-third of what it had been in the 1960s and the population of priests and nuns was graying and thinning. As many as one-fifth of priests, and an even greater proportion of nuns, had left the ministry.[24]

Despite their increasingly hard line, the bishops had even less grounds to claim a homogeny of Catholic opinion on abortion than ever before. By the mid-1980s, Catholic "support for abortions for social reasons, such as poverty, not wanting to get married, or not wanting more children, was as high among Catholics as among Protestants for the first time," according to Tom Smith of the National Opinion Research Center. Only 12 percent of Catholics agreed with the bishops that abortion should be prohibited in all circumstances. The number of strongly pro-choice Catholics, who approved of abortion for both social reasons and in cases of rape, incest, and to save the life of the woman, outnumbered "complete anti-abortion Catholics by between 2–3 to 1." Smith concluded, "The majority of Catholics are moderately pro-choice, overwhelmingly favoring abortion rights for reasons such as rape, incest, health, and birth defects and with 45–50% favoring abortions for social reasons."[25]

This split on abortion opinion between lay Catholics and the hierarchy made it evident that the bishops' ecclesiastical conference had evolved into a freestanding lobby dedicated to translating the bishops' views on social issues into public policy. As a religious nonprofit, the bishops' conference is prevented by law from engaging in lobbying to a "substantial" degree. However, "substantial" is not defined by the IRS and activities that support lobbying, such as legal affairs and media relations, are not counted as lobbying. By the mid-1980s, the bishops had an imposing public policy presence in Washington, complete with a six-story, 170,000-square-foot headquarters on five lavishly landscaped acres just a few miles from Capitol Hill that included a marble-floored chapel, a state-of-the-art conference room, and a reflecting pool. By 1990, the NCCB had an annual budget of $30 million, which paid for "[c]ongressional testimony, litigation, lobbying, media outreach, monitoring of federal legislation and regulation, participation in federal regulatory proceedings, conferences and seminars, educational ministry, pastoral letters, publications, domestic and international relief services, and grassroots organizing." It had a lobbying budget of nearly $500,000 and four full-time lobbyists who worked on Capitol Hill on seventy-four issues ranging from abortion to asbestos abatement for Catholic schools to immigration. The NCCB was supported by legal and media relations departments with $1 million budgets. The NCCB Secretariat of Pro-Life Activities had a budget of $300,000, the largest of any secretariat.[26]

The bishops also directed state-level Catholic conferences that lobbied state legislatures. After the *Webster* decision opened the door for more restrictive state abortion legislation, the Pennsylvania Catholic Conference was the "most significant lobby" behind passage of Pennsylvania's Abortion Control Act, which became the most restrictive abortion law passed to date and set up another Supreme Court challenge to the constitutionality of *Roe*. The measure required women to get their husbands' permission to have abortions and imposed a waiting period for the procedure.[27]

The bishops were leveraging their ecclesiastical authority at both the federal and state levels to pressure lawmakers to pass restrictive abortion legislation in the name of the Catholic Church and Catholic voters, who didn't necessarily agree with their positions, while at the same time bullying pro-choice Catholic politicians into silence to justify their contention that there was no such thing as a pro-choice Catholic.

·   ·   ·   ·   ·

Pro-choice advocates watched nervously through the spring of 1992 as the Supreme Court heard arguments in *Planned Parenthood v. Casey*, which challenged the constitutionality of Pennsylvania's Abortion Control Act. Many feared that a now more conservative court, which included three justices appointed by President Ronald Reagan—Sandra Day O'Connor, Antonin Scalia, and Anthony M. Kennedy—would use *Casey* to overturn *Roe*. The National Abortion Rights Action League (NARAL) had undertaken the first major advertising campaign in the history of the pro-choice movement to alert women to the danger of returning to the pre-*Roe* era.[28] On June 30, 1992, the Supreme Court issued its ruling in *Casey*, essentially upholding the fundamental right to abortion enshrined in *Roe* but reaffirming the right of states to put new restrictions on abortion access, including mandating a waiting period and requiring minors to receive parental consent for an abortion.[29]

It was a new world for the abortion rights movement. Not only were states now allowed to erect barriers to legal abortion, but the advent of AIDS and the political ascendency of the religious right had given rise to a conservative current in public policy issues related to sex. And women themselves had changed since the days of Patricia McQuillan. They had entered the workforce in unprecedented numbers and had made major strides in educational, professional, and social equality. For them, the struggle for basic equality and the right to control their reproductive functions was as distant as the fight for suffrage. As a result, the explicit link between women's rights and access to abortion had been severed and the "Keep your hands off my body" frame for abortion rights had lost resonance. "The road from *Roe* to *Casey* was a long one," Kissling wrote. "When *Roe* came down in 1973, the economy was expanding, and so were civil and individual rights. The pill had wrought a sexual revolution. Public attention was focused on limiting family size and postponing pregnancy. The painful and damaging consequences that illegal abortion wrought on women's lives and health were fresh memories. Now, as *Casey* is decided, the economy is contracting. Sex is suspect. Couples worry about infertility, not fertility."[30]

The Arthur DeMoss Foundation was running its blockbuster, $20 million "Life: A Beautiful Choice" anti-abortion campaign. The ads, with their sunlit, soft-focus images of cavorting children who had begun life as unplanned pregnancies, were ubiquitous and refocused the debate back to the question of fetal protection. The pro-choice movement grappled with finding a message that resonated in this new environment. NARAL's ad campaign focused on keeping government out of a woman's decision to have an abortion and returning to the back-alley horrors of the pre-*Roe* era. Kissling warned that an abortion rights message that was perceived as being more concerned with rights than with values would fail. She said that abortion rights supporters "must press not only—and maybe not primarily—for access to abortion, but also, tirelessly, for measures that will reduce unintended pregnancy and allow women who want to have children to do so with dignity."[31]

Catholics for a Free Choice (CFFC) increased its emphasis on measures to increase access to contraception and improve support for women who wanted to carry pregnancies to term as well as to address the needs of underserved populations. It began to work to build support for pro-choice and pro-family-planning policies in the Latino community, which lacked organized representation in the pro-choice community. "There had to be a institutional, pro-choice Latino presence somewhere, but it was really hard for two white girls to create a Latina institute," noted Denise Shannon, who joined CFFC as its communications director and soon became its first vice president. Eventually the right staffer was found, and in 1990 CFFC launched the Latina Initiative to provide networking and technical assistance to organize pro-choice Latinas. In 1994 the organization became independent as the National Latina Institute for Reproductive Health, the first independent national organization on Latina health and reproductive rights issues.[32]

Increasingly the battle over abortion was a battle for hearts and minds. In November 1990, the bishops launched their much-anticipated PR offensive featuring the slogan "The Natural Choice Is Life." With the tag line "1.6 million abortions can't be right," the campaign argued that too many abortions were being performed and for the wrong reasons. One of the ads noted, "92 percent of all abortions are performed for reasons that have nothing to do with rape, incest or protecting the health of the mother."[33]

Hill & Knowlton also counseled the bishops that they needed to put a feminine face on their anti-abortion efforts. The bishops appointed Helen

Alvare, a telegenic young lawyer, as their spokesperson on abortion, clearly hoping that she would seem more credible than a group of graying, celibate men. But the campaign was not as highly visible as many had expected and came and went without noticeably changing public opinion on abortion. The NCCB cancelled its contract with Hill & Knowlton in February 1992, saying the bishops would bring much of the work in house. But the counsel the bishops had received did change how they approached abortion—at least in the short run. The bishops took a more "conciliatory" and "less fire and brimstone" tack on abortion, according to Shannon.[34]

Their decision to have a woman make their arguments also proved key. Twenty years later, Cardinal Timothy Dolan of New York told a reporter that "the days of fat, balding Irish bishops are over" and that hiring an "attractive, articulate, intelligent" laywoman to be the bishops' front-woman on abortion was "the best thing we ever did."[35]

Catholics for a Free Choice explored the possibility of doing a TV campaign but lacked the resources to compete with the bishops or the DeMoss Foundation on television. Finally it decided on a print campaign focusing on the long-term goal of reshaping the public dialogue around abortion. In June 1992, CFFC launched its "Nobody wants to have an abortion" ads, which asked readers to "Picture a world where mothers have easy access to childcare they can afford. Where children can count on a good education no matter what school district they live in. Where people have healthcare whether or not they have a job. Where safe birth control is available to everyone who needs it. In this world abortion isn't illegal. It's unheard of. Isn't that the best choice of all?"

"The ad was really a culmination . . . of a concept we'd been advancing for a some time," noted Kissling on the twentieth anniversary of CFFC's founding. "It recognizes that at the root of unintended pregnancies are myriad issues that beg our attention." The ad ran in the *New York Times*, *Washington Post*, *National Catholic Reporter*, and *Congressional Quarterly's* Democratic National Convention issue. The response was overwhelmingly positive. Many complimented the organization for the unique approach, saying they couldn't make out the politics of who was behind the ad, and others called it subtle and surprising. One woman said "it was the best ad on the subject she had ever seen." However, a modest print advertising campaign with a $50,000 budget couldn't hope to make the impact of the DeMoss campaign, and even some in the pro-choice movement were wary that seeking middle ground would be giving up too much to the anti-abortion movement.[36]

·   ·   ·   ·   ·

Despite an occasional flaring of the culture wars, abortion was largely overshadowed by the recession in the 1992 presidential election between Democratic Arkansas Governor Bill Clinton and Republican Vice President George H. W. Bush. Clinton went out of his way to stress his broad agreement with the bishops on every issue except abortion, noting that his stance on social welfare issues like health care, welfare, and immigration was closer to the bishops' than the Republican platform. He signaled his sensitivity to the concerns of many who thought that abortion was too common when he declared that the procedure should be "safe, legal and rare." When NCCB president Archbishop William Keeler and other bishops met with Clinton in early March, they declared that they found "[m]uch common ground on poor children and families, health care, foreign affairs and other important areas," while noting "significant differences" on abortion.[37]

The election of Clinton as president marked the first time since the modern abortion rights movement came into being that advocates of legal abortion were completely on the inside of the political system. The Clinton administration had many acknowledged feminist leaders, such as Health and Human Services Secretary Donna Shalala, and, at least informally, Hillary Clinton. There were also now more women in positions of authority in agencies that dealt with family planning, like Elizabeth Maguire, who was acting director of the U.S. Agency for International Development's (USAID's) Office of Population, who contacted CFFC for input on initiatives the administration was considering to improve family planning services.[38]

Clinton marked the twentieth anniversary of *Roe v. Wade* by rescinding five Reagan–Bush-era abortion restrictions, including a federal "gag" order that had prevented federally funded family planning clinics from offering abortion counseling and the Mexico City policy that prevented any U.S. international family planning funding from going to international nongovernmental organizations (NGOs) that "performed or promoted" abortion.

With access to federal policymakers now assured, Kissling also worked to make CFFC a meaningful player among Catholic reform organizations. In 1991, CFFC helped found Catholic Organizations for Renewal (COR), an umbrella organization of Catholic reform and social justice organizations. In addition to bolstering CFFC's Catholic identity, Kissling wanted to increase acceptance of abortion rights among progressive reform groups that had shied away from the issue for fear of further alienating themselves from the institutional church and acceptance of what they considered less inflammatory issues like women's ordination and a greater role for the laity. "CFFC wanted very much to be a part of the Catholic reform movement, stressing the Catholic side of its title," says theologian Anthony Padovano, who was active in COR as the president of CORPUS, the national association of married priests. "I thought that was a very tough thing to balance and try to be identified as unmistakably Catholic. CFFC tried to steer a middle course, between those who say that in each and every instance fetal life must prevail and the absolutely frivolous way that abortion is dealt with by a small minority of people," he said.[39]

In June 1993, CFFC arranged a meeting at the White House for COR members, including the gay rights organization Dignity/USA, the social justice organization Call to Action, the Women's Ordination Conference, and CORPUS. They discussed Catholic support for pro-choice policies and assured the administration that progressive Catholic groups would not oppose a national health care plan that included abortion services, which was a major victory for CFFC.[40]

Catholics for a Free Choice's increasing leverage with other progressive Catholic groups did not go unnoticed by the bishops' conference. Camden, New Jersey, Bishop James McHugh of the Pro-Life Committee attempted to short-circuit the budding alliance when he criticized COR members for their association with CFFC. But he only further strengthened the alliance when a third of the COR members issued statements affirming their support of the right to dissent in the church.

By the time of the pope's visit to the United States for World Youth Day two months later, the Catholic pro-choice movement was better positioned than it had ever been in its history. Between 1989 and 1993, CFFC's budget and staff had nearly doubled. It now had an annual budget of $1 million, a figure that Patricia McQuillan couldn't have imagined; high-profile recognition within government and the media; and solid linkages with the Catholic reform community. CFFC had organized a successful "Papal Visit Coalition" during the pope's visit in 1987 to provide critical analysis to the media on how the Vatican's positions affected women at a time when the pope was unquestioningly revered. It intended to redouble its efforts in 1993, as more and more people questioned the hierarchy's stance on reproductive issues and the pope's personal popularity declined.[41]

The twenty-fifth anniversary of *Humane Vitae* in 1993 also served as a reminder of how far apart the Vatican and Catholics were on issues of sexual practice. Priest and sociologist Andrew Greeley wrote of the "catastrophic collapse of the old Catholic sexual ethic" as Catholics embraced premarital sex at a higher rate than Protestants. He said that the dramatic change in Catholics' attitudes about the morality of premarital sex went beyond the general societal liberalization of attitudes about sex and was "related to a special Catholic rejection of the right of church authority to dictate on sexual matters."[42]

CFFC partnered with COR to launch a major press initiative during the pope's visit that included press briefings, a public forum, and a press suite at a Denver hotel. The press coverage was immense: the *Today Show*, NPR, *This Week with David Brinkley*, the *McNeil-Lehrer Newshour*, and newspapers across the country. Kissling wasn't kidding when she bragged that the pope was her best press agent. The bishops were not amused. Shortly after the pope's visit, the NCCB released a lengthy statement pointedly noting that during the pope's visit "programs about dissent in the Catholic church often included a spokesperson for a group calling itself 'Catholics for a Free Choice'" that "attracts public attention by its denunciations of basic principles of Catholic morality and teaching— denunciations given enhanced visibility by media outlets that portray CFFC as a reputable voice of Catholic dissent." It tried to discredit the organization by noting that CFFC had "no affiliation, formal or otherwise, with the Catholic Church."[43]

Clearly CFFC had hit a nerve. The small organization was able to mount a sophisticated media operation that successfully counterbalanced coverage of one of the pope's most valuable PR tools—the grand papal tour—and used it to further discussion about dissent in the church. It was the perfect combination of an extremely capable spokesperson like Kissling and the right message at the right time. "The timing made a huge difference. The idea of dissent was in the air. The press was skeptical of the Vatican line. They needed someone to give voice to the dissent," said Mary Jean Collins, public affairs director for CFFC.[44]

For her part, Kissling noted that few would mistake CFFC for an official Catholic organization but argued that the organization was authentically Catholic in the sense that it represented the views of a majority of Catholics and was made up of Catholics "whose values and positions on a range of gender, sexuality and reproductive health issues derive from a Catholic commitment to justice and equality."[45]

The bishops and CFFC were soon embroiled in a fight over what constituted "authentic" Catholicism. Could anyone who was baptized into the religion and accepted the basic tenets of Catholicism call themselves a Catholic even if they disagreed with the bishops on abortion? Or did being an authentic Catholic mean buying into the bishops' dogma—which would mean that most Catholics were therefore not really Catholic, because only a minority bought into the totality of the bishops' positions?

The bishops' denunciation of CFFC generated even more media coverage of the issue and prompted *New York Times* columnist Anna Quindlen to write a column titled "Authentic Catholics." In it she said that the bishops' unwarranted attack on CFFC illuminated the "real crisis in the hierarchy," which was the lack of dialogue on issues of sexuality and the resulting alienation many Catholics felt. She said that no group drawn together by faith should be branded inauthentic. "The word Catholic is a description—not, like Styrofoam, a registered trademark," she wrote, noting that if the bishops said CFFC couldn't speak for Catholics, "neither can the bishops."[46]

The battle over who spoke for Catholics was not settled, but it was about to take on a whole new dimension as the fight moved beyond the United States.

·   ·   ·   ·   ·

Despite the continuing drama over the issue of public dissent from the Vatican's position on abortion, one thing was clear by the late 1980s: the

Vatican had largely lost the hearts and minds of U.S. Catholics. But there was another front opening up in the war over women's reproductive choices: the developing world. Here priests and bishops still held sway over the practices of their parishioners and had tremendous influence with lawmakers. The Catholic Church is a key provider of health care and social services in many Latin American countries, making legal abortion an impossibility and limiting access to family planning. And Pope John Paul II clearly saw the world as his stage. By 1987, he had taken thirty-six trips to more than sixty countries—far more than any of his predecessors—and used his travels to pointedly condemn abortion and conflate the use of contraception with "anti-life" practices. During a February 1982 visit to Nigeria he called divorce, contraception, and abortion the "modern enemies of the family."[47]

The Catholic Church was injecting itself into the politics of reproductive rights around the developing world. In Brazil, the church lobbied heavily to add a Human Life Amendment to the new constitution of 1988. In the Philippines, Cardinal Jaime Sin succeeded in getting funds for comprehensive family planning programs shifted to programs that promoted only natural family planning.[48]

Even the role of the United States in increasing access to contraception in the developing world became a political football in the mid-1980s as the Reagan administration and the Vatican found common ground on efforts to discredit international family planning programs. In mid-June 1984, the White House stunned the international family planning community when it released a draft proposal to cut U.S. population aid to any country or program involved with abortion in any way, even with non–U.S. funds. This would defund major nonprofit family planning groups like the International Planned Parenthood Federation as well as the United Nations Population Fund (UNFPA). The policy was unprecedented. The United States had long been a leader in international population programs and its $240 million international family planning budget accounted for about one-half of total international spending on population programs.[49]

The proposal was made in preparation for the United Nations' 1984 International Population Conference in Mexico City, the second in a series of decennial international conferences planned to develop a unified approach to tackling population issues in the developing world. The Reagan administration was coming under pressure from social conservatives who felt they had received little in the way of concrete domestic action on abortion. The administration was also eager to build ties with the Vatican. Reagan and the pope had a strong personal affinity, particularly over their shared antipathy toward communism, and there were a number of prominent conservative Catholics in the administration. In November 1983, Congress voted to end the 120-year-old prohibition on formal ties between the U.S. government and the Vatican. In January 1984, Reagan established full diplomatic ties with the Vatican, appointing William A. Wilson as the United States' first ambassador to the Vatican over the objection of Christian Right leaders and secular organizations concerned with the separation of church and state.[50]

U.S. family planning policy was a casualty of Reagan administration attempts to curry favor with the Vatican. According to Wilson, the State Department initially reluctantly agreed to an outright ban on the use of any U.S. aid funds by countries or NGOs for the promotion of contraception or abortion, although only the abortion prohibition remained in the final draft. "American policy was changed as a result of the Vatican's not agreeing with our policy," Wilson told *Time* magazine.[51]

Steven Sinding, former director of USAID's Office of Population, confirms that pressure brought by an alliance between conservative Catholics in the administration and the Vatican was to blame for the dramatic change in family planning policy. "During the years I was at USAID, after Ronald Reagan came in, we came under intense pressure brought about by Catholics through the Republican political establishment," said Sinding.[52]

Between 1981 and 1985, funding for Vatican-approved natural family planning programs in USAID's budget increased from $800,000 to $7 million. In particular, says Sinding, Mercedes Wilson, head of the Family of the Americas Foundation, was "very well connected to the Republican establishment" and used her connections to get funding for her organization, which promoted the Billings Ovulation Method of natural family planning. Wilson, a conservative Catholic who routinely criticized artificial methods of contraception, received a $1 million grant from USAID to produce a film directed by a Vatican filmmaker on the Billings method.

She sought another $1 million grant to promote the Billings method in Africa, Asia, and Latin America under USAID's family planning program. The request was denied by USAID administrator Peter McPherson under an "informed consent" policy that prohibited funding from going to organizations that refused to provide information on all forms of contraception. Representative Henry Hyde (R-IL) arranged a private meeting for Wilson with then–Vice President George Bush, whose office pressured McPherson to change the informed consent policy. He called Sinding and told him to fund the proposal. "It was a straight political directive that was part of a deal that Reagan made with American bishops and the Vatican to support their position on abortion," Sinding said.[53]

The first draft of the Mexico City policy came straight from the White House, subverting the usual procedure in which the State Department developed U.S. positions. "One day I got a call from the office of the AID administrator saying he wanted me to come over and look at something. He showed me a draft that he had just received from the White House from the office of Ed Meese," said Sinding. Former Jesse Helms (R-NC) staffer Carl Anderson had drafted the statement. In addition to completely defunding any organization or government that engaged in abortion, it expressed skepticism about the value of family planning programs, saying that free-market economies were the best way to control population. "I was totally shocked by the content and also by the cavalier way in which the process was being circumvented," said Sinding.[54]

At the same time, the Vatican was denouncing international family planning programs as coercive efforts to limit family size and promote abortion and immorality. During a June audience with UNFPA director Rafael Salas, the pope asserted that contraceptives had "increased sexual permissiveness and promoted irresponsible conduct." He charged that family planning programs facilitated a transition "to the practice of sterilization and abortion, financed by governments and international organizations."[55]

That same month, Cardinal Alfonso López Trujillo of Medellín, Colombia, who headed the influential Latin American bishops' conference, denounced Colombia's successful family planning program, charging that "castration" and "mutilation" were taking place under the auspices of a popular family planning program that provided voluntary sterilization.[56]

The vociferous anti-contraception rhetoric originated from a new ultraconservative theology of sexuality that Pope John Paul II had been refining and promulgating over the past few years. Between September 1979 and November 1984, the pope used his Wednesday general audiences at the Vatican to give 129 theologically dense teachings on his interpretation of marriage and sexuality that became known as his "Theology of the Body." John Paul reiterated the basic teaching of *Humanae Vitae* that contraception was illicit because marriage and sex were equally ordered toward the union of man and women and procreation. He lionized the self-discipline required of natural family planning, saying that it enhanced human love, but warned that even this method could be abused if it was used to avoid having children for "unworthy reasons." He spoke of the "morally correct" number of children and said that responsible parenthood means "the willingness to accept a larger family" to serve the church and society.[57]

Above all, John Paul stressed the "complementary" nature of man and woman and singled out women as unique in their "gift" for submission to the needs of others, of which motherhood was the ultimate expression. He viewed women as receptors and facilitators—of sperm, of pregnancies, of the ambitions of men—not as actors in their own right. His treatment of women and reproduction veered on the mystical when he proclaimed that "the mystery of women is revealed in motherhood."[58]

John Paul's theology of the body was criticized for being completely removed from the realities of human sexuality and relationships and for failing to recognize women as moral actors with aspirations outside of motherhood. Emory University biblical scholar and religion professor Luke Timothy Johnson wrote that it was as if the pope were observing human sexuality "by telescope from a distant planet." He said the pope was "fantasizing an ethereal and all-encompassing mode of mutual self-donation between man and woman that lacks any of the messy, clumsy, awkward, charming, casual, and, yes, silly aspects of love in the flesh."[59]

Under the Reagan administration, U.S. family planning policy had become a tool of John Paul's vision. By the time the final policy was unveiled in Mexico City in August 1984, USAID administrator McPherson had managed to soften the anti-contraception language in the policy, but it still banned NGOs that "perform or actively promote" abortion from receiving U.S. funds. Critics charged that the policy was so broad it would apply not only to the direct provision of abortion services but also to abortion counseling and referrals. They also worried that a decrease in family planning funding would lead to an increase in illegal abortions at a time when complications from illegal abortion already accounted for 70 percent of maternal deaths worldwide.[60]

As a result of the policy, the International Planned Parenthood Federation and Planned Parenthood of America, the two largest USAID-funded agencies providing family planning services in the developing world, were defunded. The following summer, Congress passed the Kemp-Kasten Amendment, which cut off funding to any organization that was determined by the president to support or participate in a "program of coercive abortion or involuntary sterilization." The Reagan administration used this provision to cut off funding for the UNFPA, which was accused of helping to facilitate China's repressive one-child policy.[61]

By 1986 it was clear that the Catholic pro-choice movement needed to spread beyond the borders of the United States to counter Vatican-influenced reproductive health policies in the developing world. "The Vatican has played a growing role in global politics on reproductive issues, and we thought the work we had done here might be useful to Catholics in other countries," said Kissling. Increasingly the organization was getting requests for its materials to be translated into Spanish. CFFC began doing outreach in Latin America to identify organizations that would be interested in its work and to establish a network of pro-choice Catholics. CFFC translated several CFFC publications into Spanish, including *A History of Abortion in the Catholic Church*.[62]

In 1987, CFFC held a symposium on Catholicism and reproductive choice at the Fifth International Women and Health meeting in Costa Rica. Dr. Chrisina Grela, a gynecologist, attended the meeting and saw the need for an indigenous Catholic reproductive rights group to address issues unique to Latin America. "[H]ere in Latin America we do have special problems," she wrote, including the poor's unquestioning acceptance of the pope's call to have large families and the fact that most hospitals were run by the Catholic Church as well as the high rate of mortality due to unsafe abortions.[63]

Grela founded Catolicas por el Derecho a Decidir (Catholics for the Right to Decide) in Uruguay in 1989 as an independent affiliate of CFFC. During the next three years, with funding provided by CFFC from U.S. foundations like the Ford Foundation, regional offices were opened in Paraguay, Brazil, and Mexico. Soon Grela and a part-time staff of four were publishing a quarterly newsletter, *Conciencia,* Spanish-language publications on contraception and abortion, and conducting training sessions on pro-choice Catholicism. It was a model that CFFC would use around the world to promote pro-choice Catholicism: identify interested and committed Catholic women, help them get local organizations off the ground, and provide them with the funding and training to create indigenous movements that reflected the social and political realities of their countries.

Kissling visited Mexico three times in 1992 during a nationwide debate on legalizing abortion in the state of Chipas to give seminars on Catholicism and abortion, including one to top staff in the local diocese. In August 1992, CFFC arranged a speaking tour of Brazil, Argentina, and Chile for Rosemary Radford Ruether, who met with local feminist leaders and delivered lectures on Catholic feminism and reproductive rights.

When the Catholic hierarchy became involved in the political process in Poland after the fall of communism, CFFC made its first foray into Europe. The bishops were lobbying heavily for a ban on abortion, which had been widely used as a method of birth control under communism, and for an end to the constitutional separation of church and state. In May 1991, CFFC organized an open letter to the Polish bishops, decrying their heavy-handed interference in the emerging democratic process in Poland and condemning their efforts to ban abortion when few Catholics supported the effort. Kissling spent ten days in Poland in April 1992 to advise pro-choice activists about marshaling pro-choice Catholic sentiment and had CFFC materials translated into Polish. Despite these efforts, in February 1993, the Polish Parliament banned abortion except when a woman's life or health was seriously threatened or in cases of rape or incest or severe fetal abnormalities. Pope John Paul II campaigned personally for the law, and just before the final vote on the measure, Cardinal Jozef Glemp, the archbishop of Warsaw, appeared in Parliament to hand out Christmas wafers, a move the

New York Times noted was a "holiday custom with strongly religious overtones."[64]

In addition to its efforts in Poland, in the early 1990s CFFC also began working on a small scale in Ireland, Yugoslavia, and the Philippines, providing support and information to pro-choice Catholics and moving to counter the increasingly international influence of Pope John Paul II.

7 Showdown at Cairo

The election of Bill Clinton as president in 1992 marked the end of Reagan-era international family planning policies. Clinton rescinded the Mexico City policy, which cheered feminists and international family planning organizations. He drew their approbation, however, when he announced the appointment of Boston mayor Raymond Flynn, an anti-abortion Catholic who had been a valuable political ally to Clinton, as ambassador to the Vatican. Catholics for a Free Choice (CFFC) president Frances Kissling organized a letter signed by thirty pro-choice and women's organizations protesting the appointment as sending the wrong signal to the Vatican about U.S. commitment to reproductive rights. Despite the protest, the Senate unanimously confirmed Flynn in July.

The skirmish over Flynn foreshadowed a larger debate over the appropriate role of the Vatican at the United Nations that would play out at a series of UN conferences designed to develop a unified international approach to population and development issues. The 1992 United Nations Conference on Environment and Development in Rio de Janeiro, known as the Earth Summit, was the first of these high-profile UN conferences. Coming at a time of increased concern about climate change and loss of biodiversity, the summit received unprecedented international attention. It also demonstrated that these UN gatherings could provide an opportunity for conservative forces to promulgate fundamentalist worldviews and to stymie international consensus on development-related issues.[1]

At Rio, the Vatican joined with the Group of 77, which represents developing countries—some of whom had firsthand experience with coercive family planning programs and were distrustful of Western efforts to reduce population growth—and left-leaning women's organizations who were suspicious of modern contraceptive methods to block any mention of family planning in the final conference document. This document was designed to reflect the consensus of the countries in attendance and serve as a roadmap for implementing the conference recommendations, so the omission of family planning was a major shortfall given the relationship between population and the environment.[2]

The International Conference on Population and Development (ICPD) was slated for Cairo in 1994, ten years after the Mexico City conference that produced the eponymous U.S. policy limiting overseas aid for organizations that provided abortion services or counseling. Feminist organizations viewed the Cairo conference as a landmark opportunity to move the discussion about population and development beyond the traditional notion of population control, which focused on meeting demographic targets. Organizations concerned with women's empowerment viewed these family planning programs as overly focused on controlling women's reproduction. Some, like India's sterilization program in the 1970s, were highly coercive. The paradigm that women's groups hoped to promote focused on improving the status of women through increased educational and employment opportunities, which would lead to a concomitant decrease in family size. The other component was situating access to birth control within the provision of a range of reproductive health services focused on improving the well-being of women and children, including maternal health services, sexuality education, and sexually transmitted disease screening and prevention.

Eager to avoid a rerun of Rio, where the Vatican was able to forge alliances with constituencies that harbored suspicions of traditional Western family planning programs, and where environmental and women's organizations often found themselves at odds over the relationship between population growth and environmental degradation, feminist organizations began laying the groundwork for Cairo long before the conference. In July 1992, CFFC held a conference on Women, Population and Environment, bringing together feminists, Catholic theologians, and environmentalists to discuss population and development from a Catholic, feminist perspective.[3]

"We found ourselves increasingly asked by funders and collegial groups to put our thinking caps on and participate in the growing discussions that are going on within population organizations, within environmental organizations, and within women's organizations about the questions of population, environment and women's rights, women's needs and particularly because of the high profile of the Vatican we feel it is important that we do make a contribution in this area," Kissling told the conference.[4]

CFFC developed a media strategy to publicize what it believed would be the Vatican's attempt to sabotage the conference. It began working to ensure that the press covering the Cairo conference would understand the issues involved, particularly regarding the Vatican's participation. The Vatican was allowed to participate in the conference as an observer because its status as a country gave it a special, although limited, role in the United Nations. In July, CFFC held a series of press conferences on the Vatican and population policies in New York, Washington, D.C., and, most important, Rome. "Frances had this brilliant idea of going to Rome and holding a press conference," said Denise Shannon, who was the top staffer at CFFC at the time and in charge of the organization's media relations. The Rome event allowed Kissling and Shannon to make connections with Vatican-based reporters from key outlets like the Associated Press and *New York Times* who would cover the Cairo conference, so that by "the time of the ICPD they knew us and knew we weren't some completely crazy American dissidents," said Shannon.[5]

The landscape going into the Cairo conference had been dramatically altered since Mexico City. Not only did the United States have a pro-choice presidential administration, but feminist organizations like CFFC now had a seat at the table. The decision had been made to give nongovernmental organizations (NGOs) a formal role at a UN conference for the first time, allowing them to participate in the preparatory conferences and to hold a parallel NGO forum. There also were now a host of women's organizations ready to participate at the international level. CFFC was not very active at the Mexico City conference, noted Kissling. "[T]here were a lot of people in the population organizations saying, 'We have got to get those Catholics down there, we have got to get them involved so they can counter the influence of the Vatican,'" said Kissling, but the organization wasn't ready to participate at the international level. "We weren't prepared in '84. We weren't big enough," she said.[6]

The decade between 1984 and 1994, however, marked the rapid growth and maturation of women's rights and reproductive rights NGOs like CFFC. These groups had honed their skills fighting anti-abortion battles at home. They also had the money to back their efforts, noted Kissling, as foundations interested in population and reproductive rights began investing in international women's reproductive health groups. The bottom line was that by the early 1990s there was a "women's movement who had been funded, who had professionalized, and who now had a place at the table," said Kissling.[7]

In March 1993, just before the second preparatory conference, or prepcom, for the Cairo meeting, the International Women's Health Coalition, a consortium of organizations interested in international women's health issues, including CFFC, released a Women's Declaration on Population Policies. It called for a "broad range of reproductive health and development issues to be incorporated into population policies." CFFC took an active role in laying the groundwork for the conference. It convened a planning group of organizations interested in women's health and reproductive rights and held a series of briefings for women's organizations. Kissling also contacted Dr. Nafis Sadik, the executive director of the United Nations Population Fund (UNFPA) and secretary-general of the Cairo conference, and informed her of CFFC's interest in taking an active role in working on the issue of religious and ethical perspectives on reproductive health and women's empowerment.[8]

CFFC board member and theologian Dan Maguire addressed a meeting organized by the NGO Steering Committee on Religious and Ethical Perspectives on Population Issues, where he stressed the need to have a Catholic perspective other than the Vatican's on population issues. He said that because progressive Catholic views on contraception and abortion are "the dominant views of Catholic theology . . . this Preparatory Committee must be aware of that if it is to do justice to the Catholic people and

Catholic thought." He noted that both contraception and abortion "are necessary options and their moral respectability must be forthrightly maintained and vigorously defended."⁹

Feminist organizations successfully lobbied Sadik to ensure that the document being prepared as a point of negotiation for the conference included a mention of the staggering worldwide public health implications of mortality due to unsafe abortions. But another force was also lobbying to have its views included in the Program of Action, which was designed to serve as a blueprint for how nations should address and fund population issues over the next twenty years. "It became evident through the course of the prepcoms starting about a year before Cairo that the Vatican was intending to play a major role in the conference," said Steve Sinding, a population expert and a member of the U.S. delegation to Cairo. "There were more and more collars showing up. The delegation of the Holy See was very active and always present."¹⁰

As in Mexico City and at Rio, the Vatican was allowed to participate in the Cairo conference and the negotiations leading up to the conference through a fluke of geography. The Roman Catholic Church is the world's only major religion that possesses a physical territory—Vatican City, the home of the Holy See, the central government of the church. The 110-acre Vatican City, which has a population of about 800, is a sovereign city-state. Vatican City is a member of the Universal Postal Union and the International Telecommunication Union because it operates postal and radio services. Early in its history the United Nations invited the postal and telecommunications unions and their members to attend UN sessions on an ad hoc basis; the Vatican did so and stuck around. Eventually, the Holy See applied for and was granted nonmember consultative status at the United Nations, a rather fuzzy designation that no other entity at the United Nations shares and that allows it to participate in, but not vote at, UN meetings and to participate in and have a voice in UN conferences—a privilege no other religion shares.

As the second prepcom for the conference, scheduled for April 1994, approached, it became clear that the Vatican intended to make a full-court press to ensure its positions held sway in the final conference document, which all nations attending the meeting would be asked to consent to in order to give it the imprimatur of an international, if nonbinding, accord.

A leaked U.S. State Department cable had alerted the Vatican that the United States intended to press for "stronger language on the importance of access to abortion services." The language on ensuring access to a broad range of reproductive health services for women and adolescents also concerned the Vatican that the international community was sanctioning sexual activity—and access to contraceptives—among unmarried adults outside of the reproductive parameters of marriage.[11]

The aging Pope John Paul II increasingly saw the Cairo conference as his last opportunity to hold the line on his traditionalist view of women and marriage. He did not want progressive ideas about women, marriage, and family, such as access to contraception, enshrined in an international, treaty-like document. On March 18, Sadik had a tense, forty-minute private meeting with John Paul at the Vatican to discuss the draft Program of Action. She had barely sat down before he unleashed a scathing criticism of the document, saying, "[W]hat is at stake here is the very future of humanity." He charged the program of action promoted an "internationally recognized right to access to abortion on demand," ignored marriage and the family, demeaned motherhood, and told adolescents they could have sex without moral consequences. He decried the terms "sexual and reproductive rights" and "women's rights," accusing the international community of attempting to create new rights for women that went beyond the purview of governments and the patriarchal confines of family.[12]

Sadik was astounded by the pope's lack of compassion for women and by his dogmatism regarding women and sexuality. "In this area there can be no individual rights and needs. There can only be the couples' rights and needs," said the pope.[13]

When Sadik tried to explain why natural family planning was an unrealistic option for women who were powerless to demand abstinence from their husbands, she was left gasping in amazement when the pope asked, "Don't you think that the irresponsible behavior of men is caused by women?"[14]

With negotiations with Sadik at an impasse, the pope marshaled all the diplomatic forces at his disposal to press his point. The day after the Sadik meeting, all the ambassadors to the Holy See were summoned to the Vatican for a meeting with Vatican Secretary of State Cardinal Angelo

Sodano. Sodano and Cardinal Alfonso López Trujillo, head of the Pontifical Council for the Family, "instructed the diplomats on the Vatican's position on population issues and decried the supposed UN 'ideology of fear for the future.'" Vatican emissary Diarmuid Martin traveled from country to country meeting with foreign ministers and the heads of development agencies to reiterate the Vatican's position. The pope sent a letter to all the heads of state saying that it wasn't the United Nations' responsibly to determine moral law.[15]

By the time the third prepcom started in April, it was clear that lines in the sand had been drawn. Pope John Paul II railed against the conference from Vatican City, saying it promoted the "systematic death of the unborn" and that 1994 "could easily become a year against the family if these projects are adopted at the Cairo conference."[16]

At the prepcom, Holy See delegate Diarmuid Martin charged the conference had no "moral vision," which drew an unprecedented personal rebuke from committee chair and former International Planned Parenthood Federation president Fred Sai. Sai drew applause from the 300 delegates in attendance—many wearing "No papal control" buttons supplied by CFFC—when he asserted that "a lot of ethical considerations" went into the development of the document. Timothy Wirth, the head of the U.S. delegation to the conference, told the meeting that abortion should be part of reproductive health measures made available to women, but, repeating the formulation used by the Clinton administration, said it should be "safe, legal, and rare." The Vatican immediately condemned the U.S. position as part of an attempt to create an international, unethical right to abortion. Kissling told the conference the Vatican was arrogant for attempting to impose its vision of sexuality on the conference when "not a single woman, not a single child is a citizen of the Vatican."[17]

The run-up to the Cairo conference illustrated that CFFC was uniquely positioned to refute positions advocated by the Vatican. During the third prepcom, CFFC hosted a session on "How to Respond to the Vatican" to help NGOs and governments counter the Vatican's aggressive lobbying efforts. Kissling called the Vatican out on its strategy of using its position within the United Nations to lobby like any other international actor and then take refuge in its status as a religion—and an international arbitrator of moral values—when it came under any criticism. "We need to be alert that the tactic of the Vatican, once criticized, is to claim that it has been personally assaulted, that it is anti-Catholicism or Catholic bashing if you criticized the Vatican," she said.[18]

CFFC assembled a briefing packet for the press to refute the Vatican's criticisms of the Cairo Program of Action and provide a history of the Vatican's view on population policies and the history of abortion and Catholic thought. It also analyzed how Catholics around the world view contraceptives and abortion and quoted theologians who opposed the Vatican's policies on reproductive health. "We worked for a long time in putting together a really incredible press list and mailed thousands of these out to every reporter who ever covered anything related to these issues," recalled Shannon. "I remember getting to Cairo and going to the press area to hand them out and I saw them everywhere. That made a huge, huge impact—it really gave reporters some meaty background about what was up, which was important because these giant UN meetings are often covered by people who don't know much about these things," she said.[19]

Behind the scenes CFFC also worked to rally pro-choice organizations in support of a progressive position on reproductive rights. They were asked to sign on to a letter to President Clinton urging the administration to stand firm in its support for access to safe, legal abortion despite pressure from the Vatican.

In May the Vatican turned up the heat once again when the Pontifical Council on the Family released a lengthy document casting doubt on the existence of a population problem and denouncing the "contraceptive imperialism" of developed countries imposing family planning programs on developing countries. The pope reiterated this message personally to President Clinton when Clinton visited the Vatican in June, saying he had "grave ethical problems" with the Cairo document. The cardinals of the church seconded that message when at the behest of Cardinal John O'Connor they voted to condemn the Cairo document.[20]

"The Vatican was trying to use this ploy that somehow Western feminists were cultural imperialists who were trying to impose Western feminism on these poor benighted third world women who couldn't think for themselves," said theologian Rosemary Radford Ruether, who attended the Cairo conference as part of a CFFC-sponsored delegation.[21]

With the Vatican pushing the notion that the Cairo document amounted to an attempt by the West to impose unwanted reproductive health policies on developing countries, CFFC released a study in July showing that Catholics in many developing countries disagreed with the Vatican's teachings on contraception and abortion. "Implicit in the pope's ultraconservative message on Cairo is that the 944 million Catholics around the world agree with him. Yet these surveys prove that the Vatican's views are out of step with the people they purport to represent throughout the world," Kissling told the *Washington Post*.[22]

The attacks by the Vatican continued. In early August, Vatican spokesman Joaquin Navarro-Valls unleashed a stinging condemnation of the conference document, saying it promoted abortion on demand. He charged that the term "reproductive health" included abortion and "sexual health" included promoting homosexuality. The Clinton administration was working furiously behind the scenes to mollify the Vatican, especially on the point that it was not promoting abortion as a method of family planning, but it was increasingly clear that the Vatican wasn't looking for compromise but was intent on using its objections to derail any consensus at the conference. One Vatican observer likened the pope's efforts to remove references to abortion, women's rights, or alternative forms of family from the conference document to his fight against communism, calling it one of the great battles of his papacy.[23]

As the opening of the conference in early September drew close, it became clear that the Vatican was seeking allies in its fight. The Vatican reached out to some Islamic nations, including the fundamentalist government of Iran and the pro-terrorist government of Libya, in an attempt to build an anti-reproductive rights voting bloc. It appealed to these nations by casting the Cairo document as an assault on traditional sexual morality. Leaders of Cairo's Al Azhar Islamic University, considered the most influential center of Islamic learning, criticized the document in language straight from the Vatican's playbook, saying it condoned extramarital sex and abortion. "[T]his alliance is a further sign of the extent that the Vatican is willing to distort the traditional social and human rights mission of the Catholic church in pursuit of an anti-woman, anti-family planning agenda," said Kissling.[24]

In the United States, the Clinton administration was coming under political pressure to back down from its strong stand on Cairo lest it alienate Catholic voters in the upcoming mid-term election. Conservative Catholics charged that the administration was anti-Catholic because one member of the U.S. delegation said the Vatican's objections to the document were driven by its regressive view of women. A group of progressive Catholic organizations, including CFFC, ran an open letter to Clinton in the *New York Times* on September 1 reminding him of the hierarchy's track record in opposing women's equality. "In the unprecedented level of criticism of the document by church officials and conservative lay Catholics, we see the heavy hand of sexism," it said.[25]

The conference opened in early September with a dizzying amount of political maneuvering. The Vatican accused Vice President Al Gore, who was leading the U.S. delegation, of misrepresenting the delegation's intent to create an international right to abortion. Bishop James McHugh, formerly the head of the U.S. bishops' pro-life committee and a Vatican delegate to the committee, appeared on *Meet the Press* and warned that American Catholics would "walk away" from the Democratic Party if the Clinton administration didn't back down from its support of abortion. For its part, the Vatican had insisted on bracketing the terms "reproductive health" and "sexual health" every time they appeared in the document—which was more than one hundred times. Because UN conferences work by consensus, objections to language from even one nation can hold up the proceedings while a phrase is laboriously renegotiated.[26]

The Vatican also took exception to language calling on governments to deal with unsafe abortion, arguing that no abortion could be "safe" for the fetus. In a setback to the Vatican's effort to build an alliance with Islamic nations, however, the Grand Mufti of Egypt, the highest religious figure in that country, issued a fatwa—an Islamic legal pronouncement—saying that family planning was not against Islam, which took much of the energy out of the emerging Vatican–Islamic bloc.

The conference opened on September 5 with word of a compromise on abortion language being developed by representatives from the European Union. Sadik had taken pains as the conference opened to assure the Vatican that the consensus document did not advocate or promote abortion. After a conciliatory speech from Gore that sought to downplay any differences with the Vatican, Norwegian prime minister Gro Harlem Brundtland electrified the conference with a call for the legalization of abortion around the world that included a sharp rebuke of the Vatican's position: "Morality becomes hypocrisy if it means accepting mothers' suffering or dying in connection with unwanted pregnancies and illegal abortions and unwanted children," she said.[27]

On September 8, Dan Maguire addressed the Cairo conference, calling the Program of Action a "thoroughly religious" document for its holistic focus on improving conditions for poor women and children, limiting Western consumption of resources, and making contraception and safe abortion available for those who want them. "Sadly, due to the Vatican's idiosyncratic fixation . . . on contraception and abortion," he told the conference, "the moral triumph of the document has been overshadowed, and religions have once again been made to look like obstructive icebergs in the shipping lanes of progress."[28]

Over the next few days the conference would be consumed with trying to find some compromise language that would satisfy the Vatican. Fifteen countries haggled for five hours on one formula that said abortion shouldn't be used as a method of family planning—a distinction sought by the Vatican—but where it was legal it should be safe and countries should make their own determinations about its legality. Conference delegates broke into boos when the Vatican rejected the language, but Vatican allies such as Iran and Pakistan agreed to accept it. CFFC and other women's groups, which initially objected to the language about abortion not being a method of family planning as demeaning to women, reluctantly agreed to accept the language. "As long as this document deals somehow with abortion it is a victory for women," said Kissling.[29]

But any sense of momentum was lost the next day when the Vatican rounded up a new alliance of a dozen conservative Latin American counties and Malta to object to the compromise language. With debate on the larger document stalled and Western negotiators warning that they had compromised as much as they intended to, critics began charging that the Vatican had hijacked the conference. "Does the Vatican rule the world?" asked an incredulous Maher Mahran, the Egyptian population minister. Buttons that read "I'm Poped Out," provided courtesy of CFFC, appeared on the lapels of delegates. The Vatican had overplayed its hand. Suddenly, everyone was wondering how it had so much power at the United Nations. Kissling asked the question that was on everyone's lips when she questioned why is Catholicism "the only religion with a permanent observer seat the UN?"[30]

The controversy turned Kissling into a rock star at the conference. "Frances was really good at advising people and strategizing," said Shannon. "She couldn't take two steps down the hall without people rushing up to her."[31]

Meanwhile, public opinion was turning against the Vatican and its allies were backing away. The surge of unhappy Catholic voters pressuring the United States to reverse its position had failed to materialize. Meanwhile, recalled Ruether, "Dan Maguire was having a heyday exposing the Vatican because he discovered that the head of the Vatican delegation was there with his mistress."[32]

Faced with overwhelming opposition and little support for its positions, the Vatican relented on the fifth day of the conference, dropping its objection to language that said countries should strengthen their commitment to dealing with unsafe abortion and allowing a phrase about the legality of abortion to stand. It also dropped its objections to the phrase "family planning." It was widely seen as a victory for women and a major defeat for the Vatican. "They have already lost the war. All they are doing now is battling over wording," said Kissling.[33]

In the end, the Vatican signed on to the final document, withholding its approval from the sections on reproductive rights and related issues. Women's health advocates hailed the consensus document as a sea change in international family planning that empowered women. "I think this conference can be seen as ending 2,000 years of ecclesiastical authority or jurisdiction over marriage and women's lives," said Margaret Sanger biographer Ellen Chesler.[34]

The conference demonstrated the power of a strong pro-choice Catholic voice in the international arena. The presence of CFFC at the conference, and especially Kissling, making pro-choice Catholics visible and providing a progressive Catholic voice in support of modern reproductive heath options for women was critical. "The success of the conference was balanced on a knife-edge," wrote Secretary-General Sadik. "In this highly charged atmosphere, Frances' energy, diplomacy and humor were like oil on what could have been very troubled waters. She has many friends in many places, and she ensured that they all knew what the stakes were and responded accordingly. The final consensus . . . owes a lot to her."[35]

.   .   .   .   .

While women's rights advocates spent much of 1994 focused on the Cairo conference, another fight was brewing at home over the Clintons' plan to reform the U.S. health system. Once again abortion was a flashpoint as conservatives sought to exclude abortion from any package of health care benefits that would be guaranteed under the reform plan. When Clinton launched the reform effort in the spring of 1993, the U.S. bishops made it clear that inclusion of abortion in the basic benefits package would compromise their support of the plan, even though the bishops' conference had long been one of the nation's most outspoken advocates for universal health coverage. The bishops cautioned Clinton that including abortion in the plan would be a "moral tragedy," as well as a "major political mistake."[36]

In addition to their basic antipathy toward the procedure, the bishops feared that including abortion in the basic benefits package would be financially debilitating to the nation's Catholic hospitals because, due to the bishops' own rules, they couldn't participate in insurance plans that covered abortion. The bishops threatened to mobilize U.S. Catholics against any health plan that included access to abortion. In early 1994, the National Committee for a Human Life Amendment (NCHLA), the bishops' anti-abortion lobby, sent 6 million postcards demanding the exclusion of abortion from any national benefits package to U.S. dioceses, nearly 85 percent of which distributed them to parishioners to send to their congressional representatives.[37]

At the same time, pro-choice groups were lobbying to ensure that abortion was included in the basic benefits package, arguing that it should not be segregated from other reproductive health services. During their June 1993 meeting at the White House, CFFC and the Catholic reform umbrella organization Catholic Organizations for Renewal had assured the Clinton administration that progressive Catholic groups would not oppose a national health care plan that included abortion, which provided an important counterbalance to the bishops' argument that the inclusion of abortion would alienate Catholics.

Access to abortion, and possible compromises that would mollify the bishops, were hotly debated during the health care reform process, but the eventual demise of the Clinton proposal at the hands of a coalition of large insurers, other health care interests, and conservatives left abortion coverage a moot point. The debate did serve, however, to heighten awareness about the critical role that Catholic institutions played in the U.S. health care system and the concomitant control that the Catholic hierarchy exercised on access to reproductive health services at these institutions. During the debate over the Clinton plan, CFFC produced the first comprehensive report on the size and scope of Catholic health care, a little understood but widely utilized component of the U.S. health care system that was becoming increasingly influential because of the nature of health care economics in the 1990s.

Many Catholic hospitals in the United States were founded by nuns from religious orders that were dedicated to caring for the poor, sick, and dispossessed. In fact, the "nursing" of the sick as a profession was largely founded by the Sisters of Charity in France. Nuns from orders such as the Sisters of Charity and the Sisters of Providence came to the United States in the nineteenth century to found hospitals in the rapidly growing cities of the East and Midwest, as well as in frontier regions that lacked any other health care. Some of these hospitals cared largely for Catholic immigrant populations, but many others served Americans of all faiths, particularly the destitute. Catholic nuns founded some 300 hospitals between 1830 and 1900. By 1915, there were nearly 600 Catholic hospitals in the United States, making them a major component of the country's health infrastructure.[38]

These nun-nurses provided excellent health care through their dedication, professionalism, and training. Florence Nightingale herself said that the training of a Catholic nun-nurse was second to none. Women religious also were excellent hospital administrators and savvy businesswomen. They were adept at raising money and leveraging government funding to found and operate hospitals and "were able to provide the best value for the money in the care of the indigent sick," noted Sioban Nelson in her history of women religious and nursing. This allowed them to successfully compete for government contracts. They were equally savvy about getting contracts from insurers, railroad and mining companies, and even the

Army. In addition, they "attracted excellent doctors, collaborated with medical schools and ran teaching facilities." They allowed doctors excluded by the medical boards of exclusive hospitals to practice at their facilities, which broadened access to private hospital care to those of more modest means. In effect, wrote Nelson, they "created the prototype for the modern twentieth-century hospital" and laid the foundation for the country's fee-for-service private health care system.[39]

Women religious continued to run the Catholic hospitals they founded as freestanding institutions throughout much of the twentieth century. That began to change, however, in the 1980s and 1990s. Rising costs and increasingly sophisticated technologies like CAT scans created health care economics that favored large regional hospitals and health systems that grouped together a number of hospitals and ancillary health care services rather than stand-alone community hospitals. The result was a wave of hospital mergers that saw local hospitals gobbled up by corporate health systems and large regional providers. Because of their excellent management and financial standing, many Catholic hospitals did quite well under this trend, buying up secular hospitals and themselves becoming large Catholic health care systems. By the mid-1990s, the 624 Catholic hospitals in the United States accounted for 16 percent of all hospital admissions, which meant that Catholic hospitals were caring for 50 million patients annually. Some 70 percent of these facilities were affiliated with one of sixty-six Catholic health systems, which in addition to one or more hospitals could include medical practices, outpatient clinics and rehabilitation facilities, nursing homes, hospices, and managed care plans.[40]

But increasingly these Catholic hospital systems were no longer run by nuns. A dearth of women religious meant that more and more Catholic facilities had lay management. While just over 3 percent of Catholic hospitals had lay leaders in 1965, that number had skyrocketed to 70 percent by 1988. Not only were these hospitals no longer run by nuns, but they were no longer primarily charitable institutions. According to the industry magazine *Modern Healthcare*, in 1992 Catholic hospitals ranked behind public hospitals, secular nonprofit hospitals, and other religious hospitals in the amount of charity care they provided, outranking only for-profit hospitals. While public hospitals spent more than 12 percent of their gross patient revenue on charity care, Catholic hospitals spent less than 2 percent.[41]

As a result, what had started as a religiously based effort to provide charity care and care to ethnic Catholic populations had evolved by the 1990s into a major competitive player in the health care arena and the single largest private sector provider of health care in the United States, collecting revenue not only from private insurers but from the taxpayer-financed Medicare and Medicaid systems.

Although Catholic hospitals increasingly had lay management, cared for patients of all faiths, and collected government-financed reimbursement for the services they provided, they were still bound to follow the *Ethical and Religious Directives for Catholic Health Care Services,* the guidelines promulgated by the U.S. bishops under the direction of the Vatican. These guidelines spell out the services Catholic hospitals cannot offer, including abortion, family planning counseling or contraceptives, and contraceptive sterilization.

As the wave of hospital mergers picked up in the 1990s, CFFC began hearing from doctors and community activists that because of these *Directives,* newly merged, formerly secular hospitals were being forced to eliminate services such as abortion, tubal ligations, and family planning clinics (most hospitals don't perform elective early abortions but do provide later-term abortion in cases of fetal abnormalities or health threats to the women and provide emergency abortions in cases of miscarriages and other catastrophic situations). In some communities, the newly merged entity was the only hospital in the area, which forced all local patients, Catholic or not, to abide by the limitations of the *Directives.*

The U.S. bishops were also worried about hospital mergers, but for a different reason—they were afraid that the merged institutions would lose their "Catholic identity." In 1994, the bishops formed the Ad Hoc Committee on Catholic Health Care Ministry to review mergers between Catholic and non-Catholic hospitals to make sure the merged institutions continued to abide by the *Directives* to the greatest extent possible. They also updated the *Directives* to deal explicitly with hospital mergers, emphasizing that the merged institutions must avoid "scandal" by following Catholic moral teaching and receive the approval of the local bishop for the joint venture, signaling a significant escalation in direct hierarchical oversight of Catholic health care whose implications would only become more apparent in the coming decade.[42]

.   .   .   .   .

The Cairo conference thrust many of the "culture war" issues that had dominated the 1980s—reproductive rights, the role of women, adolescent sexuality—back into the headlines as the Vatican fought to prevent a more progressive sexual ethic from being enshrined in international documents. The United Nations' Fourth Conference on Women, scheduled for Beijing, China, the following year, was widely anticipated as a rematch between many of the forces that had squared off in Cairo. Women's advocates feared the Vatican would use the Beijing conference to attempt to roll back many of the gains that had been made in Cairo.

Their fears appeared to be well founded when at the final preparatory meeting for the conference the Vatican objected to language on family planning and reproductive health and suggested the inclusion of language on the health risks of contraception and abortion. It and its allies also repeatedly contested the word "gender," claiming the conference was attempting to recognize five genders, including homosexuality and transexuality. And in an attempt to promote the pope's conservative anthropology of women, which held that women are primarily suited to be wives and mothers, it tried to add language to the section on the equality of men and women recognizing women's "innate dignity" and "unique role" as wife and mother, saying women are "equal but different."[43]

The Vatican's tactics went beyond merely promoting its conservative theology. On the opening day of the final preparatory meeting in March, Vatican delegate Sherri Rickert stunned attendees when she opposed the routine NGO accreditation of CFFC and its Catholics for the Right to Decide (CDD) affiliates in Mexico, Uruguay, and Brazil. The Vatican said that CFFC should be denied accreditation because it was misleading in its use of the word "Catholic." It held that an organization that "publicly promotes some fundamental positions contrary to those held by the Catholic Church . . . cannot be recognized as Catholic."[44]

The move would not only block CFFC from attending the conference but would ban it from the preparatory meeting, removing the most effective counterpoint to the Vatican's conservative theology. Within hours of the Vatican's move, Kissling was at UN headquarters in New York, where she found that CFFC had indeed been crossed off the list of approved

NGOs and the matter referred to the accrediting commission. CFFC officially objected to the Vatican's move, complaining that it was politicizing the UN accreditation process in an attempt to censor internal debate in the church about the role and status of women. "The Vatican participates in the UN as a state, not a religion, and in that capacity has no standing to comment on the religious identity of NGOs," said Kissling. More than 200 NGOs sent a letter to the accreditation committee objecting to the Vatican's attempt to "defy women's self-participation, to thwart the principles of freedom of speech and association and to politicize the accreditation process within the UN."[45]

After several days of deliberation, the committee restored CFFC's accreditation, as well as that of the CDDs. A subsequent request by the Vatican to asterisk CFFC's name every time it appeared in conference documents also was turned down. The Vatican's attempt to discredit the organization received widespread press coverage, including op-eds in the *New York Times* and *Washington Post* that compared the Vatican to the authoritarian Chinese government, which was attempting to block the accreditation of several Tibetan women's groups. Kissling couldn't have been more pleased with the publicity the controversy generated. "Now when we walk the halls of the UN, diplomats and NGOs all know who we are. Everyone now knows the name of Catholics for a Free Choice," she said.[46]

The drumbeat of criticism from the hierarchy continued as the conference approached. In late March, the pope released *Evangelium Vitae* (The Gospel of Life), a major encyclical that condemned abortion, euthanasia, and the death penalty. It outlined the great battle that John Paul II saw between the "culture of life" and the "culture of death." He accused international organizations working to ensure access to abortion and birth control in the developing world of being part of a "conspiracy against life" and decried efforts to limit population growth or create rights for women beyond the confines of family.[47]

In April, Cardinal O'Connor wrote in *L'Osservatore Romano*, the official Vatican newspaper, that the "reproductive rights" called for in the Beijing document were "thinly disguised code words for abortion on demand, or even forced abortion; contraception on demand or even forced contraception." In May, Archbishop Oscar Rodriguez, president of the Latin American bishops' conference, charged the UN meeting was attempting to create a "culture of death" and said that feminists want to "destroy family and moral values."[48]

The August announcement that the pope had appointed Harvard law professor and conservative family law scholar Mary Ann Glendon as the first woman to head the Vatican delegation, suggested, however, that the Vatican might take a different tack. Glendon did criticize the Beijing document, saying it failed to address the real problems poor women faced, such as disease and poor sanitation, and "neglects marriage, motherhood, family and religion."[49]

But as the conference got under way, it became apparent that the Vatican would forgo the obstructionist role it played in Cairo. When natural family planning advocate and frequent Vatican ally Mercedes Wilson, who was serving as a delegate from Guatemala, demanded a formal definition of the word "gender" on the second day of the conference, attempting to reopen an issue that had been extensively discussed at the prepcom, Vatican ally Malta quickly quashed the move. On the third day, Vatican negotiators made a formal announcement that they would not attempt to reopen the fight over reproductive rights language settled a Cairo. Vatican watchers agreed that the backlash from Cairo informed the Vatican's decision to take a lower-key role at Beijing. "In Beijing, there just wasn't any energy around the Vatican—partially because they took a more low-key role and partially because their insipid language about how much they love women isn't nearly as jarring as their positions on sexuality and reproduction," said Shannon.[50]

Although the Vatican took less of a publicly confrontational role, it worked behind the scenes to insert its conservative theology into the conference document. It lobbied successfully with some Islamic nations to block language on "sexual rights" and "sexual orientation" and to include some of its favored references to the importance of the traditional family. It also worked unsuccessfully to add a "conscience clause" that would allow health care providers and institutions to refuse to provide reproductive health services to which they object.[51]

Nonetheless, the final document was a landmark for women's rights. It declared the universality of women's rights—in the famous words of Hillary Clinton at the conference that "women's rights are human rights"— and that the human rights of women include the right to control their sexuality and family size. It also urged governments to review laws containing punitive measures against women who have had illegal abortions.[52]

CFFC used the Beijing conference to launch a petition calling on the United Nations to "evaluate the appropriateness of allowing the Holy See, a religious entity, to act on par with states in the United Nations." The petition, which garnered more than 1,000 signatures at the conference, said that as the governing arm of the Catholic Church, not a civil institution, the Holy See did not meet the criteria for statehood. It noted that the Holy See's status gave it special privileges at the United Nations that no other religion enjoyed and that "standards of impartiality and neutrality with respect to religion would dictate a change in the status of the Holy See to establish parity between the Roman Catholic church and other religions and nongovernmental institutions."[53]

In a *New York Times* op-ed, Kissling and Shannon called the Holy See a "nebulous, religious construct" that owed its presence in the United Nations to "happenstance and diplomatic deference." It was only the opening volley in an issue that would increasingly consume international conferences devoted to women and reproductive health and create a formidable new alliance between conservative Catholics and the Christian Right.[54]

8 Matters of Conscience

The landmark UN conferences on population and development and women's rights in the 1990s made important strides in the international recognition of civil and reproductive rights for women. But they also served to deepen the antagonism between the Vatican and the Catholic reproductive rights movement, which was now providing a counterbalance to the Vatican at the international level as well as in the United States. The Cairo conference in particular was a stinging defeat for the pope. "No issue has affected John Paul II in a more profound way in his 15-year papacy than the Cairo conference," observed former U.S. Vatican ambassador Ray Flynn.[1]

Cairo also created new alliances among fundamentalist forces that opposed the recognition of reproductive rights for women, alternative definitions of family, such as those headed by same-sex couples, and sexuality education for adolescents. The Beijing women's conference witnessed the debut of Christian Right groups that had formerly eschewed international forums, including Concerned Women for America and Focus on the Family, as they sought to tie the conference, and by implication the Clinton administration, to a radical feminist agenda. They joined with an organization called the Catholic Campaign for America, which was founded by high-profile conservative Catholics who wanted to bring "a distinctly Catholic voice to the U.S. public policy debate."[2]

Under the banner of the International Coalition for Authentic Womanhood, these organizations picked up and amplified Vatican charges that the conference denigrated women and was an attack on the family. James Dobson told Focus on the Family's 2 million members that the conference was "the most radical, atheistic and anti-family crusade in the history of the world." Mary Ellen Bork of the Catholic Campaign charged that the conference document "undermines women's role as mothers and men's role as fathers, rejects accepted definitions of the family and the moral responsibility that goes with it, and promotes sexual license."[3]

It's not surprising that conservative Catholics and the Christian Right began to eye one another as potential allies in the war against supposedly godless liberal feminists and their ilk, a cross-pollination that previously had been kept in check by conservative Protestants' historic distrust of the Vatican and their antipathy toward some aspects of Catholic theology. That distaste was formally set aside in March 1994, when a who's who of conservative Catholics and evangelicals, including Cardinals John O'Connor and Avery Dulles, Pat Robertson, Mary Ann Glendon, Father John Neuhaus, Michael Novak, George Weigel, Richard Land of the Southern Baptist Convention, and evangelical leader Charles Colson, signed the "Evangelicals and Catholics Together" declaration. Declaring that Christians "have a responsibility for the right ordering of civil society," the signers announced that they had put aside their traditional theological differences to create a unified political front against abortion and the secularization of America, foreshadowing what would become a major political trend.[4]

The following year, the Christian Coalition announced plans to create an affiliate called the Catholic Alliance to add Catholics to its 1.7 million-member electoral powerhouse. "A strong alliance between evangelical Christians and pro-family Roman Catholics could become one of the most profound developments in the history of American politics," said Ralph Reed, head of the coalition.[5] The initiative, however, failed to gain momentum after a number of Catholic bishops decried it as moving onto their turf of instructing Catholic voters and told Catholics not to join, but it would not be the last attempt to bring together these political forces.[6]

Catholics and evangelicals did find more rapport on Capitol Hill. After the 1994 mid-term election, when the Republic Party gained control of both the House and Senate for the first time in forty-two years, the U.S. Catholic Conference, the National Right to Life Committee (NRLC), and the Christian Coalition met to craft a legislative strategy to curb access to abortion. Gone were the days of infighting among anti-abortion forces; now they were on the same page—there wasn't sufficient support for an amendment to ban abortion, so they would seek ways to chip away at abortion access. They proposed to end federal Medicaid funding of abortions resulting from rape or incest, leaving a threat to a woman's life as the only condition under which poor women could get a publicly funded abortion. They also sought to prohibit federal employees from getting abortions under their health plans and women in federal prisons from getting abortions.[7]

This conservative Catholic–Christian coalition also worked to turn public opinion against abortion. In June 1995, legislation was introduced to ban a specific abortion procedure that Doug Johnson of the NRLC had termed "partial-birth" abortion. The intact dilation and extraction procedure, as it is medically known, is a procedure used in limited circumstances to terminate pregnancies over twenty weeks, most often when a fetus has deformities that are incompatible with life. Although the procedure sounds gruesome—a woman's cervix is dilated and the fetus, which has been partially moved into the birth canal, is extracted by suctioning its brain and compressing its skull—doctors argued that it was sometimes the safest option. It also gave women who had to terminate wanted pregnancies the option of spending some time with the fetus and saying goodbye. It was rarely used; most estimates were that it accounted for well under 1 percent of all abortions performed in the United States. Nonetheless, Johnson and his allies worked to create controversy over the procedure, and by inference abortion in general, by labeling it as infanticide and gleefully describing it in grisly detail. "This is an educational exercise," admitted Johnson of the entire debate.[8]

When President Bill Clinton said he would veto the ban if it did not contain an exception to allow the procedure when a doctor thought it was in the best interest of a woman's health, the bishops switched into battle mode. They ran a full-page ad in the *New York Times* that claimed the health exemption would allow the late-term procedure for "just about anything," including a woman who couldn't fit into her prom dress. When Clinton vetoed the bill several weeks later, the U.S. cardinals issued a withering critique, claiming the president had moved the nation one step closer to "acceptance of infanticide" and threatening to marshal Catholic voters against his reelection in retaliation.[9]

In May, the National Conference of Catholic Bishops (NCCB) sent a letter decrying the procedure to every diocese in the country and urged parishioners to contact their representatives to support an override. Priests, including New York's Cardinal John O'Connor, preached against it from the pulpit. And in an exceptionally harsh criticism of a specific policy action of an American president, the Vatican called Clinton's move "a shameful veto that in practice is equivalent to an incredibly brutal act of aggression."[10]

With a presidential race rapidly approaching, Catholics for a Free Choice (CFFC) president Frances Kissling met with Betsy Myers, director of the White House Office on Women's Initiatives, to assure the administration that Clinton's move would not alienate Catholic voters, who had backed him in 1992 but then swung back to the Republican Party in the 1994 mid-term election. Clinton's Republican opponent, Senator Bob Dole (R-KS), was quick to pander to the perceived priorities of Catholic voters. One of his first speeches after wrapping up the nomination was to the Catholic Press Association, where he attacked Clinton's veto of the partial-birth measure. "Though not a Catholic, I would listen to Pope John Paul II," he promised. Following the speech, Dole met with Philadelphia Cardinal Anthony Bevilacqua. In June, Dole met with Archbishop O'Connor, who praised his "wonderfully pro-life record" and posed for a picture with Dole that appeared on the front page of the *New York Times* and was widely viewed as a de facto endorsement.[11]

The bishops ran ads criticizing the veto in the *New York Times* and *Washington Post* during the Republican National Convention in August. They distributed 23 million postcards for parishioners to send to Congress. Two weeks later at the Democratic National Convention, CFFC countered with an open letter to the bishops that noted that although their 1995 statement on political responsibility listed a range of issues of importance to Catholics, the bishops were again putting a "profoundly disproportionate effort" on abortion. "So frequent, so vehement, and so condemning of individual political figures are your statements and actions on abortion as compared to other issues, that it is hard to avoid the conclusion that the United States Catholic Conference and individual diocesan leaders are conducting a partisan campaign," it said.[12]

A little over two weeks later the U.S. hierarchy made an unprecedented direct lobbying blitz when every member of the bishops' conference—eight cardinals and eighty bishops—appeared on the Capitol steps in a prayer vigil on the eve of the vote to override Clinton's veto. Kissling warned that Americans "do not want religious leaders operating as political bosses." She was correct. Despite the bishops' show of ecclesiastical authority, the override attempt failed and Clinton was reelected six weeks later with 53 percent of the Catholic vote, once again illustrating the illusionary nature of the bishops' power over Catholics.[13]

·   ·   ·   ·   ·

Jon O'Brien grew up in a country where contraception, abortion, and even sex education were illegal thanks to pressure from the hierarchy of the Irish Catholic Church to have their moral precepts codified into law. "It felt like you were living in a theocracy, not a democracy," said O'Brien. It wasn't until 1979 that the law was liberalized to allow adults to get contraceptives for "bona fide" family planning purposes, but they had to get a prescription from a doctor and have it filled by a pharmacist even for condoms. In 1985 the direct sale of condoms was legalized, but they could only be sold in pharmacies and family planning clinics and not to anyone under eighteen. By this time the AIDS epidemic was in full swing and the health consequences of unprotected sex were well known, but the hierarchy brought formidable pressure against further liberalization of the law. "Politicians would ask, 'Well, what do the bishops think about that?'" said O'Brien.[14]

Ireland's "horrible history" of denying women the right to control their fertility compelled O'Brien to join the Irish Family Planning Association, which had in 1988 begun selling condoms in defiance of the law at its safe sex information counter at a Virgin Records Megastore in Dublin. In 1992, O'Brien was arrested by an undercover police officer for selling him a condom. He was tried and convicted. His conviction became a cause célèbre after the rock band U2 offered to pay the fine on behalf of the Irish Family Planning Association. The outcry forced a change in the law despite protestations from the bishops, giving O'Brien a taste of the power of popular sentiment to challenge the Catholic hierarchy. Soon after, he heard about CFFC and invited Kissling to come to Ireland. The publicity she received was an eye-opener. "There was a big article in the *Irish Times*. There had always been a small, brave group of people who would do things to oppose the bishops, but we needed to be able to convince the larger society that your faith doesn't require you to do something that is wrong in terms of your health. I could really see the value of being able to make this argument within a moral and ethical framework," he said.[15]

O'Brien encountered Kissling again a few years later in Poland, when the bishops were trying to ban abortion and he was working for the International Planned Parenthood Federation. "I saw CFFC's importance there because of the role that religion plays in that country," he said. Inspired by the idea of being able to "make globally a message that I had seen work locally," he came to the United States and joined CFFC as director of communications in 1996.[16]

It was the ultimate irony that O'Brien, who had come from a country that had banned birth control for so long, arrived in the United States just as a new effort was gearing up to attack contraception. The Catholic hierarchy had been agnostic on the issue of contraception in public policy since they lost the battle over public funding of family planning programs in the 1960s. Part of this was because their attention was consumed by what they considered the far greater evil of abortion. Part of it was because opposing family planning programs, which had widespread bipartisan support, was a losing political issue. The only consistent opposition to contraceptives came from a fringe anti-abortion organization called the American Life League (ALL), which was founded by former NRLC staffer Judie Brown to give Paul Weyrich's New Right a foothold in the right-to-life movement.

Brown, a stanch orthodox Catholic, was happy to part ways with the NRLC because she didn't think it was sufficiently strident in its quest for a human life amendment. What set Brown apart from other opponents of abortion, however, was her equally fierce opposition to contraception

Figure 9. Jon O'Brien joined Catholics for a Free Choice in 1996 after working to legalize condoms in Ireland. (Courtesy of Catholics for Choice)

and her belief that the "contraceptive mentality" contributed to abortion. "Pro-lifers must see the connection between contraception and abortion," she insisted. According to Brown, divorcing procreation from sex conditioned people to think of babies as "accidents" that could be easily disposed of by abortion, thereby increasing the abortion rate. She also claimed that contraceptives were much more prone to failure than proponents admitted.[17]

Brown even asserted that oral contraceptives were abortifacients in disguise. She was an early proponent of the theory that the Pill could in some cases cause an abortion because it thins the endometrium—the lining of the uterus—which could in theory prevent a fertilized egg from implanting in the uterine wall if the Pill's primary and secondary mechanisms of action—preventing ovulation and increasing the viscosity of cervical mucus to impede the movement of sperm—failed.[18]

There was at the time enough uncertainty as to how exactly the Pill worked to make it impossible to discount this theory completely. Even if it were true, however, that the Pill sometimes caused a fertilized egg to fail to implant, this would still not make it an abortifacient according to the medical definition of pregnancy. The mainstream medical community, including the American College of Obstetricians and Gynecologists, defines pregnancy as beginning when the fertilized egg implants in the uterine wall—which happens about fourteen days after fertilization. Anything that prevents implantation is considered a contraceptive; anything that works post-implantation, such as the "abortion pill" mifepristone, is an abortifacient. What Brown was attempting to do was to apply Catholic doctrine, which holds that life begins "at the moment of conception" (which is in itself a misnomer since fertilization is a process that takes about twenty-four hours), to redefine some contraceptives as abortifacients. It was a distinction that would become increasingly important when the Food and Drug Administration (FDA) approved the first "morning after" contraceptive pill in 1998.[19]

For most of the 1980s and well into the 1990s, Brown's hostility to contraception made her an outlier in the anti-abortion movement. "Even in a pro-life audience, the critics will rise and scold me, stating that I damage our cause by making a connection between contraception and abortion," she wrote.[20]

Conservative Christians and mainstream anti-abortion groups had long been more or less agnostic about contraception. The Southern Baptist Convention, the largest organized fundamentalist group, accepted contraception use for married couples. The NRLC took no official position on contraception. Social conservatives had objected to allowing federally funded family planning clinics to dispense contraceptives to teens without their parents' permission and had tried to stop federal family planning money from going to domestic or international family planning organizations that provided abortions or abortion counseling, but these objections had more to do with parental authority and ways to undercut access to abortion than with contraception itself.[21]

But in the mid-1990s, electorally emboldened social conservatives began weaving attacks on family planning into the narrative of their increasingly heated culture war and were happily joined by the U.S. bishops. As part of their 1994 postelection legislative strategy, the U.S. Catholic Conference, the NRLC, and the Christian Coalition sought to defund the federal Title X family planning program, which provides contraceptives and family planning counseling to low-income and young women. They also turned on international family planning funding with renewed vigor. They tried to reinstate the Reagan-era Mexico City policy that prevented U.S. international family planning funding from going to nongovernmental organizations (NGOs) that provided or promoted abortion overseas. They proposed ending U.S. funding for the United Nations Population Fund, the United Nations' international family planning program. When the attempt to restore the Mexico City language failed, the Republican Congress slashed the family planning budget of the U.S. Agency for International Development (USAID) by 35 percent and imposed new disbursement regulations that effectively cut funding for 1997 by 87 percent, a move family planning advocates called "crippling."[22]

Despite a government analysis that concluded the cuts would force USAID to shutter family planning programs that had successfully reduced abortion rates in developing countries, conservatives mounted a campaign to assert that U.S. international family planning funding was actually promoting abortion. Republican representative Chris Smith (NJ), one of the highest-profile Catholic opponents of abortion in the House, charged that it was "fiction" that "international population-control agencies can use bookkeeping devices to spend 'their' money on abortions and 'our' money on everything else."[23] The Christian Coalition and the NRLC dubbed U.S. family planning funding part of the Clinton administration's "overseas abortion crusade." Boston Cardinal Bernard Law, who headed the NCCB's Committee for Pro-Life Activities, echoed this charge when he said that U.S. funding was effectively "subsidizing" organizations that performed abortion. The formerly fringe charge that contraception increased the abortion rate also gained new prominence. NCCB spokesperson Helen Alvare asserted, "[W]hen you give money to groups that not only promote contraception but also promote abortion in an integrated way, you actually drive abortion rates up."[24]

Concerned that conservative Catholics were making inroads in Congress against family planning funding, CFFC went on the offensive. "Support for contraception had always been in CFFC's mission statement," said CFFC's Denise Shannon, "but we felt it was important to get involved in the issue in a more direct way because there were people who were opposed to contraception not just in the abstract, but were now actually working on policies that made contraception less accessible."[25]

The organization launched "Catholics for Contraception" to highlight Catholic support for family planning. The high-profile campaign featured ads in the *Washington Post* and *New York Times* that showed a bishop's mitre under the headline, "Worn correctly, it can prevent unintended pregnancy, AIDS and abortion." The ads charged that having failed to convince Catholics not to use contraception, the bishops were inappropriately using the public policy process to limit access to birth control. CFFC also began aggressive outreach to members of Congress to educate them about Catholic support for international and domestic family planning funding ahead of a key 1997 vote, when Congress voted to restore family planning funding. International family planning funding was spared, at least in the short run, but it was clear that there was, in the words of one family planning advocate, a "concerted attack on family planning."[26]

One reason for the sudden interest in contraception was the increased viability at the state and national levels of contraceptive equity measures designed to ensure that health plans covered prescription contraceptives like the Pill just like other prescription medications. For years, insurers had omitted contraceptives from prescription drug plans—the only entire class of drugs routinely and explicitly excluded—which made women's out-of-pocket medical expenses some 70 percent higher than men's. Measures to ensure contraceptive equity had been stalled by male legislators and social conservatives who asserted that employers and insurers should not be forced to pay for what they called a "lifestyle" choice, not a health care need. Despite the fact that nearly all women use contraceptives at some point in their lives—98 percent, according to government surveys—and that at any given moment two-thirds of women of childbearing age are using a contraceptive method, the implication was that fertility management was frivolous or immoral and that "other people" shouldn't be forced to pay for it.[27]

When Connecticut considered a contraceptive equity measure in 1999, a Catholic priest, the Reverend Joseph Looney of Bethlehem, Connecticut, told the legislature that covering contraceptives would only benefit "playboys" and would fund "craziness and irresponsibility." It was a framework that conservatives had successfully applied to abortion—asserting that it must be segregated from other health services and government funding because it was immoral—and now were trying to apply to birth control.[28]

But the decision of most health insurers to cover Viagra almost immediately after it was approved by the FDA in 1998 largely negated this argument. Suddenly contraceptive coverage measures were sailing through state legislatures. A national contraceptive equity measure was introduced but failed to make it out of committee. The sponsors retooled the bill and reintroduced it as a measure that required insurance plans participating in the health insurance program for federal employees to cover contraceptives. Even this scaled-down measure would set an important precedent because the federal benefits package is often used as a model for private sector health plans. The bishops and social conservatives worked furiously to derail the measure by claiming that it would force health plans to cover abortifacients—which they now defined as anything that worked post-fertilization. Representatives Smith and Tom Coburn (R-OK) tried unsuccessfully to insert a provision prohibiting "coverage for abortifacients," claiming that newly approved emergency contraceptive pills and the intrauterine device were abortifacients because they could prevent a fertilized egg from implanting.[29]

When charges that contraceptives were abortifacients failed to halt the measure, the bishops turned to a new tack: claiming that contraception equity laws violated the religious freedom of insurers and employers who disapproved of contraception and would be forced to subsidize its use. "They force private health insurance plans and/or employers . . . to cover all 'FDA-approved' methods of contraception . . . regardless of the provider's conscientious objection or long-standing religious beliefs against such coverage," wrote Cathy Deeds of the NCCB. It was a stunning claim, suggesting that anyone who administered or paid for an insurance policy should be free to dictate what coverage was provided to policyholders based on their objection to services that they themselves would not be forced to use.[30]

The Catholic bishops now sought a broad-based conscience clause that would allow any employer or insurer to refuse to cover contraceptives for any religious or moral objection. This represented a major escalation in the grounds for claiming conscience protections. Traditionally so-called conscience clauses, like the 1973 Church Amendment, protected individuals or health care entities like hospitals only from being compelled to directly perform abortions or sterilizations in violation of their moral or religious beliefs. In 1997, the federal government expanded conscience protections to the payers of abortion-related services when it allowed Medicaid and Medicare managed-care plans to refuse to pay providers for abortion counseling or referral services. Now the bishops were attempting to extend conscience protection to any payer who had a "moral" objection to contraception. Such a measure would make contraceptive coverage mandates useless, because any employer or insurer could opt out. And it would once again leave women's reproductive health care, and only women's reproductive health care, at the mercy of individual employers and insurers and stigmatize contraceptives, like abortion, as a segregated health service that could be carved out of the continuum of women's health needs.[31]

The bishops failed to get a broader conscience clause in the bill mandating coverage of contraceptives for federal employees, but they did manage to get an exemption for the five religiously affiliated plans in the system. Having set the precedent that religious providers would be treated differently concerning the provision of reproductive health care, even in the matter of noncontroversial services such as contraception, the bishops launched a major new effort to create broad conscience exemptions. The issue was particularly contentious because the FDA recently had approved the first prepackaged "morning after" pill—a high dose of oral contraceptives that worked to prevent pregnancy if taken shortly after unprotected intercourse. Like regular oral contraceptives, emergency contraceptives (ECs) work primarily by preventing ovulation; however, at the time it was believed that this early version might in some cases prevent implantation. Public health advocates praised the widespread availability of EC as a major step forward in preventing unwanted pregnancy and reducing abortion. The Catholic bishops, however, were among the earliest and sharpest critics of EC, asserting that it was an abortifacient because it may prevent implantation and "destroy a developing embryo" despite the fact that the FDA said it could not interrupt an established pregnancy.[32]

"What is striking is how hard the bishops worked to conflate abortion and contraception, particularly around EC," said Lois Uttley, director of MergerWatch, which began tracking religiously based health restrictions in the mid-1990s. "But they said it over and over enough that they actually managed to convince many people," she said.[33]

With interest in the availability of EC running high, especially after Wal-Mart said it wouldn't carry the medication in its pharmacies because of conservative objections, CFFC conducted an undercover survey of Catholic hospitals to see if they were making it available to a particularly vulnerable population—women who had been raped. CFFC recently had documented dramatic growth in the number of Catholic hospitals as the result of more than 125 mergers or acquisitions between 1990 and 1998 that resulted in formerly nonsecular or nominally religious hospitals becoming Catholic and falling under the authority of the *Ethical and Religious Directives for Catholic Health Care Services.* In nearly half these mergers, reproductive health services were discontinued—most often contraceptive sterilization and family planning services, as well as abortions for women with health problems or medical emergencies.[34]

With five of the ten largest health care systems as measured by revenue now Catholic, CFFC and allies in the reproductive rights movement were increasingly concerned about the availability of reproductive health services, especially in communities where the only hospital was now Catholic. The availability of EC in emergency rooms was particularly critical for women who had been raped because it is most effective if used within seventy-two hours of unprotected intercourse. The *Directives* allow the provision of EC to women who have been raped provided they are not already pregnant. Some Catholic ethicists hold that it is adequate to administer a pregnancy test and then proceed with EC if a woman desires it. Others hold that an ovulation test should be administered to determine whether the woman has ovulated, because there was believed to be a small chance that EC used postovulation may prevent implantation and therefore would not be licit.[35]

The CFFC survey of some 600 Catholic hospitals found that 82 percent didn't make EC available to women who had been raped and that only 22 percent of the ERs that didn't provide it told women about its availability or where they could get it.[36] The idea of Catholic hospitals denying information about EC to women who had been raped hit a nerve. The survey was featured in more than thirty media outlets, including a hard-hitting Dewayne Wickham column in *USA Today* and on Bill Maher's *Politically Incorrect.* "You can try and talk to someone about the *Directives* and what they mean to women, but it's all very technical," said CFFC's O'Brien. "But people could imagine if it was them or their daughter in this situation. It really brought it home."[37]

As a result of the study, Catholic hospitals and the Catholic Health Association (CHA), the trade association representing Catholic hospitals, were forced to clarify that Catholic hospitals could provide EC. State legislators moved to formulate laws to require hospitals to offer EC to women who had been raped. By now, it was obvious that a new front had been opened up in the battle over Catholic doctrine and women's reproductive health. No longer was it exclusively about abortion. The Catholic reproductive rights movement was questioning the right of the Catholic bishops to impose doctrinally based health restrictions on Catholics and non-Catholics who interacted with a range of Catholic-affiliated providers such as insurers and hospitals operating in a nonsecular marketplace.

Advocacy groups working on the issue, such as MergerWatch, the National Women's Law Center, and the American Civil Liberties Union (ACLU), began working in coalition with CFFC on the issue. They held national strategy sessions, published reports, briefed legislators, and rallied community support to block mergers or insist on the inclusion of "creative compromises," such as freestanding clinics, to allow reproductive health services to continue. With widespread media coverage bringing the issue to the public's attention, the CHA complained of "biased" news coverage and charged that the widely covered CFFC reports were inaccurate.[38]

The controversy over Catholic health care restrictions further intensified when California considered a contraceptive equity measure in 1999. The California Catholic Conference fought tooth and nail for a broad conscience exemption for any organization that didn't want to provide contraceptives to its employees. Instead, lawmakers included a narrowly drawn conscience exemption that specifically recognized the moral quandary that contraceptive coverage provided for explicitly religious employers. It exempted organizations that met the IRS definition of a "church" and employed people of its own faith. This meant that Catholic churches were exempt but that organizations more loosely affiliated with the church, such as Catholic universities and social service agencies, were not. In July 2000, one such organization, Catholic Charities of Sacramento, filed a lawsuit claiming the law violated the organization's religious freedom by requiring it to provide contraceptives for its employees. The case was closely watched to see how the courts would deal with requests for broad conscience exemptions from non-church entities.

CFFC filed an amicus brief with other progressive Catholic groups in which it argued that Catholic Charities shouldn't be exempt because it was "primarily a welfare agency that employs individuals of different faiths." It also noted that a recent study it had done of Catholic health maintenance organizations found that just over half managed to cover contraceptives through a variety of creative arrangements, such as contracting with non-Catholic providers to deliver services or using third-party administrators. "If so many Catholic health plans can find ways to provide access to contraception while protecting their conscience, then Catholic Charities must be expected to do so as well," said Kissling.[39]

The California Supreme Court agreed. It ruled in July 2001 that Catholic Charities had to comply with the law, a decision that the U.S. Supreme Court let stand, which was viewed as a major endorsement of limited conscience clauses.[40]

In December 2000, *60 Minutes* did an exposé based on CFFC's research on the curtailment of reproductive health services as the result of Catholic hospital takeovers. The program featured a New Hampshire woman who had to take a cab eighty miles for an emergency abortion after the now-Catholic local hospital refused to perform the procedure, and a hospital in rural California that stopped performing tubal ligations after it became part of a Catholic chain, effectively ending access to the popular contraceptive procedure for a poor, isolated population. With an audience of 17 million viewers, the program brought unprecedented attention to the long reach of the Vatican into health care decisions. "It's not like the old days. Doctors are no longer gods. Now we have bishops who are gods," Kissling told Morley Safer.[41]

The CHA was furious. Father Michael Place, president of the CHA, complained to *60 Minutes* executive producer Don Hewitt about the program's reliance on CFFC's analysis and studies, charging it had "allowed opponents, rather than ministry leaders, to describe Catholic health care and Church teaching." Place was extensively quoted in the story and given ample opportunity to argue that it was a matter of religious freedom and conscience to allow Catholic hospitals to refuse to provide services. Once again the argument came down to who could legitimately interpret Catholic teaching and tradition, but the argument now was reaching into the daily lives of both Catholics and non-Catholics.[42]

. . . . .

By the dawn of the twenty-first century, CFFC had solidified its position as the institutional arm of the Catholic reproductive rights movement, with a staff of twenty and a budget of some $3 million. "We are the strongest we have ever been—our research capacity is unsurpassed, production levels have reached new highs, and we have hit the big leagues with major media coverage," Kissling told donors. But with the organization's increased effectiveness and visibility came new challenges: an ever-more organized and strident Catholic Right allied with the Vatican. These groups echoed the Vatican's highly orthodox view of doctrinal matters pertaining to sexuality, as well as assertions that only the hierarchy was authorized to address the morality of abortion and contraception.[43]

The Catholic League for Religious and Civil Rights had been in existence for as long as CFFC but had never attracted much attention. That changed in 1993 when William Donohue became president. Donohue had worked for the Heritage Foundation, a conservative think tank cofounded by Paul Weyrich to promote limited government and "traditional American values," where he specialized in over-the-top attacks against the ACLU. His trademark move became to assert that any criticism of the Vatican or its policies was "anti-Catholic." Donohue attracted prominent Catholic conservatives to the organization's board and put his rhetorical skills to use manufacturing made-for-the media incidents of anti-Catholicism. He generated reams of publicity by condemning an MTV bus ad in New York City that featured the Virgin Mary and by calling for a boycott of Disney when its Miramax subsidiary released a movie about a priest struggling with celibacy. The organization soon turned its eye to CFFC, attacking the organization as "a well-funded letterhead that functions as a front group for the population-control movement."[44] After the *60 Minutes* exposé, the Catholic League attacked the CBS news program as anti-Catholic, calling Kissling "the most notorious anti-Catholic bigot in the nation."[45]

Another increasingly prominent critic of CFFC was Human Life International (HLI), which was founded by Father Paul Marx, a Benedictine priest known for his outspoken anti-abortion activism, in 1981 with the help of ALL's Judie Brown. It was Marx who introduced Brown to a far-right Catholic orthodoxy on birth control. In fact, she almost got fired as the head of publicity for the NRLC after she sent an article he wrote titled "Are You Really Pro-Life?," which asserted that you couldn't be pro-life if you didn't oppose contraception, to 2,000 NRLC chapters.[46]

Marx was a pioneer of anti-abortion "shock" tactics such as displaying fetuses in jars. After his stridency got him ousted from the Human Life Center he had founded at St. John's University in Collegeville, Missouri, which sent him packing with nothing more than "a few dollars and an old car," he became something of an itinerant anti-abortion activist.[47] He ran into Judie Brown's husband, Paul, in 1977 at a pro-life rally in Syracuse, New York, and ending up crashing in his hotel room after the rectory he was supposed to stay at kicked him out for refusing to tone down the anti-contraception rhetoric in a homily he was scheduled to deliver the next day.[48]

Marx was a tireless promoter of natural family planning and traveled the world preaching its benefits and the dangers of contraception: "People who use contraception are not happy, and that is why there are so many divorces. One of the most evil protection devices is the diaphragm. The pill causes infertility. Contraception promotes homosexuality."[49] He warned in hysterical tones of an impending depopulation crisis in Western counties, which he said was caused by "the world's rejection of traditional Catholic teachings on abortion and birth control."[50]

Human Life International's fundraising letters and publications depict an ongoing battle between godless, pro-abortion feminists who "hate all that we hold dear" and the true defenders of the Catholic faith. It labeled CFFC a "group of heretics which shamelessly promotes chemical and surgical abortion, and teaches Catholics to disobey God."[51] It launched a three-part "exposé" about CFFC in 1995 that placed CFFC at the center of a conspiracy to promote the "New Age movement" in the Catholic Church in which it accused CFFC board members like Rosemary Ruether of taking part in goddess worship and promoting sexual immorality. It listed the foundations supporting CFFC, drawing specious links to population control and forced sterilization programs, and provided the home phone numbers of board members of the foundations and suggested that concerned Catholics call them or boycott other organizations associated with the foundations.[52]

These organizations were joined by a new voice criticizing CFFC: Marjorie Maguire, who, after a bitter divorce from Dan Maguire, recast herself as an opponent of CFFC and abortion rights. She trashed the organization in a letter to the *National Catholic Reporter*. "I see CFFC's agenda as the promotion of abortion, the defense of every abortion decision as a good, moral choice and the related agenda of persuading society to cast off any moral constraints about sexual behavior," wrote Maguire, who had written some of the organization's most eloquent defenses of abortion as a moral option and coauthored the Catholic Statement on Pluralism and Abortion. She gave CFFC's critics valuable ammunition when she charged that the organization was Catholic in name only and that most staff members were not practicing Catholics. "When I was involved with CFFC, I was never aware that any of its leaders attended Mass. Furthermore, various conversations and experiences convinced me they did not," she wrote.[53]

These new, explicitly Catholic anti-choice groups were on full display at the 1999 five-year review of progress made toward the goals of the Cairo Conference on Population and Development. At the March preparatory conference, a host of anti-choice NGOs made their presence felt at the United Nations for the first time. Upset by the clout of CFFC at UN conferences, the Vatican had recruited anti-choice organizations to apply for consultative status to the UN Economic and Social Council (ECOSOC). This designation, which CFFC had received the previous year, automatically accredits NGOs to attend UN conferences. "For more than a year the Vatican has appealed for more pro-life and pro-family groups to apply for ECOSOC status, since these groups can assist the Holy See and other friendly nations in lobbying the big UN conferences," wrote Austin Ruse, the head of a new group called the Catholic Family and Human Rights Institute (CAFHRI), which had been created by HLI, which itself had been denied ECOSOC accreditation because of its extremist anti-UN rhetoric.[54]

According to one HLI official, CAFHRI was to apply for UN accreditation and serve as a "spy satellite" for the Holy See in the UN NGO community. "Though not publicized, one of CAFHRI's major mandates will be to act as a real resource and information office to the Holy See delegation," said the job description for the initial staffer hired to run the organization.[55]

By the time of the Cairo review, Ruse had emerged as the Vatican's point man at the UN, coordinating efforts to get sympathetic governments to ally with the Vatican on anti-reproductive rights efforts. "[W]e will not win until we begin writing language and getting governments to introduce it for us," he wrote to supporters.[56] At the conference, Kissling observed Ruse conferring frequently with the head of the Holy See delegation, John Klink, as the Holy See and conservative Catholic and Muslim countries objected to the inclusion of terms like "sex education," which, as in Cairo, slowed the review process to a crawl.[57]

The appearance of CAFHRI coincided with a new, harder edge at UN conferences. Right-wing attendees gleefully broke long-standing rules of decorum designed to foster dialogue and agreement. At a seminar sponsored by CFFC, a woman in the audience called Kissling "the Salman Rushdie of the Catholic church." She shocked attendees when she said, "[W]e have to put a contract out on you."[58] Jon O'Brien, who was now the vice president of CFFC, was falsely accused of shoving a representative from the Couple-to-Couple League after he found him distributing materials at a CFFC seminar in violation of UN rules.[59]

In was in this atmosphere that CFFC launched a formal campaign to change the Holy See's status at the United Nations from a permanent nonmember state observer to an NGO, which would require the Holy See to participate at the United Nations on the same grounds as other religions and religious organizations.[60] The Holy See's unusual status as a permanent observer, which at the time was shared only by Switzerland (which has since become a full member), isn't in the UN charter, but evolved as a matter of custom based on the Holy See's participation in several UN agencies. Ending the Holy See's special status would end the privileges that went with it, which included full access to the negotiating floor at international conferences and the ability to directly lobby delegates, which NGOs are prevented from doing. "There was an incredible feeling of frustration that the Holy See was on the floor at these conferences and sitting next to actual nations like Haiti. They could just put their hand up and say whatever they wanted to say, and of course they were always opposed to a progressive agenda. No other religion has that ability," said Anika Rahman, who wrote a legal analysis of the Holy See's status at the United Nations.[61]

The Vatican and its attendant curia are a vestige of feudal Europe. The Vatican as an independent city-state was established by the Lateran Treaty in 1929. It was what was left of the Papal States, which encompassed most of central Italy from A.D. 756 through 1870, when they were incorporated into modern Italy. Until then, popes ruled territory and exercised temporal power much as other monarchs in Europe and were deeply involved in European political intrigue. Cardinals were like feudal lords, appointed by the pope and engaging in civic affairs and exercising power on behalf of the Vatican and themselves. As the pope's temporal power waned, he was able to continue to exercise influence by claiming spiritual and moral authority. It is no coincidence that the pope was declared to be infallible on certain spiritual matters in 1870, the same year the church was forced to cede most of its physical territory to Italy.

The Holy See is the government of the Roman Catholic Church. It is made up of the pope and the Roman Curia, the administrative apparatus of the Holy See, which is literally the pope's royal court. The Holy See is the entity given diplomatic recognition by other governments. What is especially useful for the leaders of the church is that they can move back and forth between the identities of the Vatican, a temporal city-state; the Holy See, an ecclesiastical government; and their role as the senior clerics of Roman Catholicism as it suits their needs. This fungability has helped the hierarchy survive as a powerful force in the modern world—what is essentially a feudal court exercising power in international civic affairs in the name of religion. "Why should an entity that is in essence 100 square acres of office space and tourist attractions in the middle of Rome with a citizenry that excludes women and children have a place at the table where governments set policies affecting the very survival of women and children?," asked Kissling when she announced the "See Change" campaign.[62]

Realistically there was little chance of stripping the Vatican of its special designation, but the campaign provided the opportunity to educate the public about the Vatican's role at the United Nations. "The whole point was to try and reduce their credibility as a nation-state," Rahman said.

"Our goal was to raise some hell around the fact that they didn't belong in that role."[63]

The final phase of the Cairo +5 review opened at a special session of the UN General Assembly on June 30 with tensions running high and the Vatican and its allies insisting on language that undercut the basic agreements on reproductive health made at Cairo. On the second day of the conference, Dan Maguire addressed the General Assembly and called on the Vatican to "stop their dogmatism, a dogmatism that offends many Catholics and most of the world's religions." The following day UK delegate Clare Short, who was Britain's secretary of state for International Development, made headlines around the world when she called the Vatican's partnership with conservative Catholic and Muslim nations an "unholy alliance."[64]

On the third and final day of the conference, a majority of NGOs sent a letter to UN Secretary-General Kofi Annan complaining that the conference had been diverted from its original purpose by the Vatican and its allies. It was only on the last day that the delegates reached a final consensus that largely rejected the Vatican's interventions and upheld the Cairo agreement, due in no small part, according to Joseph Fahey of the American Humanist Association, to Kissling's leadership at the conference.[65]

A similar scenario played out at the five-year review of the Beijing Conference on Women the following year. A handful of anti-abortion NGOs, including ALL, Concerned Women for America, and Focus on the Family, registered some 300 delegates to the preparatory conference in March, including 30 Franciscan Friars of the Renewal, a conservative, anti-abortion order, and set about trying to obstruct the conference. On the first day of the conference, conservative delegates emblazoned with bright red "Motherhood" buttons swarmed the gathering government delegates. "[W]e broke every single rule of UN lobbying . . . which forbids leafleting," CAFHRI's Ruse bragged. "[W]e spread out across the floor and like an Old Testament plague, handed [a leaflet] to every single person on the conference room floor . . . something like pandemonium ensued."[66]

The good friars encircled a lone women's rights advocate and "prayed" loudly for her redemption. Conservative delegates packed the various caucuses, refused to identify themselves, and copied down the names of other attendees. A group called the World Youth Alliance, which was created by CAFHRI, packed the Youth Caucus with forty delegates, who then objected to everything the moderator said. "The Youth Caucus is paralyzed because of the World Youth Alliance. They are dominating. We can't work," one delegate complained.[67]

The prepcom ended with no agreement on a final document, which had been heavily bracketed by the Holy See and its allies, and a sense of rancor over the proceedings. Again the suspected ringmaster was Ruse, who had sent out a call for anti-abortion activists to come to New York to fight the "radical and dangerous" Beijing platform for action.[68]

In addition to recruiting anti-abortion activists to disrupt UN conferences, Ruse was working behind the scenes to organize a bloc of nations to protect "traditional family life" because, he said, "a dozen states can stop anything" at the United Nations. At the World Congress of Families, a virtual lollapalooza of patriarchal family values uniting conservative Christians, Catholics, and Mormons, Ruse had met with representatives from the governments of Argentina and Nicaragua; the Archdiocese of New York; the World Family Policy Center, which was the Mormon counterpart of CAFHRI; the Organization of the Islamic Conference; and Archbishop Alfonso López Trujillo, president of the Vatican's Pontifical Council on the Family, to plot conservative strategy.[69]

In the midst of the charged Beijing +5 review, CFFC announced that the "See Change" campaign had received the backing of some 450 organizations. The day after the CFFC press conference, CAFHRI announced a countercampaign to protect the Holy See's status. It released the "Declaration of Support of the Holy See at the UN," which was coauthored by noted Princeton University natural law scholar and conservative Catholic Robert George and William Saunders of the Family Research Council and endorsed by 1,015 conservative organizations.[70]

Given that it was a presidential election year and the importance of heavily Catholic swing states in presidential elections, it was no surprise that the See Change campaign hit a political nerve. In February, Representative Smith introduced a congressional resolution voicing support for the Vatican's status at the United Nations, reportedly at the prompting of Ruse. Likewise Republican senators Bob Smith (NH), who had attended the recent World Congress of Families, and Rick Santorum

(PA) introduced a concurrent resolution in the Senate "commending the Holy See for making significant contributions to international peace and human rights and objecting to efforts to expel the Holy See from the United Nations." The resolution said the See Change campaign was an attack on the pope and was "comprised of extremist groups, pro-choice groups, some extreme environmental organizations, and anti-religious, atheist groups who want to take away this permanent status of the Holy See."[71]

Republican presidential candidate Texas governor George W. Bush in particular needed to appear friendly to Catholics because he had been harshly criticized for a stop he made during the bitterly contested GOP primary at Bob Jones University, a fundamentalist Christian school that labeled Catholicism a "cult." Following CFFC's UN press conference, Republican National Committee chair Jim Nicholson demanded that presumptive Democratic nominee Vice President Al Gore repudiate two organizations supporting him, the National Abortion Rights Action League and Women Leaders Online, because of their support of the See Change campaign. "As a Catholic, I am appalled that Al Gore has courted the support of two groups trying to throw the Vatican out of the UN," he said, labeling the campaign and the organizations supporting it "anti-Catholic." A Bush spokesperson called on Gore to repudiate CFFC for "hateful accusations" it made against the Catholic Church.[72]

The U.S. bishops were also taking note of the See Change campaign and the negative publicity for the Vatican. In May, just a month before the formal Beijing +5 review was to take place, the NCCB issued a blistering statement condemning the campaign and accusing CFFC of anti-Catholic bigotry. The bishops' statement was part of a campaign to discredit the Catholic reproductive rights movement as "one woman and a fax machine" that now went into overdrive. In mid-April, Gail Quinn, the head of the NCCB's pro-life staff, wrote an article portraying CFFC as a one-woman media campaign funded by large foundations to undermine the Catholic Church. Two weeks later, NCCB spokesperson Alvare took to the conservative *National Catholic Register* to accuse CFFC of "Catholic bashing" with the See Change campaign.[73]

Conservative organizations allied with the hierarchy continued the onslaught. Donohue of the Catholic League produced an article on "The

Real Agenda of Catholics for a Free Choice," while ALL asked, "Who Are 'Catholics for a Free Choice'?" Dean Hudson's *Crisis* magazine ran "Aborting the Church: Frances Kissling and Catholics for a Free Choice." From CAFHRI came "The War on Faith: How Catholics for a Free Choice Seeks to Undermine the Catholic Church." Human Life International gave CFFC book-length treatment in *Catholics for a Free Choice Exposed.* The attacks rehashed the same charges: from having accepted two small grants from the Playboy Foundation in its early years, CFFC was portrayed as being lavishly and continually funded by the Playboy Foundation and "pornographers." Frances Kissling's quip to *Mother Jones* magazine that she "spent twenty years looking for a government that I could overthrow without being thrown in jail. I finally found one in the Catholic Church," was offered as evidence that she wanted to destroy the Catholic Church. The population control rhetoric that infused reproductive rights organizations in the early 1970s was used as evidence that major foundations were using CFFC as a tool of a "population control movement" that had ceased to exist twenty years ago.

In late May, Bush ramped up his efforts to appeal directly to Catholics when he told a meeting of the Catholic Press Association that the Holy See "has long been an influence for good." Noting that some organizations "have been trying to silence that voice in the United Nations," he said his administration would support retaining the Holy See's special status at the United Nations. He tried to cast doubt on the Clinton administration's support for the Holy See, and by inference that of Gore's, when he noted that the U.S. mission to the United Nations had sponsored CFFC's March UN press conference—despite the fact that the mission also sponsored CAFHRI's press conference. A Bush aide said that Bush would not give CFFC access to the United Nations. For his part, Gore stated that he too supported the existing status of the Holy See at the United Nations—the Catholic vote was too important to any presidential candidate to risk it over a dispute at the increasingly maligned United Nations.[74]

Just days later the formal Beijing +5 review opened with the familiar standoff. The Vatican and conservative allies sought to delete references to sex education for girls, reproductive freedom for women, and sexual rights. Amparo Claro of the Latin American and Caribbean Women's Health Network said there was a sense of déjà vu as a handful of countries

Figure 10. See Change demonstrators sail by the United Nations to protest the Holy See's role at the UN during the Beijing +5 review in June 2000. (Courtesy of Catholics for Choice)

managed to propel negotiations into a "theater of the absurd, where basic ideas, such as the idea of women's rights as human rights, are questioned."[75]

Because of the mayhem at the preparatory conference, participation of NGOs was strictly limited to three delegates per group and the names of participants weren't circulated, which dampened the normally productive NGO networking activity. It was in the midst of this growing sense of unreality that conference delegates looked out the windows of the United Nations and saw what at first appeared to be a mirage: a stately two-masted schooner sailing up the East River flying a "See Change" banner. As the schooner sailed past the United Nations, reproductive rights advocates from around the world waved "See Change" flags and chanted, "Hey hey, ho ho, the Holy See is an NGO."

Not since Pope Patricia had mounted the steps of St. Patrick's had the Catholic pro-choice movement held such a theatrical, visible protest. It was, according to O'Brien, "a way to manifest the movement and speak truth to power. It helped end the campaign of intimidation that the Holy See was engaged in at the U.N. It gave people backbone and reminded them that what the Holy See said was wrong."[76]

In the end, the progressive delegates managed to hold the line on reproductive and sexual rights and add new language about protecting women from trafficking and domestic violence. But there was an increasing sense that the UN conferences on women's issues had been hijacked by conservative forces allied with the Vatican and were losing their potency as a tool to improve the lives of women and girls around the world.

9 Playing Politics

The controversy over the See Change campaign in the early stages of the 2000 presidential race showed how critical the Catholic vote had become to both parties in a closely divided electorate. While there is no such thing as a homogenous "Catholic vote," as the bishops found time and time again when they tried to get Catholics to vote for favored candidates or causes, Catholics are a significant portion of the electorate in crucial swing states like Pennsylvania, Ohio, and Michigan. In 2000, the electoral map for either candidate didn't add up unless they won a significant number of these swing states and, therefore, Catholics.

The importance of the Catholic vote was propelled back into the news eighteen months before the election when the U.S. bishops released their strongest statement in years on Catholics' voting responsibility. "Living the Gospel of Life" was the bishops' most concerted effort since 1976's Pastoral Plan for Pro-Life Activities to instruct Catholics on voting and abortion and was a direct reaction to the intransigence of pro-choice Catholic lawmakers on partial-birth abortion. In it, the bishops said officially for the first time that Catholic public officials being "right" on issues such as poverty, war, and hunger couldn't excuse a "wrong choice" on abortion. And they inserted bishops directly into the political process, saying bishops should "explain, persuade, correct and admonish" those who contradicted their teaching on abortion, firstly privately and then, if that failed, publicly, although the document stopped short of calling for formal ecclesiastical sanctions.[1]

The *Washington Post* called "Living the Gospel of Life" a "new era in the church's political activism," and the statement led to intense speculation about the role the bishops would play in the upcoming election. It was immediately criticized as an inappropriate intrusion by the bishops into politics—a dramatic repudiation of John F. Kennedy's famous pledge as a presidential candidate that he would not take direction from the church hierarchy. Catholics for a Free Choice's (CFFC's) Jon O'Brien called it a "slap in the face to the democratic principles that Americans expect their leaders to uphold." Bishop Howard Hubbard of Albany, who was a leading voice of moderation in the bishops' conference, said the document could create an anti-Catholic backlash by giving the impression that "Catholic bishops are trying to dictate how a politician must vote."[2]

But Boston's Cardinal Bernard Law, who was chairing the National Conference of Catholic Bishops' (NCCB's) Committee on Pro-Life Activities, was unapologetic about the new hard-line stance. At a news conference he called out pro-choice Massachusetts Democratic senators Edward Kennedy and John Kerry and Republican governor Paul Cellucci for being "wrong" on abortion. "Only I am right," he said.[3]

Shortly after the release of the document, Vice President Al Gore, the Democratic presidential candidate, was publicly embarrassed when Scranton Bishop James Timlin ordered him disinvited at the last minute from a campaign stop at a Catholic hospital in Scranton, Pennsylvania. Erie, Pennsylvania, Bishop Donald Trautman chastised Pennsylvania governor Tom Ridge (R) for his pro-choice stance and said he was no longer welcome to speak at Catholic-supported events in his diocese, which was widely believed to have torpedoed Ridge's chance to be George W. Bush's vice presidential pick.[4]

Around the same time the bishops were debating their new voting guidance, Bush strategist Karl Rove began assembling an outreach effort to marry conservative-leaning Catholics with fundamentalist Protestants in a new Republican electoral coalition he hoped would replace the fading Christian Coalition. Bush's political credo was specifically fashioned to facilitate this coupling. It was an amalgamation of the right's traditional opposition to abortion and same-sex marriage and calls for government promotion of premarital sexual abstinence and other "traditional" values with a new emphasis on a larger publicly financed role for religious organizations in addressing social problems like poverty. This "compassionate conservatism" was designed in part to assuage the social justice concerns that Republican strategists believed prevented many Catholics from throwing their support behind the Republican Party.

The Republican National Committee (RNC) launched a Catholic Task Force to conduct outreach to Catholics in key swing states, emphasizing Bush's opposition to abortion and support for "school choice"—voucher programs that allow parents to send their children to religious schools at taxpayer expense. The task force was headed by Brian Tierney, a Philadelphia public relations executive who had served as an advisor to Philadelphia Cardinal Anthony Bevilacqua. Tierney oversaw the compilation of a list of 3 million Catholics in swing states who were targeted with an unprecedented $2.5 million direct mail and telephone outreach effort. Every Catholic on the list received at least two phone calls and two mailings highlighting Catholic teaching on abortion and same-sex marriage. One flyer featured a priest on the cover and read, "Which presidential candidate represents your values?"[5]

In fact, the task force proclaimed in its mission statement, "We have studied the political record of all major political parties and we believe that the Republican Party is closest to the teaching of the Catholic church." CFFC couldn't let this claim go unanswered—especially since Bush was the governor of a state known for its enthusiastic application of the death penalty and an abysmal record of providing social services for the poor. In April 2000, CFFC president Frances Kissling asked NCCB president Bishop Joseph Fiorenza to repudiate the task force's claim. She noted that the Republican Party supported the death penalty, which the bishops opposed, as well as the denial of all but emergency public benefits to undocumented immigrants, while the bishops called for a more generous immigration policy. Similarly, the GOP opposed the bishops' long-standing call to create a national health care system.[6]

An analysis of congressional voting patterns by sociologists William D'Antonio and Jacqueline Scherer for the *National Catholic Reporter* confirmed that "aside from the Republican Party's antiabortion stand, and its support for educational vouchers and funds for Catholic schools, the party's claim to best represent Catholic views is greatly exaggerated." They concluded that "Democrats more closely reflect Catholic teachings over the broad spectrum" of social justice issues, including a commitment to nonviolence and support for society's most vulnerable members.[7]

Another organization pressing the message that the GOP was the party of God was Priests for Life, an anti-abortion group that claimed a membership of 6,000 priests but was largely a vehicle for one priest: Father Frank Pavone. Pavone was a militantly anti-abortion priest who had links to far-right abortion clinic protestors like Joseph Scheidler and Randall Terry. Pavone had implied that violence against doctors who performed abortions was justified. "When someone kills an abortion provider, he/she is practicing what pro-choicers have preached for decades: that sometimes it is OK to choose to end a life to solve a problem," wrote Pavone.[8]

In 1993 Pavone was given permission by New York Cardinal John O'Conner to leave his priestly duties and run Priests for Life full time. He had been gradually raising the organization's profile and political rhetoric since then. Pavone claimed his anti-abortion message was nonpartisan, but the organization had never endorsed a Democrat and had coordinated political strategy with anti-abortion Republicans in Congress. In May 2000, he met with George W. Bush and declared him "pro-life," while calling Gore "an apostle for abortion."[9] In July, Pavone announced a $1 million "Campaign for Life 2000" to amplify the message of "Living the Gospel of Life": that no good Catholic could vote for a pro-choice candidate. The campaign included full-page ads in the *New York Times* and *USA Today* that reminded Catholics that pro-choice public officials are a "scandal" to the church, as well as television ads in New York, Los Angeles, Washington, D.C., and the swing states of Missouri, Michigan, and Pennsylvania.[10]

One television ad featured Pavone asking, "If those elected to public office can't respect the life of a little baby, how are they supposed to respect yours?" Pavone's rhetoric on the sinfulness of voting pro-choice and the unacceptability of pro-choice candidates was significantly more inflammatory than that of the bishops, and his emergence as a political actor moved the debate about Catholics and abortion to the right without the direct involvement of the NCCB.[11]

With the election fast approaching and speculation running rampant that Bush had the Catholic vote tied up due to his campaign's unprecedented Catholic outreach, CFFC released a national poll in October that disputed the idea that pandering to Catholics on abortion would get their vote. Contrary to widely publicized GOP polling, the CFFC poll found Catholics evenly divided between Bush and Gore—although regular churchgoers did favor Bush. The majority of Catholics said the most important issues to them were the "bread and butter" issues of protecting Social Security and Medicare. Some 70 percent said Catholics didn't have a religious obligation to vote for candidates who opposed abortion and that the bishops shouldn't advance their moral opinions in the political arena.[12]

The poll received widespread media coverage, but apparently the bishops didn't get the message. As the election drew near, conservative bishops used the pulpit to back Bush, and Bush engaged in a whirlwind tour of appearances with Catholic prelates. He met with Los Angeles Archbishop Roger Mahony, Pittsburgh Bishop Donald Wuerl, Philadelphia Archbishop Bevilacqua, and New York Archbishop Edward Egan. Shortly thereafter, Egan penned a statement that was read at masses across his diocese that said voters should cast their ballots for those who "share our commitment to fundamental rights for the unborn, those advanced in age, the sick and the needy."[13] Washington Cardinal James Hickey told his parishioners that there was "one issue that rises above the others" when they vote and that Catholics "need to ask which candidate will offer even a measure of protection for the unborn."[14]

Despite concerted efforts on the part of the Catholic bishops and the Bush campaign to steer Catholics away from pro-choice candidates and toward the GOP, Gore won the much-contested "Catholic vote" by two points, 49 to 47 percent, as well as the overall popular vote, but, as history well knows, lost the electoral vote. Bush, however, did pull off victories in the key Catholic swing states of Missouri and Ohio, which were essential to his electoral vote victory, and did significantly better among Catholics than other recent GOP presidential candidates, suggesting that Republican efforts to make inroads among conservative Catholic voters were paying off.

.   .   .   .   .

By 2000 the political climate in the United States had polarized considerably. The Republicans had taken over Congress on the power of the Christian Right and Newt Gingrich's brand of hard-edged attack politics that painted political opponents in harsh personal terms as unpatriotic and out to destroy America. The politically motivated impeachment of President Bill Clinton had ratcheted up the political discord, which was then whipped into a froth by the emerging medium of twenty-four-hour cable news, particularly the conservative Fox News Channel, which debuted in 1996.[15]

Reproductive rights were both the source and the victim of this new polarization. In the mid-1990s, conservative anti-abortion groups like the Christian Coalition and the National Right to Life Committee began scoring votes on domestic and international family planning funding, in addition to abortion, on their influential congressional scorecards. Now, to get a favorable score Republican lawmakers, many of whom had traditionally supported family planning, had to vote against family planning as well as abortion. And as gerrymandering created more ideologically pure congressional districts, moderate Republicans increasingly found themselves "primaried" by Republican opponents who ran to the right of them on a position of absolute opposition to abortion and family planning funding. By the late 1990s, the moderate, pro–family planning Republican was becoming an endangered species, especially among the Republican leadership. In 1998, all the candidates for the top GOP leadership positions scored 100 percent on the Christian Coalition's scorecard, indicating opposition to both abortion and publicly funded family planning.[16]

A similar, if less dramatic, shift happened in the Democratic Party, as southern Democrats, who were often socially conservative and tied to the Democratic Party largely by antipathy toward the Republicans' historic support for civil rights, retired and were replaced by Republican Christian conservatives, who were ascendant in the South. The anti-abortion Democrat was becoming a thing of the past. While fully 57 percent of Democrats were opposed to abortion in 1979, according to sociologist D'Antonio, by 1996 that had plummeted to only 15 percent.[17]

When Democratic rising star and recently reelected Pennsylvania governor Bob Casey was refused a chance to address the 1992 Democratic convention about the party's increasingly stringent stance in favor of abortion rights, it signaled the marginalization of anti-abortion Democrats within the party. (Casey was the "Casey" in the landmark *Planned Parenthood of Pennsylvania vs. Casey* Supreme Court case that almost overturned *Roe*, which undoubtedly created some of the animosity toward him taking a major role in the convention.)[18]

Once elected, Bush and his allies in Congress wasted no time in fulfilling their promise to take the country in a more socially conservative direction. On his first day in office, Bush reinstated the Mexico City policy that prevented nongovernmental organizations (NGOs) from receiving U.S. family planning funding if they performed abortions or engaged in abortion advocacy. Congress dramatically expanded funding for "abstinence only" sex education that preached sexual abstinence to teens instead of giving them factual information about contraception and sexuality. These programs were infused with conservative religious notions about the importance of maintaining one's virginity until marriage, especially for women, and the responsibility of women to curb men's sexual appetites. They also tried to scare teens away from contraceptives by casting doubt about their effectiveness in preventing pregnancy and sexually transmitted diseases.

Then in May 2001 came word that Bush would nominate John Klink, an advisor to the Holy See's UN delegation, to head the State Department's Bureau of Population, Refugees and Migration, which is in charge of international refugee assistance. Klink was the architect of the Vatican's obstructionist strategy at the Cairo conference, where he was the floor manager of the Vatican delegation and had objected to the promotion of condoms to prevent AIDS and women's right to access family planning services. More disturbing to women's and refugee advocates was his opposition to making emergency contraception (EC) available to women refugees who had been raped as an act of war based on the Vatican's contention that the medication was an abortifacient. Klink had publicly mislabeled EC an abortifacient at the Cairo +5 review. He also served as the lead spokesperson when the Vatican defunded UNICEF in 1996 because it cosponsored a manual on emergency operations for refugee populations that mentioned providing EC to refugees when appropriate.[19]

Klink had been chosen for the position over Secretary of State Colin Powell's choice of a career civil servant in a move to curry favor with the

Vatican and Catholics. One Bush administration official called Klink the "Holy See's choice." With firsthand experience with Klink's activities at the United Nations on behalf of the Vatican, CFFC was quick to raise alarm in the larger reproductive rights community about the appointment. It produced a fact sheet about Klink detailing his opposition to condoms, family planning, and emergency contraception that was widely circulated as part of a successful lobbying effort to derail the nomination.[20]

Bush's push for Klink was part of a postelection effort to affirm his ties with conservative Catholics. The Bushes' first social engagement after they moved into the White House was a dinner at Washington Archbishop Theodore McCarrick's residence that included Archbishop Gabriel Montalvo, the Holy See's head diplomat, and Bishop Joseph Fiorenza, the current president of the NCCB. And right after Bush announced plans to launch his signature "faith-based" initiative to allow religious groups to participate in government-funded social service programs, he met with thirty Catholic leaders at the White House to solicit their support for the program. Bush also had a private lunch shortly after his election with Archbishop Egan and two high-profile conservative bishops, Paul Loverde of Arlington, Virginia, and Denver Archbishop Charles Chaput. Also at the lunch was *Crisis* magazine editor Deal Hudson, who had been instrumental in helping Rove craft his conservative Catholic–Protestant outreach strategy and who served as a conduit between Bush and conservative Catholics.[21]

Rove and Hudson were already strategizing about 2004. In April 2001, the RNC announced the formation of a Catholic Leadership Forum with Hudson as its head to begin building Catholic support for Bush's reelection. The White House also held a weekly conference call on Catholic strategy that included Hudson, Princeton University natural law scholar Robert George, and other prominent conservative Catholics. Bush's concerted outreach to Catholics prompted George to note, "[I]n 1960, John Kennedy went from Washington down to Texas to assure Protestant preachers that he would not obey the pope. In 2001, George Bush came from Texas up to Washington to assure a group of Catholic bishops that he would."[22]

The alliance between the Catholic and Christian Rights and the Republican Party was now fully realized. "What was new during the Bush administration was the common cause that anti-choice Catholics made with anti-choice Evangelicals. This made for much more formidable set of opponents," said Sara Seims, who was head of the Alan Guttmacher Institute, a leading reproductive rights think tank, at the time. This new alliance turned its sights not just on abortion, but also on family planning. In July 2002, the Bush administration announced that it would completely defund the United Nations Population Fund (UNFPA), directing the $34 million annual U.S. contribution that had been allocated for the program—12 percent of its total budget—to international programs that promoted maternal and child health.[23]

Bush said he was eliminating the funding because by working in China the UNFPA was complicit in China's strict "one child" population control program that had in the past included forced abortion and sterilization— even though by law no U.S. money could go to the China program. The right had been making the charge that the UNFPA was complicit in China's controversial program since the Reagan administration. During the 1984 Mexico City population conference, the United States required the UNFPA to certify that it wasn't engaged in abortion or coercive family planning programs. The 1985 Kemp-Kasten Amendment subsequently gave the president the authority to defund any organization that was found to take part in a "program of coercive abortion or involuntary sterilization." Although the UNFPA was at the time providing only technical support to the Chinese government about implementing voluntary programs, Presidents Ronald Reagan and George H. W. Bush both used the amendment to defund the organization. As a result, no U.S. contributions were made to the UNFPA from 1986 until Clinton came into office in 1993.[24]

A May 2002 State Department fact-finding mission to China, however, found no evidence that the UNFPA, which by the early 2000s had realized its goal of running a voluntary family planning pilot program in thirty-two districts in China, "knowingly supported or participated in the management of a program of coercive abortion or involuntary sterilization."[25]

Despite this and the UNFPA's assertion that its work in the country was aimed at moving China away from coercive programs, the Bush administration defunded the organization. It claimed that the UNFPA's presence in a district in which officials threatened to impose draconian fines on parents for having additional children was tantamount to taking part in a program of forced abortion. It also asserted that UNFPA expenditure on equipment such as computers and data-processing equipment "allows the Chinese government to implement more effectively its program of coercive abortion."[26]

Efforts to defund UNFPA had been led in Congress for years by Republican anti-abortion opponent Representative Chris Smith (NJ), who called the UNFPA "the chief apologist and cheerleader for China's coercive one-child-per-couple policy."[27] The campaign against UNFPA was orchestrated by Smith and a far-right Catholic think tank called the Population Research Institute (PRI), which was created by Human Life International founder Father Paul Marx to debunk the "myth" of overpopulation and oppose U.S. funding for international family planning programs. PRI underwrote a one-woman, three-day mission to China in 2001 to find evidence of UNFPA culpability in the Chinese program. The PRI employee, who spoke no Chinese and had no experience in family planning program evaluation, claimed to find a desk in a government family planning office in a district where coerced abortions reportedly took place that was used by an absent, unnamed UNFPA employee. Although the State Department mission couldn't find any such desk and UNFPA said it didn't have any employees outside of Beijing, PRI cited the mystery employee as the smoking gun the right had long sought as evidence of UNFPA's culpability in coerced abortions and successfully used the accusation to drum up support in Congress to defund UNFPA.[28]

The assaults on family planning continued throughout 2002. At the Fifth Asian and Pacific Population Conference in Bangkok in December, which was serving as the ten-year review of the Cairo population conference, the United States announced that it would not reaffirm the reproductive rights consensus reached at the Cairo and Beijing UN meetings because, echoing the Holy See's contention, it said the language in favor of family planning could be construed as promoting abortion. CFFC placed ads in major newspapers in Asia, Europe, and the United States to warn of the attempt by the Bush administration, the Vatican, and their allies to water down the Cairo language and support for family planning worldwide. "Bad politics is mixing with bad religion in a powerful axis of the Vatican and the newly conservative U.S. government," said Frances

Kissling. "Unless this attempt to undermine the Cairo agreement is stopped at the Bangkok meeting, we fear that the U.S. and the Vatican will turn important UN efforts to evaluate the success of family planning into polarized debates, thus blocking progress on making family planning available to all women and men."[29]

With conservative Catholic thought on family planning ascendant in U.S. policy, CFFC decided to tackle the UNFPA funding issue head-on. In September 2003, Kissling led a nine-member interfaith delegation of religious leaders, heads of faith-based organizations, and ethicists to China to conduct an assessment of UNFPA policies. The delegation visited Beijing and three Chinese provinces to assess the work of the UNFPA. The delegation, which had no restrictions placed on its activities by the Chinese government, concluded that "the charges against UNFPA made by its opponents, including PRI, are without foundation." It called UNFPA's pilot program a major catalyst in China's transition to a voluntary family planning program and said that abortion and sterilization were declining as contraceptive choices increased in the areas where UNFPA was active. "[W]e are convinced that UNFPA has made an invaluable contribution to women's reproductive health and rights in China," they concluded, calling the charges of conservatives in Congress and the Bush administration "unfounded" and saying that UNFPA funding should be restored.[30]

·   ·   ·   ·   ·

Even as the U.S. bishops were cementing their alliance with the Bush administration, the Vatican found itself increasingly under siege. In early 2002, the issue of Catholic clergy sex abuse, which had been brewing for some time, became a major national scandal after the *Boston Globe* published a series of Pulitzer Prize-winning articles detailing dozens of abuse allegations against five Boston-area priests. This followed on the heels of a scandal about the widespread sexual abuse of nuns by priests in developing countries that was revealed by the *National Catholic Reporter*. In March 2002, the Diocese of Boston agreed to pay $30 million to eighty-six victims of Father John Geoghan, who was convicted of sexually molesting a ten-year-old boy. By the end of the year, accusations were snowballing around the country. Most damaging to the hierarchy was evidence that some bishops and cardinals knew of the abuse but moved predator priests from diocese to diocese rather than removing them from contact with children or reporting them to law enforcement authorities.

With the U.S. bishops having taken little concrete action to address the scandal and the UN Special Session on Children scheduled for May 2002, Kissling announced that a coalition of progressive Catholic groups and abuse victims would ask the United Nations to hold the Vatican accountable for violating the Convention on the Rights of the Child, to which it was a signatory. She called on the Vatican to apologize and make public a plan to ensure that abuse did not occur in the future. "We come to the United Nations because there is no sign that Catholic bishops or the institutional church are prepared to deal with this problem in a definitive way that will end pedophilia in the church," she said. The meeting ended without an apology from the Vatican.[31]

In December 2003, longtime outspoken abortion opponent Cardinal Law of Boston, who just a few years before had boomed so confidently that pro-choice politicians were wrong and only he was "right," resigned, becoming the first U.S. prelate to step down as a result of the burgeoning sex abuse scandal. A June meeting of the U.S. bishops had ended with much talk of the horrors of abuse but without agreement on concrete steps to remove priests who had abused children from the priesthood or calls for bishops who had been complicit to resign.

The other issue that was damaging the hierarchy's image was its response to the AIDS epidemic, which by the early 2000s was a full-blown global health crisis. No issue so well illustrated the human cost of the hierarchy's intransigence on contraception. The Vatican insisted from the start of the epidemic that there was no room for compromise on its position that condoms could never be used, even if it was to prevent the transmission of HIV rather than thwart conception. In his first public comments on the AIDS crisis in 1989, Pope John Paul II said condom use to prevent AIDS was "morally illicit" and "profoundly damaging to the dignity of the human beings."[32]

To the hierarchy, the only answer was a return to traditional sexual morality that eschewed nonreproductive sex, including premarital sex and gay sex. They saw AIDS as a symptom of a moral failing—an "immunodeficiency in existential values" in the pope's words—that couldn't be corrected simply by blocking transmission of the virus. "The Vatican's own rhetoric made it hard for them to back down on contraception when AIDS came along. If something is intrinsically evil you can't have much movement," said theologian Anthony Padovano.[33]

Nowhere was this intransigence more devastating than in sub-Saharan Africa, which had some of the world's highest rates of HIV infection and AIDS mortality combined with influential Catholic prelates in countries with significant Catholic populations such as Angola, Congo, Kenya, Nigeria, Rwanda, Tanzania, and Uganda. In 1990, the pope visited Tanzania, which was at the time the epicenter of the African epidemic, with an estimated 1 million HIV-positive people out of a population of 24 million. The population of working-age adults was hit so hard by the disease that there were entire villages populated with nothing but orphans and the elderly who struggled to care for them. Public health officials were trying frantically to promote condom use in a desperately poor culture where premarital sexual experience was common, it was the prerogative of men to sleep with women outside of marriage, and women had little leverage to demand their partners practice safe sex. When John Paul II told the faithful that using a condom was a sin in any circumstance, AIDS activists were devastated. In one afternoon, wrote journalist Jonathan Clayton, the pope "sentenced millions of Africans to death."[34]

Paul Zeitz, who was head of the Global AIDS Alliance at the time, concurred with this assessment. "John Paul II's statement was very detrimental at a crucial moment in the epidemic. It created confusion and inaction. People don't take on prevention when there is uncertainty," he said.[35]

The sheer direness of the AIDS crisis made some in the hierarchy willing to bend the rules regarding contraceptives. The French and the German bishops' conferences spoke out in favor of condom use to protect partners in couples in which one member was already HIV-positive. In 1988, the U.S. bishops released a policy statement that condemned condoms as a primary prevention strategy but said that "accurate information about prophylactic devices" could be provided in the context of programs that stressed abstinence until marriage. The bishops also said that an HIV-positive person who was unlikely to abstain from sex could be counseled about condom use as the "lesser evil."[36] Many theologians felt that the seriousness of the AIDS epidemic and the moral responsibility of not infecting another person with HIV outweighed the ban on contraceptives, especially because the primary purpose was to prevent death, not conception. "The consistent thinking of the Catholic church has affirmed the lesser of two evils," wrote Padovano. "This approach reasons that the ambiguity of choices sometimes makes it necessary to prefer one evil in order to prevent a greater evil."[37]

The U.S. bishops' statement, however, was denounced by Cardinals O'Connor and Law and other conservatives within the bishops' conference, which split over the statement much along the same lines it had over abortion. Within six months the bishops released a new statement that unequivocally condemned safe-sex education to prevent AIDS. Days later O'Connor, who had fought to block a plan to distribute condoms in New York City's public high schools, told the Vatican's first conference on AIDS that the promotion of condoms to prevent the spread of AIDS was a lie "perpetrated often for political reasons on the part of public officials."[38]

During the next decade, members of the hierarchy asserted that the use of condoms to fight AIDS would lead to sexual promiscuity that would only worsen the epidemic. They also cast doubt on the effectiveness of condoms as a mechanism to prevent the transmission of HIV. "Parents must reject the promotion of so-called 'safe sex' or 'safer sex,' a dangerous and immoral policy based on the deluded theory that the condom can provide adequate protection against AIDS," wrote two senior members of the Vatican's Pontifical Council on the Family.[39] Another Vatican official called using condoms to protect against HIV "playing Russian roulette." The Vatican denounced the inclusion of any mention of condoms in anti-AIDS programs at the Cairo conference and the Cairo +5 review.[40]

The Vatican's intransigence on condoms had concrete implications because the Catholic Church, through its hospitals, orphanages, hospices, and outreach programs, is the largest single provider of HIV/AIDS care in the world and an especially important provider in developing countries.[41] As a result of Vatican policy, health care and social services workers associated with Catholic institutions cannot counsel patients about safe sex or distribute condoms. The result is that although Catholic institutions often provide excellent care to AIDS patients—care that in many cases no one else is willing or able to provide—they can't work to ensure that AIDS patients don't pass the virus to others in violation of accepted public health practices. "If you are found to be HIV positive and married and aren't offered condoms right there, that is dangerous," said Zeitz.[42]

There is anecdotal evidence, however, that Catholic providers do find ways to put the needs of patients first. Zeitz remembered visiting the Catholic archdiocese in Angola in the early 2000s at the height of the AIDS epidemic. No one would talk publicly about condoms, but when he went to the archdiocese he found "boxes and boxes of condoms for parishioners."[43] Peter Piot, former head of the Joint UN Program on HIV/AIDS, recalled meeting nuns in South Africa who were distributing condoms. When he asked how they could do it, one nun replied, "Rome is a long way away."[44]

Frustration with the Catholic hierarchy's official policy was running so high during an historic three-day UN meeting on AIDS in June 2001 that Piot took the unprecedented step of publically calling out the Vatican. "When priests preach against using contraception, they are committing a serious mistake which is costing human lives," he said. "We do not ask the church to promote contraception, but merely to stop banning its use."[45]

The following month South African Bishop Kevin Dowling, who was the prelate of the mining town of Rustenberg, which had a 50 percent HIV infection rate among pregnant women, made headlines when he lobbied the South African bishops to approve condom use. "My personal stance on this issue comes out of much reflection, not to say anguish over the enormity of the suffering. . . . Every week I am with people dying in their huts and shacks," he said.[46]

The South African Bishops' Conference, however, refused to sanction condom use, arguing that condoms were "one of the main reasons for the spread of HIV/AIDS." It was a wrenching example of how the Vatican was willing to put adherence to a doctrine that didn't have much credibility in the first place above human lives.[47]

"The way that poor people suffered because of this was very much on our minds," said CFFC's Jon O'Brien. It was particularly personal to him because he had campaigned to decriminalize the sale of condoms in Ireland. On December 1, 2001—World AIDS Day—CFFC launched the Condoms4Life campaign to raise awareness about the effects of the Catholic hierarchy's ban on condoms. The campaign debuted with ads in the *Washington Post* and posters throughout the Washington, D.C., transit system and was expanded internationally in early 2002. The ads declared, "Because the bishops ban condoms, innocent people die."[48]

"It was important to challenge the bishops' position," said O'Brien. "Much like the issue with emergency contraception and rape victims, a light bulb went off in people's heads. When people saw these ads, the reaction was 'I always wanted to say that.'"[49]

The D.C. subway ads quickly caused a furor, with officials from the Washington Archdiocese complaining that the ads should be removed because they contained false information—they disputed that the hierarchy had the authority to "ban" condoms. The bishops and the Catholic League also charged anti-Catholicism, saying the ads mocked the bishops. They called on local Catholics to complain to Metro authorities—which generated a total of twenty-four complaints. The campaign was covered by CNN and the BBC and by political talk shows like the *O'Reilly Factor* and *Crossfire*, where Kissling went head to head with the Catholic League's Bill Donohue, bringing further attention to the human toll of the condom ban.

As with family planning, however, conservative forces were ascendant in U.S. policy. In 2003, when Congress voted to fund President Bush's historic, five-year, $15 billion Emergency Plan for AIDS Relief (PEPFAR), Representative Smith successfully included a conscience clause pushed by the Catholic hierarchy that exempted any organization receiving PEPFAR funding from having to "endorse, utilize or participate in a prevention method to which the organization has a religious or moral objection." This provision, which codified the right of Catholic-affiliated institutions and organizations to withhold information about condoms and safe-sex practices, was a major victory for the hierarchy because Catholic Relief Services was in line to become a major recipient of PEPFAR funding. Representative Joseph Pitts (R-PA) added another amendment, supported by the bishops, that required one-third of all PEPFAR funding to go to programs that promote sexual abstinence until marriage as a remedy for AIDS.

In October 2003, AIDS activists and international public health officials were aghast when Cardinal Alfonso López Trujillo, head of the Vatican's Pontifical Council on the Family, made the patently false statement on a BBC television show that HIV could "easily pass" through condoms.[50] The statement gave new urgency to CFFC's "Condoms4Life" campaign. The organization unveiled a new series of ads for World AIDS Day 2003 with the message "Good Catholics Use Condoms." With AIDS and the hierarchy in the headlines, the campaign received extensive media coverage in *Newsweek*, Nicholas Kristoff's column in the *New York Times*, and the major wire services. "The ads were great and really effective," said Zeitz, noting the importance of progressive religious voices in arguing for condom use to prevent AIDS at a critical point in the epidemic.[51]

.   .   .   .   .

The AIDS epidemic illustrated the importance of a progressive Catholic voice in international policy forums. Nowhere was this better illustrated than in Europe in the early 2000s as historic negotiations were under way to enlarge the European Union (EU). The Catholic Church was an increasingly beleaguered institution in European countries as religious adherence and mass attendance plummeted. Surveys found that fewer than 10 percent of Catholics in France and only about 30 percent of Catholics in Italy attended mass on a regular basis.[52]

As the EU Constitution was being negotiated, the Vatican was lobbying hard for provisions to shore up its position in European affairs, including special nonstate consultative status at the European Parliament similar to the status it held at the United Nations. It also wanted a specific reference in the new constitution to God and to Europe's Christian roots. "Having experienced the desire of the Holy See for a privileged place in the United Nations, we are increasingly concerned that the Vatican is seeking similar privileges and power within the European Union," said Kissling.[53]

Catholics for a Free Choice had been active in heavily Catholic European countries such as Poland and Ireland since the 1990s. When Ireland contemplated changes to its laws banning nearly all abortions, CFFC made two submissions to the Irish Interdepartmental Working Group on Abortion that were widely covered in the *Irish Times*. It outlined why even in a majority Catholic country like Ireland laws governing access to abortion didn't need to adhere to the official Catholic position. The organization also began documenting the rise of conservative Catholic influence in Europe, as the Vatican, Vatican-allied groups like Opus Dei, and lay traditionalist and anti-abortion organizations became increasingly assertive.

In November 2001, CFFC organized the first seminar on the role of religion in European policy at the European Parliament and hired its first coordinator for European activities.

In 2003, CFFC led a coalition of nearly 200 organizations petitioning the European Convention to reject Article 51 to the European Constitution, which would grant special exemptions from European law to religious organizations. Article 51 was eventually adopted, but without mention of Europe's "Christian roots," which the Vatican had aggressively lobbied for.

CFFC founded the European Parliament All Party Working Group on the Separation of Religion and Politics to promote discussion on the role of religion in European policy forums as Vatican-allied conservative organizations made their presence felt. "These groups don't like to work in the open—if you can explain their agenda, reasonable people will distance themselves," said Neil Datta, secretary of the European Parliamentary Forum on Population and Development. He noted that much like in the United Nations, the Vatican takes advantage of the traditional deference given to an "observer state" to send delegates to ministerial meetings of the Council of Europe, where it lobbies against gay rights and abortion rights. Sometimes it lends its seat to anti-choice activists such as Austin Ruse of the Catholic Family and Human Rights Institute. In the European Union, it partners with far-right conservative groups to make many of the same claims that it makes at the United Nations—that there is a far-left conspiracy to promote widespread abortion and disrespect for the family. "The Catholic Church is reaching out to the traditionalist movement and moving further to the right. CFFC has been helpful in giving us insight on these issues from a religious perspective," said Datta.[54]

It is in Latin America, however, where Catholicism has remained vibrant—some 85 percent of the population is Catholic—and the power of the hierarchy strong, that the development of a Catholic pro-choice movement has been most critical. Frances Kissling and Rosemary Radford Ruether were the original evangelists for the idea that with the right tools and training, Catholic women could come together to challenge the seemingly unchallengeable hierarchy in Latin America. They each traveled to the region numerous times. Ruether gave lectures in feminist Catholic theology. Kissling worked to locate women who had her passion for the cause, the courage to stand up to the pressure of the hierarchy, and the skills to run a credible movement out of a one- or two-woman office. "These women for the most part are not from the elite but really understand how to appropriate the theological and canon law discourse," said Ruether, who counts helping to establish a Latin American Catholic prochoice network as among the defining accomplishments of her career. The nine-country Catholics for the Right to Decide (CDD) network now encompasses Argentina, Bolivia, Brazil, Chile, Colombia, El Salvador, Mexico, Nicaragua, and Paraguay.[55]

The growth of the Mexican group illustrates the path that many of these groups took. Maria Consuelo Mejia still remembers attending a prepcom for the Cairo conference in New York in 1993 and seeing a flyer for a workshop titled "Everything You Wanted to Know about the Vatican and Were Afraid to Ask." She was already working on reproductive health issues and had experienced firsthand the repression by the hierarchy when it orchestrated a crackdown on the nuns who operated the Marymount School she attended in Bogota because the school was following the more open social justice policies of Vatican II. "That is how I came to understand that there were a lot of positions in the church and that the Vatican didn't always appreciate a church that was committed to social justice," she said. She attended the workshop, met Kissling, and was hooked. "When I saw this social justice perspective related to women's and sexual and reproductive rights, I knew this was my mission," she said. A year later, Kissling hired her to run CDD Mexico.[56]

In the early years, the small organization received hands-on support from Kissling and the CFFC international staff. Mejia slowly built up the organization's credibility with the reproductive rights and the human rights communities—the latter being especially politically important in Mexico—and with the media. When the legislature in the state of Guanajuato passed a bill in 2000 that would remove rape as one of the few grounds for a legal abortion and sentence women who had abortions to three years in jail, CDD Mexico and other reproductive rights groups gained national attention when they occupied a makeshift jail cell in front of the legislature, "incarcerated" in solidarity with women who had had abortions. CDD Mexico also commissioned an independent poll that found that 63 percent of Mexicans opposed the new law, which was eventually vetoed by the governor. That same year CDD Mexico joined four other reproductive rights groups to found the National Alliance for the Right to Decide to work toward the decriminalization of abortion. In 2002, it received a national human rights award, which cemented its stature in the human rights community. "After that we grew up," said Mejia, and no longer required as much support from CFFC.[57]

In 2007, the Mexican reproductive rights movement registered a major triumph when the Mexico City legislature voted to legalize early abortion and provide abortion free of charge to any woman who wanted it. The hierarchy lobbied mightily against the bill. Bishops threatened to excommunicate legislators who voted for the measure, and a spokesperson for the bishops called supporters of the bill "child killers" and said that Catholics for the Right to Decide should be renamed "murderers for the right to kill children." But it the end it was to no avail; the bill passed. "We worked eighteen years to change the discourse around abortion, to inform society and widen the scope of support," said Mejia. "Our main strategy has been to document contradictions between the Catholic tradition, what the bishops say it is, and what believers think and say."[58]

.   .   .   .   .

In early 2003, the Bush administration's effort to court Catholic voters for Bush's second term got an unexpected push when Cardinal Joseph Ratzinger released the Vatican's first formal statement on the participation of Catholics in political life. In it he said that even in a democracy, Catholics must be guided by certain inalienable precepts of moral law, especially the protection of life. He cast support for abortion as part of an unacceptable trend toward moral relativism that was contrary not only to Catholicism but to the fundamental tenets of Christianity. As such, he said, it was a violation of natural law that went beyond the specifics of Catholic doctrine and could never be tolerated. He wrote that Catholic lawmakers have a "grave and clear obligation" to oppose "any law that attacks human life."[59]

Ratzinger's letter was a clear rebuff to what had become known as the "Cuomo doctrine"—personally opposed to abortion but pro-choice in voting on the issue as a matter of representing a plurality of voters. It was also a gift to conservative Catholics who had been trying to make common cause with the Republican Party, particularly *Crisis* magazine's Hudson. Hudson was serving as an advisor to Bush on courting the Catholic vote and was a major strategist behind efforts to coalesce a conservative Evangelical–Catholic voting bloc that relied heavily on Catholics who attended mass every week, who were assumed to be more traditional, to support the GOP. Calling it the "best news I have heard all year," Hudson told subscribers to his e-mail column that Ratzinger's statement meant that "Catholic politicians need to act like Catholics."[60]

Hudson also sought to discredit CFFC, the voice most capable of countering right-wing claims about the "Catholic" position on abortion, noting that Ratzinger said that "organizations founded on Catholic principles" that support "political forces or movements with positions contrary to the moral and social teaching of the Church on fundamental ethical questions" contradict "basic principles of Christian conscience."[61]

Hudson also used the doctrinal note to pillory Massachusetts Democratic senator John Kerry, who was a pro-choice Catholic and one of the front-runners for the 2004 Democratic presidential nomination, as insufficiently Catholic. "His responsibility to the Faith must always come first, or he simply isn't living that Faith," wrote Hudson to supporters.[62]

For his part, Kerry, who had been an altar boy, wore a crucifix, and attended mass most Sundays, defended his practice of Catholicism and his interpretation of Catholic doctrine as it applied to the separation of church and state. He said that he had "enormous respect for the words and teachings of the Vatican," but that "as a public servant I've never forgotten the lasting legacy of President Kennedy, who made it clear that in accordance with the separation of church and state no elected official should be 'limited or conditioned by any religious oath, ritual or obligation.'"[63]

But conservatives were arguing that the Vatican had confirmed that abortion was not a matter to which Catholics could apply such "prudential judgment"—the application of Catholic moral principles to specific policy choices—but a non-negotiable issue that trumped separation of church and state. They were agitating for bishops to make examples of pro-choice Catholics. Sacramento Bishop William Weigand was the first to take the bait. During a sermon less than a week after the release of Ratzinger's statement, he said that any Catholic who was pro-choice "is not in good standing with the church" and said that Democratic governor Gray Davis should refrain from receiving communion until he "has a change of heart."[64]

The same day, the American Life League (ALL) debuted its "Deadly Dozen" campaign in the *Washington Times* with a "wanted" ad for twelve pro-choice Catholic senators it said were "fraudulently claiming Catholic faith." The list included Kerry, Ted Kennedy, Minority Leader Tom Daschle (D-SD), and Barbara Mikulski (D-MD). ALL called on "all bishops and priests to respectfully refuse Holy Communion to these and all public figures whose unrepentant support for the killing of babies in the womb defiles the Body of Christ."[65]

Shortly thereafter it was reported that Daschle received a letter from a bishop in his home state of South Dakota telling him to remove all references to his Catholicism from his official biography. Hudson announced that *Crisis* would publish an exposé on "so-called pro-choice 'Catholic' politicians" to expose them "for the hucksters they are."[66]

In mid-September, Hudson organized a closed-door meeting of leading conservative Catholics with the leaders of the U.S. bishops' conference to press the bishops to publicly reprimand pro-choice Catholics. They wanted the bishops to say that pro-choice Catholics should be denied public honors or speaking engagements at places that were "officially" Catholic, like Catholic universities. They also wanted pro-choice Catholics to be barred from serving in leadership positions related to the church. Specifically, they were upset that former representative Leon Panetta (D-CA), who was pro-choice, had been appointed to the bishops' panel on sexual abuse in the church and that the bishops had recently met with progressive Catholics to discuss issues facing the church.[67]

With speculation growing about how Ratzinger's guidance would be applied in the upcoming election, the U.S. bishops' conference announced in November 2003 that it would create a task force under the direction of Washington, D.C., Cardinal Theodore McCarrick to formulate guidance for bishops on applying Ratzinger's statement. But in a tacit admission of what a powder keg the issue had become, the bishops said that the recommendations wouldn't be made public until after the 2004 presidential race. In late January 2004, just as it was becoming apparent that Kerry was the likely Democratic nominee, several members of the clergy took matters into their own hands. St. Louis Archbishop Raymond Burke said he would withhold communion from Kerry if he presented himself for the sacrament in his diocese. The pastor of Senator Richard Durbin's church in Springfield, Illinois, said he would refuse communion to the pro-choice Democrat.[68]

With Burke's comments in the headlines and Kerry scheduled to address a major pro-choice march, a Vatican official delivering a briefing was asked if withholding communion was the correct course of action with "unambiguously pro-abortion" Catholic lawmakers. Cardinal Francis Arinze said, "Yes. Objectively, the answer is clear. The person is not fit. If he shouldn't receive it, then it shouldn't be given." When asked specifically about Kerry, he replied that "the norm of the church is clear" and that the U.S. bishops should "interpret it."[69]

Arinze's comments reignited the question of how to reconcile Kerry's Catholicism with his pro-choice stance. Kerry, who met privately with Cardinal McCarrick, who was heading up the bishops' task force, reiterated that as a public official he had to respect the separation of church and state, but that did little to quell the growing controversy.[70]

In May, Newark, New Jersey, Archbishop John Myers wrote in the diocesan newspaper that it was "objectively dishonest" for Catholics who disagreed with the church on nonnegotiable issues like abortion to receive communion, which prompted pro-choice Democratic governor James McGreevy to say he would refrain from taking the sacrament. A week later, Colorado Springs Bishop Michael Sheridan issued a pastoral letter that said that Catholics who defied church teaching on abortion or same-sex marriage were making a "mockery" of the faith and should not receive communion.[71]

The sacrament of communion was fast becoming a political football. It was being used by the Catholic Right, in alliance with a handful of bishops, to reanimate the old question of whether a "good" Catholic could support abortion rights just as the first major-party Catholic candidate since Geraldine Ferraro stepped to the plate. With ALL still running ads urging the bishops to use communion to discipline wayward politicians, fortyeight Catholic congressional Democrats sent a letter to McCarrick decrying the tactic and warning that the bishops were "allowing the church to be used for partisan purposes."[72]

As Catholics, the group said, they did not "believe it is our role to legislate the teachings of the Catholic Church." They also said that "it would be wrong for a bishop to deny the sacrament of Holy Communion to an individual on the basis of a voting record." Among the signatories were a dozen pro-life Democrats. One of them, Michigan Representative Bart Stupak, noted that the bishops condemned the Iraq War but said he didn't "see them saying to all the people who voted for it, you can't receive communion."[73]

By Easter, speculation about whether Kerry or other avowedly pro-choice Catholics like House Minority Leader Nancy Pelosi (D-CA) would dare present themselves for communion or whether a priest would have the nerve to deny it to his or her face had turned into a full-scale media frenzy. Paparazzi clustered outside of Kerry's church on "wafer watch." With the spectacle of the media stalking churchgoers all over the national news, Kissling accused conservative Catholics of politicizing the Eucharist to score political points. "By attacking Sen. Kerry's practice of faith, conservative Bush Catholics hope to deny him the support of mainstream Catholics," she wrote.[74]

A number of bishops, however, including McCarrick, who met with pro-choice House Democrats to hear their concerns, voiced their reluctance to see communion—which to Catholics is literally the body and blood of Christ—turned into a political weapon. CFFC worked to emphasize how serious such denials would be doctrinally and how little overall support there was in the bishops' conference for such a draconian measure. It conducted a widely reported phone survey of all the U.S. Catholic dioceses and found that only 4 bishops out of some 300 said they would deny communion to pro-choice policymakers. Another 15 said they would ask them to voluntarily refrain; fully 135 said that such sanctions were not appropriate.

With the issue in the headlines and the election rapidly approaching, the bishops realized they needed to formulate some kind of guidance on the issue and announced they would do so at their upcoming June meeting. The result was "Catholics in Political Life," which said that Catholics shouldn't create a divide between "belief and public action, between moral principles and political choices." They said that Catholic public officials who consistently support abortion rights risk "cooperating in evil" and urged bishops to counsel such Catholics in the hope that they would reform and conform to church teaching. The bishops said that such politicians could be denied communion at the discretion of individual bishops but fell short of mandating ecclesiastical sanctions.

The bishops had largely maintained the status quo. Baltimore Cardinal William Keeler said sentiment against denying communion ran 3–1 at the conference. Many bishops were afraid that taking such a position was against the meaning of communion, which is what unites Catholics. Others were afraid to dilute the tradition of the all-powerful local bishop who had the power to set policies in his diocese. Still others worried that it would lead to the marginalization of Catholics in public life.[75]

Groups like ALL, which had been pushing the bishops to crack down on pro-choice Catholics, were furious. They charged that McCarrick had watered down a letter from Ratzinger to the bishops' conference that took a much tougher stance. Ratzinger said that a Catholic politician who "consistently" campaigned and voted for permissive abortion laws was formally cooperating in evil, which Catholics are never allowed to do in the case of abortion, and should be told by his pastor that "he is not to present himself for Holy Communion." If the politician refused to accept such guidance, the minister distributing communion "must refuse to distribute it," not as a sanction or a judgment of guilt but as a reaction to the "person's public unworthiness to receive Holy Communion"—in other words, to avoid the "scandal" of having a publicly pro-choice Catholic receive communion. McCarrick denied that Ratzinger's letter had been misrepresented to the bishops and said his communications with Ratzinger did not reach the conclusion that communion must be denied. The Vatican moved quickly to squash any sign of discord. McCarrick released a letter to him from Ratzinger that acknowledged receipt of the U.S. bishops' statement and said that their guidance was "very much in harmony with the general principles."[76]

The dispute inadvertently shed light on just how much theological leeway there was in decisions over the morality of abortion—particularly the question of just how close to abortion was "too close" for a Catholic politician or voter. In his letter, Ratzinger waded into the thorny theological issue of "cooperation." Catholic theology identifies various degree of cooperation with evil; the closer the degree of cooperation, the greater the sin or prohibition. Formal cooperation is the direct, intended participation in another's evil act and is never allowed in the case of what the church considers an intrinsically evil act such as abortion. Material cooperation, which itself has several degrees, occurs when one participates in some way in the wrong act but doesn't intend the outcome. Immediate material cooperation contributes to the performance of the act in an essential way and can be just as prohibited as formal cooperation. Mediate material cooperation is the provision only of assistance in the evil act and can be justified if it prevents a greater evil. Remote material cooperation only constitutes a casual contribution; it is the furthest removed from the evil act.[77]

In the case of abortion, the church considers those directly involved in the abortion—the doctor who performs the procedure and the woman who procures it—to be formal cooperators in evil. Culpability for others' degrees of involvement depends on the circumstances but generally is considered some level of material cooperation, depending both on the degree of closeness to the act and the intent of the cooperator. Ratzinger sparked a theological controversy when he said that although a Catholic would be guilty of formal cooperation and unworthy to receive communion if he or she voted for a candidate because of his or her "permissive stand on abortion," a Catholic could in good conscience vote for that candidate for other reasons. This, he said, would be remote material cooperation, "which can be permitted in the presence of proportionate reasons."[78]

Father Andrew Greeley hailed the Vatican for saying that "Catholics can vote for Kerry." But the Vatican denied it had meant to "clear the way for Catholics to vote for candidates who are in favor of laws permitting abortions." It said it was simply clarifying that such a vote did not automatically disqualify Catholics from receiving communion. But the dispute made clear that even at the highest levels of Vatican theology there was a great deal of inherent flexibility in Catholic doctrine that made it impossible to make simple pronouncements regarding pro-choice Catholics and communion.[79]

But with the election rapidly approaching, conservatives pressed their case, trying to warn Catholics away from voting for Kerry. Newark Archbishop Myers penned a *Wall Street Journal* op-ed that said nothing could excuse voting for a pro-choice Catholic. Robert George and Father Richard Neuhaus convened a conference at Chicago's Ava Maria Law

School arguing the same point, which was echoed by papal biographer George Weigel in his syndicated column. But the Catholic Right was now missing its chief strategist and most direct connection to the White House. Deal Hudson resigned as an advisor to the Bush campaign and the RNC in August after a student accused him of sexually harassing her when he was a professor at Fordham University.[80]

Catholic outreach continued under other advisors like Leonard Leo of the Federalist Society. The slack was also taken up by Bill Donohue of the Catholic League, who had been trying since the summer of 2002 to make political hay out of the fact that the Democratic National Committee (DNC) had a link to CFFC on its web page of allied organizations and no links to any other Catholic groups. Donohue accused the DNC of giving legitimacy to an "anti-Catholic front-group" that had been called a fraud by the U.S. bishops.[81]

Donohue made little headway in getting under the DNC's skin, however, until June, when he got the Kerry campaign to silence its newly hired director of religious outreach, Mara Vanderslice, after he accused her of being an "ultra-leftist who consorts with anti-Catholic bigots" because of her advocacy with progressive groups like ACT UP (AIDS Coalition to Unleash Power). The accusations were fabricated to gin up one of Donohue's made-for-cable-TV controversies. But with polls showing that fewer than 10 percent of Americans thought Kerry, who was reticent to talk publicly about his religiosity, was a man of strong faith and the debate about communion and Kerry's Catholic-ness still ongoing, the campaign backed down.[82]

Having found his point of leverage, Donohue struck again in August. Brenda Peterson, an ordained Disciples of Christ minister, served as the head of religious outreach for the DNC for a total of eight days before she was forced to resign after Donohue turned up the fact that she had signed an amicus brief in favor of removing "under God" from the Pledge of Allegiance.

With Kerry faltering in the polls and questions about his religiosity lingering, Donohue had successfully torpedoed both people the Democrats had hired to get out the message that Kerry was a committed Catholic despite his disagreement with the bishops on abortion. In fact, Senator Durbin had his staff compare the voting records of Catholic Democrats in the Senate with the stated legislative priorities of the U.S. bishops and found that Kerry had the single highest rating, supporting the priorities of the bishops 60 percent of the time. But Kerry's overall consistent support for the teachings of the church were lost in the noise surrounding communion and abortion. In hindsight, said Peterson, the short-lived head of religious outreach, the DNC hadn't understood "who Donohue was or where he fit on the Catholic-religious continuum." They didn't understand, she said, that he was "a partisan, a member of the religious right intent on discrediting people of faith who signed on with Kerry."[83]

As Kerry's religious outreach faltered, the RNC was fielding a massive Catholic mobilization effort that included a staff of paid field coordinators, 3,000 volunteer Catholic team leaders, and 52,000 field volunteers. RNC head Ed Gillespie coordinated a swing-state speaking tour for well-known Catholic Republicans. The RNC collected directories from Catholic churches, reanimating a technique that had been successfully used to build lists of Republican-leaning voters for the religious right. It launched the "KerryWrongForCatholics.com" website to point out all the ways in which the Democratic candidate disagreed with the bishops on "life" issues.[84]

When the bishops' conference failed to agree on wording for its quadrennial preelection statement on voting guidance for Catholics, with hardliners pushing to elevate abortion above other issues, a little-known Catholic apologetics organization called Catholic Answers stepped in to fill the void. Millions of copies of its *Voter's Guide for Serious Catholics* were distributed in parishes around the country. The guide listed five "nonnegotiable issues" that it said disqualified candidates from consideration by Catholics: support for abortion, euthanasia, same-sex marriage, embryonic stem cell research, and human cloning. The bishops of Phoenix and St. Louis gave the guide their official blessing, even as other bishops refused to distribute it and the bishops' conference steered voters to its 2000 voting statement.[85]

Individual bishops continued their politicking. Denver Archbishop Chaput, who discussed Catholic voting priorities in fourteen of his twenty-eight columns in the diocesan newspaper in 2004, made news around the country when he said that a vote for Kerry was a sin that must be confessed before a Catholic would be fit to receive communion. His archdiocese organized a massive voter registration drive. Archbishop Raymond Burke of St. Louis also issued a statement saying voting for Kerry was a sin. Pittsburgh Cardinal Justin Rigali, who had preached that Catholics had an obligation to vote for pro-life candidates, made an appearance with Bush in the critical swing state of Pennsylvania.[86]

The *National Catholic Reporter* decried the bishops' statements as part of "a deliberate and decided attempt to delegitimize the Democratic Party in the eyes of American Catholic voters." It said that "never has such a small band of ideological partisans attempted to make their narrow reading of a political race the undisputed view of the church."[87]

With time to the election dwindling, CFFC formally filed a complaint with the IRS against the Archdiocese of St. Louis, the Archdiocese of Denver, Catholic Answers, and Priests for Life for violating their non-profit, tax-exempt status by explicitly urging Catholics to vote against Kerry. Kissling said the "level of electioneering by Catholic conservative bishops and lay people is unprecedented" and needed to be stopped, but she acknowledged that little could happen before the election.[88]

As the election approached, this band of ideological partisans— Republican political operatives and conservative Catholic leaders and organizations—worked hand-in-glove to create the impression of a Catholic groundswell for Bush as far-right Catholic doctrine, political activism, and party politics fused. Few understood the depth or extent of the coordinated, far-right conservative Catholic effort that was directed against Kerry. For example, when the *Catholic Register* interviewed one of the thousands of volunteers who were out the Sunday before the election distributing 75,000 Catholic Answers voting guides in church parking lots across the swing states, it failed to mention that the "volunteer" who represented herself as one of thousands of Catholics activated by Kerry's abortion stance was a Bush political appointee. Jacqueline Halbig was the deputy director of the Center for Faith-Based and Community Initiatives at the Department of Health and Human Services, which was one of Bush's signature programs to infuse religion into civic life. Halbig, who had worked as a lobbyist for the Christian Coalition, the Family Research Council, and Concerned Women for America, helped found the National Catholic Prayer Breakfast, one of the most successful and high-profile GOP Catholic outreach efforts, with, among other Republican political operatives, Austin Ruse of the Catholic Family and Human Rights Institute and Leonard Leo of the Federalist Society.[89]

In the end, Kerry lost the election and the Catholic vote by an embarrassing 5 percentage points to a non-Catholic. Bush beat Kerry by more than 10 points among Catholics in über-critical states like Ohio and Florida. As with most unsuccessful candidates, Kerry lost for a number of reasons. His campaign lacked the nimbleness to respond in an increasingly polarized and "post-fact" media environment and didn't successfully refute the "Swift Boat" charges designed to discredit his military service at a key point in the campaign. He was unable to capitalize on Bush's weaknesses as president to make a compelling case for why he should be elected. He failed to articulate an authentic progressive Catholic identity at a time when politics was increasingly infused with religious discourse.

Republicans crowed that they had proved that a crucial margin of Catholics would not vote for a pro-choice Democrat and boasted of a lasting political realignment of religious churchgoers. The reality, however, was never that clear. Kerry's poor performance with Catholics was a reflection of his poor performance with voters in general; he also performed relatively poorly with other traditional Democratic constituencies such as women, Hispanics, and urbanites. At the same time, he won Catholics in hotly contested Pennsylvania, where he also won regular churchgoers by 4 percentage points.[90]

An exit poll that indicated that "moral values" were voters' number one concern and that 80 percent of these "values voters" had supported Bush was widely used to support the contention that Kerry was abandoned by religious voters. The poll, however, didn't define which "moral values" the voters were being asked about, which led some pollsters to question the validity of such a catchall term and the wisdom of relying on the 2004 exit polling to make future predictions about party preference.[91]

What is unmistakable about the election of 2004 is that the controversy over Kerry and communion created by the Vatican, a handful of Catholic bishops, and what Kissling termed an "ultraconservative lay movement developed and supported by the Vatican" spooked the Democratic Party on the issue of Catholics and abortion and spooked it badly. The simplistic conclusion was that the party was doomed to lose at the presidential level unless it could find a way to attract religious voters, and that meant distancing the party from its historic support of abortion rights. "You can't have everybody who goes to church vote Republican; you just can't," lamented Democratic strategist Al From.[92]

.   .   .   .   .

By the time of the 2004 election, CFFC had moved beyond merely working to represent progressive Catholic voices and was putting "the Vatican and the Catholic bishops on the defensive on many fronts," said Kissling. She noted that the organization's work on restrictions in the Catholic health care system, the See Change campaign, and the Condoms4Life campaign had "caused the world to see the church as answering questions, not asking them."[93]

CFFC was established as a key player at the intersection of religion, reproductive rights, and public policy. It remained a small organization with fewer than twenty employees, but its reach greatly outstripped its size because of its unique niche and Kissling's skill as a communicator. When Father Michael Place stepped down as head of the Catholic Health Association in 2004, he named "the sustained challenges that have come from Catholics for a Free Choice" as among the most trying issues of his tenure.[94]

But the organization, like the reproductive rights movement as a whole, faced challenges. Kissling was a brilliant strategist who had a knack for finding leverage points and making the most of them. But Kissling's high-profile persona could overshadow other individuals in the movement, possibly giving credence to the oft-repeated conservative claim that CFFC was "one woman and a fax machine." The organization had difficulty retaining mid- and senior-level staff, which hampered its effectiveness in policy areas in which a consistent effort was critical. The movement as a whole struggled to remain relevant at a time when political conservatism was ascendant and reproductive rights appeared to many women to be secured—at least to the extent that it concerned them. The 2004 March for Women's Lives attracted close to 1 million women to the National Mall to protest the Bush administration's rollback of reproductive rights, yet his reelection ensured the onslaught would continue through his second term.

Figure 11. CFFC president Frances Kissling addresses supporters of reproductive rights at the 2004 March for Women's Lives in Washington, D.C. (Courtesy of Catholics for Choice)

Then, in April 2005, the man at the heart of many of the church's most bitter controversies, Pope John Paul II, died. He was replaced by the man known as "God's Rottweiler"—Cardinal Joseph Ratzinger. As head of the Vatican's powerful Congregation for the Doctrine of the Faith, the guardian of church doctrine on faith and morals, it was Ratzinger who was more responsible than anyone in the church other than John Paul for the Vatican's emphasis on doctrinal conformity and obedience, policing dissent with a heavy hand appropriate to the man who ran what was once the Inquisition.

It was Ratzinger who in 1986 revoked Charles Curran's theological teaching authority and stripped Seattle Archbishop Hunthausen of control of his diocese for allowing gay Catholics to openly celebrate mass and some Catholic hospitals to quietly perform sterilizations. It was Ratzinger who chastised the U.S. bishops in 1988 for saying that AIDS education programs might include information about condoms and who that same year declared in a contentious meeting with U.S. bishops that absolute obedience to Rome was the only solution to the problem of dissent in the church. Shortly after that he imposed a "gag order" on theologians, warning that they had no right to publicly dissent from the Vatican. In 1995, he had stirred controversy when he declared that the pope's teaching that women could never be priests was to be considered infallible, even though it wasn't a matter of doctrine. In 2004, he issued a strongly worded critique of the "lethal effects" of feminism that said women should cultivate "feminine values" such as "listening, welcoming, humility, faithfulness, praise and waiting."[95]

"Ratzinger has drawn lines in the sand and wielded the tools of his office on many who cross those lines. Whether necessary prophylaxis or a naked power play, his efforts to curb dissent have left the church more bruised, more divided, than at any point since the close of Vatican II," concluded *National Catholic Reporter* Vatican columnist John Allen. Now as Pope Benedict XVI, he was the man in charge of an increasingly fractured Catholic Church.[96]

10 Health Care and Politics Redux

After John Kerry's loss in the 2004 presidential election and the implication that the Democratic Party was in serious trouble if it couldn't attract religious voters, debate about the direction of the party raged for the next two years. Political pragmatists counseled the party to downplay its support of abortion rights. They said the party should embrace what they viewed as "moderate" restrictions on access to abortion, like parental notification laws and waiting periods for women seeking abortion. They also advised the party to distance itself from traditional allies like the National Abortion Rights Action League (NARAL) and Planned Parenthood, which they feared were at the core of perceptions that the party was a bastion of immorality and irreligiousness.

Others in the party, like Representative Rosa DeLauro (CT), argued that the Democratic Party had let others, particularly the far right, frame the narrative that allowed this perception to flourish by failing to publicly embrace progressive religious values. She said Democrats needed to do a better job of speaking to religious voters within the context of the party's traditional values, like reducing poverty and expanding access to health care, and stress how these efforts were in line with the Catholic Church's emphasis on economic and social justice. "Our values were being challenged in a very fundamental way," she said. "So many members were told they couldn't receive the sacraments. People were so troubled by that effort. We had come full circle since John F. Kennedy's speech on religion and we knew the issue was not going to end with the election."[1]

Beyond a matter of political strategy, the very future of the abortion rights movement was at stake. Since NARAL's "Who Decides" campaign of the early 1990s, which capitalized on voter concern with government overreach by suggesting that abortion rights were about keeping government out of personal decisions, the movement had been moving away from the more explicit woman's rights framework of its early days. NARAL's framing allowed pro-choice politicians to attract moderate and conservative voters because, according to William Saletan, these voters could construe the "who" in "Who Decides" to include anyone they thought should be included in the abortion decision, such as other family members or clergy. This tactic allowed pro-choice candidates to win races and partially constrained the rising conservative tide in the 1990s. It also made NARAL a political powerhouse within the Democratic Party. But it inadvertently gave anti-abortion groups an opening to push for specific regulations that codified the right of others to have a say in a woman's abortion decision. They proposed new measures at the state level that required spousal or parental permission or notification for an abortion. They also capitalized on anti-government sentiment to suggest that taxpayer dollars shouldn't go toward funding abortions for poor women, further limiting access to already restricted Medicaid-funded abortions.[2]

An increasingly sophisticated anti-abortion movement was able to portray these new restrictions as sensible, moderate limitations that addressed the concerns of voters who were troubled by easy access and frequent recourse to abortion. Reproductive rights advocates countered that the restrictions were designed to return access to abortion to a pre–*Roe v. Wade* situation by making it difficult for young women and poor women to get abortions. These new restrictions put many Democrats on the spot. If they refused to embrace so-called moderate abortion restrictions like parental notification, which was approved by a majority of voters, they feared being branded as pro-abortion liberals and losing elections to more extreme opponents of abortion.[3]

As a result, Democrats began creeping to the middle on abortion rights, and NARAL began endorsing moderately pro-choice candidates who supported measures that had once been anathema to the movement, such as parental notification and government funding limitations. When Bill Clinton ran for president in 1992, he ran as a moderate pro-choice Democrat who had signed a parental notification law while governor of Arkansas and who picked as his vice president Tennessee senator Al Gore, who opposed public funding of abortions.[4]

That same year, the Supreme Court's *Planned Parenthood v. Casey* decision opened the door to a raft of new state-based abortion restrictions that were implicitly designed to impede access to abortion. For the next decade, the liberal wing of the Democratic Party and abortion rights supporters tried to hold the line against an onslaught of state and federal legislation that threatened to swamp *Roe:* increasingly extensive and logistically complicated waiting periods; state-written monologues on the supposed physical and mental dangers of abortion designed to scare women away from the procedure; and budget-busting new building codes manufactured to put abortion clinics out of business. State legislatures enacted forty-five measures designed to incrementally limit access to abortion in 2003 alone—out of an avalanche of 558 that were introduced.[5]

Now, in the wake of the 2004 election, the Democratic Party increasingly was pressured to move to the right on abortion to court critical Catholic voters. There was also internal debate about the future of the movement. Less than a month after John Kerry lost, Catholics for a Free Choice (CFFC) president Frances Kissling stirred controversy with her essay, "Is There Life after *Roe:* How to Think about the Fetus," as she attempted to reframe the abortion debate in light of the seeming ascendency of pro-life ideology.

In the essay, Kissling contended that the abortion rights movement was losing ground because it had failed to "even consider whether or not a fetal life has value" for fear that to do so would give credibility to the contention that fetuses are persons and further efforts to limit abortion. Kissling said that the discourse surrounding abortion had changed as a result of anti-abortion measures designed to focus attention on fetuses, such as laws requiring pain medication for later abortions, and the availability of 3D fetal ultrasound images, and argued that the movement needed to respond to this new environment. She contended that although the movement often won legal battles related to abortion, it was losing the fight for the hearts and minds of the public. "I am deeply struck by the number of thoughtful, progressive people who have been turned off to the prochoice movement by the lack of adequate and clear expressions of respect for fetal life," she wrote.[6]

Kissling criticized pro-choice leaders for failing to "express any doubt about any aspect of abortion," especially "partial-birth" abortion, which she said had surfaced "broader unrest about abortion." She acknowledged that most of the abortion-related legislative initiatives were designed to limit access, but said that for many people supporting such measures was the only way to demonstrate that "pro-choice does not mean pro-abortion." She went against pro-choice orthodoxy by suggesting that the parents of younger teens should be included in the abortion decision and by questioning whether women having later abortions should be offered fetal anesthesia.[7]

Many abortion rights leaders, however, like the National Organization for Women's Eleanor Smeal, disagreed that they ignored the moral components of abortion or failed to acknowledge that abortions could include sadness and loss. They expressed doubt that moving to the right on abortion would be useful in countering efforts to limit access thinly disguised as concern for women and children. Political scientist Rosaline Petchesky, who had written extensively about the abortion rights movement, wrote to Kissling, "If and when those who dominate anti-abortion politics could for a minute take seriously the rights to a decent life and health of born children, maybe then we could start to talk about advancing respect for fetal life, early or late."[8]

The debate was further amplified in early 2005, when Senator Hillary Clinton (D-NY), a longtime advocate of abortion rights who was a potential presidential candidate for 2008, said in a speech to a family planning meeting that abortion "in many ways represents a sad, even tragic choice to many, many women." She voiced her respect for opponents of abortion and called for both sides of the debate to come together around common ground initiatives designed to prevent unwanted pregnancies and reduce the need for abortion.[9]

Catholics for a Free Choice now found itself at the heart of the debate over the future of the abortion rights movement. The values that it had long espoused—situating access to abortion within a broader Catholic social justice framework and creating common-ground solutions—was potentially the only way forward for the Democratic Party, as some in the party soon recognized. In early 2006, fifty-five House Democrats, including long-time abortion rights supporters like DeLauro and pro-life Democrats like Bart Stupak (MI) and James Oberstar (MN), released a "Statement of Catholic Principles" that placed abortion within the context of reducing poverty and increasing access to education, social services, and health care. They said, "We envision a world in which every child belongs to a loving family and agree with the Catholic Church about the value of human life and the undesirability of abortion—we do not celebrate its practice. Each of us is committed to reducing the number of unwanted pregnancies and creating an environment with policies that encourage pregnancies to be carried to term. We believe this includes promoting alternatives to abortion, such as adoption, and improving access to children's healthcare and child care, as well as policies that encourage paternal and maternal responsibility."[10]

The statement could have come straight from CFFC's 1992 "Nobody Wants to Have an Abortion" campaign. "We reinforced our commitment to the basic principles of Catholic social justice teaching," said DeLauro. She then worked with Representative Tim Ryan (D-OH), who identified himself as a pro-life Catholic, and groups across the political spectrum, including CFFC, to craft a bill around the shared value of reducing the need for abortion. "We tried to bring together groups that were traditionally opposed to one another—groups such as CFFC and NARAL with the Christian Coalition—to find common ground," said DeLauro.[11]

The "Reducing the Need for Abortions and Supporting Parents Act" was introduced in late 2006 and again in 2007. It was a comprehensive approach to reducing abortion that included increased funding for family planning programs, measures to improve insurance coverage for pregnant women, programs to reduce teen pregnancy, tax incentives for adoption, and expanded child care services for low-income parents. Kissling said the resulting "two pronged approach" of working to reduce unintended pregnancies by increasing access to contraception and expanding services to help women carry their pregnancies to term "avoids an ideological stalemate and bridges the gap between sensible, well-motivated members of Congress who hold differing views on abortion."[12]

It was the realization of a vision that CFFC had been promoting for a long time. It was also one of the last things that Kissling would do as the head of the organization. A month later, she announced her retirement after twenty-five years at the helm of CFFC, saying she was afraid she might become "predictable" if she remained any longer. Coming just three years after Kate Michelman stepped down as head of NARAL, Kissling's retirement marked a changing of the guard for the abortion rights movement, as the generation of women who came of age when abortion was illegal and steered the nascent movement from political obscurity vacated leadership roles.

The movement was at a turning point. Piecemeal efforts to limit access to abortion were succeeding, largely because they operated in a stealth manner at the state level and avoided the big national discussion about the general legality of abortion, which the movement was better equipped to address. Bush had appointed two conservative justices, John Roberts and Samuel Alito, to the Supreme Court, which in April 2007 upheld the constitutionality of the "partial-birth" ban without an exemption for the health of a woman. It marked the first time a specific abortion procedure was banned and the first time since *Roe* that the court had discarded women's health as a nonnegotiable consideration in the constitutionality of abortion limitations. It was becoming clear that the outcome of the 2008 presidential election would determine much about the future conversation regarding abortion as well as about access to abortion itself.

President Barack Obama's eventual winning strategy was to embrace the call for Democrats to discuss their pro-choice position within a continuum of progressive religious values and not to shy away from calling abortion "a moral issue" that many struggle with. "I don't think that the government criminalizing the choices that families make is the best answer for reducing abortions. I think the better answer . . . is to figure out how do we make sure that young mothers, or women who have a pregnancy that's unexpected or difficult, have the kind of support they need to make a whole range of choices, including adoption and keeping the child," Senator Obama (IL) said in the closing months of the campaign.[13]

At the same time, Obama upheld core pro-choice values. He criticized the Supreme Court decision on partial-birth abortion, voiced support for rolling back the Hyde Amendment, and said if elected he would sign the Freedom of Choice Act, a federal measure that would guarantee abortion rights for women. He told a Planned Parenthood conference that "reproductive care is essential care" and said that any health reform plan he proposed would include a public health plan that "will provide all essential services, including reproductive services," which his staff confirmed included abortion.[14]

On the strategy side, the campaign successfully co-opted many of the GOP's tactics from 2004. It created a Catholic leadership council and fielded an extensive Catholic outreach staff that operated phone banks targeting Catholics and organized post-mass brunches to "push the message that Obama is a Christian man who welcomes religious voters" and wanted to reduce the need for abortion. The campaign touted endorsements by prominent pro-life conservative Catholics such as Pepperdine University law professor Douglas Kmiec and canon lawyer Nicholas Cafardi.[15]

Democratic operatives created groups like Catholics in Alliance for the Common Good and Catholics United to push the idea that "pro-life" meant voting for the "common good," which subsumed the importance of abortion as the most important Catholic issue. They distributed voter guides that focused on a range of social justice issues to compete with conservative voting guides stressing abortion, which the bishops' conference had banned parishes from distributing.

Even the bishops, who surely were chagrined at having seen the Holy Eucharist turned into a political sideshow in the 2004 election, gave Obama an unexpected boost when their 2008 voting guide stated, "There may be times when a Catholic who rejects a candidate's unacceptable position may decide to vote for that candidate for other morally grave reasons." It was a fuller analysis of then-Cardinal Joseph Ratzinger's guidance that a vote for a candidate who did not agree with the church on an issue like abortion could be acceptable if the voter disagreed with the candidate's position and voted for the candidate for other proportionally important reasons. With the Iraq War increasingly seen as ill considered and unjust and the economic collapse of 2008 revealing the huge gap in economic inequality presided over by the Republican Party, the need to consider formerly abstract social justice issues such as war and poverty took on a concreteness that they hadn't had since the days of the nuclear arms race. This put Democrats in a position to make the case that a candidate like Obama, who opposed the war and supported social welfare programs and access to health care, had a claim to the moral attention of Catholics, while simultaneously dampening the ability of Republicans to claim that abortion should be the only issue concerning Catholics.

At the same time, few individual bishops spoke out against Obama or Senator Joe Biden (PA), his Catholic vice presidential pick, who embraced the privately opposed/publicly pro-choice position. A bishop in Biden's childhood home of Scranton, Pennsylvania, had priests condemn pro-choice candidates as supporting "homicide" and said he wouldn't give Biden communion. Archbishop Charles Chaput of Denver publicly disagreed with the bishops' new voting guidance and the idea that Democrats could be called "pro-life" because of their support for programs for vulnerable women and children, but these bishops found themselves largely speaking alone. Not coincidently, the bishops' 2008 voting statement was the first to be voted on by the entire bishops' conference.[16]

Beyond rhetoric, Democrats made an effort to show that the party welcomed pro-life Democrats, coming full circle when it asked Senator Bob Casey Jr. (PA), the son of Pennsylvania governor Bob Casey, to address the Democratic convention a full sixteen years after his father was exiled for his anti-abortion stance. Casey, who was an outspoken supporter of Obama's candidacy, said, "I believe that as president, he'll pursue common ground by seeking common ground, rather than trying to divide us." When the election results were tallied, Obama won the Catholic vote by 54 percent to GOP challenger Senator John McCain's 45 percent and made gains among regular churchgoers compared to Senator John Kerry, which seemed to confirm that Catholics weren't turned off by support of abortion as much as by candidates who couldn't place it within a broader moral framework.[17]

For Jon O'Brien, who took over as president of the newly renamed Catholics for Choice (CFC)—the organization dropped the "Free" from its name because it had lost its cultural relevance—the debate showcased the need to return to the theme of justice for women, from supporting those who needed late-term abortions to federal funding for abortion for poor women, and away from political calculation. "We don't care if that's a feminist thing, or a reproductive health thing, or a reproductive justice thing. CFC is here to remind the community that something is wrong if choice isn't extended to everyone," said O'Brien.[18]

.   .   .   .   .

Suzie Bassi remembers the exact moment she knew her ten-year career as an Illinois state legislator was over. It was in 2010, the Sunday before the Republican primary in her district. She walked out of mass and saw an enormous banner hanging across the street that said her campaign was financed by abortionists. "It was Catholics from other parishes who did it. They hung banners in front of every church in the parish," said Bassi, an abortion rights supporter. "I was a high school teacher. I have three kids and grandkids and here they were calling me a baby killer," she said. The charge was untrue and nasty, but it worked. Bassi lost the primary to a man who was against abortion in all circumstances, even to save a woman's life.[19]

By the late 2000s, what happened to Bassi was a microcosm of what was happening nationally. The issue of reproductive rights had become hopelessly politicized, as conservatives demanded increasingly stringent levels of ideological purity and worked to hound Republican moderates out of office in all but the safest districts. "I was elected in 1998 and it has gotten progressively worse—more vindictive and nasty, with Catholic and Protestant anti-abortion groups teaming up to defeat abortion-rights supporters," Bassi said.[20]

The realities of governing in this polarized atmosphere hit the new administration early on. With the economy still unraveling and conservative Republicans united in unexpectedly fearsome opposition to the new president, Obama began equivocating on his previously strong pro-choice stance. He revoked the Mexico City language on international family planning funding but backed down from a proposal in the 2009 stimulus package to allow states to expand Medicaid family planning services after it came under ridicule from Republicans as unnecessary and wasteful—even though it was expected to save $200 million. He dismissed the

Freedom of Choice Act as "not his highest priority." When CFC and other pro-choice organizations were invited to the White House to discuss reproductive health, they found themselves face to face with conservative promoters of abstinence-only sex education and asked to defend access to contraception as a strategy to reduce unintended pregnancy. "This was the Democratic Party wanting us to persuade them that contraception works," said O'Brien, who like many in the movement and on Capitol Hill expressed growing concern that women were being "thrown under the bus" in the name of political expediency.[21]

When Obama announced that his first major domestic policy initiative would be health care reform, it was clear that abortion was a potential flashpoint, just as it had been during the 1993 debate over the Clinton plan. Like most policy issues in the United States, the debate over expanding health care access had evolved in a conservative direction. Obama embraced a largely incremental strategy of using subsidies to increase access to private sector health insurance, creating new consumer protections, and mandating that all Americans carry some type of health insurance. Progressives pushed for a government-sponsored "public option" to compete with for-profit insurers. There were the predictable spats with the various stakeholders, but physicians, hospitals, and insurers were more subdued than in the 1990s, sobered by the reality that the economy was increasingly hobbled by soaring health care costs and a growing uninsured population. More unexpected was the hijacking of the debate in the summer of 2009 over charges of fictional "death panels" fermented by Sara Palin–leaning far-right, anti-government conservatives who teamed up with anti-abortion organizations and other traditional opponents of progressive policies in an attempt to sink health reform.[22]

At the same time, the U.S. bishops began warning about the inclusion of abortion coverage. They told Congress and lay Catholics that health reform was in danger of becoming "a vehicle for promoting an 'abortion rights' agenda" unless abortion was explicitly excluded from any public plan or basic benefits package and a Hyde Amendment–like restriction on federal funding was included. They worked to gin up opposition in the broader anti-abortion movement when they made the completely unsubstantiated claim that language in the bill requiring timely access to services could be used to override state-level abortion restrictions. Cardinal

Justin Rigali, who was chairing the bishops' Pro-Life Activities Committee, sent a letter to the House Energy and Commerce Committee insisting that health reform be "abortion neutral."[23]

Although the bishops' opposition was not surprising, the dynamics of their lobbying on the issue had changed in an important way. Now lobbying wasn't just coming from the conservative-leaning pro-life committee but also from the more progressive Committee on Domestic Justice and Human Development, which was in charge of social justice issues. This committee had strong ties to Democratic members of Congress whom it worked with on issues like poverty reduction, immigration, and access to health care. On July 17, Bishop William Murphy, chair of the Justice and Human Development Committee, sent a letter to Congress calling for universal access to health care but warning that any attempt to include government funding or mandatory coverage for abortion would be "politically unwise."[24]

By August, the National Right to Life Committee was echoing the bishops' charges that health care reform would "greatly expand abortion in America." It claimed that the plan would establish a government-run "nationwide insurance plan to cover elective abortions" and could "require health networks to establish new abortion-providing sites" or recruit abortion providers.[25]

The drumbeat against abortion continued throughout the fall. In October, the bishops' conference, which had been renamed the U.S. Conference of Catholic Bishops (USCCB) dispatched a notice to church bulletins around the country instructing parishioners to oppose health care reform if it didn't contain the bishops' anti-abortion language. The Obama administration tried to mollify critics. It abandoned any pretense that it would try to roll back Hyde restrictions and announced that health reform would maintain the status quo on abortion: no federal dollars would go to abortion.

By fall, the public option was dead, discarded by the administration in an increasingly elusive attempt to find the "middle" on health reform. The plan was now limited to expanding the public Medicaid system to cover the very poor and giving working poor and lower-middle income uninsured individuals and families subsidies to buy into private plans offered through government-run exchanges. This appeared to be moving toward approval when, at the eleventh hour, negotiations ground to a halt. Democrats were dumbfounded to learn that one of their own, Representative Bart Stupak of Michigan, had rounded up a bloc of some forty pro-life Democrats who were refusing to vote for the plan unless it contained restriction favored by the bishops that would prevent any federal subsidy monies from going to private health plans that covered abortion. Abortion rights supporters like DeLauro asserted that this would force any health plan that wanted to participate in health insurance exchanges to stop covering abortions altogether. With some 50–85 percent of health plans covering abortion, this would result in a dramatic reduction in coverage for women and could effectively end private abortion coverage by major health plans.[26]

Abortion rights proponents offered a proposal to segregate federal subsidy funds from the private premiums used to pay for abortion coverage. The bishops, aided by allies like Representative Chris Smith (R-NJ), had been claiming since the summer, however, that any attempt to keep the two funding streams separate was just an accounting ploy. "[T]he plan itself will be subsidizing abortion-on-demand, with taxpayer funding comingled, and the number of abortions will go up significantly," charged Smith.[27]

It was an argument that the bishops had been building for years: that funding any plan or provider who provided abortions was illicit because even segregated funding would free up other money for abortions. They were now trying to use this argument to force private health plans to stop covering abortion, with major implications for women's access. Private health plans aren't a major source of payment for abortions. Many women who get abortions don't have private coverage, and of those who do, apparently few submit claims for a procedure they would rather keep private. But such plans do pay for abortions for women who have them for health reasons or if a fetus has substantial deformities, which can be an expensive procedure if performed later in a pregnancy. And with more young, previously uninsured women covered through plans in exchanges, lack of abortion coverage would be a serious shortcoming that would also serve to further stigmatize abortion services.[28]

It soon became public knowledge that the Stupak Amendment had been drafted by Richard Doerflinger, the USCCB's chief lobbyist, who had worked closely with Stupak's staff. The bishops were also a major lobbying force behind the amendment. Doerflinger had buttonholed Democratic members to support it and sat in Stupak's office counting votes. Members of the hierarchy personally lobbied key Democrats. Former Washington Archbishop Theodore McCarrick called House Speaker Nancy Pelosi (D-CA) from Rome. Boston Cardinal Sean O'Malley cornered Obama at Senator Ted Kennedy's funeral in the summer of 2009 and urged him to adopt the bishops' provisions.[29]

Now, in November, with the clock ticking on health reform, members of the clergy and USCCB lobbyists sat in Pelosi's office and threatened to turn Catholics against the reform bill if they didn't get their amendment. Pelosi needed the forty-odd Democrats represented by Stupak's coalition; with just about every Republican opposed to health reform, she couldn't get it through without them. She relented and the House passed the measure. It was a bitter pill for pro-choice advocates, who saw the health reform effort go from an opportunity to reassert the importance of abortion to comprehensive women's health care to an attempt to further limit the procedure.

It was especially bitter for Catholics. "As a Catholic and a member of Congress, it was very hard dealing with the fact that the bishops were willing to destroy the bill over a manufactured issue. To deny health care to 45 million people because they would like to overturn *Roe* was so troubling," says Representative DeLauro.[30]

The blatant show of force by the bishops sent shockwaves through Washington. *National Journal* reported that the bishops' role in drafting the Stupak Amendment "raised eyebrows both on and off Capitol Hill." Hill staffers expressed amazement at the politicking and said the bishops came out of nowhere on the issue.[31]

But the reality was that the bishops had been there all along. They created the anti-abortion movement out of whole cloth. They were the first to politicize abortion in a presidential campaign. They helped craft the original Hyde Amendment, which was in many ways the single most debilitating piece of anti-abortion legislation because it not only denied poor women access to abortion but set the pattern of segregating abortion from other health services. And, as *Mother Jones* noted, Doerflinger had been "involved in almost every major pro-life initiative in Congress since 1980."[32]

For many years the bishops' lobby had been overshadowed by the more high-profile Christian Right. The evangelical movement was so associated with anti-abortion activism that it had obscured the bishops' own persistent anti-abortion activism for the past thirty years. The Christian Right had what the Catholic hierarchy had never been able to muster: the electoral troops to oppose abortion. Instead, the bishops worked in a more low-key, personal way, using their ecclesiastical clout to lobby legislators directly. Since they weren't dependent on fundraising for their war chest, they had no need to brag about their accomplishments on the Hill. They just took money from parishioners and used it to lobby for policies that advanced their institutional interests but were often counter to majority Catholic opinion. "The challenge is that many Catholics have 'divorced' themselves from the bishops, but now the bishops and the politicians are in cahoots," noted CFFC's O'Brien.[33]

For instance, when George W. Bush's PEPFAR (President's Emergency Plan For AIDS Relief) program was up for reauthorization in 2008, the Democrats pressed to ease Bush-era restrictions that promoted abstinence-only programs and limited spending on family planning. They thought they had a deal until the night before the bill was set for a vote in the House, when they found that USCCB and Catholic Relief Services lobbyists were on the Hill renegotiating the bill. Family planning and AIDS activists were stunned to find a completely different bill the next day. The bill now applied the global gag rule to PEPFAR funds, erased any linkage of family planning services to HIV prevention, and expanded the conscience clause to allow faith-based groups not only to refuse to distribute condoms but to refuse to refer to organizations that did.[34]

What made the bishops' efforts suddenly more visible? For one thing, the environment had changed. The evangelical political movement that had dominated U.S. politics for nearly thirty years was waning. The Christian Coalition was gone. Moral Majority founder Jerry Falwell was dead. Younger evangelicals were turned off by politics and what had turned out to be empty promises to remake the culture by suppressing abortion and gay rights. They had discovered causes like AIDS, and Darfur and global warming, and were living a more personal, less political form of evangelism typified by Saddleback pastor Rick Warren and his "purpose driven" life. And anti-abortion activism itself had changed. Much of the action was no longer at the national level. It was in the states, where groups like Americans United for Life pushed laws designed to impede abortion access. As the clout of national anti-abortion groups declined, the bishops' anti-abortion activism became more apparent. For the first time, many people saw the bishops for what they really were: a powerful political lobby nakedly pursing its own interests.

Even the bishops' clout, however, didn't extend to getting the Senate to accept the Stupak Amendment. The Senate passed an alternative amendment that restricted public money from going to abortion but allowed private plans in health exchanges to cover abortion if they used segregated premiums to do so. It was a compromise that managed to anger pro-life forces, who claimed that public money would still be used to subsidize abortion, and pro-choice groups, who called it a "shameful" concession that further stigmatized and limited abortion. The health care package moved toward a final vote in March 2010 with the issue still unresolved and the bishops and Stupak insisting that only the House abortion limitations would suffice.[35]

But "official" Catholic opposition to the measure was shattered in mid-March, when Sister Nancy Keehan, who had replaced Michael Place as head of the Catholic Health Association (CHA), announced the CHA's endorsement of the Senate measure, which she said was adequate to prevent federal funding of abortion. The Leadership Conference of Women Religious (LCWR), which is made up of the heads of the major women's religious orders in the United States, representing some 80 percent of nuns, weighed in with its approval. It said that "despite false claims to the contrary, the Senate bill will not provide taxpayer funding for elective abortions."[36]

The backing of the CHA and the LCWR gave the plan the official Catholic imprimatur it needed. Their approval was especially influential because many of the nuns endorsing the plan, such as Keehan, were directly involved in the provision of health care. As a result of the nuns' backing, a number of pro-life Democrats who had been opposed to the Senate bill said they would change their votes. Stupak held out until the last minute, and then, fearing that failure to compromise might doom the whole reform effort, accepted a proposal under which Obama issued an executive order stipulating that no federal funds could go toward abortion. The Affordable Care Act passed, leaving the bishops alone and fuming in their opposition and abortion yet again stigmatized as a segregated procedure.

.   .   .   .   .

In November 2009, as the battle over health reform raged in Washington, a twenty-seven-year-old woman nearing the end of her first trimester of pregnancy was admitted to St. Joseph's Hospital and Medical Center in Phoenix, Arizona, suffering from pulmonary hypertension. Doctors told the mother of four that she had a nearly 100 percent chance of suffering heart failure and dying if she carried the pregnancy to term. They recommended an immediate therapeutic abortion to save her life. The recommendation went to the Catholic hospital's ethics committee, which included Sister Margaret McBride, a Sister of Mercy who was an administrator at the hospital. The ethics committee approved the abortion under the rationale that its primary purpose was to save the woman's life, not terminate the pregnancy. The abortion was performed and the woman survived. Six months later the decision came to the attention of Phoenix Bishop Thomas Olmstead. He condemned the hospital for approving the abortion and announced that Sister McBride was automatically excommunicated because of her participation in the decision to allow the abortion. "In the decision to abort, the equal dignity of mother and her baby were not both upheld," Olmstead said.[37]

Olmstead was suggesting that a woman who could otherwise be saved be allowed to die to protect the letter of the *Ethical and Religious Directives for Catholic Health Care Services*, which said that direct abortion couldn't be allowed under any circumstance. Hospital administrators and Sister McBride defended the abortion as the correct decision because both the woman and the baby would have died without it. "Morally, ethically, and legally, we simply cannot stand by and let someone die whose life we might be able to save," said hospital president Linda Hunt. In December 2010, Olmstead stripped the hospital of its Catholic affiliation after it refused to promise that it would never again perform an abortion to save a woman's life.[38]

The McBride case was a dramatic example of the willingness of the Catholic bishops to place Catholic dogma over patients' needs and raised serious concerns about their oversight of Catholic hospitals. "The need to accommodate religious doctrine does not give health providers serving the general public license to jeopardize women's lives," said a *New York Times* editorial.[39]

It also illustrated the bishops' insistence that they alone had the right to define the parameters of the provision of health care at any institution related to the Catholic Church. It was an issue on which the bishops were increasingly intransigent and on which they had found an accommodating partner in the Bush administration. The administration had included a Catholic health plan in the federal employees' health program that tailored its benefits to comply with the restrictions in the *Directives*. It excluded coverage for abortion, sterilization, contraception, and artificial insemination even though the plan, OSF Health, offered contraception coverage through a third-party provider under other programs.[40]

Because obviously no one could force Catholics to utilize banned services if they didn't want to, the implication now was that their premiums couldn't even go toward a plan that offered such services. And since the federal employees' health program was already prohibited by law from covering abortion, it was clear that an effort was under way to elevate less controversial services such as contraception to the same level of moral approbation as abortion.

But it was on the issue of conscience clauses that the Bush administration was especially accommodating to the bishops. Bush's PEPFAR program included an exemption for religious providers who didn't want to distribute condoms, which was custom-made for Catholic agencies like Catholic Relief Services. Bush signed an appropriations bill in 2005 that included the first federal conscience clause. This broadened the abortion exemption to a wide range of health care entities, including health maintenance organizations and other insurers, and included the right to refuse to refer for abortions.

By this time, the issue of conscience refusals was becoming increasingly contentious, as the bishops were joined by elements of the Christian Right in asserting the need for greater conscience protections for health care workers, who they charged were regularly being forced to violate their faith in the provision of certain services. Organizations like Pharmacists for Life campaigned for the right of pharmacists to refuse to dispense or refer for oral contraceptives or emergency contraception (EC) on the discredited grounds that they were potentially abortifacients. Reports of conscience-based service refusals mushroomed. There were hospital nurses who refused to care for patients before or after emergency abortions, doctors who refused to prescribe the Pill to unmarried women, and infertility clinics that turned away lesbian patients. Conscience exemptions were now being used as a political tool to block access to services to which some objected or to make moral judgments about the provision of care to certain patients.

In 2008, the health care community was in an uproar after the Bush administration used the regulatory process to codify the right of almost any health worker—including those ancillary to a procedure like schedulers or janitors—to opt out of providing any service to which he or she had a religious or moral objection. Women's health advocates, medical associations, and even drugstore chains were quick to express alarm about the regulation, not only because of its unprecedented scope and potential impact on patients' access to care but because it seemed to purposely conflate abortion and contraception. They said the rule could be used to circumvent laws that required insurers to cover prescription contraceptives or hospitals to provide EC to women who had been raped—two issues of special importance to the Catholic bishops.[41]

By the dawn of the Obama administration, however, the bishops were losing ground on conscience exemptions. They lobbied unsuccessfully in Arizona to broaden that state's narrow religious exemption to its contraceptive equity law, which covered only churches, to include any religious employer, such as Catholic hospitals and universities. The bishops in Connecticut lost a bruising two-year battle for an exemption to that state's new "EC in the ER" law despite putting up a fierce fight. The Obama administration undid the sweeping Bush conscience exemption, noting that federal law still protected providers from being compelled to participate in abortions. Then, in August 2011, the Department of Health and Human Services (HHS) announced that all employer-based health plans would be required to provide contraceptives to women at no cost under its proposed rules for the preventive services guaranteed to all individuals under the Affordable Care Act.

In deference to the Catholic bishops, HHS proposed a narrow conscience clause that exempted nonprofit organizations directly involved in the inculcation of religion that primarily employed individuals of the same religion, like Catholic churches and other houses of worship. However, Catholic-affiliated institutions like universities and hospitals that served the general population and employed non-Catholics would have to provide contraception through their plans. Many of these employers had chosen to self-insure—that is, serve as their own insurers—to circumvent state contraception mandates, but they would be required to comply with federal law.

The type of narrowly drawn conscience clause proposed by the administration had been sanctified by two closely watched state supreme court decisions in New York and California. The U.S. Supreme Court let both decisions stand, which was seen as a major victory for a limited application of conscience clauses. But in the ensuring years since the 2006 New York decision, not only had the Christian Right become activated on the issue, but the question of conscience clauses had spilled beyond health care as efforts advanced to ensure equality for same-sex couples. Catholic Charities affiliates in Boston and Illinois closed their well-respected adoption agencies rather than comply with state mandates that they provide adoptions to gay and lesbian couples.

Then in September 2011, shortly after the Obama administration announced the contraceptive mandate, HHS announced that it would not renew a contract with the USCCB to provide assistance to victims of international human trafficking because the bishops' organization refused to provide women who had been subjected to rape or forced prostitution with access to comprehensive reproductive health care, including abortion, EC, and family planning and sexually transmitted disease counseling. Where HHS saw the need to provide all medically appropriate services to these women, the bishops claimed anti-Catholic discrimination, especially because political appointees at HHS had overruled a program evaluation that rated the USCCB as the top-performing contractor in terms of service provision. Sister Mary Ann Walsh, a spokesperson for the USCCB, said that there was a "new, albeit unwritten rule of HHS, the ABC rule—Anybody But Catholics."[42]

It was a dramatic charge and signaled that the bishops were going to make a full-court press on the issue of exemptions for Catholic providers.

In mid-November, USCCB president Archbishop Timothy Dolan of Milwaukee, Wisconsin, announced a new Committee for Religious Liberty to counter what he said was a move to "neuter religion" in the public square. The committee was put under the direction of Bridgeport, Connecticut, Bishop William Lori, an outspoken conservative who was formerly the head of the Pro-Life Committee, and staffed by Anthony Picarello, a rising young lawyer at the USCCB who had worked as a litigator for the Becket Fund for Religious Liberty, which had pursued a number of high-profile religious freedom cases.[43]

In addition to the contraceptive mandate, Dolan named the dropping of the USCCB from the HHS contract: state marriage equality laws that required same-sex couples be allowed to adopt; and the Obama administration's failure to defend the Defense of Marriage Act, which prohibited federal recognition of same-sex partnerships, as government actions that "infringe upon the right of conscience of people of faith." The bishops were charging that efforts to make them play by the same rules as other health and social service providers were affronts to religious freedom—their freedom to discriminate against others or deny services in the name of religion.[44]

There was more at stake than just the bishops' authority over services provided by Catholic institutions. Domestic and international social service agencies affiliated with the church, like Catholic Charities USA and Catholic Relief Services, receive hundreds of millions of dollars in government contracts each year to provide social services to the poor, run adoption agencies, and manage international development projects. Catholic Charities affiliates received nearly $3 billion in government funding in 2010, accounting for more than 60 percent of their revenue. Religiously affiliated hospitals in the United States, of which 70 percent are Catholic, receive some $40 billion in government funding each year through Medicare and Medicaid and other government programs.[45]

The bishops were making the preservation of their right to participate in these federally funded programs and discriminate based on religious doctrine their most high-profile crusade since *Roe v. Wade* provoked their anti-abortion activism. Between the launch of the religious freedom committee and the election of Dolan, who was selected over the organization's more moderate vice president, the bishops were trying to reclaim the national leadership role on social issues that they had enjoyed under pugnacious, outspoken conservatives like the late Cardinal John O'Connor.[46]

With the bishops' newly aggressive stance, all eyes turned to the White House to see if Obama would accept the HHS rule, with its narrow conscience exemption, or seek to pacify the increasingly outspoken bishops. He came under ferocious lobbying from the reproductive rights community to maintain the mandate after a private meeting with Dolan at the White House that left the archbishop "feeling a bit more at peace about this issue," which many took to mean that he had received assurances from Obama that he would soften the mandate.[47]

But no one was prepared for the firestorm that broke loose when the mandate, with its narrow religious exemption intact, was announced on January 20. That the bishops screamed bloody murder shouldn't have come as any surprise. They had announced their intention to make this their defining issue. But the mandate was also denounced by Sister Keehan, who had proved such a critical ally to the White House on the health reform bill, and a handful of mostly male, liberal-leaning Catholic columnists and pundits, who seemed to think the administration was asking nuns in habits to stand on street corners handing out condoms rather than proposing a reasonable compromise on the issue that had been affirmed by two influential high courts. Also lost in the debate was the fact that many Catholic health plans like the OSF Health Plan in Illinois already routinely covered birth control through a third-party administrator, an arrangement that proved adequate for these plans for at least a decade.

The Obama administration announced that religiously affiliated employers would be given an additional year to figure out how to apply the mandate, but that didn't mollify the bishops, who contended that the mandate was an affront to rank-and-file Catholics—even though some 98 percent of Catholic women have used birth control and nearly 60 percent of all Catholics supported the mandate.[48] In addition, many of the 650,000 employees of Catholic hospitals aren't Catholic, which meant that the bishops had absolutely no moral authority over their reproductive health choices. Dolan argued in a video made even before the administration released the final rule, however, that the mandate was a violation of religious freedom because it would force Catholics "to go out into the marketplace and buy a product that violates their conscience."[49]

It was a radical new way of viewing conscience rights—not as the right of an individual to decline to use or participate in a service, but as their right to deny that service to others based on their mere participation in an insurance pool in a commercial marketplace.

But with Catholic use of birth control nearly universal, Dolan needed to raise the stakes. He drew on years of efforts by the bishops to conflate abortion and contraception, and particularly abortion and emergency contraception, to charge that the mandate would require Catholic insurers and employers to cover "abortion-inducing drugs" in a reference to EC. He made the charge even though the official journal of the CHA had published an article nearly two years earlier saying that Plan B, the most widely used emergency contraceptive, was not an abortifacient—even under the bishops' definition—because it worked to prevent fertilization, not implantation. The general medical community also was increasingly in agreement that postfertilization effects of EC, like those of oral contraceptives in general, were virtually nonexistent.[50]

The Christian Right was particularly receptive to the bishops' arguments, helping to fuel opposition to the mandate. The National Association of Evangelicals parroted the bishops, asserting, "Employers with religious objections to contraception will be forced to pay for services and procedures they believe are morally wrong." The first lawsuit against the contraception mandate was filed by the Becket Fund on behalf of Belmont Abbey College, a Catholic college in North Carolina, and Colorado Christian University, an evangelical university.[51]

In fact, fundamentalists were more and more receptive to the Catholic position on birth control. In 2004, Albert Mohler, president of the influential Southern Baptist Theological Seminary, which is the closest thing the Baptists have to a Vatican-like teaching authority, acknowledged the transformation of conservative Christian thought on birth control in an essay titled "Can Christians Use Birth Control?" He noted that although "birth control use has been an issue of concern only for Catholics . . . [a] growing number of evangelicals are rethinking the issue." He urged evangelicals to reject the "contraceptive mentality" and "look closely at the Catholic moral argument as found in *Humanae Vitae*," agreeing with Pope John Paul II that widespread use of the Pill and the delinking of sex from reproduction has led to "near total abandonment of Christian sexual morality."[52]

Although Mohler rejected the idea that married Christians must eschew birth control altogether, some young evangelicals were doing just that, attracted to the orthodox Catholic position by what they saw as a countercultural rejection of materialism wedded to the conservative Christian disposition toward traditional roles for women. Even more far-right evangelicals embraced the "quiverfull" movement that lionized large families and women's submission to the will of God—and their husbands—in matters of procreation.

That same year, the Evangelicals and Catholics Together coalition released a statement in which they noted a "new pattern of convergence and cooperation" between Catholics and evangelicals on a "culture of life" that not only rejected abortion but featured a growing appreciation for the "relationship between unitive and procreative sexual love within the bond of marriage." The Christian Right was now officially infected with the anti-contraceptive mentality of the Catholic hierarchy.[53]

This shift had implications for the anti-abortion movement and nascent efforts to find common ground on measures to reduce the need for abortion. In 2009, Representative Tim Ryan, who had fought for common-ground legislation, was kicked off the board of Democrats for Life because of his pro-contraception stance. "The new fault line is not between pro-life and pro-choice people," he said. "It's within the pro-life community. The question now is: 'are you pro-life and pro-contraception, therefore trying to reduce the need for abortions, or are you pro-life and against contraception'."[54]

The implications of this convergence also reverberated in the Republican Party, which now completely abandoned its traditional support for contraception, rejected common-ground measures and began a full-out assault on family planning funding, marrying the right's antagonism toward contraception with the tax-cutting, anti-government fervor of the Tea Party.[55]

In April 2011, the GOP unsuccessfully tried to end funding for the Title X family planning program, the major federal funding source for domestic family planning programs, as part of the budget showdown with President Obama. Legislators in eight states defunded Planned

Parenthood, which had long been on the wish list of far-right anti-abortion groups like the American Life League, echoing fringe claims that family planning funding was facilitating abortions.[56]

It was against this backdrop of efforts to decrease access to contraception that the Obama contraceptive mandate was announced. Reproductive health advocates implored Obama to maintain the policy and not marginalize contraceptive access. CFC ran a full-page ad in the *Washington Post* graphically depicting that 98 percent of Catholic women who used birth control versus the tiny number of male bishops opposed to it to remind legislators that Catholic voters overwhelming approved of contraceptive use. A few days later, however, after seeing the issue turn into a political football and deciding that his position was politically untenable, Obama announced a new iteration of the mandate that would allow religiously affiliated employers to push responsibility for providing contraceptives on to insurers.

CFFC's O'Brien praised the administration for not completely caving in to the bishops but noted it had given them their first victory on their "'religious liberty' shopping list" and said they would move on to demand more special treatment, like exemptions from marriage equality laws. Liberal pundits applauded it as an elegant solution that protected religious freedom and contraceptive access, effectively ending the firestorm from the left. More important, the compromise satisfied Obama's key Catholic allies in the health and social service fields. Sister Keehan of the CHA, Catholic Charities, the LCWR, and the social justice lobby Network pronounced themselves satisfied with the Obama plan, as did Planned Parenthood. The bishops expressed optimism that they would find it acceptable. It seemed Obama had managed to walk a fine line between political expediency and commitments to his core constituencies and allies.[57]

But no sooner had all the parties breathed a sigh of relief than the bishops backtracked and denounced the compromise, saying Catholics were still "being called upon to subsidize something we find morally illicit." It was a rehash of the bishops' long-running contention that funding streams could never be adequately segregated in the case of morally illicit services, but now they were applying it to birth control. Conservative Catholics like Robert George and Mary Ann Glendon took up the bishops' tack and called the compromise a "cheap accounting trick." But many Catholic moral theologians disagreed, saying that Catholic institutions' role in the provision of contraception under the compromise would be remote material cooperation, which was acceptable and widely used in the realm of health care to allow Catholic hospitals to operate in secular society.[58]

But the bishops wouldn't back down. Instead, they took their demands one step further, calling for a broad conscience clause that would allow any employer who had a moral objection to contraception to refuse to provide it. Increasingly it looked as if the fight wasn't about finding a reasonable compromise that would allow Catholic employers to distance themselves sufficiently from the provision of contraception to satisfy at least the letter of the widely ignored Catholic teaching on contraception. It was an attempt to block the federal enshrinement of contraception as a basic women's health care right.

The full scope of the issue didn't become apparent to most people until a few days later, when the Republican-run House Committee on Oversight and Government Reform held a hearing on the mandate and its supposed impediment to religious freedom. Within hours a picture from the first panel of witnesses was ricocheting around the Internet and social media sites like Twitter. It showed five middle-aged men—half in clerical garb—testifying about women's access to birth control. There was Bishop Lori, testifying for the USCCB; the Reverend Matthew Harrison, president of the Missouri Synod of the Lutheran Church, a conservative Lutheran sect that has long been prominent in the anti-abortion movement; Meir Soloveichik, a conservative rabbi; and two conservative Christian theologians. When Georgetown University law student Sandra Fluke, a non-Catholic whose student health insurance excluded contraception, was denied the right to testify on the basis that the hearing wasn't about women's access to birth control but religious freedom, the picture became clear to many for the first time. It was like looking through a time machine to the 1969 hearing on abortion reform in New York City, where an all-male panel, and one nun, debated women's access to abortion.

Women's health advocates and political pundits expressed amazement that contraception could be so controversial in 2012. But they shouldn't have been surprised. That's because the forty-year fight over reproductive rights had never really been about abortion; it had always been about women and sex—specifically, the ability of women to have sex without the

Figure 12. USCCB president Rev. William Lori; Rev. Dr. Matthew Harrison, president of the Lutheran Church Missouri Synod; Professor C. Ben Mitchell of Union University; Rabbi Meir Soloveichik of Yeshiva University; and Craig Mitchell of the Southwestern Baptist Theological Seminary testify about women's access to birth control before the House Oversight and Government Reform Committee, February 16, 2012. (AP/Carolyn Kaster)

consequence of pregnancy. That's why it was the shot heard 'round the world when in the midst of the flap over the all-male birth control panel radio talk show host Rush Limbaugh called Fluke a "slut" for wanting her insurance to treat birth control like any other prescription medication. Limbaugh had revealed what the right really believed about women and sex: Women who wanted to have sex—especially outside of marriage—and control their fertility were doing something fundamentally illicit and shouldn't expect anyone else to pay for it. To them, birth control was just a lesser form of abortion.

Once the right had successfully limited access to abortion for any group it could control through public policy—mainly poor and young women who relied on public funding or lacked the money or time to jump through logistical hoops—it turned to contraception and began a similar campaign to suppress access. If the right could get Obama to back off the contraception mandate by making the conscience clause so broad that any employer could refuse to provide contraceptive coverage, it would have scored a major victory for the remarginalization of contraception. (Lost in the debate was the fact that the health reform plan also forbade insurers from requiring women to buy expensive, separate "pregnancy riders" to cover childbirth.)

And it wasn't just about birth control. The religious freedom, anti-Catholic narrative was essential to the bishops' efforts to beat back the rising tide in favor of same-sex marriage. As Sister Simone Campbell, executive director of Network, told Chris Matthews on *Hardball*, "They are claiming that the administration is persecuting Catholics and other religions in the United States. This for me is a huge fallacy, but if they accepted the [contraceptive] accommodation then they would lose their position as being oppressed by the administration."[59]

In mid-March, the bishops officially rejected the Obama compromise. A month later, they announced their "Fortnight for Freedom," a campaign for the two weeks leading up to the Fourth of July to assert that contraceptive equity and same-sex marriage were violations of Catholics' constitutional rights.

The bishops also leveraged their contacts in Congress to try to insert their doctrinal preferences into law. Longtime allies Chris Smith and Joe Pitts introduced legislation that would undo the compromise over the health reform legislation by making it illegal for any women to buy into a private health plan that covers abortion under the Affordable Care Act. The "Protect Life Act" also would allow hospitals to refuse to provide emergency abortions like the one in the McBride case. The "Respect for Rights of Conscience Act" was also reintroduced to create a blanket exemption to the Affordable Care Act that would allow any employer to refuse to provide any health care service to which it had a moral or religious objection.

Bishops Lori and Dolan called on the U.S. bishops to rally parishioners in support of the legislation. The bishops and their allies campaigned to whip Catholics into a frenzy over the religious liberty issue in anticipation of the 2012 presidential election. One bishop likened Obama and his "anti-Catholic bias" to Hitler and Stalin. Carl Anderson, head of the 1.8 million-member Knights of Columbus, addressed the National Catholic Prayer Breakfast in April, telling an audience of high-profile Catholics, "Never in the lifetime of anyone present here, has the religious liberty of the American people been as threatened as it is today."[60]

Catholics had fought for some hundred-plus years for an equal role in society by showing they could play by the same rules as everyone else. Now the bishops were telling them to thrust that aside and ask the government to give religious beliefs that emanated directly from the Vatican special preference under the law. But as in the days of the debate over a constitutional amendment to ban abortion, Catholics failed to rally to the bishops' cry. Polls still showed that a solid majority of Catholics were in favor of religiously affiliated institutions providing birth control. The conscience measure failed in the Senate and lingered on the House calendar. The Fortnight for Freedom fell flat. Again it appeared that the bishops stood alone.

.　　.　　.　　.　　.

The bishops may have been losing the battle, but as usual the Vatican was determined not to lose the war. The debate over the contraceptive mandate put the issue of the role of Catholic doctrine in public policy more firmly in the public eye than at any time since the Catholic Statement on Pluralism and Abortion. And like that famous confrontation, this one also was followed by a blowback against dissent.

In mid-April 2012, in the midst of the controversy over the contraception mandate, the Vatican's Congregation for the Doctrine of the Faith (CDF) announced that it was disciplining the LCWR for what it called "serious doctrinal problems." The nuns' group had been critical to providing a religious imprinter to the abortion compromise in the health reform plan. It had explicitly rebuked the bishops' claim that the Senate version of the reform bill would allow federal funding of abortion. It also endorsed Obama's contraception compromise, helping to remove any leverage the bishops had to claim they alone represented official Catholic opinion.[61]

The LCWR had long been a target of Vatican conservatives for what they believed was its lack of obeisance to the hierarchy. It first vexed the Vatican in 1971, when the fifteen-year-old Conference of Major Superiors of Women changed its name to the Leadership Conference of Women Religious to reflect the new, more autonomous role granted to nuns by Vatican II. The Vatican objected to the organization's use of the word "leadership," which it felt suggested the nuns were equal in authority to male clerics. Sister Margaret Brennan, who was head of the conference at the time, requested an audience with Pope Paul VI to discuss their rationale for the name change. The pope refused the audience in a message pointedly delivered through National Conference of Catholic Bishops president Cardinal John Krol, who told Brennan that the pope said that if she was "more obedient" she might get in to see him.

In 1979, LCWR president Sister Theresa Kane electrified progressive Catholics around the world when in her official welcome to Pope John Paul II on behalf of American nuns during his visit to the Shrine of the Immaculate Conception during his much-ballyhooed first visit to the United States she stood up and told him, "The church must regard the possibility of women being included in all ministries of the church." The pope had given a speech opposing women's ordination the day before. John Paul didn't deign to respond to her respectful request but did subsequently scold her for failing to wear a habit. After that, he showed marked favoritism to a conservative splinter group of the LCWR that eventually became the Council of Major Superiors of Women Religious, a smaller organization of women religious leaders that represents traditionalist orders of nuns who wear habits, support Vatican teaching on abortion and other sexuality-related issues, and leave politics to the menfolk of the church.[62]

In 2001, after years of prodding by conservatives, then-Cardinal Ratzinger, head of the CDF, issued a doctrinal warning against the LCWR. It was reportedly Baltimore Archbishop Lori, head of the bishops' Committee on Religious Liberty, who successfully petitioned the CDF to open the formal review of the LCWR in 2009 with support from Cardinal Bernard Law, who had been appointed to a position in Rome after being forced to resign from his post in Boston due to charges that he mishandled clerical sex abuse.[63]

Most of the problems identified by the Vatican investigation revolved around the nuns' lack of deference to the authority of the all-male magisterium. The LCWR was criticized for dissenting from the Vatican's teaching on women's ordination and homosexuality and for hosting speakers who claimed that "dissent from the doctrine of the Church is justified." The Vatican also condemned the "prevalence of certain radical feminist themes" in the organization's programs and presentations. Additionally, the Vatican reprimanded the LCWR for publicly challenging the bishops as "the Church's authentic teachers of faith and morals." It also said the LCWR and Network, with which it worked closely, spent too much time working on social justice issues to the exclusion of promoting the Vatican's agenda on banning abortion and gay marriage.[64]

The LCWR said it was "stunned by the severity" of the assessment, calling the process that reached it "flawed" and the charges "unsubstantiated." Many believed that politics were behind the accusations. "I would imagine that it was our health care letter that made them mad," Network's Sister Campbell told the *New York Times*, referring to their endorsement of the Obama health plan. She denied that the nuns had violated church teaching, saying they had "just been raising questions and interpreting politics."[65]

But this was exactly what the Vatican was complaining about. According to the hierarchy, the nuns had no right to make any interpretation of doctrine or policy. It was the old schism in the church reopened: progressives versus conservatives; an inclusive view of moral authority in the church that included nuns and lay Catholics versus an authoritarian, top-down approach. Except now, with progressive theologians and bishops purged or dead, the nuns were the last bastion of official progressive thought. As long as there were nuns publicly representing an even moderately progressive Catholic position, the bishops would be undercut. The nuns would need to be silenced.

The Vatican announced that Seattle Bishop J. Peter Sartain and two other bishops would oversee the "reform" of the LCWR, including a rewriting of their statutes regarding the organization's mission and responsibilities; oversight of all the organization's programs, publications, and speakers for the next five years; and the development of new materials to better inculcate the leaders of women religious about their responsibility to accept the teaching of the hierarchy. Archbishop Gerhard Müller, the current head of the CDF, said the nuns should focus on their vows of chastity, poverty, and obedience.[66]

The LCWR wasn't the only target of the Vatican crackdown on nuns. The Vatican was simultaneously conducting an investigation, or a "visitation," of all women's religious communities in the United States to examine the "soundness of their doctrine." The visitation was reportedly backed by Law and was at least partially funded by the Knights of Columbus, which has close ties to Archbishop Lori.[67]

Individual nuns also came under fire. In 2011, with little advance warning and almost no dialogue with its author, the USCCB's Committee on Doctrine denounced *Quest for a Living God*, a popular book by Fordham

University theologian Sister Elizabeth Johnson. The book had been widely praised for Johnson's attempt to explore the meaning of God within a modern context and was used by many Catholic universities and parish discussion groups. The bishops criticized Johnson not only for not hewing to a traditional understanding of God and the Trinity, but for suggesting that the use of exclusively male language to describe God created an "unequal relationship between women and men." The suddenness and ferocity of the condemnation of the widely respected scholar brought protests from noted theologians and the Catholic Theological Society of America.[68]

A little over a year later, in June 2012, the Vatican's CDF condemned another respected theologian, Sister Margaret Farley, who had taught at Yale Divinity School, for her book *Just Love: A Framework for Christian Sexual Ethics,* which found a theological justification for same-sex marriage and masturbation. The attack on two of the most prominent, progressive women theologians in the United States, both of whom had served as president of the Catholic Theological Society, left little doubt that Vatican was in the midst of a full-blown crackdown on women religious who dared explore Catholic doctrine beyond the rigid confines sanctioned by the hierarchy.[69]

Just weeks later, Sister Keehan of the CHA unexpectedly reversed her endorsement of the Obama contraception compromise. She now characterized the solution she had praised as "unduly cumbersome" and "unlikely to meet the religious-liberty concerns of our members." She joined the bishops in calling for a broad-based exemption for Catholic-affiliated institutions, echoing the bishops' assertion it was impossible to differentiate between the church and its health care and educational ministries.[70]

It was a blow to the Obama administration. With the election approaching and the bishops working to gin up the religious liberty issues, many questioned whether the CHA's change of heart was due to pressure from the bishops. Keehan was a longtime supporter of broad conscience exemptions for Catholic providers. But her experience running hospitals made her pragmatic about the grassroots realities of health care provision and she had shown herself willing to compromise to meet the greater social justice goal of expanding access to care.

Keehan was uniquely influential when it came to health care. *Modern Healthcare* magazine routinely ranked her among the most powerful people in the industry and she was named as one of the hundred most influential people of 2010 by *Time* magazine for her role in the passage of the health reform plan. Her willingness to chart an independent course for the CHA had ruptured the coordinated policy front among the CHA, Catholic Charities, and the USCCB that the bishops had been cultivating for some time. USCCB head Cardinal Francis George personally blamed her for passage of the Affordable Care Act.[71]

It must have galled the bishops that Obama personally called Keehan, a nun, along with Dolan, who would soon be elevated to a prince of the church, to get her blessing on the compromise. For her part, Keehan denied that the CHA and USCCB were at cross-purposes and would only acknowledge that the bishops "would love to see everybody saying exactly the same thing on the issue."[72]

With the CHA neutered on the issue, the bishops and a coalition of conservative Christian employers moved to quash the contraceptive mandate. Some forty Catholic universities, including Catholic University and the University of Notre Dame, Catholic dioceses, and social services agencies filed a lawsuit against the mandate. They were joined by conservative-owned companies such as Hercules Industries, a Catholic-owned manufacturing company, and Hobby Lobby, a chain of arts and crafts stores owned by a conservative Christian who objected to covering EC.

But the election of 2012 came and went without the "religious liberty" issue becoming a major flashpoint and polls showing a reawakening of interest by moderate and women voters in issues of reproductive health access, fanned by far-right efforts at the state and national levels to suppress access to abortion and birth control. Realizing the electoral power of the issue, especially after the controversy over the all-male birth control panel, the Democratic Party rushed to reembrace reproductive rights, as Republican presidential candidate Mitt Romney and conservatives struggled to explain why they would defund Planned Parenthood or redefine rape to further restrict access to abortion.

In February 2013, with the issue of the religious exemption in the contraceptive mandate looking likely to head to the Supreme Court, the Obama administration announced the draft final rules for the compromise. It altered the definition of a religious employer to comport with the IRS definition, which would allow a religious entity that ran a program that served individuals of other faiths, such as soup kitchen or school, to quality for the exemption. This would slightly broaden the exemption to make it clear that dioceses and parochial schools qualified. But the administration maintained its proposed treatment of religiously affiliated institutions such as hospitals and universities, specifying that insurers would arrange, provide, and pay for contraceptives for women employees of such organizations who objected to coverage. It even outlined a specific mechanism for institutions that self-insured that would completely remove them from the payment or administration of the contraceptive benefit through a stand-alone plan run by their insurance administrators.

Church watchers again hailed it as a reasonable compromise. *Washington Post* columnist E. J. Dionne said it was a "clear statement that President Obama never wanted this fight." He counseled the bishops to take the expansion of the definition of a religious employer as "the victory it is" and end their ill-considered war over religious freedom. The Reverend Thomas Reese, who was now the former editor of *America* magazine after a run-in with the CDF over the magazine's liberal tendencies, said the administration had "gone out of its way" to address the bishops' concerns. The CHA's Keehan also accepted the compromise, saying it would allow its members to continue to offer health insurance. The bishops rejected the compromise. As usual, they stood alone.[73]

.   .   .   .   .

Nearly fifty years after Rosemary Radford Ruether suggested that not all Catholic wives welcomed an endless string of pregnancies, Jane Furlong Cahill wrote that contraception was women's redemption, and Catholic women turned en masse to modern contraceptives, the hierarchy was trying to hijack the public policy process to enforce dogma that had long been rejected by its own followers. Pioneers of the Catholic reproductive rights movement like Ruether had seen the debate go from contraception to abortion and back to contraception, but of course it had always really been about women and sex.

Figure 13. Rosemary Radford Ruether today. Her career as a groundbreaking Catholic feminist theologian has spanned more than fifty years. (Courtesy of Rosemary Ruether)

But thanks to Ruether and Cahill and Farians and McQuillan and the women and men who took up their work in the decades following their founding of the movement, there was now a vibrant debate within the church and the public square about Catholic doctrine and reproductive health. "The main contribution of the Catholic reproductive rights movement has been giving intellectual respectability to an alternative theological ethical argument. Without it, the assumption would have been that those who critiqued the official Catholic position, especially women, were just deviant, immoral people," said Ruether.[74]

It is impossible to overstate the importance of this alternative theology to modern Catholics and their ability to grapple with issues of sexuality within the context of their religion—especially because they have been abandoned by the hierarchy on the issue. "The most important value of Catholics for Choice has been in working out a pastoral way of being Catholic—teaching people how to be Catholic in a way that gives them a measure of peace and comfort with their decisions," said theologian

Anthony Padovano. In particular, the organization's groundbreaking work on abortion dissent has had major implications for Catholics. "If you can address people on a wrenching issue like abortion and convince them that they are still Catholic, you open up the possibility that they can dissent on other issues and still be Catholic," said Padovano.[75]

The Catholic reproductive rights movement has also provided an important backstop to the enduring political power of the bishops by making pro-choice Catholicism visible. Time and time again when the bishops assert in the public square that they alone speak for Catholics, they have run headfirst into the reality of a vibrant pro-choice Catholic presence. "The work of CFC is enormously important as public policies are being debated because they are evidence on a daily basis that the ultra-conservative Catholic bishops don't represent views of Catholics in the pews," said Lois Uttley of MergerWatch, which works to curb the discontinuation of health services by Catholic providers. "For our work, having a progressive Catholic voice representing 98 percent of Catholic women is extremely helpful."[76]

Others inevitably view the movement in relationship to what the years since the *New York Times* ad have revealed about the church's leadership. "We thought there were differences of theology that we were grappling with," said theologian Mary Hunt. "We thought we were dealing with people of good will. What we didn't know then was that we were up against criminal behavior—people participating in criminal behavior and ignoring criminal behavior. The hierarchy blew issues like abortion out of proportion as cover for their long-term duplicity on issues like pedophilia," she said. Hunt credits pro-choice Catholics, gay and lesbian Catholics, and Catholic feminists for laying the groundwork for the reassessment of the church that many undertook when the pedophilia scandal hit.[77]

It is this disillusionment on the part of lay Catholics that is the fundamental reality of the church. The pedophilia scandal, combined with the hierarchy's failure to deal with issues of sexuality and women's role in the church, has resulted in not only an exodus from the church, with ex-Catholics now the single largest group of dispossessed believers in the country, but in an erosion of the church's moral authority. The church's once-vibrant voice has been muted on issues like global peace, poverty, and human rights, even as the bishops toil furiously to influence politics in the United States and elsewhere.[78]

The election of Argentinean Cardinal Jorge Mario Bergoglio as Pope Francis in March 2013 initially seemed to hold little hope of change given the overwhelmingly conservative composition of the College of Cardinals, from which the pope is both selected and elected. His election came as a surprise, although he was reportedly the runner-up in the 2005 papal conclave, and not much was known about the new pope other than he was a Jesuit who was known for his humble manner and outreach to the poor and marginalized. He was believed to be a doctrinal conservative and was an outspoken opponent of efforts to legalize same-sex marriage in Argentina when he was head of the Argentinian bishops conference.

From the start, Pope Francis impressed Catholics and non-Catholics alike with his common touch and the pronounced lack of dogma in his public addresses, which focused on the gospel messages of concern for the poor, peace, love, and mercy. Within six months of his election, it became clear that the new pope was something that the Vatican hadn't seen in some fifty years—a reformer prepared to take on entrenched power structures with the Roman Curia and who thought the Catholic Church should be more concerned with proclaiming the good news of Jesus Christ than with following an increasingly orthodox rule book.

"We cannot insist only on issues related to abortion, gay marriage and the use of contraceptive methods," Pope Francis said in an electrifying interview with *America* magazine. He acknowledged that the teaching on these matters was clear, but said the church had become "obsessed" with imposing the rules on the faithful. "We have to find a new balance; otherwise even the moral edifice of the church is likely to fall like a house of cards," warned the new pontiff.[79]

It was a profound commentary on how the division and rancor over sexuality-related issues created by the hierarchy's narrow focus had consumed the church and eroded its moral credibility. The new pontiff, who had reaffirmed the Vatican's reprimand of the LCWR shortly after he became pope, also decried the habit of conservative Catholics calling on the Vatican to discipline dissenters. He said such matters should be handled locally, or the Vatican's various congregations "run the risk of becoming institutions of censorship."[80]

And as if to prove that someone really had been listening all these years, Pope Francis said, "Women are asking deep questions that must be addressed." He said the church must think about "the specific place of women" within institutions of authority in the church, perhaps signaling the rebirth of a conversation that Pope Patricia tried to have more than forty years ago.[81]

Epilogue

The photo that accompanied the *New York Times* article about the teeming public maternity hospital in the Philippines capital of Manila told the whole story. It showed dozens and dozens of postpartum women and their newborns packed two to a bed in an overcrowded, outdated hospital ward. Some women stared blankly ahead as their newborns suckled. Others were curled in fetal positions, trying to get some sleep in the din. Many already had half a dozen children at home. Most wanted to use birth control to slow the onslaught of babies but were too poor to buy commercially available contraceptives. "I would take the pills, but we don't have money to buy those," one woman told the *Times*.[1]

In the 1990s, the Philippines had a thriving government-sponsored family planning program that made modern contraceptives available to poor women in the overwhelmingly Catholic country. But when President Gloria Macapagal-Arroyo came to power in 2001 she paid the country's Catholic bishops back for their political support by ending the family planning program. Her administration promoted natural family planning as the country's official method of birth control. Contraceptive use sagged, especially among the many poor women who could not afford to buy contraceptives in the private sector. Maternal mortality increased. Between

2003 and 2006, the number of poor in the Philippines soared by nearly 4 million.[2]

Meanwhile, other similarly situated countries in Southeast Asia, like Thailand, supported comprehensive family planning programs and flourished. Thailand saw its birthrate drop by 30 percent and its gross domestic product increase dramatically, while in the Philippines the birthrate remained high and the economy lagged. Today, just over one-quarter of the Filipino population is officially poor. Nearly 30 percent of poor women have an unmet need for contraception, meaning they would like to prevent additional pregnancies but do not have access to modern methods of birth control.[3]

Family planning advocates tried for more than a decade to restore a publicly funded family planning program in the Philippines but were stymied by the powerful Catholic Bishops' Conference of the Philippines, which is close to many elected officials. "Bishops still have a lot of political influence in the country," said Magdalena Lopez, a local reproductive rights activist.[4]

But the lessons of the Catholic reproductive rights movement in the United States were not lost on progressive Catholics in the Philippines. They formed a group called Catholics for Reproductive Health to advocate for the proposed Reproductive Health (RH) Bill to restore family planning support and make public Catholic support for access to contraceptives. "There are more thinking Catholics than the bishops are saying," said Lopez. "We needed to let people know we are out here and they can support reproductive health."[5]

Catholics for Choice organized a communications training to help activists speak to the media and their fellow Catholics. "In the Philippines fifteen years ago it was really hard to get people to stand up. Now there is a huge groundswell both politically and socially of people who want contraception and are willing to stand up for it," noted CFFC president Jon O'Brien. Professors from Ateneo University, a leading Jesuit university, issued a widely publicized statement that said Catholics could support the RH Bill in good conscience. Jesuit priest Joaquin Bernas, dean emeritus of the Ateneo de Manila Law School, came out and said the use of family planning was a personal choice.[6]

Despite overwhelming public support for the bill, the bishops fought it tooth and nail. They claimed the bill would lead the nation down a slippery slope to abortion on demand, even though it did not legalize abortion. "Yes to Life? No to RH Bill!" was the slogan of their widespread anti-RH Bill advertising campaign. Banners in front of churches castigated the measure as an "abortion bill." Nuns and priests in clerical garb testified against the bill at public hearings. Two bishops called on President Arroyo and got her to pressure the speaker of the house to stall the bill when it appeared to be gaining momentum in 2009. A bishop told the house minority leader that he was "excommunicating himself" by supporting the bill. U.S.-based anti-choice groups like Human Life International made their presence felt, amplifying the bishops' charges that the bill would end up legalizing abortion.[7]

The bill made it out of committee for the first time in 2011. When new President Benigno Aquino voiced his support for the measure, the bishops threatened him with excommunication. They said they would issue voting guidelines for the upcoming elections telling Catholic voters to reject anyone who supported the bill. They said that "contraception is corruption" and warned of an epidemic of marital infidelity and an "abortion generation" if sex were divorced from procreation. But a planned rally of 50,000 Catholics to demonstrate grassroots opposition to the bill in August 2012 netted just 7,000 protestors milling about in the rain. More and more politicians spoke out in favor of the measure. The RH Bill passed in December 2012, guaranteeing all women access to contraceptives and bringing modern sex education programs to the country.[8]

Lopez, who like O'Brien came to the United States to work for CFC to put into practice globally what she had learned locally in the Philippines, credited the thousands of activists who struggled against the bishops for years. "We look forward to seeing reductions in maternal mortality and HIV rates," she said, "as well as increases in the sort of things you can't measure—the dignity and personal autonomy that are affirmed by choice."[9]

In July 2013, under continued ferocious lobbying from the Catholic bishops, the Supreme Court indefinitely delayed implementation of the law while it considered the bishops argument that the law violated the country's constitutional protection of "the life of the unborn from conception."

Notes

The following abbreviations have been used throughout the notes to identify periodicals or sources:

BG   *Boston Globe*
CFC   *Catholics for Choice Archives*
LAT   *Los Angeles Times*
NCR   *National Catholic Reporter*
NYT   *New York Times*
WP   *Washington Post*

INTRODUCTION

1. Letter of Pope John Paul II to Women, June 29, 1995.
2. See chapter 1.
3. As Sarah Blaffer Hrdy has noted, as "new food sources became available, and as people spent more time in fewer places, birth intervals shortened," due to a combination of earlier age at menarche, increased fertility due to better nutrition, and earlier weaning thanks to the availability of cooked gruels to replace breast milk. See Hrdy, *Mother Nature*, 195–202.

CHAPTER 1. THE FOUR WISE WOMEN

1. Jane Furlong Cahill, interviewed by Patricia Miller, May 18, 2010.

2. Rock, *The Time Has Come*, 186–87.

3. The most exhaustive treatment of the evolution of Catholic theology on contraception is John T. Noonan's *Contraception*. According to Noonan, the "Christian Fathers derived their notions on marital intercourse—notions which have no express biblical basis . . . chiefly from the Stoics." He discounts the widely held belief that the story of Onan provides the biblical basis for the church's ban on contraception. Onan was commanded by God to have sexual intercourse with his dead brother's wife and "raise up seed for your brother." Onan practiced coitus interruptus and allowed his seed "to be lost on the ground" because any offspring would not be his. God punished him, however, for disobeying his command, not for the spilling of his semen. See *Contraception*, 34, 46–47.

4. From *Marriage and Concupiscence* (1418). Ironically, Augustine had himself been in a long-term, live-in sexual relationship with a woman to whom he was not married and with whom he had a son. The relationship ended when his mother pressured him to marry a more socially suitable woman. After that, he abandoned his more liberal philosophy about sex and adopted the Stoic idea that intercourse was sinful if it did not hew to its natural, that is, procreative, purpose. See Noonan, *Contraception*, 135–38.

5. Stern, legalistic, and decidedly celibate monks eager to develop clear norms for the church and strict distinctions between right and wrong were largely responsible for the codification of the church's strict sexual ethic between 550 and 1100, according to Noonan. In addition to being fearful of sex itself, the monks often associated contraceptive potions with paganism and forbidden magic *(maleficium)*. See Noonan, *Contraception*, 144–50, 173.

6. Rosemary Radford Ruether, "A Catholic Mother Tells: 'Why I Believe in Birth Control,'" *Saturday Evening Post*, April 4, 1964.

7. Ibid.

8. See Westoff and Ryder, "United States: Methods of Fertility Control," 1–5. By 1965, 20 percent of Catholic women using contraception were using the Pill, 17 percent were using condoms, 4 percent were using diaphragms, and 4 percent were using other methods like contraceptive foam and the intrauterine device (IUD), for a total of 45 percent using contraceptives. When figures assessing whether a woman had ever used contraception were included, 53 percent of Catholic women were not compliant with church rules.

9. French theologian Martin le Maistre was the first to posit in the fifteenth century that it was acceptable for married couples to have sex for the sake of pleasure, ending, according to Noonan, "the tie between procreative purpose and lawful intercourse," and beginning a new conversation about sex and pleasure within marriage. See *Contraception*, 306–8. The teaching on the purpose of marital intercourse would not undergo "substantial evolution," however, until the period between 1850 and 1964. See Noonan, *Contraception*, 491–43.

10. Ibid., 497.

11. Ruether, "A Catholic Mother Tells."

12. Noonan, *Contraception*, 426–27.

13. It condemned contraceptive sterilization, but from the perceptive of its then-current use as a forced eugenic instrument for individuals labeled undesirable rather from the perspective of a voluntary method of birth control.

14. Pius wrote that intercourse was licit for couples "even though, through natural causes either of time or of certain defects, new life cannot thence result." There was some theological controversy over exactly what Pius meant. Some said he was referring only to menopause. But the moral theologians Father John Ford and Father Gerald Kelly note in their definitive *Contemporary Moral Theology:* "The fact that the licit use of the sterile period was already at that time a commonplace among theologians, the fact that the phrase 'through natural reasons . . . of time' was used, rather than 'reasons of age' or some similar expression, and the fact that the immediate context of the encyclical itself was concern for the difficulties of married people tempted to onanism—all these considerations convinced the great majority of theologians that Pius XI was here referring to the permissible use of the sterile periods as a means of avoiding conception." See *Contemporary Moral Theology*, 387.

15. Couples had been trying to use the sterile period as a form of birth control since Felix Archimedes Pouchet reported in 1845 that the human egg matured and released as part of the menstrual cycle, indicating that there should be a "safe period" during the cycle when conception was impossible. However, most scientists incorrectly pegged ovulation to menstruation, which caused them to recommend intercourse during the period when many women were most fertile, rendering success with the method highly variable. Brodie, *Contraception and Abortion*, 79–86.

16. The Vatican had indicated since the 1850s that such a use of a natural sterile period would be acceptable as an alternative to the greater evil of contraception. The question had first been asked in 1853 by a French bishop after reports of couples trying to use a primitive version of the rhythm method surfaced. The Vatican had replied that such couples "are not to be disturbed provided they do nothing by which conception is prevented." In 1873 a French theologian was the first to take on a detailed examination of the issue and concluded that use of the sterile period offered a way to limit family size without resorting to the greater evil of contraception, a conclusion that was given qualified Vatican approval in 1880. Noonan, *Contraception*, 439–42.

17. Pope Pius XII, Moral Questions Affecting Married Life, address given October 29, 1951, to the Italian Catholic Union of Midwives; Noonan, *Contraception*, 446.

18. Noonan, *Contraception*, 461–63.

19. The theologians were Jouis Janssens, William van der Marck, and Joseph Mary Reuss. Noonan, *Contraception*, 470–72, 512–13.

20. Like many moral theologians, his greatest concern was that the Pill would lead to "anti-babyism." Bernard Häring, "Theology and the Pill," *Catholic Herald*, May 29, 1964.

21. Noonan, *Contraception*, 532–33.

22. See "The Catholic Revolution," *Look*, Feb. 9, 1967; and "Growing Unrest in the Catholic Church," *US News & World Report*, March 27, 1967.

23. Cahill, "Contraception and Eve," 469.

24. Ruether, *The Church against Itself*, 223–24.

25. Daly, *The Church and the Second Sex*, 190.

26. Mary Luke Tobin, "Women in the Church since Vatican II," *America*, Nov. 1, 1986.

27. Daly, *The Church and the Second Sex*, 9.

28. Ibid., 10.

29. *Gaudium et Spes*, Pope Paul VI, Dec. 7, 1965.

30. Henold, *Catholic and Feminist*, 46; Daly, *The Church and the Second Sex*, 123.

31. Daly, *The Church and the Second Sex*, 81–82.

32. Ibid., 89, 93.

33. Ibid., 83.

34. Ibid., 87.

35. Ibid., 86.

36. Ibid., 148–49.

37. For a full account of the commission, see McClory, *Turning Point*.

38. Like Noonan, they found that the teaching on contraception "developed in the argument and conflict with heretics such as the Gnostics, the Manichaeans and later the Cathari, all of whom condemned procreation or the transmission of life as something evil." It was "intended to protect two fundamental values: the good of procreation and the rectitude of marital intercourse" but over the centuries the "expressions and formulas proper to the times" and "the words with which it was expressed and the reasons on which it was based were changed by knowledge which is now obsolete." Pontifical Commission on Birth Control Commission, "Responsible Parenthood," 1966.

39. Pope Paul VI, *Humanae Vitae*, July 25, 1968.

40. McClory, *Turning Point*, 110.

41. Patty Crowley, one of the laywomen on the commission, is said to have answered, "Do you really believe God has carried out all your orders?" Ibid., 122. Documents released in 2011 from one of the conservative commission members confirmed the long-suspected belief that the pope had no intention of changing the contraception teaching. When the majority report recommending contraception was delivered to the pope, Cardinal Alfredo Ottaviani, head of the Vatican Congregation for the Doctrine of Faith, asked conservative Jesuit John Ford, who was a member of the commission, to write the "minority report" to rebut the majority report. Ford said Pope Paul VI told him privately in 1966 that

he was not going to change the teaching on contraception. See Gerald Slevin, "New Birth Control Commission Papers Reveal Vatican Hand," *NCR*, March 23, 2011.

42. George Dugan, "Working Mothers Called Harmful," *NYT*, March 27, 1954.

43. De Lestapis, *Family Planning*, 74–78.

44. Deirdre Carmody, "Catholic Experts in Strong Dissent on Edict by Pope," *NYT*, July 31, 1968.

45. *Truth and Consequence*. Washington, DC: CFC, 2008.

46. Anthony Padovano, interviewed by Patricia Miller, April 9, 2012.

47. Elizabeth Farians, interviewed by Patricia Miller, July 20, 2010; and Henold, *Catholic and Feminist*, 73.

48. Farians, "Theology and Animals," 104.

49. Elizabeth Farians, "How NOW Got Religion," NOW Papers on Women and Religion, 1971–72; NOW's other founding task forces were Equal Opportunity of Employment; Legal and Political Rights; Education; Women in Poverty; the Family; and the Image of Women.

50. Farians, interviewed by Miller, July 20, 2010.

51. Elizabeth Farians, "Struggle for Women's Rights in the Catholic Church," Spring 1973. Self-published pamphlet.

52. Ibid, 2.

53. "Churches Feel Pressure of Women's Rights Drive," *NYT*, May 3, 1970.

54. Henold, *Catholic and Feminist*, 78.

55. Farians, "Struggle for Women's Rights," 3.

56. Farians, "How NOW Got Religion," 4.

CHAPTER 2. THE DREAD SECRET

1. John Leo, "Pope Bars Birth Control by Any Artificial Means," *NYT*, July 30, 1968; and Mosher and Goldscheider, "Contraceptive Patterns," 101–11.

2. The definitive history of abortion practice in early America is James C. Mohr's *Abortion in America*.

3. See Brodie, *Contraception and Abortion*, for a discussion of the role of contraceptives and abortion in the nineteenth-century decline in the birthrate in the United States.

4. See ibid.; and Reagan, *When Abortion Was a Crime*, 46–79, for a discussion of the availability of various abortifacients.

5. Mohr, *Abortion in America*, 50.

6. The pills were "combinations of aloe, hellebore, powdered savin, ergot, iron, and solid extracts of tansy and rue," while the liquid medications were "oils of savin, tansy, or rue dissolved in alcohol and improved in taste by wintergreen." Brodie, *Contraception and Abortion*, 225.

7. Ibid.; Mohr, *Abortion in America*, 48–53.

8. Mohr, *Abortion in America*, 87–90.

9. Ibid., 207–8.

10. Ibid., see especially chapter 6, "The Physician's Crusade against Abortion."

11. Ibid., 240.

12. Joffe, *Doctors of Conscience*, 110.

13. For a history of abortion practice in early twentieth-century America, see Joffe, *Doctors of Conscience;* and Reagan, *When Abortion Was a Crime.* For the increase in abortions during the Depression, see Reagan, 134–38.

14. Reagan, *When Abortion Was a Crime*, 164.

15. Ibid., 179.

16. Ibid., 201–2.

17. In 1958 lawyer Herbert Packer and lawyer-physician Ralph Gampell surveyed twenty-six hospitals in California regarding their therapeutic abortion practices. They asked each hospital whether it would allow an abortion in eleven hypothetical cases that the authors created. Two of the cases were designed to be legal, two were in a gray area, and seven were clearly illegal. They found a wide variation in which abortions would be allowable in each hospital. At least one hospital would provide an abortion in each of the seven cases designed to be clearly illegal. The study found an abortion rate ranging from 1 therapeutic abortion per 126 live births to 0 therapeutic abortions per 7,615 live births. "Therapeutic Abortion," 417–55.

18. See Lader, *Abortion*, 24–31.

19. Ibid., 3, 24.

20. Joffe, *Doctors of Conscience*, 64.

21. Rachel Benson Gold, "Lessons from Before *Roe:* Will Past Be Prologue?" *The Guttmacher Report on Public Policy*, March 2003.

22. Reagan, *When Abortion Was a Crime*, 197; Martin Tolchin, "Doctors Divided on Issue," *NYT*, Feb. 27, 1967.

23. Messer and May, *Back Rooms*, 11–12.

24. Martin Tolchin, "Doctors Divided," *NYT*, Feb. 27, 1967.

25. Reagan, *When Abortion Was a Crime*, 113–30.

26. Joffe, *Doctors of Conscience*, 60.

27. Reagan, *When Abortion Was a Crime*, 211, 214.

28. Lader, *Abortion*, 3.

29. Estimates of the annual number of illegal abortions at the time ranged between 200,000 and a Planned Parenthood estimate of 1.5 million. See ibid., 1–2.

30. Up until this point, notes Kristin Luker, the hospital review committee system reflected a tacit compromise. "The presence of a strict law satisfied those who wanted to believe that virtually all abortions should be outlawed whereas the much broader interpretation of the law in actual medical practice satisfied

those who felt . . . that embryonic rights were far less compelling than the rights of mothers." See *Abortion and the Politics of Motherhood*, 77.

31. James Voyles, "Changing Abortion Laws in the United States," *Journal of Family Law*, 7: 496–511.

32. Reagan, *When Abortion Was a Crime*, 221.

33. Luker, *Abortion and the Politics of Motherhood*, 128.

34. For a discussion of how the U.S. hierarchy's relationship to the American political process evolved over the course of the twentieth century, see Byrnes, *Catholic Bishops in American Politics*, 11–53.

35. See *Gaudium et Spes*, Dec. 7, 1965, which called abortion and infanticide "unspeakable crimes."

36. "Hayes Denounces Birth Control Aim," *NYT*, Nov. 21, 1921. The church's insistence on policing the sexual morality of everyone in the society around it went back to the earliest days of Christianity, according to Jack Goody. From its founding as a sect within Judaism until well into the Middle Ages, the Catholic Church imposed its own rules regarding sex and marriage on society in an attempt to weaken pagan practices and to direct inheritances that would have otherwise gone to heirs to building up the church. "By insinuating itself into the very fabric of domestic life, of heirship and marriage, the Church gained great control over the grass roots of society itself." See Goody, *The Development of Marriage and Family*, 34–47.

37. Keith Monroe, "How California's Abortion Law Isn't Working," *NYT*, Dec. 29, 1968; Paige, *The Right to Lifers*, 56.

38. Voyles, "Changing Abortion Laws in the United States," 497.

39. Ibid; George Dugan, "Bishops Ask Fight on Abortion Bill," *NYT*, Feb. 13, 1967.

40. Sydney Schanberg, "State's 8 Catholic Bishops; Bill's Backer Loses Post," *NYT*, Feb. 12, 1967.

41. "Catholic Conference Is Sued as Lobbyist," *NYT*, May 21, 1974.

42. Haley worked for the NCCB from 1967 to 1973, according to McHugh. "Martin Ryan Haley: RIP," National Right to Life Committee, http://www.nrlc. org/news/1998/NRL3.98/rip.html. See also Segers, "The Catholic Church as Political Actor," 87–129; and Nossiff, *Before Roe*, 47.

43. Risen and Thomas, *Wrath of Angels*, 19.

44. Nossiff, *Before Roe*, 114.

45. Right to Life League of Southern California, History, http://rtllsc.org/ AboutUs/OurStory.aspx; and John Dart, "Catholic Church United by Opposition to Abortion Issue," *LAT*, April 4, 1971.

46. The measure had widespread support that evaporated after a hard-hitting advertising campaign from a coalition of anti-abortion groups, including the Michigan Catholic Conference. The conference launched a major campaign targeting Catholic voters that included the distribution of 1.5 million brochures and

exhortations from the pulpit for Catholics to vote against the measure. Karrer, "The Formation of Michigan's Anti-Abortion Movement," *Michigan Historical Review*, 22, no.1 (Spring 1996): 67–107.

47. The Virginia Society for Human Life was founded in 1967, following a call for abortion reform by Virginia's public health director. The society was quickly assisted by Richmond Bishop John Russell, who let them use church buildings for meetings and provided the fledging organization with secretarial assistance. Risen and Thomas, *Wrath of Angels*, 19. New York Right-to-Life founder Ed Golden admitted the organization got help from the Catholic Church with political races, and the New York Archdiocese said that local anti-abortion groups had received "office space, telephones, mailings and the like from the church." Fred Shapiro, "'Right to Life' Has a Message for New York State Legislators," *NYT*, Aug. 20, 1972; Tom Buckley, "Both Sides Gird for Battle on Abortion," *NYT*, Jan. 2, 1973.

48. In 1969, NARAL described local right-to-life groups as "clumsily disguised arms of the Roman Catholic Church." Gorney, *Articles of Faith*, 108.

49. Karrer, "The Formation of Michigan's Anti-Abortion Movement," 67–107.

50. Staggenborg, *The Pro-Choice Movement*, 192. In 1972 the NRLC received half its $50,000 budget from the conference. Buckley, "Both Sides Gird."

51. These states were Colorado, Arkansas, California, Delaware, Georgia, Kansas, Maryland, New Mexico, North Carolina, Oregon, South Carolina, and Virginia. Reagan, *When Abortion Was a Crime*, 331.

52. Peter Kihss, "Bill for Liberalizing New York Statue Goes to State Senate," *NYT*, June 8, 1965.

53. Kristin Luker, interviewed by Patricia Miller, Oct. 8, 2010.

54. *Voice of the Women's Liberation Movement*, 3, Jan. 1969, 3, 5–6.

55. Ibid.

56. Edith Evans Asbury, "Women Break Up Abortion Hearing," *NYT*, Feb. 14, 1969.

57. The hearing and protest was also covered by the *Daily News* under the headline "Gals Squeal for Repeal."

58. As quoted in Baehr, *Abortion without Apology*, 42.

59. See Greenhouse and Siegal, *Before* Roe v. Wade, 44.

60. Baehr, *Abortion without Apology*, 8.

61. Greenhouse and Siegal, *Before* Roe v. Wade, 39.

62. Mainstream organizations endorsing repeal by 1970 included the President's Commission on the Status of Women, Planned Parenthood, and the YWCA. Even the American Medical Association, which had opposed abortion for a hundred years, said doctors should be allowed to perform abortions for "social and economic" reasons, although they still wanted two doctors to sign off on the procedure. As a result, Catholic physicians threatened to resign. Richard Lyons, "Social Reason Accepted," *NYT*, June 25, 1970.

63. Fred Graham, "A Priest Links Easing of Abortions with Racism," *NYT,* Sept. 8, 1967.

64. Lader, *Abortion II,* 126.

65. Bill Kovach, "Final Approval of Abortion Bill Voted in Albany," *NYT,* April 11, 1970.

66. Fred Shapiro, "'Right to Life' Has a Message," *NYT,* Aug. 20, 1972.

67. Ibid.

68. In 1972, reform efforts failed in George, Indiana, Rhode Island, Colorado, Delaware, Maine, Kansas, Iowa, Illinois, Michigan, Pennsylvania, Massachusetts, and Connecticut. Jurate Kazickas, "Counterattack on Abortion Gains Ground," *NYT,* Aug. 14, 1972.

69. See Garrow, *Liberty and Sexuality;* and Critchlow, *Intended Consequences,* for a history of the bishops' efforts to suppress state and federal funding for birth control.

70. Gene Burns argued that the bishops were successful in their efforts to inhibit the legalization of birth control because they were able to tap into a generally conservative climate about sex and broader societal concerns about widespread availability of contraception. "[W]hile Catholic natural law doctrine provided specifically Catholic reasons to see birth control as intrinsically immoral, an appeal to broader moral distaste for contraception, and to presumed deleterious consequences of its use, was the mainstay of Catholic doctrine," he notes. *The Moral Veto,* 129–49.

71. Ti-Grace Atkinson, president of the New York chapter of NOW, criticized the organization for not taking on the church directly, which was one reason she left to join a more radical group of feminists. "If you've got a position on abortion, you've got one on the church," she said. See Hole and Levine, *Rebirth of Feminism,* 90.

72. Lader, *Abortion II,* 133.

73. Drinan, "The Morality of Abortion Laws," *Catholic Lawyer* 14 (Summer 1968): 264.

74. Nossiff, *Before* Roe, 107–8.

75. "Catholics Ask for Free Choice in Abortions," *Pittsburgh Post-Gazette,* Sept. 25, 1971.

76. Letter to the Members of the Commonwealth of Pennsylvania General Assembly, from Mary S. Robison, Roman Catholics for the Right to Choose, Sept. 1971, Pennsylvania State Archives, Harrisburg, PA, Pennsylvania Historical and Museum Commission.

77. Testimony given before the Abortion Commission in Harrisburg, PA, Feb. 9, 1972, by Dr. Jane Furlong Cahill, Pennsylvania State Archives, Harrisburg, PA, Pennsylvania Historical and Museum Commission.

78. Jane Furlong Cahill, interviewed by Patricia Miller, May 18, 2010.

CHAPTER 3. POPE PATRICIA

1. "Estimated Median Age at First Marriage, by Sex: 1890 to Present," U.S. Census Bureau, *Annual Social and Economic Supplement: 2003 Current Population Survey, Current Population Reports,* Series P20–553; and Blake, "The Americanization of Catholic Reproductive Ideals," 27–43.

2. Joffe, *Doctors of Conscience,* 25.

3. The divorce rate began its historic increase around 1960. See Table 1: Estimated number of divorces and children involved in divorces: United States, 1950–90, in Sally C. Clarke, "Advance Report of Final Divorce Statistics, 1980 and 1990," *Monthly Vital Statistics Report,* 43(9), 1–6. Where just under 38 percent of women over the age of sixteen worked in 1960, by 1970 that percentage increased to just over 43 percent. See Howard N. Fullerton Jr., "Labor Force Participation: 75 Years of Change, 1950–98 and 1998–2025," *Monthly Labor Review,* Dec. 1999.

4. My mother was a successful buyer for a large department store in New York City in the early 1960s before she married. When she was interviewing for a new job, the man interviewing asked her point-blank if she planned to get married and have children. She got the job as head buyer, but she knew that no matter how good she was at the job, only men would be promoted up the ladder to vice president. Sociologist Kristin Luker recalls getting turned down for a fellowship when she was in graduate school in the late 1960s and being told that the slot went to a man under the assumption that she would have a family and leave academia. Kristin Luker, interviewed by Patricia Miller, Oct. 8, 2010.

5. Martha Weinman Lear, "The Second Feminist Wave," *NYT,* March 10, 1968.

6. "'Sexism in Religion' Criticized by Women," *Virgin Island Daily News,* March 8, 1974.

7. "You Can Be a Catholic and Favor Abortion, She Says," *Cleveland Press,* March 6, 1974.

8. Noonan, "An Almost Absolute Value in History," 8–11.

9. St. Jerome wrote that "the seeds are gradually formed in the uterus, and it is not reputed homicide until the scattered elements receive the appearance and members." Noonan, "An Almost Absolute Value in History," 8–9, 16.

10. From the canon Aliquando compiled by Gratian. Ibid., 20; and Hurst, *The History of Abortion,* 15.

11. This was a minority view for a time but became the majority view in the 1500s, when the Spanish theologian Martin de Azplicueta, the leading canonist of the times, ruled that doctors may abort an unensouled fetus to save the life of a woman. Spanish Jesuit Tomás Sanchez held that abortion would be licit in this case, as well as in the case of a betrothed woman who had illicit sex and feared

she may bear the child of another man to her husband. The Sacred Penitentiary in the time of Pope Gregory XIII considered saving a woman's reputation as a mitigating factor that lessened the penalty for later abortions. Noonan, "An Almost Absolute Value in History," 27–28, 32–33.

12. Ibid., 36–42.

13. Curran, "Abortion: Law and Morality," 162–83.

14. Traina, "Catholic Clergy on Abortion," 151–56.

15. Patricia McQuillan, address at Cleveland State University, March 6, 1973, CFC.

16. Elizabeth Farians, interviewed by Patricia Miller, July 20, 2010.

17. Judy Klemesrud, "Feminist Organization Is Fighting 'Oppression' in the Catholic Church," *NYT*, Dec. 1, 1973.

18. Catholics for the Elimination of All Restrictive Abortion and Contraception Laws press release, Dec. 11, 1972, CFC; McQuillan, address at Cleveland State University.

19. *Roe v. Wade*, Sec. IX, 1973.

20. For a complete discussion of the sociological implications of abortion positions, see Luker, *Abortion and the Politics of Motherhood.*

21. John Cardinal Krol, "Statement on Abortion," Jan. 22, 1973; NCCB, "Pastoral Message on Abortion," Feb. 13, 1973.

22. According to McQuillan, nuns from the Sisters of Charity, the Sisters of Mercy, and the Marymount Sisters joined the organization. Reuters, "Work to Repeal Laws Regulating Birth Control," Feb. 23, 1973.

23. Cosigners included NOW, Planned Parenthood, NARAL, the Board for the Homeland Ministries of the United Church of Christ, and the Central Conference of American Rabbis. "Maude's Dilemma Is Your Problem Too!" *LAT*, Aug. 21, 1973, p. 14.

24. The "free" in "free choice" referred to women's ability to have true choice when it came to abortion, which included not only the legal availability of abortion but economic and physical access to abortion services as well as the moral right to choose abortion. See Rosemary Radford Ruether, "Reflections on the Word 'Free' in Free Choice," *Conscience*, Summer 1994.

25. Beatrice Blair to Frances Kissling, May 5, 1993, CFC.

26. The text of McQuillan's address on the steps of St. Patrick's is taken from her letter to the editor, *Time*, Feb. 1, 1974, and Mel Juffe, "Both Sides Make Their Points on Abortion," *New York Post*, Jan. 23, 1994.

27. Ibid.

28. McQuillan, letter to editor, *Time*, Feb. 1, 1974.

29. Patricia Carbine, interviewed by Patricia Miller, June 15, 2010.

30. Harriman to S. Harmany, Pennsylvania Abortion Coalition, June 13, 1974, CFC.

31. Luker, interviewed by Miller, Oct. 8, 2010.

32. McQuillan, address at Cleveland State University.

33. Planned Parenthood provided CFFC with a small office with a desk, typewriter, file cabinet, and telephone line, first at its office a 810 Seventh Ave. and then at its new location at 515 Madison Ave. Pamela Veerhusen, Planned Parenthood Federation of America, to Harriman, April 30, 1974, CFC; and Harriman to Ilse Darling, RCAR, March 22, 1974, CFC.

34. CFFC brochure circa 1974, CFC. McQuillan also wrote to Daly to keep her apprised of the movement and even asked her if she would be willing to lend her name to the newly formed Religious Coalition for Abortion Rights, perhaps thinking Daly would be more inclined to support an ecumenical abortion rights organization, but apparently she was not, because she didn't lend her name to the organization. McQuillan to Daly, Feb. 18, 1974, CFC.

35. *Conscience*, June 1974.

36. "Patricia Fogarty McQuillan," *Conscience*, July 1974.

37. John Cardinal Krol, Testimony before the Subcommittee on Constitutional Amendments of the Senate Committee on the Judiciary, March 7, 1974.

38. Marjorie Hyer, "Abortion Issue Stains Ecumenism," *WP*, April 5, 1974.

39. Ibid.

40. The Office of Pro-Life Activities operated directly out of the bishops' conference under Monsignor James McHugh, who had been in charge of anti-abortion activities for the bishops since 1967. Risen and Thomas, *Wrath of Angels*, 20.

41. Fred Shapiro, "'Right to Life' Has a Message," *NYT*, Aug. 20, 1972.

42. Karrer, "The Formation of Michigan's Anti-Abortion Movement," 67–107.

43. The National Right to Life Committee was formally incorporated on May 14, 1973. At its first convention in June 1973, Ed Golden was elected president and Marjory Mecklenburg was elected chair of the board. Karrer, "The Formation of Michigan's Anti-Abortion Movement," 67–107.

44. Byrnes, *Catholic Bishops*, 57.

45. Lester Kingsolving, "Campaign Crumbles," *The Day* (New London, CT), June 22, 1974. NCHLA head Robert Lynch denied that the committee posed a threat to the NRLC, but he laid out a short-term strategy for the new organization that included bringing together all the various pro-life groups in the country and creating state-level groups. Lynch, "The National Committee for a Human Life Amendment," 303–10.

46. In a hand-written P.S. she asks Harriman to let her know whether air mail made any difference in how fast her letter got to her, so obviously she was looking for ways to speed up communication between DC and New York. Ellefson-Brooks to Harriman, n.d., CFC.

47. Meta Mulcahy to L. Van Haste, Aug. 27, 1974, CFC.

48. Judith Cummings, "Jesuit Dismissed on Abortion Issue," *NYT*, Sept. 7, 1974.

49. "O'Rourke, Teacher Uphold Abortion," *NCR*, n.d., 1974, CFC.

50. "Abortion: The Double Standard," Testimony by Jane Furlong Cahill, before the United States Senate Subcommittee on the Judiciary, Washington, DC, Sept. 12, 1974.

51. Harriman envisioned Catholic Alternatives as a direct service organization that would provide counseling and education about responsible sexuality, contraception, and abortion to Catholics through dedicated centers. It opened one counseling center in Manhattan in November 1976. In 1978, John D. Rockefeller III provided Catholic Alternatives with $10,000 in general support, a grant that in one publication is mistakenly attributed to CFFC. The organization ceased to function after about 1980. See Patricia McCormack, "Catholic Laity Organizes Center," UPI, Nov. 2, 1976, and e-mail from Mary Ann Quinn, archivist, Rockefeller Archive Center, to Patricia Miller, Jan. 25, 2011.

52. "New CFFC President," *Conscience*, February/March 1975.

53. Everett Holles, "Abortion Backers Denied Eucharist," *NYT*, April 14, 1975; Everett Holles, "Target of Bishop's Ire Explains Her Views on Abortion," *NYT*, April 23, 1975.

54. Cahill and Farians remained lifelong activists. Cahill, who passed away in September 2011, was a longtime advocate for mental health programs. At the age of eighty-one she led a petition drive in Chattanooga, TN, to keep libraries open seven days a week. Farians founded Animals, People and the Earth (APE). In 2001 she successfully persuaded Cincinnati Archbishop Daniel Pilarczyk to call for an end to the use of turtles and other live animals in parish festivals.

55. "Pastoral Plan for Pro-Life Activities," NCCB, Nov. 20, 1975.

56. Robert N. Lynch, "'Abortion' and 1976 Politics," *America*, March 6, 1976.

57. Richard Rashke, "Bishops Urge Nationwide 'Pro-Life Citizens Lobbies,'" *NCR*, Nov. 28, 1975.

58. "The Catholic Party," *NCR*, Nov. 28, 1975.

59. Michele Magar, "Abortion Politics and the American Catholic Church," *Conscience*, July 1981.

60. Paige, *The Right to Lifers*, 73.

61. The policy reversal was at the suggestion of advisor Pat Buchanan, who said that abortion was "a rising issue and a gut issue with Catholics." See Greenhouse and Siegal, "Before (and after) *Roe v. Wade*," 2054.

62. Robert McFadden, "President Supports Repeal of State Law on Abortion," *NYT*, May 7, 1972; "Mr. Nixon's Intervention," *NYT*, May 8, 1972.

63. Byrnes, *Catholic Bishops*, 65.

64. Ibid, 70, 75–76.

65. CFFC Statement, Sept. 15, 1976; Ibid., 77.

66. Two other amendments limiting access to abortion had successfully passed but neither was as broad in scope as the Hyde Amendment. The federal Church Amendment, passed in 1973, decreed that no individual or institution could be required to perform an abortion or sterilization that violated their

moral or religious convictions. The Helms Amendment, first enacted in 1973, prohibited the use of any foreign aid money for abortions.

67. Martin Tolchin, "On Abortion, the House Still Remain Miles Apart," *NYT*, Nov. 27, 1977.

68. Byrnes, *Catholic Bishops*, 58.

69. Laurie Johnson, "Abortion Foes Gain Support as They Intensify Campaign," *NYT*, Oct. 23, 1977; one CFFC member forwarded an envelope she received at mass at Our Lady of Mercy Church in Potomac, MD, for a special collection for the Pro-Life Congressional District Action Committee, CFC; Lawrence Lader, "Abortion Opponents' Tactics," *NYT*, Jan. 11, 1978.

70. Virginia Andary, "We Lose Hyde," *Conscience*, Sept. 1976.

71. Joan Stanley to Joseph O'Rourke, Feb. 13, 1979, CFC.

CHAPTER 4. COMING OF AGE

1. Elizabeth (Pat) McMahon, interviewed by Patricia Miller, June 14, 2010.

2. Pat McMahon to Mary Gordon, Nov. 20, 1979, CFC.

3. The $15,000 had been raised by Andary as seed money to help secure the movement's future, according to former CFFC board president Carol Bonosaro. Carol Bonosaro, e-mail communication with Patricia Miller, June 9, 2010.

4. Pat McMahon to Jennie Lifrieri-Ries, May 27, 1981, CFC.

5. Pope John Paul II had participated in the Second Vatican Council, "but felt its teaching had been badly misapplied through an uncritical embrace of modernity and a too-hasty abandonment of elements of church practice and doctrine." See John Allen, "He Was a Magnificent Pope Who Presided over a Controversial Pontificate," *NCR*, 2005, http://www.nationalcatholicreporter.org/update /conclave/jp_obit_main.htm.

6. UPI, "Pope, Criticizing Abortion, Calls Human Life Too Sacred a Value," *NYT*, Nov. 15, 1978.

7. Paige, *The Right to Lifers*, 135.

8. Laurie Johnson, "Abortion Foes Gain Support as They Intensify Campaign," *NYT*, Oct. 23, 1977; Nathaniel Sheppard, "Group Fighting Abortion Planning to Step Up Its Drive," *NYT*, July 3, 1978.

9. Paige, *The Right to Lifers*, 136. Credit for the term "pro-family" goes to ERA opponent Phyllis Schlafly, who organized a "pro-family" rally in response to the 1977 federally sponsored National Women's Conference in Houston, which marked the International Year of the Woman. Attendees heard from the NRLC and the National March for Life, and Anita Bryant, a prominent opponent of gay rights, and passed a resolution against "abortion, the proposed equal rights amendment, and lesbian rights." Other groups in attendance included Howard Phillips' Conservative Caucus and the John Birch Society. Judy Klemesrud,

"Equal Rights Plan and Abortion Are Opposed by 15,000 at Rally," *NYT*, Nov. 20, 1977.

10. Paige, *The Right to Lifers*, 135.

11. The Life Amendment Political Action Committee was founded in 1977 and the American Life League in 1979. See Byrnes, *Catholic Bishops*, 88, and Paige, *The Right to Lifers*, 146–51.

12. Weyrich met with Falwell and told him, "Out there is what you might call the moral majority." Weyrich remembered that Falwell turned to an aide and said, "If we get involved, that's the name of the organization." Dan Gilgoff, "How Paul Weyrich Founded the Christian Right," *US News & World Report*, Dec. 18, 2008.

13. Robert Lynch, "'Abortion' and 1976 Politics," *America*, March 1976.

14. The May 14, 1976, issue of *Triumph* reported that NCCB president Bernardin was "threatening the existence of right to life in Cincinnati and Cleveland" because the organizations were urging Ohio legislators to support a human life amendment when the Catholic Conference had "hired a staffer to lobby for a states' rights amendment." See *Conscience*, July 1976; Lynch, "'Abortion' and 1976 Politics."

15. Byrnes, *Catholic Bishops*, 87.

16. Francis X. Clines, "Pope Ends U.S. Visit with Capital Mass Affirming Doctrine," *NYT*, Oct. 8, 1979.

17. "An Open Letter Concerning Human Rights to His Holiness, Pope John Paul II," *WP*, Sunday, Oct. 7, 1979. The *Post* refused to publish the ad in a special commemorative section because it wasn't "congratulatory," so McMahon had to raise $20,000 to run it in the regular paper at a much higher rate. "It was a very respectful ad but they felt they would lose money from other advertising if they put it in there," said McMahon. McMahon, interviewed by Miller, June 14, 2010.

18. McMahon, interviewed by Miller, June 14, 2010.

19. "History of CFFC," unpublished, CFC.

20. McMahon, interviewed by Miller, June 14, 2010. The "Abortion in Good Faith" series included "The History of Abortion in the Catholic Church"; "My Conscience Speaks," in which Catholic women discussed their abortions; and "I Support You but Cannot Sign My Name," which took its title from a note scrawled across a response coupon included in the *Washington Post* ad directed to Pope John Paul II, which chronicled the experiences of Catholics confronted by the reproductive crises of others in their professional or personal lives.

21. McMahon interviewed by Miller, June 14, 2010.

22. Bonosaro, e-mail communication to Miller, June 9, 2010.

23. Michele Magar, "Abortion Politics and the American Catholic Church," *Conscience*, July 1981.

24. AP, "U.S. Bishops Urging Rome to Re-Examine Birth Control Issue," *NYT*, Sept. 29, 1980.

25. Padovano, interviewed by Miller, April 9, 2012.

26. Ibid.

27. Francis X. Murphy, "Of Sex and the Catholic Church," *Atlantic Monthly*, February 1981.

28. Pope John Paul II, *Familiaris Consortio*, Nov. 22, 1981.

29. The *Directives* were subsequently revised in 1975, 1994, 2001, and 2009. The original version of the *Directives* was released in 1948 and updated in 1956 but was not official policy unless it was adopted by the bishop of the diocese in which the hospital was located. When some hospitals began interpreting the prohibitions on sterilization and contraceptives more liberally in the late 1960s, the Catholic Hospital Association asked the NCCB to "compose and promulgate a set of *Directives* that would be uniform for the entire country." O'Rourke, Kopfensteiner, and Hamel, "A Brief History," 18–21.

30. Lawrence Lader, "The Family Planning Ploy," *NYT*, Dec. 12, 1985.

31. *Encyclopedia of Women and Religion in North America*, Keller and Ruether, eds., 1103–4.

32. NCCB: Statement on Tubal Ligation, July 9, 1980.

33. Marjorie Hyer, "Catholics Tighten Sterilization Ban," *WP*, July 10, 1980.

34. Drinan, "The Morality of Abortion Laws," 190–98.

35. See Mark Feeny, "Congressman-Priest Drinan Dies," *BG*, Jan. 29, 2007.

36. UPI, "Bishop Hopes Reagan Keeps Vow on Abortion Ban," *NYT*, Nov. 10, 1980.

37. "Church Jumps into Hatch Fray," *Conscience*, Nov./Dec.1981.

38. Ibid.

39. "Bishops Convene for Surprise Abortion Disarray," *Conscience*, Nov./Dec. 1981.

40. The Reverend Edward Bryce, Statement on CFFC, undated, CFC.

41. William McGurn, "Catholics & 'Free Choice,'" *National Catholic Register*, Feb. 14, 1982.

42. McMahon, interviewed by Miller, June 14, 2010.

43. C. McKenna, "Church Enlists Massgoers in Hatch Amendment Push," *Conscience*, March/April 1982.

44. Nadine Brozan, "Opposing Sides Step up Efforts on Abortion Measure," *NYT*, Feb. 15, 1981.

45. Frances Kissling, interviewed by Rebecca Sharpless, transcript of audio recording, September 13–14, 2002, Population and Reproductive Health Oral History Project, Sophia Smith Collection, Smith College, Northampton, MA, 5–6.

46. Ibid., 7.

47. Ibid., 59.

48. Ibid., 81.

49. Sheila Caudle, "The Triumph of Coalition Politics," *Ms.*, Jan. 1983.

50. Ann Crittenden, "Pro-Abortion Group Sets a Major Political Drive," *NYT*, June 14, 1982.

51. Steven Roberts, "Senate Kills Plan to Curb Abortion by a Vote of 47–46," *NYT,* Sept. 16, 1982.

52. The rift among the bishops was on full display at the NCCB annual meeting less than two weeks after their endorsement of the measure, when several prominent bishops complained that the NCCB had sacrificed its hard-line position on a human life amendment for political expediency. Cardinal Cooke was forced to call for an impromptu resolution voicing the bishops' support for the amendment, but it took a prolonged, closed-door session before the bishops rounded up enough votes to affirm their commitment to it. "Bishops Convene," Nov./Dec. 1981.

53. CFFC press release, April 19, 1982, CFC.

54. "Catholic Women Meet the Press," *Conscience,* Nov./Dec. 1982.

55. Phyllis Trible, "The Creation of a Feminist Theology," *NYT,* May 1, 1983.

56. Rosemary Radford Ruether, interviewed by Patricia Miller, Oct. 29, 2010.

57. Frances Kissling, "A Greeting from Our New Director," *Conscience,* March/April 1982.

58. David Anderson, "Independent Catholic Group Offers Abortion Guidelines," UPI/*Raleigh Times,* Feb. 25, 1984.

59. Dan Maguire, interviewed by Patricia Miller, August 10, 2010.

60. Mary Jean Collins, interviewed by Patricia Miller, August 20, 2010.

61. Joseph Bernardin, "A Consistent Ethic of Life," Fordham University, Dec. 6, 1983.

62. Byrne, *Catholic Bishops,* 115.

63. Joseph Bernardin, "Exploiting the Pastoral," *Chicago Catholic,* March 25, 1983.

CHAPTER 5 THE CARDINAL OF CHOICE

1. Kurt Anderson, "For God and Country," *Time,* Sept. 10, 1984.

2. Ari Goldman, "New York's Controversial Archbishop," *New York Times Magazine,* Oct. 14, 1984.

3. See "Archbishop Contends Abortion Is Key Issue," *NYT,* June 25, 1984; and Sam Roberts, "Cuomo to Challenge Archbishop over Criticism of Abortion Stand," *NYT,* Aug. 3, 1984.

4. Michael Oreskes, "Cuomo Adds to Debate with Church on Policy," *NYT,* Aug. 13, 1984.

5. Former Jesuit priest Albert Jonsen, who was present at the gathering, recalled it in his book *The Birth of Bioethics,* 290–91.

6. J. Giles Milhaven, "Catholic Theologians and the Abortion Debate," *Conscience,* July/Aug. 1984.

7. Jonsen, *The Birth of Bioethics,* 291.

8. Milhaven, "Catholic Theologians."

9. Fox Butterfield, "Archbishop of Boston Cites Abortion as 'Critical' Issue," *NYT*, Sept. 6, 1984.

10. Robert McFadden, "Archbishop Calls Ferraro Mistaken on Abortion Rule," *NYT*, Sept. 10, 1984.

11. Frances Kissling, "Afterword," in *The Abortion Issue in the Political Process*. Washington, DC: CFFC, 1982.

12. Jim Castelli, "Abortion and the Catholic Church"; Martire, "Polling the Catholic Public"; and Ken Swope, "Successful Political Responses," in *The Abortion Issue in the Political Process*.

13. Dan Maguire, "Catholic Options in the Abortion Debate," in ibid.

14. Cover letter from Geraldine A. Ferraro, Leon Panetta, and Tom Daschle, for *The Abortion Issue*, Sept. 30, 1982.

15. See AP, "O'Connor Critical of Ferraro Views," *NYT*, Sept. 9, 1984; Robert D. McFadden, "O'Connor-Ferraro Dispute on Abortion Unresolved," *NYT*, Sept. 11, 1984; and Jane Perlez, "Ferraro Acts to Still Abortion Dispute," *NYT*, Sept. 12, 1984. A week later in a letter to the editor of the *New York Times*, Maguire said that O'Connor should criticize him since he authored the offending line that the Catholic position on abortion was not "monolithic." Letter to the Editor, *NYT*, Sept. 16, 1984.

16. Wayne Barrett, "Holier Than Thou," *Village Voice*, Dec. 1984; and John Herbers, "Catholic Activism: Reasons and Risks," *NYT*, Sept. 23, 1984. Anti-abortion organizations were in possession of the CFFC briefing materials. In its June 1984 issue of *LifeLetter*, the Ad Hoc Committee in Defense of Life noted that Ferraro "sent out a memo (on her own house letterhead) introducing CFFC's printed pro-abort 'Briefing for Catholic Legislators.'" *LifeLetter* no. 6, 1984.

17. Ellen Goodman, "Bishops as Bosses," *WP*, Sept. 11, 1984.

18. He made the speech after 150 protestant ministers, led by well-known Methodist minister Norman Vincent Peale, issued a letter urging Americans not to vote for a Catholic. The National Conference of Citizens for Religious Freedom said that although Kennedy claimed he wouldn't be influenced by the hierarchy, "his church insists that he is duty bound to admit to its direction." "Protestant Groups' Statements," *NYT*, Sept. 8, 1960.

19. John F. Kennedy, speech to Greater House Ministerial Association, Sept. 12, 1960.

20. John Herberts, "Abortion Issue Threatens to Become Profoundly Divisive," *NYT*, Oct. 14, 1984.

21. Mario Cuomo, "Religious Belief and Public Morality: A Catholic Governor's Perspective," Speech delivered at the University of Notre Dame, Sept. 13, 1984.

22. Dan Maguire, interviewed by Patricia Miller, Aug. 10, 2010. According to Marjorie Maguire, the model was the 1966 statement by the Catholic Committee on Population and Government Policy, which endorsed public financing of

family planning programs when Congress was considering federal support of such programs. Many lawmakers were afraid to support family planning because of a feared backlash from the Catholic hierarchy. Some 500 Catholic academics, including the dean of the Notre Dame Law School, doctors, and lawyers, as well as forty-five priests and twenty-one nuns, signed on in support. See Marjorie Maguire, "Pluralism on Abortion in the Theological Community: The Controversy Continues," *Conscience*, Jan./Feb. 1986; and John Cogley, "500 Catholics Support Family Planning Programs, *NYT*, May 11, 1966.

23. Catholic Statement on Pluralism and Abortion, *NYT*, Oct. 7, 1984.

24. Ibid.

25. Maguire, interviewed by Miller, Aug. 10, 2010.

26. Kenneth Briggs, "Bishops Describe View of Politics," *NYT*, Oct. 14, 1984.

27. Kenneth Briggs, "Fight Abortion, O'Connor Urges Public Officials," *NYT*, Oct. 16, 1984; Kenneth Briggs, "Cardinal Presses Catholics to Attack Wide Range of Social Issues," *NYT*, Oct. 26, 1984.

28. Adam Clymer, "Religion and Politics Mix Poorly for Democrats," *NYT*, Nov. 25, 1984.

29. "Abortion and 'Free Choice,'" Statement by Committee on Doctrine of the NCCB, Nov. 15, 1984.

30. "Dear Sister," *Conscience*, Winter 1984/1985.

31. Barbara Ferraro, interviewed by Patricia Miller, Aug. 13, 2010.

32. Rosemary Radford Ruether, "Why This Issue, At This Time?" *Conscience*, Winter 1984/1985.

33. AP, "Cardinal Insists Nuns Retract Abortion View," *NYT*, Aug. 25, 1985.

34. Russell Chandler, "Bishops Warn against Dissent on Church's Anti-Abortion Stance," *LAT*, Oct. 3, 1985; AP, "Church Officials Permitting Nuns to Clarify Opinions on Abortion," *WP*, Nov. 9, 1985.

35. St. Martin's College wrote Maguire in January 1985 that the college's board "determined that the St. Martin's religious studies program should avoid the hiring of personnel who advocate teachings that may be contrary to the tenets of the Roman Catholic Church." The College of St. Scholastica cancelled an agreement with Maguire to be the keynote speaker at their summer ministry institute. In April, Boston College cancelled a year-old contract with Maguire to teach a summer course on Christian ethics, telling him his "presence was not desired." In March, Villanova University withdrew its invitation for Maguire to give the opening address at its annual theology institute because of his "involvement in public controversy." See Report of a Special Committee, "Academic Freedom and the Abortion Issue," *Academe*, July–Aug. 1986.

36. Joanne Ball, "Teacher Says Abortion View Cost Him BC Job," *BG*, April 26, 1985.

37. "Academic Freedom," July–Aug. 1986.

38. Mary Hunt, interviewed by Patricia Miller, Sept. 15, 2010.

39. Carol Coston, "Temporal Solutions to the Very Noble Art of Politics," *Conscience*, May 1983.

40. The committee included Kissling, Hunt, Ruether, Marjorie Maguire, and two nuns who refused to recant their support of the statement, Barbara Ferraro and Patricia Hussey.

41. "Don't Sign the Abortion Ad," *NCR*, Sept. 27, 1985.

42. Frances Kissling, "The NCR and the Infamous Ad: A Pariah Responds," *Conscience*, Sept./Oct. 1985.

43. Pat Windsor, "Dissent Legitimate, Ad Claims," *Catholic Herald*, March 6, 1986.

44. AP, "R.I. Planned Parenthood Director Excommunicated by Catholic Church," *BG*, Jan. 23, 1986; "Roman Catholics: A Rare Excommunication," *Time*, Feb. 3, 1986.

45. Committee of Concerned Catholics, "Declaration of Solidarity," March 2, 1986, CFC.

46. One nun signed a statement saying she "agrees in principle that abortion is always wrong." Two days later, six Sisters of Loretto met with the archbishop and signed a statement that read: "We had no intention of making a pro-abortion statement. We regret the statement was misconstrued by some who read it that way. We hold, as we have in the past that human life is sacred and inviolable. We acknowledge this as the teaching of the church." Mary Hunt and Frances Kissling, "The 'New York Times' Ad," 115–27.

47. UPI, "11 Nuns Deny Statement by Vatican on Abortion," *NYT*, July 25, 1986.

48. Pat Hussey, interviewed by Patricia Miller, Aug. 13, 2010.

49. Joseph Berger, "Order of Nuns to Resist Move to Oust 2 Dissenters," *NYT*, June 19, 1986.

50. Hunt and Kissling, "The 'New York Times' Ad."

51. Denise Shannon, "A Mouse that Roars Turns 20," *Conscience*, Spring/Summer 1993.

52. Janet Wallach, "The Cardinal of Choice," *WP Magazine*, Aug. 24, 1986.

53. Richard Doerflinger, "Who Are Catholics for a Free Choice," *America*, Nov. 16, 1985.

54. Ibid.

55. Marjorie Maguire, "Pluralism on Abortion."

56. Kissling, "The NCR and the Infamous Ad."

57. Tom W. Smith, "Catholics' Attitudes on Abortion, 1962–1982," *Conscience*, July/Aug. 1984.

58. Mary Jean Collins, interviewed by Patricia Miller, Aug. 20, 2010.

59. Frances Kissling, Editorial, *Conscience*, May 1983.

60. "The density and extensiveness of the pro-life mobilization is importantly the result of the leadership by the hierarchy of the American Catholic Church

and the consequent widespread availability to activists of the structures of the church and its community organizations," he wrote. McCarthy, "Pro-Life and Pro-Choice Mobilization," 53.

61. John McCarthy and Mayer Zald first recognized the evolution of social movements in their landmark 1973 paper, "The Trend of Social Movements in America: Professionalization and Resource Mobilization," in which they noted that the "picture of movements composed of aggrieved individuals banding together to fight for their due seems to us seriously inadequate." While social movement organizations traditionally were dependent on members for both funding and the manpower, in a modern, affluent society these functions have been "increasingly taken over by full-time employees" and funded by outside sources such as philanthropic foundations. McCarthy and Zald, "The Trend of Social Movements in America," 1–30.

62. Frances Kissling, interviewed by Rebecca Sharpless, transcript of audio recording, September 13–14, 2002, Population and Reproductive Health Oral History Project, Sophia Smith Collection, Smith College, Northampton, MA, 102.

63. Collins, interviewed by Miller, Aug. 20, 2010.

64. "'Catholic' Abortion Lobby Termed Fraud by Coalition President," *Wanderer*, Dec. 19, 1986.

65. Doerflinger, "Who Are Catholics for a Free Choice."

66. Joseph Berger, "Catholic Dissent on Church Rules Found," *NYT*, Nov. 25, 1985.

67. Greeley, *American Catholics since the Council*, 81.

CHAPTER 6. THE BISHOPS' LOBBY

1. They called the measure scripturally and theological flawed. "Bishops Reconsidering Appointee Who Supported Women as Priests," *NYT*, July 16, 1986; and AP, "Professor Is Awarded Tenure Despite Views," *NYT*, Aug. 29, 1986.

2. Ari Goldman, "Vatican Curbs U.S. Theologian over Liberal Views on Sex Issues," *NYT*, Aug. 19, 1986.

3. Marjorie Hyer, "600 Theologians Support Curran," *WP*, March 26, 1986.

4. Russell Chandler, "Results of Controversial Survey by Former Jesuit," *LAT*, Aug. 20, 1986.

5. AP, "Vatican Moves to Curb Power of a Liberal Prelate in Seattle," *NYT*, Sept. 5, 1986.

6. Ari Goldman, "Catholic School Expels Girl over Abortion Stand," *NYT*, Aug. 16, 1986.

7. "Cardinal Law: Protests Won't Detract from Pope's Visit," *BG*, March 23, 1987.

8. "The Cologne Declaration," *Conscience,* March/April 1989.

9. "Joseph Cardinal Ratzinger's Report Issued on Seattle Archbishop Raymond Hunthausen," *Seattle Catholic,* http://www.seattlecatholic.com/misc_20040105.html.

10. Russell Chandler, "Americans Spoke Their Minds in 4-Day 'Summit' at the Vatican," *LAT,* March 18, 1989; Peter Steinfels, "Meeting with Vatican Soothes U.S. Archbishops," *NYT,* March 12, 1989.

11. Peter Steinfels, "The Vatican Warns Catholic Theologians over Public Dissent," *NYT,* June 27, 1990.

12. CFFC filed an amicus brief in the case with the National Coalition of American Nuns, Women's Alliance for Theology, Ethics and Ritual, Chicago Catholic Women, and other organizations that stated, "Today, as in 1973, the question of whether abortion is morally right or wrong in particular circumstances is a matter which involves competing claims based on divergent moral and religious beliefs . . . There is no constant teaching in Catholic theology on the commencement of personhood . . . Constitutional mandates of privacy and religious neutrality require government to be completely neutral in the face of competing religious beliefs and claims of moral conscience." *Brief for Catholics for a Free Choice et al. as Amici Curiae 5, Webster v. Reproductive Health Services,* 1989.

13. Linda Greenhouse, "Supreme Court, 5–4, Narrowing *Roe v. Wade,* Upholds Sharp State Limits on Abortions," *NYT,* July 4, 1989.

14. By the mid-1980s, a more militant breed of abortion opponent, disenchanted with the lack of progress made by groups like the National Right to Life Committee, was using new direct action tactics aimed at abortion clinics. They harassed women coming to clinics under the guise of "sidewalk counseling," followed doctors and their families, and blockaded clinics to shut down services. Violence against abortion clinics also had become commonplace, as a spate of arson fires, acid attacks, and clinic bombings occurred across the country. There were 319 acts of violence against 238 clinics between January 1983 and March 1985. Risen and Thomas, *The Wrath of Angels,* 114.

15. NCCB Resolution on Abortion, Nov. 7, 1989; Laura Sessions Stepp, "Catholics Press Fight on Abortion," *WP,* Nov. 8, 1989.

16. Jay Mathews, "Abortion-Rights Win Follows Bishops' Rebuke," *WP,* Dec. 7, 1989; Russell Chandler, "Bishops Facing a Dilemma on Pro-Choice Politicians," *LAT,* Nov. 22, 1989.

17. Frances Kissling, "Introduction," *Guide for Prochoice Catholics,* Washington, DC: CFFC, 1990.

18. Sam Verhovek, "Cleric Assails Cuomo Stand on Abortion," *NYT,* Jan. 24, 1990; Ari Goldman, "New Brooklyn Bishop to Bar Cuomo over Abortion," *NYT,* Feb. 21, 1990.

19. Peter Steinfels, "Knights Aiding Anti-Abortion Effort," *NYT,* May 13, 1990; Dan Baltz, "Bishops Enlist PR Firm in Abortion Battle," *WP,* April 6, 1990.

20. Cardinal John O'Connor, "Abortion: Questions and Answers," *Catholic New York,* June 14, 1990.

21. Nancy Evans and Denise Shannon, "BishopSpeak: A Chronology of the U.S. Catholic Clergy's Involvement in Abortion Politics," *Guide for Prochoice Catholics,* Washington, DC: Catholics for a Free Choice, 1990.

22. Ed Blazina, "Bishops Raise Church's Role in Abortion Controversy," *Pittsburgh Press,* April 15, 1990; Robert Steutville, *Press Intelligencer* (Doylestown, PA), April 10, 1990; Evans and Shannon, "BishopSpeak;" Dean Olsen, "Bishop Restricts Abortion Views," *Journal Star* (Peoria, IL), June 2, 1990.

23. In November, Elva Bustamante, director of the New Women's Clinic of Corpus Christi, and Dr. Eduardo Aquino, a local obstetrician who performed abortions, also received letters of excommunication from Gracida. Nancy Evans, "The Excommunication of Rachel Vargas," *Conscience,* July/Aug. 1990.

24. Andrew Greeley, "Going Their Own Way," *NYT,* Oct. 10, 1982.

25. Tom W. Smith, "Catholics' Attitudes on Abortion, 1962–1982," *Conscience,* July/Aug. 1984.

26. Denise Shannon, "The Bishops Lobby," Washington, DC: CFFC, 1991; Michele Mager, "Abortion Politics and the American Catholic Church," *Conscience,* July 1981.

27. Thomas O'Hara, "The Catholic Conference and the Pennsylvania Abortion Law," *Conscience,* Autumn 1992.

28. The print ads featured a full-page picture of a coat hanger with the caption: "For most of our daughters, this looks like a coat hanger. Let's keep it that way." The multimillion-dollar television campaign featured a woman walking up a dark alley to get an illegal abortion. Tribe, *Abortion,* 174–75.

29. Linda Greenhouse, "High Court, 5–4, Affirms Right to Abortion but Allows Most of Pennsylvania's Limits," *NYT,* June 30, 1992.

30. Frances Kissling, "Imagine a World," *Conscience,* Summer 1992.

31. Ibid.

32. Denise Shannon, interviewed by Patricia Miller, Dec. 17, 2010.

33. Peter Steinfels, "New Voice, Same Words on Abortion," *NYT,* Nov. 20, 1990.

34. Jim Castelli, "PR Firm's Legacy: Kinder, Gentler Pro-Life Stance," *NCR,* Feb. 14, 1992.

35. Tim Stelloh and Andy Newman, "Dolan Urges Catholics to Become More Active in Politics," *NYT,* March 3, 2012.

36. Denise Shannon, "A Mouse That Roars Turns 20," *Conscience,* Spring /Summer 1993; CFFC received some 200 phone calls and letters in response to the ad. Report on "Picture a World" response. Minutes from meeting on Middle /Ground Dialogue, April 3, 1992, CFC.

37. *Catholic Trends,* March 13, 1993.

38. Elizabeth Maguire to Frances Kissling, April 26, 1993, CFC.

39. Anthony Padovano, interviewed by Patricia Miller, April 9, 2012.

40. Religion News Service, "Dissident Catholics Welcomed to White House," *The Wanderer*, July 18, 1993.

41. Although teens named the pope as their most admired person in 1979, by the early 1990s he had been replaced in their estimation by Michael Jordan and Arnold Schwarzenegger. AP, August 12, 1993.

42. Andrew Greeley, "Sex and the Single Catholic: The Decline of an Ethic," *America*, Nov. 7, 1992.

43. NCCB, "Statement Regarding CFFC," Nov. 4, 1993.

44. Mary Jean Collins, interviewed by Patricia Miller, Aug. 20, 2010.

45. CFFC, "Response to NCCB Statement on CFFC," n.d., CFC.

46. Anna Quindlen, "Authentic Catholics," *NYT*, Nov. 18, 1993.

47. "Papal Quotes," Women's Rights Are Human Rights press kit, 1987, CFC.

48. Frances Kissling, "International Update," *Conscience*, March/April 1986.

49. Congress had already banned direct U.S. foreign aid funding "for the performance of abortions as a method of family planning or to motivate or coerce any person to perform abortions" under the Helms Amendment to the Foreign Assistance Act.

50. Among those objecting to the appointment were Jerry Falwell of the Moral Majority, the National Council of Churches, the National Association of Evangelicals, the Seventh-day Adventists, the Baptist Joint Committee on Social Affairs, and Americans United for the Separation of Church and State. Kenneth Briggs, "Diplomatic Ties with the Vatican: For U.S., an Old and Divisive Question," *NYT*, Dec. 12, 1983.

51. See Carl Bernstein, "The U.S. and the Vatican on Birth Control," *Time*, Feb. 24, 1992; and Bill Keller, "U.S. Revises Stand on Aid and Abortion," *NYT*, July 13, 1984.

52. Steven W. Sinding, interviewed by Patricia Miller, Oct. 13, 2010.

53. Ibid.

54. Ibid.

55. Peter Wilson, "White House Population Aid Draft Sparks Abortion Controversy," *Conscience*, May/June 1984.

56. Alan Riding, "Battleground in Colombia: Birth Control," *NYT*, Sept. 5, 1984.

57. Pope John Paul II, "Responsible Parenthood Linked to Moral Maturity," General Audience, Sept. 5, 1984.

58. Pope John Paul II, "The Mystery of Women Is Revealed in Motherhood," General Audience, March 12, 1980.

59. Luke Timothy Johnson, "A Disembodied 'Theology of the Body': John Paul II on Love, Sex and Pleasure," *Commonweal*, Jan. 26, 2001.

60. Frances Kissling, "An Open Letter to the Vatican Delegation at the 1984 UN International Population Conference," *Conscience*, May/June 1984.

61. Legislative Background: The Kemp-Kasten Amendment, http://www. planetwire.org/wrap/files.fcgi/2469_kempkasten.htm.

62. Shannon, "A Mouse that Roars"; and Pauline Nunez-Morales to Elsa Clay, June 10, 1986, CFC.

63. Cristina Grela, "Life Is Not a Banquet," *IPPF People*, 17, no. 4, 1990.

64. Open Letter to the Bishops of Poland, May 9, 1991; John Darton, "Tough Abortion Law Provokes Dismay in Poland," *NYT,* March 11, 1993.

CHAPTER 7. SHOWDOWN AT CAIRO

1. Signers include Planned Parenthood and the Association of Reproductive Health Professionals. Letter from Frances Kissling to President Bill Clinton, March 18, 1993, CFC.

2. Language referring to the need for "high-quality family planning" was changed to language urging governments to "take active steps to implement, as a matter of urgency, in accordance with country specific conditions, measures to ensure that women and men have the right to decide freely and responsibly on the number and spacing for their children, to have access to the information, education and means, as appropriate, to enable them to exercise this right in keeping with their freedom, dignity and personally held values taking into account ethical and cultural considerations." See Cohen, "The Road from Rio," 61–66.

3. Attendees included representatives from the Cousteau Society, the World-watch Institute, the National Academy of Science's Committee on Population, the Population Council, Rosemary Radford Ruether, and Jesuit priest David Toolan, the associate editor of the progressive Jesuit magazine *America*.

4. CFFC Conference on Women, Population and Environment, July 21, 1992, transcript, CFC.

5. Denise Shannon, interviewed by Patricia Miller, Dec. 17, 2010.

6. Frances Kissling, interviewed by Rebecca Sharpless, transcript of audio recording, September 13–14, 2002, Population and Reproductive Health Oral History Project, Sophia Smith Collection, Smith College, Northampton, MA, 128.

7. Ibid., 146.

8. McIntosh and Finkle, "The Cairo Conference," 223–60; and letter from Frances Kissling to Nafis Sadik, March 18, 1993, CFC.

9. Azizah al-Hibri and Daniel Maguire in James B. Martin-Schramm, *Religious and Ethical Perspectives on Population Issues*. Washington, DC: The Religious Consultation on Population, Reproductive Health and Ethics, 1993.

10. Steven W. Sinding, interviewed by Patricia Miller, Oct. 13, 2010.

11. McIntosh and Finkle, "The Cairo Conference," 246.

12. Pope John Paul II remarks to Nafis Sadik, March 18, 1994, *Origins,* March 31, 1994.

13. Bernstein and Politi, *His Holiness,* 521.

14. Ibid.

15. Gordon Urquhart, "The Vatican and Family Politics," Washington, DC: CFFC, pp. 8–9.

16. Stephen Addison, "Pope Rails against 'The Culture of Death,'" Reuters, April 6, 1994.

17. Patricia Lefevere, "Church, U.N. at Odds over Population Policy," *NCR,* April 15, 1994; and "Abortion: Hot Issue at Population Conference," *Christian Century,* April 27, 1994.

18. Gerald Fraser, "Vatican Draws Continuing Fire," *Earth Times,* April 14, 1994.

19. Letter from Rachel Pine, Center for Reproductive Law and Policy, and Frances Kissling, CFFC, to President Bill Clinton and Vice President Al Gore, April 14, 1994, CFC; Shannon, interviewed by Miller, Dec. 17, 2010.

20. Pontifical Council for the Family, Ethical and Pastoral Dimensions of Population Trends, May 13, 1994, http://www.ewtn.com/library/curia/pcftrend. htm; Alan Cowell, "An Embrace for Berlusconi but Friction with the Pope," *NYT,* June 3, 1994; and Alan Cowell, "Vatican Fights U.N. Draft on Women's Rights," *NYT,* June 15, 1994.

21. Rosemary Radford Ruether, interviewed by Patricia Miller, Oct. 29, 2010.

22. Boyce Rensberger, "Vatican 'Out of Step' on Birth Control, Group Finds," *WP,* July 20, 1994.

23. Alan Cowell, "Vatican Attacks Population Stand Supported by U.S.," *NYT,* Aug. 9, 1994; and Alan Cowell, "Vatican and U.S. Battle over Document for Population Talks," *NYT,* Aug. 11, 1994.

24. Geneive Abdo and Collen O'Connor, "Vatican, Muslims Join Forces against Population Conference," *Dallas Morning News,* Aug. 25, 1994.

25. Open Letter to President Clinton, *NYT,* Sept. 1, 1994.

26. "Vatican Tones Down, Praises Gore," *WP,* Sept. 6, 1994.

27. Barbara Crossette, "Population Meeting Opens with Challenge to the Right," *NYT,* Sept. 6, 1994.

28. CFFC organized an ecumenical delegation to the conference under the Religious Consultation on Population, Reproductive Health and Ethics that included Ruether and Dan Maguire, feminist Muslim theologian Dr. Riffat Hassan, Jesuit priest David Toolan, and Cristina Grela of CDD. Daniel Maguire, "Good Religion, Good Politics," A Speech to Delegates to the UN Conference, Cairo, Egypt, Sept. 8, 1994, *Conscience,* Winter 1995/1996.

29. "Conference Compromises on Abortion," *Detroit News,* Sept. 7, 1994.

30. Barbara Crossette, "Vatican Holds Up Abortion Debate at Talks in Cairo," *NYT,* Sept. 8, 1994.

31. Shannon, interviewed by Miller, Dec. 17, 2010.

32. Ruether, interviewed by Miller, Oct. 29, 2010.

33. David Gibson, "Pope Paid Dearly for Scant Gain," *Hackensack Record,* Sept. 10, 1994.

34. Barbara Crossette, "Population Debate: The Premises Are Changed," *NYT,* Sept. 14, 1994.

35. Nafis Sadik, "For Frances, It's Personal," *Conscience,* Spring 2007.

36. The bishops first went on record as supporting universal access to health insurance in 1919. In a 1981 pastoral letter, the U.S. bishops said, "It is the responsibility of the Federal Government to establish a comprehensive health care system that will insure a basic level of health care for all Americans." Gustav Niebuhr, "Catholic Leaders' Dilemma: Abortion vs. Universal Care," *NYT,* Aug. 25, 1994; Richard Berke, "Hillary Clinton Resumes Campaign to Sell Overhaul of U.S. Health Care," *NYT,* April 17, 1993.

37. Steve Askin, *A New Rite: Conservative Catholic Organizations and Their Allies,* Washington, DC: CFFC, 1994.

38. For a comprehensive discussion of the role of Catholic nuns in the provision of health care in the United States, particularly in the founding of Catholic hospitals, see Nelson's *Say Little, Do Much.*

39. Ibid., 32–33, 54.

40. Cynthia Gibson, *The Catholic Health Care System and National Health Care Reform,* Washington, DC: CFFC, 1994.

41. Ibid.; "Annual Hospital Systems Survey," *Modern Healthcare,* 1992.

42. "Ad Hoc Committee on Catholic Health Care Named," NCCB press release, April 21, 1994.

43. "Report of the Holy See in Preparation for the Fourth World Conference on Women," March 1995.

44. "Holy See Delegation Challenges NGO Accreditation to United Nation's Women's Conference," Holy See press release, March 21, 1995.

45. "Vatican Tries to Gag Catholic Women's Groups at UN," CFFC press release, March 15, 1995.

46. Carole Collins, "Vatican Applies Muscle at UN," *NCR,* March 31, 1995.

47. Laurie Goodstein, "Nations Conspire 'against Life,' Pope Declares," *WP,* March 31, 1995.

48. "The Campaign for a Conservative Platform," *Conscience,* Autumn 1995.

49. Reuters, "Papal Delegate to Women's Conference Slams Document," Aug. 27, 1995.

50. "A Kinder, Gentler Vatican on Stage at Beijing," *Wanderer,* Sept. 14, 1995; Shannon, interviewed by Miller, Dec. 17, 2010.

51. As in Cairo, the Holy See officially withheld its assent from large parts of the final document. Glendon said the document paid "disproportionate attention to sexual and reproductive health" and had "ambiguous language concerning

unqualified control over sexuality and fertility" that "could be interpreted as including societal endorsement of abortion or homosexuality." Statement by Professor Mary Ann Glendon, head of the Delegation of the Holy See at the Concluding Session of the Fourth International Conference on Women," Beijing, China, Sept. 15, 1995.

52. Patrick E. Tyler, "Forum on Women Agrees on Goals," *NYT,* Sept. 15, 1995; and Hillary Clinton, Remarks to the Fourth World Conference on Women Plenary Session, Sept. 5, 1995.

53. "A Call to the United Nations to Consider the UN Status of the Holy See," Sept. 1, 1995, CFC.

54. Frances Kissling and Denise Shannon, "A National unto Himself," *NYT,* Sept. 30, 1995.

CHAPTER 8. MATTERS OF CONSCIENCE

1. Prakash Naidoo, "Catholic Pro-Choice Groups Take on Vatican," *Sunday Independent* (Johannesburg), Feb. 21, 1999.

2. The heavily Republican membership of the Catholic Campaign included former secretary of Education William Bennett; Nixon strategist Pat Buchanan; anti-ERA crusader Phyllis Schlafly; Mary Ellen Bork, the wife of conservative judge Robert Bork; Thomas Monaghan, the owner of the Dominos pizza chain; and Father Richard J. Neuhaus, editor of the conservative Catholic journal *First Things.*

3. Laurie Goodstein, "Debating Focus of Conference," *WP,* Aug. 27, 1995; George Archibald, "Religious Groups Say U.N. Platform Undermines Family," *Washington Times,* July 28, 1995.

4. "Evangelicals and Catholics Together: Christian Mission in the Third Millennium," *First Things,* May 1994.

5. Deborah Kovach Caldwell, "Christian Coalition Courts Catholics," *Dallas Morning News,* Feb. 3, 1996.

6. Albany Bishop Howard Hubbard warned the NCCB that the alliance would "create massive confusion not only among lawmakers in local, state and federal governments, but among the Catholic faithful as to who it is that speaks legitimately on matters of public policy." Three Colorado bishops forbade churches from distributing the alliance's material and Los Angeles Cardinal Roger Mahony and the bishop of Richmond, VA, warned Catholics to avoid the alliance. See "Bishops Blasts Coalition-Alliance Campaign," *NRC,* Dec. 22, 1995; "Bishop Slams Catholic Alliance," *National Catholic Register,* March 17, 1996; and Esther Diskin, "Bishop Rebuffs Christian Coalition," *Virginia Pilot,* Sept.12, 1995.

7. Jerry Gray, "Issue of Abortion Is Pushing Its Way to Center Stage," *NYT,* June 19, 1995.

8. The original inflammatory description of the procedure and accompanying graphic illustrations were published in the NRLC newsletter and widely circulated by the anti-abortion community. See Tamar Lewin, "Method to End 20-Week Pregnancies Stirs a Corner of the Abortion Debate," *NYT,* July 5, 1995.

9. Letter from Cardinals Joseph Bernardin, Anthony Bevilacqua, James Hickey, William Keeler, Bernard Law, Roger Mahony, Adam Maida, John O'Connor, and Most Reverend Anthony Pilla to President William Clinton, April 16, 1996.

10. Frank Bruni, "Clinton Veto on Abortion Is Criticized by O'Connor," *NYT,* April 15, 1996; AP, "Abortion Bill's Veto Assailed by Vatican," *NYT,* April 21, 1996.

11. John Swomley, "The Vatican Connection: How the Catholic Church Influences the Republican Party," *Humanist,* Nov./Dec. 1996.

12. "An Open Letter to the Bishops of the United States," *National Journal's Convention Daily,* Aug. 25, 1995.

13. Ginger Thompson, "Cardinals, Bishops Lead Anti-abortion Vigil," *The Sun* (Baltimore), Sept. 13, 1996.

14. Jon O'Brien, interviewed by Patricia Miller, April 20, 2011.

15. Ibid.

16. Ibid.

17. Judie Brown, "Contraception and Abortion: The Deadly Connection," American Life League, 2000.

18. "Birth Control: The Abortion Connection," ALL, http://www.all.org/nav/index/heading/OQ/cat/Mzc/id/NjgwOA/.

19. See Rachel Benson Gold, "The Implications of Defining When a Woman Is Pregnant," *The Guttmacher Report on Public Policy,* May 2005; and the *Catechism of the Catholic Church,* no. 2270: "Human life must be respected and protected absolutely from the moment of conception."

20. Brown, "Contraception and Abortion."

21. The Southern Baptist Convention had long decried the fact the minors could get contraceptives at federally funded family planning clinics without their parents' permission. It passed resolutions on "Permissiveness and Family Planning" in 1977, 1980, and 1981. The Reagan administration promulgated the global gag rule that prevented U.S. funding from going to nongovernmental organizations that performed or promoted abortions. In 1988, the Reagan administration promulgated a federal gag rule that prevented clinics that received Title X family planning funding from providing any information or referrals about abortion. The rule never took full effect due to court challenges and was repealed by President Clinton. "Title X 'Gag Rule' Is Formally Repealed," *Guttmacher Report on Public Policy,* Aug. 2000.

22. Gray, "Abortion Is Pushing Its Way," *NYT,* June 19, 1995; Barbara Crossette, "U.S. Aid Cutbacks Endangering Population Programs," *NYT,* Feb. 16, 1996.

23. U.S. General Accounting Office, "Impact of Funding Restrictions on USAID's Voluntary Family Planning Program," March 25, 1997, GAO/NSIAD-97-123; Crossette, "U.S. Aid Cutbacks."

24. Stephen Sawicki, "And Baby Makes . . . Too Many?" *E: The Environmental Magazine,* Nov./Dec. 1998; "Cardinal's Letter to Congress Cites Abortion, Suicide Concerns," NCCB press release, Jan. 31, 1997; "Funding Family Planning," *McNeil-Lehrer Newshour,* Feb. 12, 1997, http://www.pbs.org/newshour/bb/health/february97/pop_2-12.html.

25. Denise Shannon, interviewed by Patricia Miller, Dec. 17, 2010.

26. This was according to Judith DeSarno, president of the National Family Planning and Reproductive Health Association. See Sawicki, "And Baby Makes."

27. As of 1995, 98.2 percent of women in the United States who had had sexual intercourse had used at least one method of contraception. See Table 1: Number of Women Age 15–44 Years Who Have Ever Had Sexual Intercourse and Percentage Who Have Ever Used the Specified Contraceptive Method: United States, 1992, 1995, 2002, and 2006–2008. As of 1995, 64.2 percent of women between the ages of 15 and 44 were using contraception. See Table 4: Number of Women Aged 15–44 Years by Current Contraceptive Status and Method: United States, 1982–2008. Both in *Use of Contraception in the United States: 1982–2008,* National Center for Health Statistics, Aug. 2010.

28. Diane Levick, "'Pill Bill' Returns, Fervor and All," *Hartford Courant,* March 10, 1999.

29. By 1999, a dozen states had passed or were close to passing contraceptive equity legislation. Carey Goldberg, "Insurance for Viagra Spurs Coverage for Birth Control," *NYT,* June 30, 1999; Patricia Miller, "Coburn Defines Contraception," *Kaiser Daily Reproductive Health Report,* June 26, 1998.

30. Cathy Deeds, "Forced Choice?" *Life Issues Forum,* March 6, 2000.

31. Jody Feder, *The History and Effect of Abortion Conscience Clause Laws,* CRS Report for Congress, Jan. 14, 2005.

32. Emergency contraception has been shown to prevent ovulation if taken before ovulation occurs. According to James Trussell, a leading expert on EC, combined oral contraceptive used as emergency contraception, the first method approved in 1999, "prevent[s] pregnancy primarily by delaying or inhibiting ovulation and inhibiting fertilization, but may at times inhibit implantation of a fertilized egg in the endometrium." Newer versions of EC appear to have no postfertilization effects. James Trussell and Elizabeth Raymond, "Emergency Contraception: A Last Chance to Prevent Unintended Pregnancy," September 2012, http://ec.princeton.edu/questions/EC-Review.pdf; and "Contraceptive Coverage Mandate in FY 2000 Treasury Postal Appropriations," USCCB, Secretariat for Pro-Life Activities, Jan. 25, 2000.

33. Lois Uttley, interviewed by Patricia Miller, April 12, 2012.

34. *When Catholic and Non-Catholic Hospitals Merge: Reproductive Health Compromised.* Washington, DC: CFFC, 1998.

35. Directive 36 states, "A female who has been raped should be able to defend herself against a potential conception from the sexual assault. If, after appropriate testing, there is no evidence that conception has occurred already, she may be treated with medications that would prevent ovulation, sperm capacitation, or fertilization. It is not permissible, however, to initiate or to recommend treatments that have as their purpose or direct effect the removal, destruction, or interference with the implantation of a fertilized ovum." *Ethical and Religious Directives for Catholic Health Care Services,* 5th ed., USCCB, 2009.

36. Catholic Health Restrictions Updated. Washington, DC: CFFC, 1999.

37. O'Brien, interviewed by Miller, April 20, 2011.

38. Letter from Rev. Michael Place, president and CEO, CHA, to David Westin, president, ABC News, July 23, 1998.

39. "Catholic Lay Groups Support Contraception Equity Act in Court," CFFC press release, Feb. 14, 2001.

40. Grace Lee, "Court Rules Catholic Charity Group Must Cover Contraception," AP, July 2, 2001.

41. CBS New Transcript, "*60 Minutes:* God, Women and Medicine," Dec. 10, 2000.

42. "Father Place to '60 Minutes': Segment about Catholic Health Encourages Misperceptions," *Catholic Health World,* Dec. 19, 2000.

43. 2000 Program Report, Catholics for a Free Choice, CFC.

44. Robert Strong, "League Fights for Catholics' Religious, Civil Rights," *El Paso Times,* Sept. 24, 1995.

45. "'60 Minutes' Accused of Catholic-Bashing in Hospital Report," *Catholic New York,* Dec. 21, 2000.

46. Judie Brown, "A Tribute to a Giant among Men: Father Paul Marx, O.S.B," March 22, 2009.

47. *Human Life International,* Washington, DC: CFFC, 2011.

48. Brown, "Father Paul Marx, O.S.B," March 22, 2009.

49. Valerie Finkelman, "Human Life International: Dallas Regional Conference," *Body Politic,* December 1995.

50. Father Paul Marx, "The World Sex Mess Confirms Catholic Teaching," http://www.hli.org/index.php/video-audio/audiopodcasts/603-fr-paul-marx-the-world-sex-mess-confirms-catholic-teaching-around-the-world.

51. HLI Fundraising Letter from Father Richard Welsh, Aug. 7, 1998, CFC.

52. "CFFC Exposed; Part I: The Dirty Ideas," *HLI Reports,* Jan. 1995; and "CFFC Exposed; Part II: Dirty Money," *HLI Reports,* Feb. 1995.

53. Marjorie Maguire, Letter to *NCR,* April 21, 1995.

54. Austin Ruse, *Friday Fax,* May 29, 1998; CFFC, *Bad Faith at the UN,* Washington, DC: CFFC, 2001. HLI had accused the UN of attempting to

"turn pro-lifers into 'war criminals'" and creating new human rights that would give pedophiles "unrestricted access to your children." It charged that the United Nations Population Fund and the International Planned Parenthood Federation go "into the tiny African villages to insist mothers contracept and abort." See HLI fundraising letter from Father Richard Welsh, Aug. 7, 1998, CFC.

55. CFFC, *Bad Faith at the UN*, 2001. HLI bragged in a fundraising letter: "[E]ven though the UN has officially blocked us from being present—we've set up an 'alternative' method of watching what goes on there and informing the world. I'm talking about the office we set up (with your help) right near the UN a little less than a year ago. I can't reveal the office's name, because it still flies under feminist radar! . . . And it's like a 'spy satellite' that watches every move the UN makes related to the life issues." See HLI fundraising letter from Father Richard Welsh, Aug. 7, 1998, CFC. CAFHRI documents suggest it was receiving significant funding from HLI. See CFFC, *Bad Faith at the UN*, 2001.

56. Druelle, *Right-Wing Anti-Feminist Groups at the United Nations*.

57. Frances Kissling, "The Vatican at the United Nations," *Conscience*, Summer 1999.

58. Statement made from the floor by a woman at the March 24 panel discussion "Challenging the Vatican's Status at the United Nations," CFC.

59. O'Brien denied the charge in a written statement to ECOSOC. "Pro-Family Rep Allegedly Accosted at Seminar," *Vivant!*, March 26, 1999; and statement of O'Brien to Michele Fedoroff, NGO Section, Department of Economic and Social Affairs, March 29, 1999.

60. CFFC was joined by seventy NGOs, including the Latin American and Caribbean Women's Health Network, the Center for Reproductive Law and Policy, Women Living Under Muslim Laws, and the National Organization for Women.

61. Anika Rahman, interviewed by Patricia Miller, April 19, 2012. See also Anika Rahman, *Church or State? The Holy See at the United Nations*, Center for Reproductive Law and Policy, 1994.

62. "International Campaign Calls Into Question Vatican's Seat at UN," CFFC press release, March 24, 1999.

63. Rahman, interviewed by Miller, April 19, 2012.

64. Joseph J. Fahey, "Cairo Plus Five and How It Almost Failed," *Humanist*, Sept./Oct. 1999; "Short in Clash with Vatican over 'Unholy Alliance' on Birth Control," *Birmingham Post*, July 2, 1999.

65. Fahey, "Cairo Plus Five."

66. CFFC, *Bad Faith at the UN*, 2001.

67. One of the two cofounders of the World Youth Alliance was Diana Kilarjian, a CAFHRI employee. The other cofounder, Anna Halpine, "responded to a call in

1999 from Catholic Family and Human Rights Institute to assist pro-family organizations at the United Nations as an answer to abortion-rights NGOs." See Mary Jo Anderson, "World Youth Alliance at World Youth Day," *Women for Faith & Family*, XVII, no. 3, 2002; "Radical NGOs React Angrily to Presence of Pro-Family Youth," *Vivant!*, March 8, 2000.

68. Druelle, *Right-Wing Anti-Feminist Groups*, 2000.

69. Jennifer Butler, "300 Religious Right Participants Attend Beijing Prep-Com," Global Policy Forum, June 1, 2000.

70. Signers included Focus on the Family, the Family Research Council, the NRLC, and the Catholic Campaign for America. Mary Jo Anderson, "The Vatican on Trial at the United Nations," *Crisis*, April 28, 2000.

71. Senate Concurrent Resolution 87, March 1, 2000. The resolution passed by the House by a 416–1 vote; only Representative Pete Stark (D-CA) voted against it. It was never voted on in the Senate.

72. Jodi Enda, "This Time, It's Gore Whose Stance on Catholics Is Questioned," *Philadelphia Inquirer*, March, 17, 2000.

73. "NCCB President Issues Statement on CFFC," NCCB press release, May 10, 2000; Gail Quinn, "What Media and Money Can Do for You," *Catholic Health World*, July 10, 2000; Helen M. Alvare, "The 'Catholics' Are Heaven Sent for Gullible Press," *National Catholic Register*, April 30–May 6, 2000.

74. Alison Mitchell, "Bush Sides with Vatican on Its Status at the U.N.," *NYT*, May 27, 2000.

75. Ellen Sung, "Vatican Role at U.N. Questioned," Policy.com, June 9, 2000.

76. O'Brien, interviewed by Miller, April 20, 2011.

CHAPTER 9. PLAYING POLITICS

1. U.S. Catholic Conference, *Living the Gospel of Life*, 1998.

2. Hanna Rosin and Thomas Edsall, "Catholics Open Major Campaign against Abortion," *WP*, Nov. 19, 1998.

3. Ibid.

4. Teresa Malcolm, "Pennsylvania Governor Warned on Abortion Stand," *NCR*, Dec. 4, 1998.

5. Ryan Lizza, "Salvation," *New Republic*, April 12, 2001; Larry Williams, "Bush to Court Catholic Voters," *Washington Times*, Oct. 1, 2001.

6. Frances Kissling to Most Reverend Joseph A. Fiorenza, April 12, 2000, CFC.

7. William D'Antonio and Jacqueline Scherer, "Research Challenges Bold GOP Boast," *NCR*, Aug. 11, 2000.

8. Frank Pavone, "Inciting Violence," http://www.priestsforlife.org/columns/document-print.aspx?ID = 279.

9. Pavone had addressed the House Pro-life Caucus in 1996 after the GOP took over Congress and met privately with Speaker Newt Gingrich, pledging to aggressively speak out on abortion despite limits on the political activity of non-profit organizations. Brian Caulfield, "Moral Crisis: Priests for Life Director Meets with Gingrich, Addresses House Caucus," *Catholic New York*, March 14, 1996; "Priests for Life Political Campaign Raises 'Serious Legal Questions,' Says Church-State Watchdog Group," Americans United for the Separation of Church and State press release, July 2000.

10. "Father Frank Raises Anger of 'Catholics for a Free Choice,'" Columbus (OH) *Dispatch*, October 13, 2000.

11. "Interest Groups Hope Campaign Ads Make Them Campaign Forces," *WP*, Sept. 27, 2000.

12. Belden, Russonello, & Stewart, "Winning the Catholic Vote," Dec. 2000.

13. Lisa Colangelo, "Egan Edict Spurs Anger," *Daily News*, Oct. 31, 2000.

14. "Cardinal Hickey on the 'Catholic Vote,'" Archdiocese of Washington, Oct. 26, 2000.

15. In a 1996 memo to GOPAC, "Language: A Mechanism of Control," Gingrich recommended describing Democrats with negative words such as *traitor, anti-flag, corrupt, destructive, disgrace, pathetic, radical, sick,* and *incompetent*.

16. See quote from Robert Gustafson in "The Secret History of the GOP and Choice," *Conscience*, Oct. 11, 2011. "When the very conservative groups started including international family planning on their scorecards—things like funding for the UN Population Fund and population programs—and scoring them as if they were abortion votes, things really changed," he said.

17. Joe Feuerherd, "Bishops Seek to Bring Pro-Choice Catholic Politicians in Line," *NCR*, May 23, 2003.

18. Casey wrote to Ron Brown, chair of the Democratic National Committee, that the party's platform draft "has the effect of placing the national party even more squarely within the abortion-on-demand camp. I believe this is a serious mistake for the party and would like the opportunity to present this point of view." See Casey, *Fighting for Life*, 149–50.

19. Background—John M. Klink, CFFC fact sheet, May 31, 2001, CFC.

20. Jane Perlez, "White House Rejects Powell's Choice to Run Refugee Bureau," *NYT*, May 24, 2001.

21. Attendees included Fiorenza, Cardinals Francis George of Chicago and Egan of New York, and Domino's Pizza magnate Thomas Monaghan, who was a major backer of conservative Catholic causes.

22. Patricia Miller, "Setting Up Shop at the GOP," *Conscience*, Summer 2001.

23. Sara Seims, interviewed by Patricia Miller, May 7, 2012.

24. See Luisa Blanchfield, *International Family Planning Programs: Issues for Congress*, Washington, DC: Congressional Research Service, June 26, 2012.

25. Ibid.

26. Analysis of Determination that Kemp-Kasten Amendment Precludes Further Funding of UNFPA, Bureau of Population, Refugees, and Migration, July 18, 2002, http://2001–2009.state.gov/g/prm/rls/12128.htm.

27. Chris Smith, "The United Nations Population Fund Helps China Persecute Women and Kill Children," http://www.nrlc.org/news/2004/NRL08/united_nations_population_fund_h.htm.

28. Smith arranged for both the PRI employee who went to China and PRI head Steven Mosher to testify before Congress about the empty desk. Jodi Enda, "Small Advocacy Group Influences American Policy," Knight Ridder Newspapers, Sept. 18, 2002.

29. "International Ad Campaign Exposes New Attack by Bush Administration and Vatican on Women and Family Planning," CFFC press release, Dec. 9, 2002.

30. Interfaith Delegation to China, *The United Nations Population Fund in China: A Catalyst for Change.* Washington, DC: CFFC, 2003.

31. William Reilly, "Catholics Seek UN Action against Vatican," UPI, May 8, 2002.

32. John Paul II, address to the Fourth International Conference of the Pontifical Council for the Pastoral Care of Health Care Workers, Nov. 15, 1989.

33. Anthony Padovano, interviewed by Patricia Miller, April 9, 2012.

34. Jonathan Clayton, "John Paul's 1990 Speech 'Sentenced Millions to Die,'" *Times* (UK), March 18, 2009.

35. Paul Zeitz, interviewed by Patricia Miller, April 12, 2012.

36. U.S. Catholic Conference, "The Many Faces of AIDS: A Gospel Response," November 1987.

37. Anthony Padovano, "Catholics, Conscience and Condoms," *Conscience,* Autumn 2001.

38. AP, "Vatican AIDS Meeting Hears O'Connor Assail Condom Use," *NYT,* Nov. 14, 1989.

39. Alfonso Lopez Trujillo and Elio Sgreccia, "The Truth and Meaning of Human Sexuality," *Origins,* Feb. 1, 1996.

40. Father Jacques Suaudeau writing in the Catholic journal *Medicina e Morale,* as reported in *Our Sunday Visitor,* Nov. 2, 1997.

41. According to the Vatican's Pontifical Council for Health Care, 27 percent of institutions caring for AIDS patients around the world are Catholic. See "Church Operating 117,000 Centers for AIDS Patients Worldwide," Catholic News Agency, May 27, 2011.

42. Zeitz, interviewed by Miller, April 12, 2012.

43. Ibid.

44. Michael Carter, "Condoms, Cardinals and the Catholic Church," Aidsmap, April 18, 2005.

45. "Church's Stand against Contraception Costs Lives," Agence France Presse, June 22, 2001.

46. Carmel Richard, "Catholic Bishops Says Yes to Condoms," *Sunday Times* (South Africa), July 16, 2001.

47. Karen DeYoung, "AIDS Challenges Religious Leaders," *WP*, Aug. 13, 2001.

48. Jon O'Brien, interviewed by Patricia Miller, April 20, 2011. The campaign was expanded to Brussels, Belgium; Cape Town, South Africa; Nairobi, Kenya; Harare, Zimbabwe; La Paz, Bolivia; Santiago, Chile; Mexico City, Mexico; and Manila, the Philippines.

49. O'Brien, interviewed by Miller, April 20, 2011.

50. Steve Bradshaw, "Vatican: Condoms Don't Stop AIDS," *Guardian* (UK), Oct. 9, 2003.

51. Zeitz, interviewed by Miller, April 12, 2012.

52. Noelle Knox, "Religion Takes a Back Seat in Western Europe," *USA Today*, Aug. 10, 2005.

53. "European Parliament Addresses Growing Role of Religion in European Policy," CFFC press release, Nov. 28, 2001.

54. Neil Datta, interviewed by Patricia Miller, April 5, 2012.

55. Rosemary Rather Ruether, interviewed by Patricia Miller, Oct. 29, 2010.

56. Maria Consuelo Mejia, interviewed by Patricia Miller, May 4, 2012.

57. Ibid.

58. In Catholic Circles, *Conscience*, Summer 2007; Mejia, interviewed by Miller, May 4, 2012.

59. Congregation for the Doctrine of the Faith, "Doctrinal Note on Some Questions Regarding the Participation of Catholics in Political Life," Nov. 24, 2002.

60. Deal Hudson, *Crisis* magazine e-letter, Jan. 17, 2002. CFC.

61. Ibid.

62. Ibid.

63. Joe Feuerherd, "Bishops Seek to Bring Pro-Choice Catholic Politicians in Line," *NCR*, May 23, 2003.

64. Pamela Martineau, Jennifer Garza, and Christina Jewett, "Bishop Challenges Governor Davis on Abortion," *Sacramento Bee*, Jan. 23, 2003.

65. "The Deadly Dozen," American Life League, April 2003.

66. Jennifer Block, "Playing the Anti-Catholic Card," *Conscience*, Autumn 2003.

67. Hudson complained in one of his mass e-mails that the bishops had met with "liberal and dissident Catholics." Joe Feuerherd, "Conservative Catholics Urge Bishops to Challenge 'Dissenters,'" *NCR*, Sept. 19, 2003.

68. See Laurie Goodstein, "Kerry, Candidate and Catholic, Creates Uneasiness for Church," *NYT*, April 2, 2004; and Joe Feuerherd, "Does GOP Get a Free Ride?," *NCR*, July 2, 2004.

69. CNN, "Vatican Cardinal Fuels Religious Dispute," April 23, 2004.

70. Shailagh Murray, "Church Leaders Enter the Political Fray," *Wall Street Journal,* May 6, 2004.

71. "Archbishop to Dissenting Politicians: Stop Receiving Communion," CNS, May 6, 2004; Laurie Goodstein, "Bishop Would Deny Rite for Defiant Catholic Voters," *NYT,* May 14, 2004.

72. Laurie Goodstein, "Democrats Criticize Denial of Communion by Bishops," *NYT,* May 20, 2004.

73. Ibid.

74. Frances Kissling, "Politicizing the Sacraments," *San Francisco Chronicle,* May 3, 2004.

75. Jerry Filteau, "Cardinal Keeler: Many Think Sanctions on Politicians a Bad Idea," Catholic News Service, June 29, 2004.

76. Joseph Ratzinger, "Worthiness to Receive Holy Communion: General Principles," July 2004; Joseph Ratzinger to Theodore McCarrick, July 9, 2004.

77. See "Key Ethical Principles: Principles of Formal and Material Cooperation," Ascension Health, http://www.ascensionhealth.org/index.php?option = com_content&view = article&id = 82:principles-of-formal-and-material-cooperation&Itemid = 171.

78. Ratzinger, "Worthiness to Receive Holy Communion."

79. John Thavis, CNS, Sept. 17, 2004.

80. See, "Partisans Try to Narrow Catholic Choices," Editorial, *NCR,* Sept. 24, 2004.

81. "Democratic National Committee Offends Catholics," Catholic League press release, July 31, 2002.

82. Kevin Eckstrom, "Catholic League Raising its Profile," Religion News Service, Aug. 15, 2004; Jim VandeHei, "Kerry Keeps His Faith in Reserve," *WP,* July 16, 2004.

83. Joe Feuerherd, "Kerry Religion Advisor Recalls Effort," *NCR,* Dec. 8, 2004.

84. Michael Kranish, "GOP Urges Catholics to Shun Kerry," *BG,* Sept. 26, 2004.

85. David Kirkpatrick and Laurie Goodstein, "Group of Bishops Using Influence to Oppose Kerry," *NYT,* Oct. 12, 2004.

86. Ibid.

87. "Partisans Try to Narrow," NCR.

88. Cheryl Wittenauer, "Abortion Rights Group Accuses Archdiocese with Violating Tax-Exempt Status," AP/*Kansas City Star,* Oct. 26, 2004.

89. Keith Peters, "Grass-Roots Effort Made a Difference in Vote 2004," *National Catholic Register,* Nov. 28, 2004.

90. Paul Kengor, "Kerry Loses His Faith," *American Spectator,* Nov. 5, 2004.

91. Jim Rutenberg, "Poll Question Stirs Debate on Meaning of 'Values,' *NYT,* Nov. 6, 2004.

92. Peters, "Grass-Roots Efforts."

93. CFFC Program Report, 2001, CFC.

94. Arthur Jones, "Health Association Head to Resign," *NCR,* Dec. 17, 2004.

95. John Allen, "Vatican Document Rejects Combative Feminism, Seeks 'Active Collaboration' for Men and Women," *NCR,* July 31, 2004.

96. John Allen, "The Vatican's Enforcer," *NCR,* April 16, 1999.

CHAPTER 10. HEALTH CARE AND POLITICS REDUX

1. Representative Rosa DeLauro, interviewed by Patricia Miller, July 11, 2012.

2. For a full discussion of how the abortion rights movement went from a women's rights frame to a "who decides" frame, see William Saletan's *Bearing Right,* especially 1–84.

3. Ibid., 108–35.

4. Ibid., 147–57.

5. Patricia Miller, "Aborted Rights," *Ms.,* Spring 2004.

6. Frances Kissling, "Is There Life after *Roe:* How to Think about the Fetus," *Conscience,* Winter 2004/2005.

7. Ibid.

8. Sharon Lerner, "The Fetal Frontier: Pro-Choice Advocates Wrestle with the Uncomfortable," *Village Voice,* Nov. 30, 2004.

9. Patrick Healy, "Clinton Seeking Shared Ground over Abortions," *NYT,* Jan. 25, 2005.

10. "Catholic Statement of Principles," Feb. 28, 2006.

11. DeLauro, interviewed by Miller, July 11, 2012.

12. "Statement of Frances Kissling on 'Reducing the Need for Abortion and Supporting Parents Act,'" CFFC press release, Feb. 15, 2007.

13. Kate Phillips, "As a Matter of Faith, Biden Says Life Begins at Conception," *NYT,* Sept. 8, 2008.

14. "Planned Parenthood Says Obama Promised to 'Put Reproductive Health Care at the Center' of Health Reform," PolitiFact.com, http://www.politifact.com/truth-o-meter/statements/2009/nov/10/planned-parenthood/planned-parenthood-says-obama-promised-put-reprodu/.

15. Krissah Thompson and Jacqueline Salmon, "Among Catholics, Political Rifts over Abortion Have Grown," *WP,* Oct.19, 2008.

16. Previous statements were approved only by the bishops' Administrative Committee, which was made up of the executive officers of the conference, elected committee chairs, and elected regional representatives. Nancy Frazier O'Brien, "New Political Document Drafted," *NCR,* Nov. 2, 2007.

17. Michael Luo, "Catholics Turned to the Democrat," *NYT,* Nov. 5, 2008.

18. Jon O'Brien, interviewed by Patricia Miller, April 20, 2011.

19. Suzie Bassi, interviewed by Patricia Miller, April 11, 2012.

20. Ibid.

21. O'Brien, interviewed by Miller, April 20, 2011.

22. See Jim Rutenberg and Jackie Calmes, "False 'Death Panel' Rumor Has Some Familiar Roots," *NYT,* Aug. 13, 2009. The National Right to Life Committee was warning of health care rationing in its July/August 2009 newsletter. See Roger Stenson, "'Comparative Effectiveness' and Rationing," *National Right to Life,* July/Aug. 2009. Attendees at a raucous late August town hall meeting in Reston, VA, with Representative Jim Moran (D) that was repeatedly disrupted by "death panel" protestors reported that longtime abortion foe Randall Terry was present and was a ringleader of the disruptions (personal communication with Patricia Miller).

23. Letter from Cardinal Justin Rigali, USCCB Committee on Pro-Life Activities to Members of the House Energy and Commerce Committee, July 29, 2009.

24. Letter to all Members of Congress from Bishop William Murphy, Chair, USCCB Committee on Domestic Justice and Human Development, July 17, 2009. In it he said, "[N]o health care reform plan should compel us or others to pay for the destruction of human life, whether through government funding or mandatory coverage of abortion."

25. "Congress to Vote in September on Obama-Backed Health Bills That Would Greatly Expand Access to Abortion," *National Right to Life News Report,* Aug. 6, 2009.

26. See David Herszenhorn, "Abortion Fight Erupts in Health Care Debate," *NYT,* Nov. 7, 2009; and David Herszenhorn, "Abortion Was a Heart of Wrangling," *NYT,* Nov. 8, 2009.

27. "Congress to Vote," *National Right to Life News Report,* Aug. 6, 2009.

28. According to the Alan Guttmacher Institute, 13 percent of all abortions in 2001 were directly billed to private insurance companies. This did not include women who later submitted a claim for reimbursement. See "Guttmacher Institute Memo on Insurance Coverage of Abortion," July 2009.

29. See Lisa Miller, "When the Bishops Play Politics," *Newsweek,* March 4, 2010; and Peter Overby, "Catholic Bishops' Lobby a Force on the Hill, npr.com, Nov. 13, 2009.

30. DeLauro, interviewed by Miller, July 11, 2012.

31. Eliza Newlin Carney, "Did Catholic Bishops' Advocacy Cross the Line?" *National Journal,* Nov. 23, 2009.

32. Nick Baumann, "The Man Who Almost Killed Health Care Reform," *Mother Jones,* March 29, 2010.

33. O'Brien, interviewed by Miller, April 20, 2011.

34. Jodi Enda, "Negotiating with Peoples Lives," *Conscience*, Winter 2008–9.

35. Katharine Q. Seelye, "Abortion Compromise Draws Fire from Both Sides," *NYT*, Dec. 19, 2009.

36. Letter from the Leadership Conference of Women Religious to Members of Congress, March 17, 2010.

37. Amanda Lee Myers, "Arizona Hospital Loses Catholic Status over Surgery," AP/*Seattle Times*, Dec. 21, 2010.

38. Ibid.

39. "A Matter of Life or Death," *NYT*, Dec. 23, 2010.

40. Milt Freudenheim, "Federal Health Plan to Include One Shaped by Catholic Tenets," *NYT*, Sept. 25, 2004.

41. The Bush administration received more than 200,000 letters opposing the proposed regulation, including objections from the American Medical Association, the American College of OB/GYNs, the National Association of Chain Drug Stores, and Planned Parenthood. An early version of the regulation contained the bishops' preferred definition of abortion as anything that prevented the implantation of a fertilized egg. Adam Sonfield, "Proposed 'Conscience' Regulation Opposed Widely as Threat to Reproductive Health and Beyond," *Guttmacher Policy Review*, Fall 2008.

42. Sister Mary Ann Walsh, "The ABC Factor at HHS—Anybody But Catholics," USCCBLOG, Oct. 13, 2011. http://usccbmedia.blogspot.com/2011/10/abc-factor-at-hhs-anybody-but-catholics.html.

43. Laurie Goodstein, "Bishops Open 'Religious Liberty' Drive," *NYT*, Nov. 14, 2011.

44. Letter from Archbishop Timothy Dolan, Sept. 29, 2011.

45. Laurie Goodstein, "Bishops Say Rules on Gay Parents Limit Freedom of Religion," *NYT*, Dec. 28, 2011; MergerWatch, "Religious Health Restrictions Threaten Women's Health and Endanger Women's Lives," September 2004.

46. William Wan and Michelle Boorstein, "U.S. Catholic Bishops Buck Tradition, Choose N.Y. Archbishop as President," *WP*, Nov. 17, 2010.

47. Goodstein, "Bishops Open Drive."

48. Jones and Dreweke, *New Evidence on Religion and Contraceptive Use*, 2011; and Laurie Goodstein, "Obama Shift on Providing Contraception Splits Critics," *NYT*, Feb. 14, 2012.

49. Laurie Goodstein, "Bishops Were Prepared for Battle over Birth Control Coverage," *NYT*, Feb. 9, 2012.

50. See "Cardinal-Designate Dolan Speaks Out against HHS Rule, Calls For Action in New Web Video," USCCB Press Release, Jan. 20, 2012; and "Catholic Journal Says Plan B Does Not Cause Abortions," *NCR*, March 31, 2010. Newer versions of EC that contain only progestin or ulipristal acetate appear to have no postfertilization effects. See James Trussell and Elizabeth Raymond,

"Emergency Contraception: A Last Chance to Prevent Unintended Pregnancy," September 2012, http://ec.princeton.edu/questions/EC-Review.pdf.

51. Robert Pear, "Obama Reaffirms Insurers Must Cover Contraception," *NYT*, Jan. 20, 2012..

52. Albert Mohler, "Can Christians Use Birth Control?" AlbertMohler.com, May 8, 2006.

53. Evangelicals and Christians Together, "That They May Have Life," *First Things*, Oct. 2006.

54. Christina Page, "Will the Real Pro-Lifer Please Stand Up?" *RH Reality Check*, Jan. 22, 2010. http://www.rhrealitycheck.org/commonground/2010 /01/22/will-real-prolifer-please-stand-up.

55. In 1999, a measure to restore United Nations Population Fund support after it had been eliminated by social conservatives in Congress received the support of fifty Republicans. A similar vote four years later received only thirty Republican votes. By the end of the 2000s, fewer than a dozen Republicans would go on record as supporting family planning funding. See "The Secret History of the GOP and Choice," *Conscience*, Oct. 11, 2011.

56. The states were Colorado, Indiana, Kansas, Michigan, North Carolina, Tennessee, Texas and Wisconsin. American Congress of OB-GYNs, 2012 Legislative Update. The American Life League has been running the Stop Planned Parenthood (STOPP) campaign since 1998. See "ALL's new meta-study shows Planned Parenthood not delivering on promises—time to defund," http://www.stopp.org/article.php?id=12611.

57. "Campaign by US Bishops Forces White House to Concede," CFC press release, Feb. 10, 2012.

58. Goodstein, "Obama Shift on Providing Contraception." For a full discussion of the material cooperation agreement as it applies to the HHS mandate, see David Gibson, "Contraception Objections Fail Catholic's Moral Reasoning," Religion News Service /*USA Today*, Feb. 14, 2012.

59. Sister Simone Campbell interviewed on *Hardball*, May 21, 2012.

60. Tom Roberts, "Bishops Are Picking a Fight This Election Year," *NCR*, May 7, 2012.

61. Laurie Goodstein, "Vatican Reprimands a Group of U.S. Nuns," *NYT*, April 18, 2012.

62. Ken Briggs, "They Took Leadership and Incurred Wrath," *NCR*, May 1, 2012.

63. James Martin, "The Tablet: Who Was Behind the LCWR Investigation?" *America*, May 3, 2012. http://americamagazine.org/content/all-things/tablet-who-was-behind-lcwr-investigation.

64. Congregation for the Doctrine of the Faith, "Doctrinal Assessment of the Leadership Conference of Women Religious," http://www.usccb.org/loader. cfm?csModule = security/getfile&pageid = 55544.

65. Laurie Goodstein, "American Nuns Vow to Fight Harsh Criticism from the Vatican," *NYT,* June 1, 2012; Goodstein, "Vatican Reprimands U.S. Nuns."

66. John Allen, "Vatican Doctrine Czar on LCWR: We Expect 'Substantial Fidelity,'" *NCR,* Oct. 13, 2012; and Joshua McElwee, "Vatican's Doctrinal Head LCWR Must Not Be 'Anti-Rome,'" *NCR,* Oct. 4, 2012.

67. Lori serves as the fraternal organization's supreme chaplain. Martin, "The LCWR Investigation."

68. John Allen, "U.S. Bishops Blast Book by Feminist Theologian," *NCR,* March 30, 2011.

69. Laurie Goodstein and Rachel Donadio, "Vatican Denounces Nun over Book on Sexuality," *NYT,* June 4, 2012.

70. David Gibson, "Catholic Hospitals Reject Obama's Birth Control Compromise," RNS/*WP,* June 15, 2012.

71. In 2003, the *National Catholic Reporter* reported that a key theme of the 2002 joint meeting between the CHA and Catholic Charities was "closer coordination at the top among CHA, Catholic Charities and the U.S. Conference of Catholic Bishops" on the issue of conscience clauses. See Arthur Jones, "Public Battle of Conscience," *NCR,* June 20, 2003; "Bishops Conference Blasts Nuns for Health Care Endorsement," CNN.com, June 16, 2010.

72. Mary Agnes Carey, "Catholic Hospital Leader Defends Split with Obama Administration on Contraceptives," Kaiser Health News, June 19, 2012, http://www.kaiserhealthnews.org/stories/2012/june/19/sister-carol-keehan-contraception-compromise.asp.

73. E. J. Dionne, "From Obama, an Olive Branch to the Catholic Church on Contraception Coverage," *WP,* Feb. 1, 2013; Sarah Kliff and Michelle Boorstein, "Obama Proposal Allows Contraceptives to Go under Stand-Alone Insurance Policy," *WP,* Feb. 2, 2013. Reese was ousted as editor of *America* by Cardinal Ratzinger when he was the head of the Congregation for the Doctrine of the Faith, for, among other things, running essays that explored the moral arguments for allowing condoms to prevent AIDS and challenging bishops' refusal to give communion to pro-choice Catholic politicians. See Tom Robert and John Allen, "Editor of Jesuits' *America* Magazine Forced to Resign under Vatican Pressure," *NCR,* May 20, 2005.

74. Rosemary Rather Ruether, interviewed by Patricia Miller, Oct. 29, 2010.

75. Anthony Padovano, interviewed by Patricia Miller, April 9, 2012.

76. Lois Uttley, interviewed by Patricia Miller, April 12, 2012.

77. Mary Hunt, interviewed by Patricia Miller, Sept. 15, 2010.

78. One-third of those in the United States who were raised as Catholics no longer describe themselves as Catholics. Ex-Catholics now account for 10 percent of all Americans. The Pew Forum on Religion & Public Life, *U.S. Religious Landscape Survey.* Washington, DC: Pew Forum, 2008.

79. Antonio Spadaro, "A Big Heart Open to God: The Exclusive Interview with Pope Francis," America, Sept. 30, 2013.

80. Ibid.

81. Ibid.

EPILOGUE

1. Floyd Whaley, "Manila Hospital, No Stranger to Stork, Awaits Reproductive Health Bill's Fate," NYT, Nov. 9, 2012.

2. Chino Leyco, "Philippines Trails in Poverty Reduction, Says UN Report," Manila Times, April 3, 2008.

3. "Facts on Barriers to Contraceptive Use in the Philippines," Alan Guttmacher Institute, May 2010.

4. Magdalena Lopez, interviewed by Patricia Miller, March 9, 2012.

5. Ibid.

6. Jon O'Brien, interviewed by Patricia Miller, April 20, 2011.

7. Rina Jimenez-David, "Under the Influence of the Bishops," Conscience, Summer 2010; and Magdalena Lopez, "Philippines Reproductive Health Bill Passes House of Representatives Despite Aggressive Opposition from Bishops," RH Reality Check, http://www.rhrealitycheck.org/article/2012/12/13/catholic-advocate-heralds-passage-reproductive-health-bill-in-philippines; "The Philippines Rejects U.S. Extremism," In Catholic Circles, Conscience, Summer 2005.

8. Kristine Alave, "Contraception Is Corruption," Philippine Daily Inquirer, Aug. 5, 2012.

9. "Catholics Applaud Final Passage of Reproductive Health Law," CFC press release, Dec. 17, 2012.

Bibliography

Baehr, Ninia. *Abortion without Apology.* Boston: South End Press, 1990.

Bernstein, Carl, and Marco Politi. *His Holiness: John Paul II and the History of Our Time.* New York: Penguin, 1996.

Blake, Judith. "The Americanization of Catholic Reproductive Ideals." *Population Studies,* 20, no. 1 (July 1966): 27–43.

Brodie, Janet Farrell. *Contraception and Abortion in 19th Century America.* Ithaca, NY: Cornell University Press, 1994.

Burns, Gene. *The Moral Veto: Framing Contraception, Abortion and Cultural Pluralism in the United States.* New York: Cambridge University Press, 2005.

Byrnes, Timothy. *Catholic Bishops in American Politics.* Princeton, NJ: Princeton University Press, 1991.

Cahill, Jane Furlong. "Contraception and Eve." *New Blackfriars,* 47, no. 553 (June 1966): 466–83.

Casey, Robert Jr. *Fighting for Life.* Dallas: Word, 1996.

Cohen, Susan A. "The Road from Rio to Cairo: Toward a Common Agenda." *International Family Planning Perspectives,* 19, no. 2 (June 1993): 61–66.

Critchlow, Donald T. *Intended Consequences: Birth Control, Abortion and the Federal Government in Modern America.* New York: Oxford University Press, 1999.

Curran, Charles. "Abortion: Law and Morality in Contemporary Catholic Theology." *Jurist,* 33, no. 2 (1973): 162–83.

Daly, Mary. *The Church and the Second Sex*, 3rd ed. Boston: Beacon Press, 1985.

De Lestapis, Stanislas. *Family Planning and Modern Problems: A Catholic Analysis*. New York: Herder and Herder, 1961.

Drinan, Robert F. "The Morality of Abortion Laws." *Catholic Lawyer*, 14 (Summer 1968): 190–98, 264.

Druelle, Anick. *Right-Wing Anti-Feminist Groups at the United Nations*. Montreal: University of Quebec, 2000.

Farians, Elizabeth Jane. "Theology and Animals." In *Sister Species: Women, Animals and Social Justice*, edited by Lisa A. Kemmerer and Carol J. Adams, 102–16. Champaign: University of Illinois Press, 2011.

Ford, John C., and Gerald Kelly. *Contemporary Moral Theology, Vol. II: Marriage Questions*. Long Prairie, MN: Newman Press, 1964.

Garrow, David J. *Liberty and Sexuality: The Right to Privacy and the Making of* Roe v. Wade. New York: Macmillan, 1994.

Goody, Jack. *The Development of Marriage and Family in Europe*. Cambridge: Cambridge University Press, 1983.

Gorney, Cynthia. *Articles of Faith*. New York: Touchstone, 1998.

Greeley, Andrew. *American Catholics since the Council*. Chicago: Thomas Moore, 1985.

Greenhouse, Linda, and Reva Siegal. *Before* Roe v. Wade: *Voices That Shaped the Abortion Debate before the Supreme Court's Ruling*. New York: Kaplan, 2010.

———. "Before (and after) *Roe v. Wade:* New Questions about Backlash." *Yale Law Journal*, 128 (2011): 2028–87.

Henold, Mary J. *Catholic and Feminist: The Surprising History of the American Catholic Feminist Movement*. Chapel Hill: University of North Carolina Press, 2008.

Hole, Judith, and Ellen Levine. *Rebirth of Feminism*. New York: Quadrangle, 1971.

Hrdy, Sarah Blaffer. *Mother Nature: A History of Mothers, Infants, and Natural Selection*. New York: Pantheon, 1999.

Hunt, Mary E., and Frances Kissling. "The 'New York Times' Ad: A Case Study in Religious Feminism." *Journal of Feminist Studies in Religion*, 3, no. 1 (Spring 1987): 115–27.

Hurst, Jane. *The History of Abortion in the Catholic Church*. Washington, DC: Catholics for a Free Choice, 1989.

Joffe, Carol. *Doctors of Conscience: The Struggle to Provide Abortion before and after* Roe v. Wade. Boston: Beacon Press, 1995.

Jones, Rachel K., and Joerg Dreweke. *Countering Conventional Wisdom: New Evidence on Religion and Contraceptive Use*. New York: Guttmacher Institute, 2011.

Jonsen, Albert R. *The Birth of Bioethics.* New York: Oxford University Press, 1998.

Karrer, Robert. "The Formation of Michigan's Anti-Abortion Movement." *Michigan Historical Review,* 22, no. 1 (Spring 1996): 67–107.

Keller, Rosemary Skinner, and Rosemary Radford Ruether, eds. *Encyclopedia of Women and Religion in North America,* Vol. 3. Bloomington: Indiana University Press, 2006.

Lader, Lawrence. *Abortion.* Boston: Beacon Press, 1966.

——. *Abortion II.* Boston: Beacon Press, 1973.

Luker, Kristin. *Abortion and the Politics of Motherhood.* Berkeley: University of California Press, 1984.

Lynch, Robert N. "The National Committee for a Human Life Amendment, Inc.: Its Goals and Origins." *Catholic Lawyer* (Autumn 1974): 303–10.

McCarthy, John D. "Pro-Life and Pro-Choice Mobilization: Infrastructure Deficits and New Technologies." In *Social Movements in an Organizational Society,* edited by Mayer N. Zald and John D. McCarthy, 49–66. New Brunswick, NJ: Transaction, 1987.

McCarthy, John D., and Mayer N. Zald. "The Trend of Social Movements in America: Professionalization and Resource Mobilization." Morristown, NJ: General Learning Corporation, 1973.

McClory, Robert. *Turning Point: The Inside Story of the Papal Birth Control Commission.* New York: Crossroad, 1995.

McIntosh, Alison C., and Jason Finkle. "The Cairo Conference on Population and Development: A New Paradigm?" *Population and Development Review,* 21, no. 2 (June 1995): 223–60.

Messer, Ellen, and Kathryn May. *Back Rooms: Voices from the Illegal Abortion Era.* New York: St. Martin's, 1988.

Mohr, James C. *Abortion in America.* New York: Oxford University Press, 1978.

Mosher, Steven, and Calvin Goldscheider. "Contraceptive Patterns and Racial Groups in the United States, 1955–76: Convergence and Distinctiveness." *Studies in Family Planning,* 15, no. 3 (May–June 1984): 101–11.

Nelson, Sioban. *Say Little, Do Much: Nursing, Nuns and Hospitals in the Nineteenth Century.* Philadelphia: University of Pennsylvania Press, 2001.

Noonan, John T. "An Almost Absolute Value in History." In *The Morality of Abortion: Legal and Historical Perspectives,* edited by John T. Noonan Jr., 1–59. Cambridge, MA: Harvard University Press, 1970.

Noonan, John T. *Contraception: A History of Its Treatment by the Catholic Theologians and Canonists,* enl. ed. Cambridge, MA: Harvard University Press, 1986.

Nossiff, Rosemary. *Before* Roe: *Abortion Policy in the States.* Philadelphia: Temple University Press, 2001.

O'Rourke, Kevin D., Thomas Kopfensteiner, and Ron Hamel. "A Brief History: A Summary of the Development of the Ethical and Religious Directives for Catholic Health Care Services," *Health Progress*, 82, no. 6 (November–December 2001): 18–21.

Packer, Herbert, and Ralph Gampell. "Therapeutic Abortion: A Problem in Law and Medicine," *Stanford Law Review*, 11, no. 3 (May 1959): 417–55.

Paige, Connie. *The Right to Lifers: Who They Are, How They Operate, Where They Get Their Money*. New York: Summit, 1983.

Reagan, Leslie J. *When Abortion Was a Crime: Women, Medicine and the Law in the United States, 1867–1973*. Berkeley: University of California Press, 1997.

Risen, James, and Judy Thomas. *Wrath of Angels: The American Abortion War*. New York: Basic Books, 1998.

Rock, John. *The Time Has Come: A Catholic Doctor's Proposals to End the Battle over Birth Control*. New York: Knopf, 1963.

Ruether, Rosemary Radford. *The Church against Itself*. New York: Herder and Herder, 1967.

Saletan, William. *Bearing Right: How Conservatives Won the Abortion War*. Berkeley: University of California Press, 2004.

Segers, Mary C. "The Catholic Church as Political Actor." In *Perspectives on the Politics of Abortion*, edited by Ted Jelen, 87–129. Westport, CT: Praeger, 1995.

Staggenborg, Sydney. *The Pro-Choice Movement: Organization and Activism in the Abortion Conflict*. New York: Oxford University Press, 1994.

Tatalovich, Raymond, and Byron Daynes. *The Politics of Abortion: A Study of Community Conflict in Public Policy Making*. New York: Praeger, 1981.

Traina, Frank. "Catholic Clergy on Abortion: Preliminary Findings of a New York State Survey." *Family Planning Perspectives*, 6, no. 3 (Summer 1974): 151–56.

Tribe, Laurence H. *Abortion: The Clash of Absolutes*. New York: Norton, 1992.

Westoff, Charles F., and Norman B. Ryder. "United States: Methods of Fertility Control, 1955, 1960, & 1965." *Studies in Family Planning*, 1, no. 17 (February 1967): 1–5.

Index